Distant
Neighbors

Distant Neighbors

A Portrait of the Mexicans

Alan Riding

Vintage Books
A Division of Random House, Inc.
New York

Vintage Books Edition, October 1989

Library of Congress Cataloging in Publication Data
Riding, Alan.
Distant neighbors.
Reprint. Originally published: New York:
Knopf, 1985, c1984.
Bibliography: p.
Includes index.
1. Mexico—Politics and government—1970–
2. Mexico—Economic conditions—1970–
3. Mexico—Social conditions—1970–
I. Title.
[F1236.R53 1986]   972.08′3   85-40137
ISBN 0-679-72441-9 (pbk.)

Manufactured in the United States of America

B98765432

To my parents and Marlise

Contents

Acknowledgments   ix

Foreword   xi

1. The Mexicans   3

2. The Roots of the Nation   22

3. From Revolution to Institution   42

4. The System: Myths and Rewards   66

5. The (Generally) Loyal Opposition   94

6. Corruption: Oil and Glue   113

7. Economic Models, Miracles and Mistakes   134

8. "The Oil Is Ours!"   157

9. Land Sí, Liberty No   180

10. Indians Body and Soul   199

11. The Social Crisis:
    Catching Up with the Population   219

12. The Family Safety Net   238

13. Mexico City: Magnet and Monster   254

14. The Other Mexicos   274

15. Culture for Some and for Many   295

16. ". . . And So Close to the United States"   316

17. Foreign Policy: Facing Central America   340

18. Shaping an Uncertain Future   364

Selected Bibliography   373

Index   377

Acknowledgments

This book was so long in its gestation that sooner or later all my Mexican friends were recruited into helping me to decipher a fascinating and complex nation. That the book was eventually completed is a tribute to their patience, frankness and generosity. During my more than twelve years as a journalist in Mexico, people of all regions, classes and ideologies also responded openly and warmly to my questioning interest in their country. And when it came to writing this book, my dependence on others increased. I am grateful to *The New York Times* for granting me a leave of absence from daily journalism at the end of my assignment in Mexico. The Ford Foundation provided me with financial assistance during this period, for which I am appreciative. The president of El Colegio de México, Victor Urquidi, and the director of its Center of International Studies, Rafael Segovia, welcomed me to the institution and found space where I could work. My colleagues in El Colegio were always available to answer my queries, although special thanks are due to Lorenzo Meyer, Soledad Loaeza, Francisco Gil Villegas, René Herrera, Manuel García y Griego, Mario Ojeda, Rodolfo Stavenhagen, Vicente Sánchez, Elena Urrutia and Miguel Wionczek for catching the mistakes and adding to the ideas in several chapters. Numerous other friends also kindly read sections of the book, among them Francesco Pellizi, Gobi Stromberg, David Winder, Luis Ortiz Monasterio, Kenneth Shwedel, William Chislett, Rogelio Ramírez, Alejandro Gertz Manero, Anne Reid, Ralph Murphy, Andrés Rozental and Fausto Zapata. I am particularly indebted to Jorge G. Castañeda, who patiently and meticulously accompanied me through various drafts and endless debates. My research assistant, Rosario Molinero, provided me with invaluable assistance. My thanks also go to Marlise Simons, who as my wife urged me to keep going, and as a tough editor improved the final result. Finally,

I am grateful to Ashbel Green at Knopf and Helen Brann, my agent, for their patience and encouragement. Such is the scope of this book, however, that none of my friends could agree with it all. Any errors of fact or judgment are exclusively my responsibility.

ALAN RIDING

Foreword

Probably nowhere in the world do two countries as different as Mexico and the United States live side by side. As one crosses the border into Mexico from, say, El Paso, the contrast is shocking—from wealth to poverty, from organization to improvisation, from artificial flavoring to pungent spices. But the physical differences are least important. Probably nowhere in the world do two neighbors understand each other so little. More than by levels of development, the two countries are separated by language, religion, race, philosophy and history. The United States is a nation barely two hundred years old and is lunging for the twenty-first century. Mexico is several thousand years old and is still held back by its past.

Over the past 150 years, Mexico has come to know and feel American power: in the nineteenth century, it lost half of its territory to its northern neighbor; in the twentieth century, it has become economically dependent on the United States. In contrast, the United States until recently barely looked south. Mexico's stability was taken for granted, its flourishing economy welcomed American investment, credits and products, its foreign policy was no more than a minor irritation, its rural poverty provided American farmers with cheap labor. Even after massive oil finds gave Mexico new political stature and economic impetus in the late 1970s, there seemed to be little reason to "understand" Mexico and the Mexicans.

Today, things are different. The failure of Mexico's postwar economic model has thrust the country into its most serious crisis since the 1910 Revolution. Not only are millions of poor Mexicans finding the daily struggle for survival increasingly difficult, but industrial workers, bureaucrats and the middle classes in general have watched new dreams of prosperity abruptly recede. The country's political system seems also to have lost some of its legendary flexibility and sensitivity. In the process, the people's faith in their leaders has been badly eroded. Mexicans have been extraordinarily tolerant of bad and abusive government, but their patience is being tested more than at any time in memory.

The implications for the United States are self-evident. Already, Washington fears that the violent struggle between Left and Right in Central America could spread to Mexico. And although the "domino theory" is less worrisome than the ingredients for unrest apparent inside Mexico's own frontiers, the repercussions in the United States would be little different. A tidal wave of Mexicans of all classes entering the United States would be impossible to contain. The United States' huge industrial, financial and commercial stakes in Mexico would unavoidably be threatened. The flow of oil from Mexico, now the United States' single largest foreign supplier, could be affected. The U.S.-Mexico border, which epitomizes the growing interdependence between the two countries, could suddenly be militarized, provoking serious tensions between the Hispanic and Anglo populations within the United States. And in response to chaos next door, Washington might be tempted to intervene, which would aggravate and prolong instability.

For the United States, "understanding" Mexico—its "distant neighbor"—has become a matter of self-interest and even of national security. To avoid policies that could prove counterproductive, the United States must learn to look beyond the surface crisis to the inner subtleties of an ancient, complex and unpredictable nation. To gain insight into Mexico's future, it must sift through the country's entire past and present for clues. The task is not easy. Mexico does not surrender its secrets willingly, because they are the secrets to its survival. It is fierce in its judgment of itself, but resents the probings of foreigners as assaults on its defenses. Yet Mexico is of such importance to the United States that it cannot be permitted to remain permanently shrouded in mystery.

The purpose of this book is to make Mexico more accessible to non-Mexicans. It is inspired not by a desire to expose the country's vulnerabilities but by the belief that Mexico would also be served if better understood by its northern neighbor. In a sense, the book represents a search for an invisible "black hole" that embraces the entirety of Mexico in a single concept: to know what it contains requires a journey through the history of the country, through the minds of its people and through the diverse sectors of society. Each element can be analyzed in isolation, but it can be understood only when related to all the others to form an idea, at once diffuse and precise, of Mexico today.

Distant
Neighbors

I

The Mexicans

I

Amidst the noise and fumes of Mexico City, there is a quiet square where
the modern Foreign Ministry building and a sixteenth-century Spanish
Colonial church look onto the remains of the pre-Hispanic pyramids of
Tlatelolco. The government has named it the Plaza of Three Cultures to
venerate Mexico's mixed-blood heritage, or *mestizaje*. In front of the
church, a plaque carries these simple but moving words: "On August
13, 1521, heroically defended by Cuauhtémoc, Tlatelolco fell into the
hands of Hernán Cortés. It was neither a triumph nor a defeat: it was
the painful birth of the *mestizo* nation that is Mexico today."

Yet, the birth pains of the new *mestizo* race are not over. More than
460 years after the Conquest, neither the triumph of Cortés nor the defeat
of Cuauhtémoc has been properly assimilated, and the repercussions of
that bloody afternoon in Tlatelolco continue to be felt. Today, in strictly
ethnic terms, 90 percent of Mexicans are *mestizos,* but as individuals they
remain trapped by the contradictions of their own parentage. They are
the sons of both Cortés and Cuauhtémoc, yet they are neither Spanish
nor Indian. They are *mestizos,* but they cannot accept their *mestizaje*.
As a nation too, Mexico searches endlessly for an identity, hovering
ambivalently between ancient and modern, traditional and fashionable,
Indian and Spanish, Oriental and Western. And it is in both the clash
and the fusion of these roots that the complexity of Mexico resides.

The Mexicans have no difficulty in understanding each other. They do
so through the secret codes—the customs, language and gestures—that
they learn unconsciously from childhood, accepting the consistency of
their inconsistencies as part of an established pattern which they are
merely repeating. Yet they anguish when it comes to explaining themselves. They realize that they are different—not only from Americans

and Europeans but also from other Latin Americans—but they seem unsure why. Poets, novelists, philosophers, sociologists, anthropologists and psychologists have been called on to define "Mexicanness"—or *Mexicanidad*—but even they become dizzy trying to distinguish the "masks" from the "real" faces of the Mexican personality. There is a magical, almost surreal air about the Mexicans that refuses to be captured. Still more frustratingly, when it is trapped by a description, it disguises itself as a caricature.

The key lies in the past, a deep subconscious past that stays alive in Mexicans today. It is a continuous past, but not a consistent past. In it, Mexicans must conciliate being conquered and conqueror, retaining many of the racial characteristics and personality traits of the Indians and even glorifying their pre-Hispanic heritage, while speaking Spanish, practicing Catholicism and thinking of Spain as the mother country. As a society, the legacy of the past is no less overwhelming. On the ruins of a long line of theocratic and militaristic empires, Cortés imposed the values of a profoundly Catholic and intellectually repressed Spain. The Conquest therefore reinforced a powerful tradition of political authoritarianism and divine omnipotence that to this day resists the incursions of Western liberalism.

Other countries of Latin America were also conquered and colonized by Iberia, but with different results. The sparsely populated colonies of the Caribbean and Atlantic coasts were shaped by migrants from Europe and, later, by slaves from Africa. In the countries of Central America and the Andes, where large Indian populations survive, pure-blooded Europeans still comprise the ruling classes. Mexico alone is truly *mestizo:* it is the only nation in the hemisphere where religious and political—as well as racial—*mestizaje* took place; it has the only political system that must be understood in a pre-Hispanic context; and its inhabitants alone are still more Oriental than Western. In few countries of the world are history, politics and social structure so mirrored in—and a mirror of—the character of its people.

At times, it seems as if the Spaniards took over the bodies of the *mestizos* and the Indians retained control of their minds and feelings. In the end, mind prevailed over matter. Most Mexicans are meditative and philosophical, they are discreet, evasive and distrustful, they are proud and consumed by questions of honor, they are forced to work hard but dream of a life of leisure, they are warm, humorous and sentimental and occasionally also violent and cruel, they are enormously creative and imaginative yet impossible to organize, they are internally set in their ways and externally anarchic. Their relationship with each other—and with society as a whole—is guided by tradition rather than principles, pragmatism rather than ideology and power rather than law.

Perhaps the strangest contrast is the ritual and disorder that seem to coexist within the Mexican, yet this too illustrates the predominance of the spiritual over the material. A powerful religiosity, adherence to traditions, a ceremonious mode of behavior, the formality of language, all involve caring for the emotional and spiritual side of life. The mechanical efficiency, punctuality and organization of an Anglo-Saxon society, in contrast, seem purposeless. What counts to the Mexican is what he is rather than what he does, the man rather than the job: he works to live and not the inverse. He can deal with external chaos if his spiritual concerns are cared for, but he cannot allow his identity to be obliterated by man-made forces. Rather, he interprets the world in accordance with his emotions. In an environment of apparent disorder, he can improvise, create and eventually impose his own personality on events. And in the end, in the name of expressing his individuality, he contributes to disorder.

This basic attitude is evident in all facets of life. The Mexican is not a team player: in sports, he excels in boxing but not in soccer, in tennis but not in basketball. He finds it difficult to subscribe to any ideology that demands strict coherence between his ideas and his actions. Even legal rights must often be filtered through the discretionary power of individuals to become personal favors. And while a Mexican's influence may be derived from his political position, he exercises it as a projection of his personality. Perhaps recognizing that some substitute for self-discipline and respect for the law is needed to make society function, he also accepts the dictates imposed by an authoritarian ethos. Thus, from family to nation, the rules that operate are virtually tribal. If he wishes to belong and benefit, those rules must be respected.

Carrying the accumulated beliefs, customs and passions of centuries, the Mexican possesses enormous internal strength. And just as this expresses itself in a metaphysical sense of solitude, it also erupts in almost uncontrolled creativity. The temples, sculptures, jewelry and pottery bequeathed by the pre-Hispanic civilizations belong to an unbroken tradition of artistic expression. Today, not only Indians but also *mestizos* remain extraordinary craftsmen in a tradition that still regards a punctilious sense of detail and design as more important than mass production. Their weaving, their pottery, their metalwork and woodwork all carry their distinctive personal imprints. Their defiant use of colors—wild pinks, purples, greens and oranges—is no less original, reflecting both the real and the paper flowers that decorate their lives. The endless variety and careful presentation of Mexican food provide an arena that combines ritual and improvisation. And Mexicans burst into song at the least provocation.

Even the Western sense of time has been resisted by Mexicans. Cultures that view birth as a beginning and death as an end can have no sense of a living past. For Mexicans, neither birth nor death is seen to interrupt the continuity of life and neither is considered overly important. In songs, paintings and popular art, death is even mocked. On the Day of the Dead each November, Mexicans crowd the country's cemeteries, carrying flowers and even food and drink to the graves of their ancestors, much as the Aztecs did. Belief in communion with the dead is widespread, not in a psychic or spiritualist sense or as a function of a Christian faith in the afterlife, but simply as an outgrowth of the knowledge that the past is not dead.

Conversely, the future is viewed with fatalism, and as a result, the idea of planning seems unnatural. If the course of events is predestined, Mexicans see little reason to discipline themselves to a routine. Businessmen gamble on large, fast profits rather than long-term expansion of a market, individuals prefer spending to saving—they may save for a fiesta but not for a bank—and even corruption reflects the concept of seizing an opportunity now and facing the consequences later. In government, planning bureaus have long existed, but their plans belong to the realm of fantasy, serving as idealistic expressions of goodwill rather than sets of objectives that must be achieved. Ambition, in a meritocratic American sense, barely exists outside the urban middle classes. The Mexican may work as hard as his Indian forefathers, but he dreams of emulating his Spanish ancestors, who arrived to conquer and not to labor: the image of success is more important than any concrete achievement.

Time itself involves rules that must be defied. On a daily basis, punctuality seems unimportant, since nothing enjoyable or important now is worth truncating for the sake of a future appointment: arriving an hour or more late for a dinner party does not merit an apology; to the contrary, it is arriving on time that is considered rude. From a senior official to a neighborhood plumber, appointments may be made with little expectation that they will be honored, and little offense is taken when they are ignored. The practice of absenteeism after a weekend is even institutionalized in "San Lunes"—"St. Monday"—which by itself is considered sufficient explanation. Logic often does not apply: a maid may leave a job the day before her wage is due for no better reason than *ganas*—that she felt like it. The *mañana* syndrome is therefore not a symptom of chronic inefficiency or laziness, but rather evidence of an entirely different philosophy of time. If the past is safe, the present can be improvised and the future will look after itself.

Thus, the disasters that befall Mexicans are not major disappointments, because they are considered unavoidable. *Ni modo*—meaning "tough luck" or, more literally, "no way" that a setback could have been averted—is the traditional response to failure or accident. Physical defeats even serve to enhance the value of spiritual victories and underline the supremacy of soul over body. The fatalism is familiarly Indian. The pre-Hispanic civilizations would seek "signs" to the future in the behavior of Nature—or their gods—but in no way did they feel able to influence events. In the post-Colonial period, the Virgin of Guadalupe played the same role, providing the hope of miracles but engendering no bitterness if petitions went unanswered. "Until now, Mexicans have only known how to die," Samuel Ramos wrote darkly in his classic *The Profile of the Mexican and His Culture,* in the 1930s, "but it is time for them to acquire the knowledge of life."

In reality, the country's own historical record of defeats and betrayals has prepared Mexicans to expect—and accept—the worst. The official heroes—from Cuauhtémoc to Emiliano Zapata—have invariably been murdered, while the ideals enshrined in laws and constitutions have been universally betrayed. "The hero's tomb is the cradle of the people," the poet Octavio Paz wrote in *The Labyrinth of Solitude,* his controversial analysis of the Mexican personality. And he added: "We are nihilists, except that our nihilism is not intellectual but instinctive and therefore irrefutable."

It was the very first "defeat" of the Conquest that enabled the Spanish colonizers to inculcate a sense of ethnic inferiority in the Indians. Inherited by the *mestizos,* this led to a form of racism that is manifested to this day in disdain for pure Indians and special respect for *güeros,* or whites: to be accompanied in public by *una güera,* a blond woman, is considered by many men to be the height of status. More important, this also led to self-denigration and insecurity, which were in turn hidden, though not obliterated, by the masks of *machismo* and bravado behavior. Imitation—first of Spaniards, then of the French and, more recently, of Americans—provided additional protection, and even innate pessimism served as a defense against disappointment. The Mexican thus flees from a reality that he cannot handle into a world of fantasy where pride, idealism and romance can safely flourish and passion dominates reason.

Beyond the cautious ceremoniousness of the Mexican, there hides great warmth and humanity. The extended family is the principal safe haven where emotions can be shown without risk, where unquestioning loyalty is guaranteed, where customs are maintained. Within the family are included the key figures of the *compadre* and *comadre,* the godparents of a child. The Mexican also feels strong ties to his barrio, or rural village, where the rules are familiar and the threats minimal. Even among casual acquaintances, he seems almost anxious to lower his defenses, to share in a degree of trust. Once an emotional bond is established, once a *cuate*—literally, twin—relationship exists, he is open and generous, willing to confide and hospitable to extremes. All he asks is that his sincerity be reciprocated. To invite a stranger to his home becomes an act of great symbolism: he is showing the real face of how he lives by sharing the intimacy of his family.

The Mexican male's insecurity is best illustrated by his constant fear of betrayal by women. A contemporary anthropological explanation remains appealingly neat: Mexico's *mestizaje* began with the mating of Spanish men and Indian women, thus immediately injecting into the male-female relationship the concepts of betrayal by women and conquest, domination, force and even rape by men. Just as the conqueror could never fully trust the conquered, today's *macho* must therefore brace himself against betrayal. Combining the Spaniard's obsession with honor and the Indian's humiliation at seeing his woman taken by force, Mexico's peculiarly perverse form of *machismo* thus emerges: the Spaniard's defense of honor becomes the Mexican's defense of his fragile masculinity.

In practice, this takes the form of worship of the female ideal, exemplified by the image of the long-suffering, abnegated and "pure" Virgin of Guadalupe and personified by each Mexican's own mother, who is seen as the giver of life and therefore incapable of betrayal. Conversely, the wife, who as an object of sex is considered an aberration from feminine perfection, must be humiliated, since a husband's faithfulness or excessive affection would imply vulnerability and weakness. Mistresses provide the man the opportunity to conquer and to betray in anticipation of betrayal. The wife's resentment toward her husband is then translated into smothering love for her son, who in turn elevates her to the status of female ideal but adopts his father's example as a husband.

Whether or not this neo-Freudian analysis is wholly valid, the male-female relationship in Mexico is often marked by tension and distrust. Like men, women therefore also spend most of their time with members of their own sex, not least their *comadres.* Contact with men is too complicated to be casual, and even at social gatherings a woman will either cling to her husband or gather with a group of other women. Women, too, are thus assigned a ritual to which they must adhere, acting as mothers and homemakers and suffering enormous social and family pressure when they decide to seek careers. But in both cases they remain the pivot of the family, the most reliable point of reference in a society where the phenomena of illegitimate children, broken homes and absentee fathers are widespread.

While seeking points of security, the Mexican lives much of the time introspectively. For this solitude and self-restraint, the fiesta provides a vital catharsis. The excuse could be a religious or patriotic occasion, a birthday or a saint's day or perhaps one of myriad special days: mothers, fathers, children, *compadres,* teachers, builders, postmen, taxi drivers, garbage collectors, secretaries, soldiers and many more all have a day assigned to them for the receipt of presents and *abrazos* and the organized pursuit of happiness. Firecrackers, trumpets, songs and shouts break the inner silence of Mexican men. Then, unlocked by alcohol, sentimentality, self-pity and frustration pour out, usually channeled harmlessly into popular songs* that articulate the bitterness of unrequited love and the honor of violent death and at times expressed in unexpected outbursts of aggression.

The Plaza Garibaldi in Mexico City, with its crowded bars and mariachi musicians, is a monument to this instinctive psychoanalysis, where Mexicans go to bare their hearts and weep over what they see. "The fiesta is at once sumptuous and intense, lively and funereal," Octavio Paz wrote. "It is a vital multicolored frenzy that evaporates in smoke, ashes, nothingness. In the aesthetics of perdition, the fiesta is the lodging place of death." Getting drunk is itself a ritual, an opportunity to express love and hate. Mexicans even refer, only half jokingly, to the four stages of a *borrachera,* or binge, among friends: toasts to their friendship; reminders of past offenses; criticism of the clergy and the government; songs and folkloric dances. Without the release of the fiesta, Mexican society would be more unstable and unpredictable.

II

The high walls that surround most Mexican homes, including frequently those of the poor, serve as both real and symbolic frontiers of security and authority. When the Mexican male steps outside them, he acts as if confronting a hostile society with which he feels minimal solidarity. The concept of commonweal barely exists and community approaches to

---

*The lexicon of such songs is rich, but one illustrates their mood: "Life is worth nothing / Nothing is what life's worth / It always begins with crying / And crying is how it ends / So that's why in this world / Life is worth nothing."

shared problems are rare. In the countryside, the determination of peasants to farm their own tiny plots condemns them to perpetual poverty. Efforts to organize voluntary work to build a school or a health clinic invariably fail. In urban areas, strewn garbage, undisciplined traffic and acute air pollution are functions of this same social egoism. Even among the wealthy, the idea of supporting charities is alien, with the result that many orphanages in Mexico depend entirely on contributions from the foreign community.

Society as a whole functions through relationships of power, while individual rights are determined by levels of influence. With all intimacy shielded by masks of formality, Mexicans seem like actors, constantly adapting their roles to circumstances without risk of spiritual exposure or commitment. They also perform against an invisible background of latent violence that discourages explosions of temper or frustration: since the consequences of a test of wills can be bloody, confrontation is avoided and conciliation becomes second nature. The poet Andrés Henestrosa once contrasted the attitudes of Spaniards and Mexicans: "The Spaniard speaks axiomatically, bossing and ordering, while we are always seeking concord when we discuss—you're half right and I'm half right." Even in the madness of Mexico City's traffic, horns are rarely blown and insults only occasionally exchanged because many drivers still carry weapons in their glove compartments. In politics, this attitude is still clearer: fear of another revolution keeps the negotiating spirit alive.

Reluctant to risk emotional contact, Mexican men touch each other physically in a familiarly Latin way, automatically shaking hands or, more intimately, walking arm in arm. Women also kiss each other upon introduction and whenever they meet. The principal ceremony is the embrace, and since the purpose is mutual reassurance rather than pledge of friendship, it follows a strict pattern. First comes the handshake, followed by the *abrazo* and two hearty coordinated back slaps and, finally, a second handshake and shoulder slap. Even this ritual involves social perils. An attempt to embrace a superior who resists the gesture is considered a humiliation; a voluntary *abrazo* from a boss, preferably in public, is to be celebrated. Above all in the world of politics, the quality of embraces is scrutinized for evidence of favor: on numerous occasions each year, politicians—men and women—will line up for hours in the hope of receiving an *abrazo* from the President.

Status and appearances are crucial throughout society. The poor spend ostentatiously to hide the "shame" of their poverty, going into debt to pay for village fiestas, lavish weddings, birthday parties and funerals. Among the more affluent, similar symbols proliferate. An ex-

pensive present reflects the wealth of the donor as much as the importance of the recipient. Men wrestle for the privilege of picking up the
check in a restaurant, while the American practice of "going Dutch" is
considered offensive. In public life, perhaps the most valued evidence of
status is an entourage of underemployed aides and bodyguards. They
may carry out such chores as whispering telephone messages and opening a way through traffic bottlenecks for the *jefe*'s dark limousine, but
their principal function is simply to constitute a retinue. In government
circles as in families, *machismo* can almost be measured by the number
of dependents.

The use of titles reinforces the sense of hierarchy that pervades society.
Titles of nobility were banished by the 1910 Revolution, but new ones
appeared. Such titles as *Don* and *Doctor,* commonly used in other Latin
American countries, are seldom encountered in Mexico. But at lower
levels of the bureaucracy and in business, to be a *licenciado,* or university
graduate, in itself implies a sphere of influence and requires the wearing
of suit and tie as evidence of clout. Academic achievement is less important than social style, and not a few self-confident politicians assume the
title *Licenciado* without possessing a degree. More subtly, the head of
an office is referred to, not as *Licenciado* So-and-So, but as *El Licenciado,*
as if no other existed. At more senior levels of power, the President or
a minister is known simply as *El Señor,* a title which normally means
"Mr." but preceded by the definite article becomes "The Lord" in a
manorial or religious sense and is the most deferential form of reference.
The title *Maestro* has several functions. A plumber, painter or carpenter
will expect his skills to be recognized in this way, but many senior
officials consider it important to give classes at the university, if only to
be addressed as *Maestro*—teacher—by both their students and their
former students.

Formal and obscure language is probably the Mexican's prime weapon
of self-defense. Using seemingly meaningless words and phrases, he can
protect his emotions, avoid the risk of committing himself and even
lavish praise without feeling servile. The concept is simple: language has
a life of its own, almost as if words rather than people communicated
with each other. Even pre-Hispanic paintings illustrated conversation by
means of balloons hovering detached in front of the speakers. Empty
promises and outright lies come easily since the words have no intrinsic
value of their own. Excessive frankness or directness is considered rude,
and even substantive discussions must be preceded by small talk about
family or political gossip. Language serves as the neutral ground on
which people can relate without danger of confrontation.

In public life, the independence of words is crucial since senior officials expect to be flattered. The talents attributed to each President—while he is in office—verge on the ridiculous. Yet the flock of acolytes surrounding each *jefe* are not expected to justify their servility after the official leaves power; rather, they simply transfer their praise to the next *jefe*. The rhetoric used by officials to discuss public issues is still more bemusing. Any aspiring politician can launch into oratory at a moment's notice with the intention of crowding the air with fine words and phrases rather than elucidating. Since the use of direct language would imply commitment, much of the official discourse is conceptual, defending principles and values that most governments in practice ignore. Electoral platforms are built around grandiose phrases sustained by wishful thinking. Myriad messages—from the nationalist pontifications of historical figures to direct moral admonitions—are painted on walls as if they have the power to influence the ordinary Mexican's thinking.

When a real political message must be conveyed, it is usually disguised in a secret code that foreigners, even Spanish-speaking foreigners, must struggle to decipher. Presidents may refer to "emissaries from the past" or "external mirrors." The head of the ruling party once viciously attacked "those who from dark cabals establish shameful alliances that the people reject," a reference that only a handful of politicians could understand. (He was referring to a meeting between conservative opposition politicians and United States diplomats.) At times, the chosen words may even contradict the intended meaning, leading the uninitiated to the wrong conclusion. On other occasions, a strong denial—"There is no crisis"—serves to confirm official recognition of a problem. The country's newspapers generally contribute little enlightenment: they usually avoid the perils of analysis and in-depth reporting by publishing endless interviews, while more pertinent political columns frequently require decoding before they can be comprehended.

Caution is the norm. When Mexican officials are invited to speak abroad, no amount of tough questioning will elicit admissions of failures of the system. Even Mexican historians, political scientists and sociologists are reluctant to be frank in public, and some avoid appearing on a podium with opposition politicians intent on embarrassing the regime. Because of the risks involved in defining oneself, most important academic treatises about Mexico have been written by foreigners. Yet this entire ritual serves an important political purpose. It provides a smoke screen behind which real power can be exercised while the illusion of a political debate is preserved. And although each President can determine the ideological tint of his administration, the unchanging rhetoric gives continuity to the system, if only by perpetuating its myths.

The language of public life essentially mirrors the language used by Mexicans in their day-to-day relationships. It is a language of formality in which endless subtleties can be hidden. Some ornate phrasing is used unconsciously. A child is taught to introduce himself by giving his name and adding *para servirle,* or "ready to serve you." A Mexican will refer to himself in the third person as *su servidor,* or "your servant." He will describe his own home as *su casa,* or "your house," to which a mumbled *gracias* is expected. But among close friends, the language is enormously flexible. There are words for all seasons, and talking—wittily and cynically—is what counts. (The *mitotero*—someone who literally creates myths or stories to inflate his own importance—is particularly mocked if he can be exposed.) Meanings are tucked between lines, in pauses, emphasis or intonation, even in odd sounds or gestures. Jokes are usually self-mocking or derogatory about Mexico in general, while close friends will constantly joust verbally with each other. Many words from Nahuatl —the language of the Aztecs—have been assimilated into Spanish and carry special significance, while *jeux de mots,* biting sarcasms and sexual double entendres are scattered through conversation, with some highly charged words used in a dozen different ways.

One word in particular, *chingar,* dominates the vernacular of curses and serves almost as a pivot of the conversation of lower-class urban men. Meaning literally "to rape," its weighty significance has been traced to the Spanish conquistador's taking of the Indian woman who became the original *chingada.* The traditional Spanish expletive *hijo de puta,* or "son of a whore," therefore became in Mexico *hijo de la chingada,* or "son of a raped woman." Endless variations on the concept have since emerged. The climactic insult of *chinga tu madre,* or "rape your mother," is invariably a prelude to violence, while *vete a la chingada* is the local variant of "go to hell." A *chingadazo* is a heavy physical blow, and a *chingadera* is a dirty trick. A Mexican can warn, jokingly or threateningly, *no chingues,* meaning "don't annoy me," and if he loses out in some way, he will admit that *me chingaron.* It is high praise to describe someone as *chingón*—that is, he is clever enough to *chingar* others—although an irritating person is *chingaquedito.*

Many words are juggled with a similar spectrum of meanings, although few more than *madre,* or mother, rich in psychosexual and religious connotations. *Nuestra madre* refers to the Virgin Mary, yet, puzzlingly, the word is usually used negatively. The insult of *chinga tu madre* can be reduced to *tu madre* with little loss of intensity, while *una madre* can mean something is unimportant and *un desmadre* converts a situation into chaos. A *madrazo* is a heavy blow, a *madreador* is a bouncer or hired thug and *partir la madre*—to "divide" the mother—means to shatter someone or something. A person with *poca madre*—"little mother"—is without shame, *a toda madre* is equivalent to a superlative and *me vale madre*—literally, "it is worth mother to me"—means "I don't give a damn." A son will use the diminutive form *madrecita* to address his own mother, but *mamacita* is a vulgar street comment to a passing girl or a term of endearment for a mistress. In contrast, the father figure—*el padre*—plays a lesser linguistic role. A *padrote,* or "big father," is a pimp, while something that is excellent is *muy padre.* Perplexingly, a mother will call her young boy *papito,* "little father," and her husband *mi hijo,* "my son." In these endless linguistic contortions, the Mexican's fascination with detail and obsession with nuance are constantly satisfied.

III

The past remains alive in the Mexican soul. Not all Mexicans of all regions and all classes are alike: in the provinces, they resent the imposition of what they consider the Aztec-rooted *mestizo* culture, and the middle-class minority struggles to shake off the past, sacrificing the present for a future of Americanized values and rewards. History, revised and adjusted to suit contemporary needs, is therefore mobilized to maintain the cohesion of modern society. When ancient and modern clash, emotions invariably favor the past. In late 1983, the mayor of Mexico City was forced to cancel plans to build a subway line under the capital's main plaza after angry protests from other government departments that construction would destroy hidden remains of the Aztec Empire: the only surprise was that the mayor had lacked the sensitivity to avoid the controversy. Compared to the past, urban planning is unimportant.

History is also actively promoted. There are statues galore, streets around the country are named after past—including pre-Hispanic—heroes and historic dates, while the entire calendar is peppered with occasions to be celebrated. On March 18, the anniversary of the nationalization of Mexico's oil industry in 1938, Mexico recalls its patriotic valor in standing up to pressure from the United States. May 5, the anniversary of the battle of Puebla, when a French occupation force was temporarily defeated in 1862, is used to reaffirm the country's determination to defend its territory. The entire month of September is given over to ceremonies commemorating Mexico's independence from Spain.

Even the official past remains highly topical. Interviews and columns in the press will often discuss "news" a half-century old. In 1983, the government financed a weekly supplement, distributed free with all newspapers, which reprinted selected articles from the period between 1910 and 1970. Posters of a long-deceased former President may suddenly appear in subways above some conceptual political phrase. Some symbols are taken from pre-Hispanic times: in 1978, a new monument to policemen and firemen who died in the line of duty comprised a statue of Coatlicue, the goddess of death, with a fallen Aztec warrior at her feet. Key figures of Mexican history have been divided into good and evil and, in a distinctly Oriental fashion, are used to personify such concepts as heroism, nationalism and revolutionary ideals or, alternatively, cowardice, treason, greed and repression.

Contemporary politicians commonly "adopt" a spiritual mentor from the past. In the early 1970s, President Luis Echeverría Alvarez held up as his political model the late General Lázaro Cárdenas, who in the 1930s had carried out a major land reform and expropriated foreign oil companies. Through frequent tributes to Cárdenas, Echeverría sought to associate himself with the former President's image as a strong nationalist and loyal friend of the peasantry. Upon taking office in 1976, President José López Portillo expressed identification with Quetzalcóatl, the mythical pre-Hispanic "White God" known as the Plumed Serpent. Years earlier, he had written a book about Quetzalcóatl, which was immediately reprinted and translated, and he even named his official aircraft and bus after the legendary god. President Miguel de la Madrid in turn let it be known that José María Morelos, one of the leaders of Mexico's fight for independence early in the nineteenth century, was his favorite historical figure. As the author of Mexico's first draft constitution, Morelos is a symbol of respect for law, a quality which De la Madrid wished to emphasize.

Many of those now on the same side of history fought each other viciously in their lifetimes. During the 1910–17 Revolution, Emiliano Zapata rebelled against Francisco I. Madero, and Venustiano Carranza persecuted Francisco "Pancho" Villa, but all four names are now listed together in gold letters in the Chamber of Deputies. The past, though, is not always forgiven. When in 1925 President Plutarco Elías Calles moved the remains of Mexico's Independence heroes to a new monument, he excluded the bones of Agustín de Iturbide, who finally won the war against Spain in 1821, because he still represented conservative Catholicism. In 1977, the veteran Communist leader Valentín Campa launched a campaign to have the muralist Diego Rivera expelled from the local Communist Party—twenty years after his death. Rivera's purported offense was to have flirted with Trotskyism, yet Campa's real purpose was to use the trial as the occasion to denounce the growing penetration of the party by Eurocommunist ideas. Recognizing his "Stalinist" motives, less orthodox Communists then blocked Campa's move.

One explanation for this constant reliving of the past is that honor and glory must somehow be extracted from the dizzying array of defeats and humiliations suffered by Mexicans since the Conquest. So often, those who fought on the side of "good" were vanquished, but their principles can be vindicated decades or centuries later. Typically, the Child Heroes of Chapultepec are remembered for resisting United States troops in 1847, although they died and the United States subsequently seized half of Mexico's territory. Conversely, uncomfortable features of Mexican history can be quietly buried and forgotten. Mexicans prefer to ignore evidence that their Aztec ancestors practiced cannibalism. History textbooks gloss over the entire Colonial period as well as the territorial losses to the United States, the French occupation and the Porfirio Díaz dictatorship in the nineteenth century, choosing to concentrate on the "glorious" pre-Hispanic civilizations, the fight for Independence and the achievements since the Revolution.

Extraordinary passions can be stirred by historical controversies. In 1983, the National University planned a production of a play entitled *The Martyrdom of Morelos,* by Vicente Leñero. In view of De la Madrid's fascination with Morelos, the presentation was presumed to be simple cultural opportunism. But the play revealed that, while being tortured prior to execution by a Spanish firing squad in 1815, Morelos betrayed the names, strategies and troop strengths of other key rebel commanders. Before the opening night of the play, university authorities intervened to suspend rehearsals, worried not only about offending the President but also about denigrating an immaculate hero. Assorted civic associations then mobilized to defend "the honor and glory" of Morelos, a leading politician devoted an entire speech to praising the "founder of the nation" and excoriating his critics, a controversial actor playing the part of Morelos was replaced and the producers took precautions against violent protests when the play was eventually opened to the public.

Even more dramatically, the final battle between Cortés and Cuauhtémoc is still being fought, usually as part of Mexico's continuing struggle to come to terms with its *mestizaje,* but occasionally as a symbol of the confrontation between the Third World and "imperialism." Today, the vanquished has become the victor: since the Revolution, Mexican history has been reinterpreted by nationalists, with Cuauhtémoc presented as the hero and Cortés as the villain; and in Diego Rivera's post-revolutionary murals, Cuauhtémoc is shown as an idealized youth, while Cortés is portrayed as a syphilitic hunchback. On such an emotionally charged subject, the past will not lie peacefully: most recently, the dispute moved into the arena of bones and statues.

Upon his death in Spain in 1547, Cortés' remains were returned to Mexico and placed in the wall of the Hospital de Jesús, which he had founded. The bones were then forgotten until rediscovered in the 1940s. Almost immediately, Cuauhtémoc's bones were also "discovered" in the small town of Ixcateopán in Guerrero state, and although two scientific commissions could not verify their authenticity, they were enshrined in a glass case in the local church. In 1975, President Echeverría appointed a new commission to study the bones, this time driven by even loftier motives. "In the bold fight waged by the Third World to end the process of colonialism imposed by the world powers," he explained, "Cuauhtémoc is the germinal antecedent that began the organized resistance against colonial dependence and exploitation." To authenticate Cuauhtémoc's bones, it seemed, was to legitimize the "struggle" of the Third World. Only after Echeverría left office did the commission dare announce that the identity of the bones in Ixcateopán could still not be confirmed. On the anniversary of Cuauhtémoc's death each year, officials still stand before the bones and pronounce nationalist speeches.

President López Portillo was immensely proud of his Spanish heritage, and in 1981 he reopened the Cuauhtémoc-versus-Cortés controversy by personally unveiling a bust of the Conquistador in the Hospital de Jesús. Until that time, there was only one known statue of Cortés in Mexico —in the Casino de la Selva in Cuernavaca. The following year, another monument to Cortés was placed in the main square of the Mexico City neighborhood of Coyoacán. Dedicated to Mexico's *mestizaje,* it showed Cortés and his Indian mistress, La Malinche, sitting behind their young *mestizo* son, Martín. But as soon as López Portillo left office, it was removed, to the delight of local nationalists. Justifications for the censorial measure kept the issue alive. "Cortés represents military conquest and genocide," one historian, Gastón García Cantú, noted. "In my view, no conqueror deserves a statue. And the idea of recognizing Cortés as the founder of our nationality is a profound and reactionary mistake." Another prominent writer, Gutierre Tibón, argued that Cortés deserved a statue, although he conceded that "Mexico's spiritual climate does not yet permit it because Mexicans have still to strike a balance between Cuauhtémoc and Cortés."

This ambivalence has continued to affect Mexico's relations with Spain. The Spanish Civil War, viewed in Mexico as the struggle between progressive good and fascist evil, enabled Mexico to give particular vent to its resentment toward Spain for its colonialist past. Not only did President Cárdenas support the Republican cause and, subsequently, give asylum to thousands of refugees, but successive Mexican governments refused to recognize the Franco regime. General Francisco Franco, it seemed, had come to personify Cortés, who could thus be symbolically punished. When diplomatic relations were restored following Franco's death, however, the main celebration was in Mexico and, soon afterwards, President López Portillo trekked to the Navarre village of Caparroso, where his forefathers had lived.

Mexico's relationship with Spain will always be passionate. Debates still rage over whether the Conquest destroyed civilization or barbarism, whether Aztec human sacrifices were any worse than the Spanish Inquisition, whether the country's endemic corruption has pre-Columbian or Spanish roots, whether bureaucracy was an import from Spain or a natural product of Indian ritual. Today, Mexicans resent the arrogance of many Spanish migrants, with their well-earned reputation for "exploiting" local workers, but they feel drawn to all things Spanish, from singers and bullfighters to food and wines. At a national level, even though Mexico is today richer, more populous and more influential than Spain, it continues to look, perhaps subconsciously, for the mother country's approval. During a visit by Spain's Prime Minister Felipe González in June 1983, De la Madrid could not resist pointing to the significance of holding their official dinner in the Plaza de Tlatelolco, "a place that recalls the lights and shadows of our conscience" and "synthesizes the twin columns, Indian and Spanish, that explain and determine our being."

The individual insecurities of ordinary Mexicans frequently become shimmering images reflected by the country as a whole. Nowhere is this more evident than in Mexico's almost aggressive sense of nationalism. The threats, attacks, invasions and occupations that have come from abroad since the time of Independence are more than sufficient to justify Mexico's unspoken xenophobia. Yet nationalism also reflects the country's continuing feeling of vulnerability and, like *machismo,* it serves as a mask both to hide internal doubts and to display external self-confidence. Mexico's nationalism is therefore not ideological but rather part of its survival instinct. And every government since the Revolution has bolstered the twin pillars of nationalism—strengthening a sense of national identity at home and stressing the country's independence abroad —as a way of consolidating its own power.

The mirror of Mexican nationalism today is no longer Spain or even France, but exclusively the United States. Even here the faces that Mexico shows to its neighbor are not consistent. There is resentment bequeathed by the loss of so much territory in the nineteenth century and by U.S. military interventions as recently as 1916. There is resistance to the oppressive weight of continuing U.S. political and economic influence in Mexico. There is intellectualized contempt for the materialistic culture exported by the United States. And there is the reassuring belief that "clever" Mexicans can always outwit "naïve" Americans. But among ordinary Mexicans there is also admiration for the United States and, above all, for its organization, honesty and affluence. And they happily watch American-made television programs, adopt American consumer tastes and prefer imported or contraband goods from north of the border to locally made products.

While much of Mexico's foreign policy is dedicated to exhibiting the country's independence from the United States, governments also tap the unifying resource of patriotism to keep alive a sense of nationhood. Inheriting a severe economic crisis in December 1982, President De la Madrid ordered that the national anthem be played at midnight on all radio stations and at the end of the day's programming on television: one television channel preceded the national anthem for several weeks with recitations of a poem entitled "Mexico, I Believe in You." All ministries or government departments were instructed to hold regular ceremonies honoring the Mexican flag. Through a decree aimed at "reaffirming and strengthening devotion to national symbols," the government also organized a competition of poetry and prose dedicated to the national flag and the national anthem.

At a cultural level, it has been more difficult to prevent erosion of formal "Mexicanness," although one interesting attempt in 1982 involved a Commission for the Defense of the Spanish Language to combat incursions by anglicisms. Above all in Mexico City, restaurants and shops had discovered that foreign names were good for business, resulting in the likes of Shirley's, Paco's and Arthur's. The commission declared war on the apostrophe—which does not exist in Spanish orthography—as the principal symbol of cultural infiltration. Radio and television spots also mocked those who said "bye" instead of *adios* or called themselves Charlie instead of Carlos. Lines from poems paying homage to the Spanish language were added to existing propaganda decorating walls around the capital. But nationalist contradictions continued to surface: one reference to the "immortality" of Spanish was altered with spray paint one night, with the word "Spanish" replaced by "Nahuatl." Soon afterwards, a Council to Defend Indigenous Languages was formed.

Just as alcohol melts the mask of *machismo,* it is during moments of crisis that the country's endemic self-doubts become visible through the screen of nationalism. The myths of progress and hope sustained so avidly in public suddenly give way in private to a self-defeating cynicism and exaggerated self-deprecation. Former President López Portillo, who claimed insight into the *mestizo* nature of the Mexican psyche, once addressed himself to this mesmerizing nihilism, trying vainly to break the trance. "Frequently, we Mexicans are given to underlining our defects," he said. "Perhaps because of the dark paths of our Indian roots, we like to tear ourselves apart, to sacrifice ourselves. It's an activity that many Mexicans seem to enjoy—to denigrate ourselves, to tear ourselves in pieces, to admit we have all the defects in the world. We have a right to do so. We have many rights. But we also have a right to agree, a right to underline the positive, the right to say we have done something well and will do it still better."

Just three months after he spoke, the Mexican economy collapsed in disarray and released a new flood of pessimism. The financial crisis was serious, but the psychological response was more dangerous. Many Mexicans resigned themselves to the demise of the entire system and, in panic, acted accordingly. Others seemed consumed by the sheer drama of the occasion, as if the futility of rules and plans was being proved. Among the urban middle classes, the crisis revealed that the internal conflicts over *mestizaje* had now been complicated by the competition between Mexican and American ways of life. For the newly affluent, the preceding four-year boom had seemingly placed the American way of life within easy grasp. When the bubble burst, their minimal nationalism was exposed. The reaction of poor Mexicans, in contrast, was less hysterical. Since the economic boom had brought them few benefits, their expectations had not been inflated and their stoicism remained largely intact.

Not for the first time, a principal obstacle to rebuilding the economy was the perception that Mexicans had of themselves. To be positive was to have hope and risk betrayal. And even though Mexico has enjoyed enviable political stability for over six decades, the memory of a past that seemingly repeats itself conspired to preserve self-doubt. The choice exists with individuals as with nations: some meditate on past misfortunes, others overcome setbacks and never look back. Mexico and the Mexicans seem unable to detach themselves from a past to which they still belong. Preferring to look back, they have ample material on which to contemplate: in the history of Mexico as perceived today lies the past that overshadows the present and continues to shape the future.

2

The Roots of the Nation

I

To romanticize the Indians from the monumental ruins and folkloric remnants evident today is to distort the lot of most Indians even before the Spanish Conquest. Then as now, the majority suffered under an inequitable social system: they fought and died as foot soldiers; they sustained the superstitions that gave life to the ruling theocracies; they worked the fields, carried water and built the temples and pyramids; they ate only corn tortillas and beans; and they lived in wooden and adobe huts not far from the stone palaces occupied by their masters. Successive conquering lords gave them different gods to worship, but their lot rarely changed. After the Conquest, it was just another god who arrived, in whose name the Indians were subjected to new exploitation.

But surprisingly little is known about ordinary Indians before the Conquest. From around 3500 B.C., some 40,000 years after they crossed the Bering Strait, they stopped being nomadic and started to cultivate the land. Corn soon replaced wild fruit and hunted animals as the basis of the Indian diet and, given its importance, it assumed a religious significance. Good harvests were vital for survival, so gods appeared who could provide the rain and protect the crops. And as the cultures developed, corn took on even greater symbolism, representing life itself and eventually being seen as the source of all life. In many ancient legends, man was born from corn. Even today, corn dominates the Mexican's diet and, for some Indians, remains sacred. The Indian's philosophical harmony with nature derives from this: corn is a gift from the gods.

Greater insight into the pre-Hispanic peoples of Meso-America in fact comes from studying these gods, at different times numbering in the hundreds. Domination by one or another god identified periods of wealth or hardship, fertility or famine, conquest or defeat, health or disease.

Similarly, the spreading influence of a particular god announced the military expansion of a certain tribe, while worship would include varied expressions of art dedicated to the gods and their priests. Nevertheless, because most pre-Columbian codices were destroyed by the Spanish conquerors, experts have only ruined temples, stelae, sculptures, jewelry and pottery as guides to the past. Their conclusions are therefore frequently based on hypotheses, deductions and guesses.

The Olmecs, it is believed, created the first important civilization of central Mexico, around 1200 B.C., in the coastal areas of the Gulf of Mexico in today's southern Veracruz and Tabasco states. It flourished for about 700 years, reaching a population of perhaps 350,000, and it built three important cities—known today as La Venta, San Lorenzo and Tres Zapotes—before disappearing. From its jewelry and pottery, perhaps the most exquisite of pre-Hispanic artifacts surviving today, it was evidently a race of great artistic talent and religious sensitivity. It lacked local supplies of stone, so few large Olmec buildings remain, although its rulers had stone brought from the western sierra to be carved into huge heads, thirteen of which have been discovered, puzzling archaeologists with their broad noses and thick lips. (Some students claim this proves North African influence in the New World long before the Conquest.) Stone stelae also point to an advanced dating system that included the concept of zero, unknown to their Roman contemporaries.

Most of all, the importance of the Olmecs is evidenced by their influence over the Mayas to the southeast and the emerging highland civilizations to the west: their principal symbol, the jaguar, can still be found as far south as El Baúl in Guatemala and as far west as Tula. But they were not warriors; rather, their influence seemed to spread through trade and religion. The Olmecs are perhaps all the more mysterious because no tribe exists today that can be traced to them. No one knows why they settled where they did, why they developed more than others, how they lived, how their political and religious structures functioned and why their civilization finally disappeared or, more likely, was absorbed by others.

The civilizations that followed in the Yucatán Peninsula and the central highlands are less remote because, ethnically at least, they survive today. Colonization of the Maya region—covering the Yucatán, Guatemala, Belize and parts of Honduras and El Salvador of today— began around 1500 B.C. But not until around A.D. 150 did the first city-states emerge in the central lowland area now known as El Petén in Guatemala, with Tikal the architectural jewel and religious center of this early empire. By 900 the area had been largely abandoned and the focus of development moved north to the Yucatán, where such cities as Palenque, Uxmal, Chichén Itzá and Tulum grew up, frequently reflecting new influence from the central highlands.

Within 300 years, however, many of these cities had also been abandoned, often mysteriously and abruptly, giving rise to speculation about conquest, disease or prolonged drought. What seems clear, however, is that by 1200 the Maya Empire as such—a region held together by politics, language, trade and religion—had broken up into dozens of different tribes and city-states, speaking different dialects, wearing different costumes and worshipping different gods, albeit maintaining an extraordinary artistic tradition in their temples and pottery. A few city-states, such as Mayapán, remained important, but were independent. Further, in contrast to the relative peace of the Classic era, reflected in the unwarlike motifs of Maya stelae, these cities often fought each other. Mayapán, for example, destroyed much of Chichén Itzá and brought Uxmal under its control until, in 1441, Uxmal itself rose up and destroyed Mayapán.

To the west, the Zapotecs first appeared in the region of Oaxaca around 300 B.C., building the extraordinary mountaintop city of Monte Albán which was to dominate the area for some 900 years. The Zapotecs then abandoned the city and moved to Zaachila, but the Mixtecs, who had migrated into the Oaxaca valleys and built their principal religious center at Mitla, continued to use Monte Albán as a ceremonial cemetery. Long before the Conquest, both tribes broke up into multiple city-states and even village-states, establishing a tradition of community fragmentation that remains a problem to this day in the region.

Their influence never stretched into central and northern Mexico and, from before the time of the birth of Christ, the construction of Teotihuacan for the first time established the domination of the highland civilizations over the rest of Mexico. By definition it was an important religious center, its temples decorated by stelae, statues and brightly colored paintings, its gods dominating smaller city-states in the region. Given its sophisticated social structure, Teotihuacan undoubtedly had military might, but its conquests were attributed to its priests and gods, while its wealth came from its merchants, who ranged as far as Guatemala. At the height of its power, Teotihuacan was probably the most populous city in the world, with some 200,000 inhabitants. Today, the remains of its huge pyramids of the Sun and the Moon and its two-mile-long Avenue of the Dead testify to its vastness.

The end of the Teotihuacan culture is also shrouded in mystery. The city appears to have been sacked and burned, probably between 650 and

700, although it remained an important religious shrine for several centuries longer. But the political cohesion of the region disintegrated and city-states subservient to Teotihuacan returned to self-government. "Whatever the motives and agents of the disaster, the fact is that Teotihuacán died and, with it, its great culture," Ignacio Bernal, former head of the National Museum of Anthropology, has written. "But it left an immense legacy whose influence is still felt and whose legend barely ended with the Spanish Conquest." Such was this legacy, in fact, that Teotihuacan became the reference point for all future highland civilizations, the first "glorious past" to which the subsequent Toltecs and Aztecs related.

Over the centuries, the city had attracted migrants who had created something of a cultural melting pot. After the empire's collapse, many Indians again abandoned the city, carrying with them talents and traditions. The emergence of the Toltecs can thus be traced directly to Teotihuacan. In particular, the legend of Quetzalcóatl, or the Plumed Serpent, already recorded in stone in Teotihuacan and recognized as the inventor of medicine, agriculture, astronomy and royalty, assumed greater importance and even physical identity under the Toltecs. The Toltecs were much given to human sacrifice when ruled by Ihitmal, who had seized power by murdering his brother, Quetzalcóatl's father. The young prince, then called Ce Acatl Topitzin, was saved and brought up by priests, who, impressed by his holiness, named him Quetzalcóatl. He then murdered his uncle and became leader of the Toltecs at the city of Tula. But by banning human sacrifice and stimulating artistic creativity, Quetzalcóatl alienated the priests and their god of evil, Tezcatlipoca, who in turn deceived him into breaking his vows of chastity and forced him to abandon his throne. He fled to Cholula and, according to legend, twenty years later took to sea in a boat, promising to return one day. Soon afterwards, he supposedly landed in the Yucatán, where he was named Kukulcán and where he died thirty years later on a self-made funeral pyre. As a god, however, he continued to be present until well after the Spanish Conquest.

With the departure of Quetzalcóatl, the Toltecs resumed their sacrificial rites and, around 1200, fell victim to new warrior tribes, known variously as the Chichimecas or "barbarians," who dominated the highland city-states at the time the Aztecs or Mexicas first appeared in the region. They came from northwestern Mexico—the mythical Aztlán—although the circumstances of their arrival in the central highlands are not known. Legend has it that in 1325 they settled on two islands in the middle of Lake Texcoco, since it was there that they sighted a predestined sign—an eagle perched on a cactus with a writhing snake in its beak. (After Independence, this image was adopted as Mexico's national emblem.) More likely, though, the Aztecs were forced onto the lake by the rulers of the nearby cities, who considered the new arrivals to be unrepentant savages. But within 100 years, through wars and alliances, the Aztecs succeeded in dominating the entire region, establishing probably the largest empire in pre-Hispanic times.

Although still given to human sacrifice, necessary to provide the blood demanded daily by their gods, the Aztecs had also developed considerable artistic talents by the beginning of the fifteenth century. Their huge temples on the principal island of Tenochtitlan—the name they gave their capital—and the nearby island of Tlatelolco were covered with ferocious carvings, some of them of Quetzalcóatl, while their pottery was unusually ornate. Some 80,000 people lived on the islands, which were in turn linked to each other and the mainland by broad causeways and two aqueducts. Every day, farmers and traders would walk or canoe to Tenochtitlan to spread their wares in the huge plaza in front of the Palace of the Emperor and the Great Temple—or Templo Mayor—dedicated to Huitzilopochtli and Tlaloc, gods of war and water.*

In 1502, Moctezuma II became Emperor and High Priest of Huitzilopochtli. He had already proved himself a valiant warrior, but he was also an enlightened ruler, a refined and sensitive man, deeply religious and superstitious. He lived in a manner appropriate to an emperor. Since his empire stretched east to the Gulf coast, west to the Pacific and south as far as present-day El Salvador, he, his court and the nobility and merchants benefited from products brought from afar. Moctezuma would eat fish daily. He wore richly woven robes, fine jewelry and a feathered headdress. He possessed a vast treasure of gold and was revered as a god-king.

While Moctezuma reigned in splendor, unaware that the West Indies had already been discovered, a young Spaniard named Hernán Cortés joined the adventurers heading for the New World, drawn like most of his contemporaries by the dream of wealth. Yet even he had little idea of what awaited him when he sailed west from Cuba early in 1519 with some 500 men and sixteen horses crowded aboard ten galleons. A short wiry man, at the time thirty-five years old, he first touched land at the island of Cozumel off the Yucatán, where he found a Spanish priest,

---

*The "imperial" domination by these gods was confirmed only recently when excavations of the Templo Mayor uncovered jewelry and pottery brought there from all over Mexico.

Gerónimo de Aguilar, who had been shipwrecked there seven years earlier and had become fluent in Maya. With Father Aguilar on board, the flotilla continued west across the Gulf of Mexico, finally going ashore at what is now Veracruz.

Moctezuma, hearing of their arrival and fearing that Cortés might be the returning god Quetzalcóatl, sent carriers loaded with gifts of gold and silver, jade and embroidered cloth, in the apparent hope of bribing the invaders into leaving. The gifts had the opposite effect. "The Spaniards are troubled with a disease of the heart for which gold is a specific remedy." Cortés is said to have remarked. He then told Moctezuma's ambassadors that he could not depart without personally saluting the great emperor in his palace at Tenochtitlan. A local Tabascan Indian leader gave him a concubine, La Malinche, who spoke both Maya and Nahuatl, the language of the Aztecs, and communicated with Cortés through Father Aguilar until she learned Spanish. Thus equipped with interpreters, the group marched inland, a few hundred adventurers in a nation of over seven million Indians.

Working in Cortés' favor was the resentment of many of the conquered Indian tribes toward the Aztec Empire. One city-state that had fought off total submission to Moctezuma was Tlaxcala, about a hundred miles east of Tenochtitlan. When Cortés arrived in the region, the Tlaxcalans also tried to beat off the new arrivals, but they were slaughtered by the Spanish cannons and cavalry—they had never seen horses before—and soon agreed to form an alliance against the Aztecs. Cortés then traveled to the religious center of Cholula, where he ordered the massacre of some 3,000 Indians in reprisal for a plot, uncovered by La Malinche, to kill the Spaniards. Thus warned, Moctezuma agreed to receive Cortés and, in November 1519, the invaders and several thousand Tlaxcalan allies marched along causeways into the magnificent city of Tenochtitlan, marveling at the giant temples, pyramids, palaces, crowded markets and, finally, the imperial extravagance of Moctezuma and his court.

"When we came near to Mexico," Bernal Díaz del Castillo, a captain in Cortés' army, recalled in *The Conquest of New Spain*, "the great Moctezuma descended from his litter and these other great *caciques* [Indian chiefs] supported him beneath a marvelously rich canopy of green feathers, decorated with goldwork, silver, pearls and chalchuites, which hung from a sort of border. . . . [These *caciques*] carried the canopy above their heads and many more lords walked before the great Moctezuma, sweeping the ground on which he was to tread and laying down cloaks so that his feet should not touch the earth. Not one of these chieftains dared look him in the face. All kept their eyes lowered most reverently except those four lords, his nephews, who were supporting him."

Having been entertained lavishly for several weeks, however, Cortés sensed the vulnerability of his small army. He therefore decided to risk all by arresting Moctezuma, a move that could have sparked an Indian uprising had the Emperor resisted but which placed Cortés at the head of the Aztec Empire when Moctezuma surrendered peaceably. The Conquest had hardly begun, however. A few months later, angered that Cortés had rebelled against his authority, the Spanish governor of Cuba sent an expedition to arrest the conquistador. Cortés quickly headed east, defeated the force and added a further 1,000 Spaniards to his own army. But during his absence from Tenochtitlan, soldiers had fired on a crowd during a wild religious festival, killing over 4,000 Indians and sparking the first native uprising. Cortés managed to re-enter Tenochtitlan but found his army besieged in its palace. Moctezuma was ordered to beg his people to end their attacks, but he was struck on the head by a stone and died shortly afterwards. As water and food ran out, Cortés decided to abandon the city. The retreat was a disaster, with hundreds of Spaniards and Tlaxcalans killed or drowned as they fought their way along the causeways in the dark, frequently overloaded with gold. The debacle became known as *la noche triste,* or "the Sad Night."

Pursued by the Aztecs, the remnants of the conquering army struggled across the valley of Texcoco until they reached the friendly territory of Tlaxcala, where they remained for five months. Finally, in May 1521, a new offensive was launched, a lightning attack along the causeways and in boats which the Aztecs, under their new emperor, Cuauhtémoc, successfully fought off. Cortés then changed his tactics. Having cut off Tenochtitlan from supplies on the mainland, his army slowly advanced on the city, destroying everything in its path. Finally, by August 1521, the Aztec warriors were trapped in the area of Tlatelolco. It was there, surrounded by sacred temples, with all the symbolism that has dominated subsequent Mexican history, that the Aztec emperor was captured, the Aztec gods were defeated and the Aztec Empire died.

Cortés reigned only briefly over New Spain, as Mexico and Central America were now named. He appeased his top commanders by giving them land and Indians to work it, and having intimidated the highland Indians into subservience by the savagery of the final conquest of Tenochtitlan, he sent new expeditions to find trade routes and to subjugate more distant tribes. After one conquistador, Cristóbal de Olid, rebelled against his authority in Honduras, Cortés marched south, taking the emperor Cuauhtémoc with him. Earlier, he had burned Cuauhtémoc's feet in the hope of extracting the secret of the Aztec gold treasure, but on this trip he trumped up charges of plotting, and hanged the deposed monarch. "The execution of Cuauhtémoc was most unjust and was thought wrong by all of us," lamented Bernal Díaz del Castillo.

But by then the Indians were too broken to protest. Cortés' absence from the capital city, however, cleared the way for him to be maneuvered out of power by envoys from Madrid. He went into semi-retirement in his palace at Coyoacán, on the banks of Lake Texcoco, and, though named Marquess of Oaxaca a few years later, he never again ruled the country he had conquered. He died at the age of sixty-three during a visit to Spain, and was later buried in Mexico. The power of the conquistadors had been broken by the Church and the Crown, and New Spain had become in every sense a colony.

II

After the fall of Tenochtitlan, the Aztecs assumed the role of a defeated people. More thoroughly than the tribes that had not previously formed part of their empire, they were immediately enslaved. Their first task was to clear the rubble of their destroyed capital and then, using the stones from their temples and pyramids, to build the churches and palaces of their new masters. The architects were Spanish, but the craftsmen were Indian and their skills and tastes added to the ornateness of the stone carvings covering the new edifices. From the early sixteenth century, in fact, a new *mestizo* style—Mexican Colonial—was born, combining the baroque and the Aztec, creating magnificent buildings that seemed to capture the deep melancholy of the conquered race.*

In "urban" areas, the Indians resigned themselves to their fate, recognizing their defeat as the defeat of their gods and therefore gradually transferring their loyalty to the god of the Spaniards. Catholic missionaries in turn accepted a blending of Christianity with the religious traditions of the Indians. The concept of building churches on or near the sites of temples enabled the Indians to continue their pilgrimages. And by no

---

*Many of these churches and palaces survive today. In the Plaza de Tlatelolco, the Church and Convent of San Francisco sit astride the central section of an Aztec temple. In Mexico City's main plaza, or *zócalo,* the remains of the Templo Mayor lie close to the National Palace and the Metropolitan Cathedral. At Cholula, where pilgrim groups had raised hundreds of temples to dozens of gods, over 350 churches or chapels were built, many of which still stand, including the Church of Our Lady of the Remedies built atop a huge pyramid.

small chance, it was close to the sanctuary of the goddess Tonantzin on the Hill of Tepeyac outside Mexico City that the "dark" Virgin of Guadalupe first appeared to a humble Indian, Juan Diego, on December 12, 1531. Religious syncretism thus took place easily: not only did the profusion of Catholic saints match the myriad pre-Hispanic gods, but both religions included much pomp and ceremony and sustained precepts of punishment and reward which made even the Inquisition understandable.

As the conquistadors struck out from Mexico City to tame the Indians, they spread death, not only through destruction and massacres but also through European diseases that took the lives of perhaps two-thirds of Mexico's Indians during the sixteenth century alone. Missionaries followed—first Franciscans and later Dominicans, Augustines and Jesuits—and in their effort to repair the damage caused by the conquistadors, they left a trail of churches, convents and schools in their path. Through the campaigning of one priest, Bartolomé de Las Casas, the Council of the Indies freed all Indians from slavery in 1542. The Indians were still regarded as minors who required spiritual education, but the new practice of placing them under the guardianship, or *encomiendas*, of landowners was also banned by Spain, which preferred that they depend directly on the Crown than on new fiefdoms. Some Indians successfully retreated into mountains, jungles and deserts—to lands that the conquistadors had little interest in exploiting. But most could only withdraw into their souls: already, pride and tradition sought to live on behind a mask of subservience and formality.

The society that emerged soon reflected many of the worst features of Spanish military and religious authoritarianism. Madrid maintained tight control over its richest and most important colony by replacing its viceroy on average every four years. Anxious to remain in the King's good graces, the viceroys were duly absolutist. One such envoy noted tartly: "The colonists were born to be silent and obey and not to discuss or proffer advice on the higher affairs of government." Corruption—the trafficking in offices and the defrauding of the Crown—was widespread and seemingly tolerated. And despite the formal equality of all subjects, society was broken up into a tight caste system reminiscent of earlier European feudalism. The fearsome weapon of the Inquisition was also used to suppress all reformist thought or political nonconformity and to limit artistic and intellectual expression to religious themes.

What happened to the majority of Indians during the Colonial period, however, can be deduced from their economic function. Mexico's wealth derived from its Indian work force as well as its natural resources.

Usually the Indians worked on large estates, living in miserable huts outside the hacienda mansion, permanently indebted to the hacienda store, or *tienda de raya,* and growing corn on tiny plots rented—in exchange for tithe of corn—from the landowner. When silver and gold mining assumed greater importance, their cheap labor spawned opulent mining towns and provided the Spanish Crown with unprecedented wealth that helped finance its other colonies as well as its European wars. All manufacturing was officially banned in the New World in order to protect goods sent from Spain. But the cost of Spanish products was beyond the reach of most consumers in New Spain and, in time, Indians were brought to work in small factories, known as *obrajes,* that supplied rough textiles and metalwork and provided a focal point for subsequent urban growth.

Yet even by the eighteenth century, when Indians still constituted 70 percent of the population and *mestizos* another 20 percent, most continued to live in traditional style, far from cities, haciendas or mines, speaking their own languages, wearing local costumes, growing only corn and maguey cactus, ruled by their governors and worshipping their own gods. Some were too remote to be of interest to the Spaniards, but a few continued to resist domination. The Yaquis in northwestern Mexico, for example, first fought off the conquistadors in 1533 and continued to resist the advance of the white man, or *yori,* until early in this century. But even for those Indians gradually being absorbed by the system of economic exploitation, political developments in New Spain meant nothing. And when Independence from Spain finally came, it did nothing to change their lives.

The War of Independence was essentially a struggle between the economic interests of the *criollos*—the Spanish families that had settled in the New World—and the *peninsulares*—the Spaniards sent over by Madrid to govern the colony. Always latent, this conflict had grown in the eighteenth century as Mexico had rapidly expanded in population, urban development, wealth and even geography. It was then that Mexico incorporated the sparsely populated semi-arid regions that became Texas, New Mexico, Arizona and California a century later. The mood of the country was optimistic. Having dropped to two million in the sixteenth century, its population was now up to six million. Large cities, such as Mexico City, with 100,000 inhabitants, and Puebla, with 60,000, were emerging as important centers of *criollo* power. Silver production equaled that of the rest of the world, while new industries were being established to satisfy the needs of the one million *criollos* and 50,000 *peninsulares.* Foreign trade—no longer just with Spain—was growing, although this was controlled by the *gachupines,* as the *peninsulares* were known derogatorily. In all, at the end of the eighteenth century, Mexico was in no mood to be ruled from afar.

It was nevertheless Europe that created the conditions for Independence. As elsewhere in Spanish America, the American War of Independence and the French Revolution inspired many *criollo* priests, academics and liberal politicians to think anew about the nature of the society in which they lived. But few showed concern for the misery and backwardness of the 3.5 million Indians and 1.5 million *mestizos.* Nor would they have shared the view of the German traveler Alexander von Humboldt, who visited the country in 1803 and noted that "Mexico is a country of inequities [where] there is no equality in the distribution of wealth and culture." Rather, they were interested mainly in such concepts as "freedom" and "rights" for the enlightened minority.

As early as 1793, plots against Spanish rule began to be uncovered, but the first real chance for Independence came in 1808 after Napoleon conquered Spain and installed his brother Joseph as king. "Open your eyes, Mexican people, and use this opportunity," said one verse that appeared painted on walls in Mexico City. "Beloved compatriots, fate has placed freedom in your hands; if you do not shake off the Spanish yoke, you will indeed be wretched." At first, the *criollos* urged the viceroy to pledge loyalty to the ousted Ferdinand VII and declare that, until his reinstatement, Mexico would rule itself. The *peninsulares,* on the other hand, saw this as a move toward Independence and instead replaced the viceroy and accepted the authority of a junta operating in southern Spain. With that, the *criollos* decided to prepare a revolution.

Miguel Hidalgo y Costilla was the fifty-seven-year-old parish priest of Dolores, a poor, largely Indian town about 120 miles northwest of Mexico City. Although Hidalgo was unusual in his concern for the Indians, he was also an impatient and energetic political thinker who would frequently attend the meetings of conspiratorial groups organized by a Captain Ignacio Allende in the nearby city of Querétaro. Eventually, they set December 8, 1810, as the date for an insurrection. But one plotter, Josefa Ortiz de Domínguez, the wife of the *corregidor,* or magistrate, of Querétaro, learned that their plans had been discovered and, on the night of September 15, she sent a messenger to Dolores to advise Hidalgo and Allende.

Rather than fleeing, the two decided to act. Guns in hand, they released the town's prisoners and then filled the cells with Spaniards. Soon after daylight on September 16, with the church bells ringing out, Hidalgo climbed into the pulpit. "My children," he told the assembled

Indians and *mestizos,* "a new dispensation comes to us this day. Are you ready to receive it? Will you be free? Will you make the effort to recover from the hated Spaniards the lands stolen from your forefathers three hundred years ago?" He then proclaimed: "Mexicans! Long live Mexico! Death to the *gachupines!*" In reality, Hidalgo made no mention of Independence, preserving the myth that the battle was against those *peninsulares* who had betrayed Ferdinand. But the War of Independence, which was to continue for eleven years and take some 600,000 lives, had nevertheless begun.

Following a banner to Our Lady of Guadalupe, Hidalgo's ragged army of Indians and *mestizos,* carrying shovels and machetes, grew rapidly to some 20,000 strong as it stormed San Miguel, Celaya, Salamanca and Guanajuato. The rebellion took on a racial ferocity as Spanish homes and towns were burned and prisoners summarily executed. With new uprisings occurring in other cities, Hidalgo and Allende captured Valladolid (now Morelia) and then turned south toward Mexico City, engaging Spanish troops for the first time on October 30 at a mountain pass known as Monte de las Cruces. The insurgents seemed to gain the advantage, but Hidalgo unexpectedly ordered his army to withdraw. He was clearly no military commander, but he was a charismatic idealist, even freeing slaves and restoring communal lands to Indian groups in northwestern Mexico before his luck ran out. He was defeated at Aculco and again at Guadalajara, finally being captured and executed on July 30, 1811, just weeks after Allende suffered a similar fate.

The years that followed were chaotic. Another village priest, José María Morelos, continued the rebellion, seizing the region south of Mexico City and eventually convening a National Assembly in Chilpancingo in 1813 which formalized the Declaration of Independence. The following year, at Apatzingán, Morelos announced the new constitution, an idealistic document influenced by a French constitution drafted in 1793, but he was himself executed in December 1815. By then, Ferdinand was back on the Spanish throne and showed no sympathy for those *criollos* who had revolted in his name years earlier. He sent reinforcements to Mexico and soon only a handful of unimportant rebel leaders remained alive.

But in 1820 new developments in Spain again created conditions for insurrection. Ferdinand was forced by his generals to accept the Constitution of Cádiz, which was too liberal to appeal to the *peninsulares* and rich *criollos* of New Spain. They therefore now saw Independence as a necessary step to prevent the social reforms that Madrid was suddenly sponsoring. The enlightened ideas of Hidalgo and Morelos were replaced

by the need to preserve the status quo. The charming, cruel and coura-
geous military leader Colonel Agustín de Iturbide was called upon to
carry out their plans. Within weeks, Iturbide made a pact with the
remaining rebel leader, Vicente Guerrero, and together they proclaimed
the Plan of Iguala (also known as the Plan of Three Guarantees), which
stated that Roman Catholicism was Mexico's only religion, that all
Mexicans were equal and that an independent Mexico would be ruled by
a constitutional monarch brought from Europe. The rest followed easily.
The new army met little resistance, and on August 24, 1821, the Spanish
viceroy, Juan O'Donojú, recognized the Plan of Iguala in the Treaty of
Córdoba. On September 27, 1821, the triumphant army marched into
Mexico City, and the following day Iturbide was appointed head of the
new government.

III

Once the initial euphoria had subsided, new instability soon confirmed
that 300 years of authoritarian Spanish rule had ill prepared the colony
for freedom. In February 1822, Iturbide presided over the first session of
a new Constituent Assembly, but Republicans and Monarchists squab-
bled endlessly. Finally, on May 8, popular demonstrations were orchestrated calling on Iturbide to take over and, the following day, the Assembly agreed. On July 21, Iturbide was crowned Emperor Agustín I, the
first member of a new hereditary dynasty assigned, in the words of the
Assembly's proclamation, "not to exercise over you his absolute authority, such as was exercised by the former Spanish monarchs, but to fulfill
toward you the tender duties of a father toward his children." But
plotting against him immediately began. In December, General Antonio
López de Santa Anna, a man who was to plague Mexico over the next
three decades, rose up against Iturbide in favor of a republic. Other
mutinies followed and, rather than face a new war, Iturbide abdicated
on March 19, 1823, and left for Europe. He foolishly returned to Mexico
a year later, but his new bid for power was short-lived. He was executed
on July 19, 1824.

The new nation, it seemed, was born into political chaos. At the heart
of the instability that lasted until the 1870s, though, was the country's
economy. Not only was it weakened by the long War of Independence
—mining, agricultural and industrial production had all fallen sharply
—but the elite was also unwilling to provide adequate fiscal revenue to
enable successive governments to survive. In despair, several govern-

ments reached for the largest single concentration of wealth—the Church—but this immediately provoked feverish plotting by the Roman Catholic hierarchy. Sensing both the weakness and the potential wealth of Mexico, the United States and Britain also meddled brazenly in its domestic affairs, while lodges of the Scottish-Rite Masons and York-Rite Masons frequently resorted to violence in their competition for power.

For the Indian and *mestizo* peasants, the loss of the minimal protection offered by the Spanish Crown following Independence brought new injustice, and large landholdings, known as *latifundios*, grew rapidly at the expense of communal land. The disappearance of the viceroy's highly centralized power and its replacement by weak central governments also encouraged the emergence of provincial warlords, or *caciques*, who were in turn sustained by the powerful *latifundistas*. As a result, on the rare occasions when laws were passed in distant Mexico City to improve the lot of the Indians, they were ignored in the provinces. The *caciques*, who were invariably also generals, seemed to play a role similar to that of the rulers of the city-states under the Aztec Empire: they owed formal allegiance to some central authority, but in practice ran their regions with considerable autonomy in exchange for payment of tribute; and when taxation became too onerous, they simply rebelled.

General Santa Anna was the country's first *caudillo*, a kind of national *cacique*. From his hacienda in Veracruz he would set out with motley armies, alternately sparking or putting down uprisings, frequently accepting the invitation to become President, only to resign or be overthrown months later. Of the fifty governments formed during Mexico's first thirty years of independent life, eleven were headed by Santa Anna. But even he could not impose his authority on the whole country. And he would be remembered by history for presiding over the dismemberment of the new nation.

In the distant province of Texas, American settlers resented Mexico's tax demands, and in 1835 they overran the Mexican garrison there. Infuriated, Santa Anna personally led an army of 6,000 to punish the rebels, savagely massacring the defenders of an old mission house at El Alamo. But within two months an American force led by Sam Houston not only defeated the Mexican Army at San Jacinto—attacking to the cry "Remember the Alamo!"—but also captured Santa Anna. In exchange for his life, the general recognized Texas' independence and signed the Velasco Agreement, promising to keep Mexican troops south of the Rio Grande and to persuade Mexico's Congress to ratify the state's independence. Santa Anna was then sent handcuffed to Washington to confer with President Andrew Jackson before being allowed to return home in disgrace to Veracruz. In the meantime, the Mexican Congress rejected the Velasco Agreement.

Within two years, however, Santa Anna had somehow redeemed himself. On hearing that France had blockaded Veracruz to press for payment for damages caused to French citizens during Mexico City riots a decade earlier, he set off for the port. In reality, France won the conflict —known as the Pastry War because of compensation demanded by a French baker—since the government eventually agreed to pay its debts, but in the process Santa Anna lost his foot to a cannon and became a hero anew. Once recovered, he helped overthrow the government, buried his foot with full military honors and then was in and out of power three times in as many years.

Mexico was clearly ill equipped to deal with the external threat that was brewing. Not only did the U.S. Congress admit Texas into the Union in 1845, but Washington was also increasingly covetous of the unpopulated Mexican lands to the west. Some Mexican generals decided that Texas' incorporation into the United States was itself cause for war, and in 1846 they sent troops north of the Rio Grande. The United States, on the other hand, immediately saw the challenge as the excuse it needed. First, U.S. forces secured Texas and occupied Los Angeles and Santa Fe, then, led by General Zachary Taylor, they marched south, defeating an army commanded by Santa Anna in February 1847. Meanwhile, General Winfield Scott landed troops at Veracruz and began advancing toward the capital, also defeating Santa Anna in the process.

Scott finally took Mexico City in September of that year, and the American flag was raised above the National Palace. The last Mexican resistance came from young cadets at Chapultepec Castle, some of whom, according to legend, wrapped themselves in the Mexican flag and jumped off the ramparts to their deaths rather than surrender. On February 2, 1848, in exchange for $15 million, the Mexican government signed the Treaty of Guadalupe-Hidalgo and surrendered half its territory— 890,000 square miles, which included California, Arizona and New Mexico as well as Texas—to the United States. Soon afterwards, American troops withdrew, leaving a mutilated nation in danger of even greater disintegration.

A year earlier, the landed class of the Yucatán had formed a Maya army to confront the advancing American forces should they continue marching south. It was a near-fatal mistake. For the first time in centuries, the Mayas were given weapons, and almost immediately they turned their new guns against their masters. The *criollos* and *mestizos* fled by the thousands to the cities of Mérida and Campeche, and the War of the Castes began. The Indians, however, were more interested in recovering their communal lands than in killing the invaders of three centuries earlier. Rather than besieging Mérida, not a difficult task given the disarray in the rest of Mexico at the time, the Mayas returned to cultivating their land and re-establishing their traditional form of self-government.

Unable to obtain help from Mexico City, the governor of the Yucatán tried in vain to persuade Spain, Britain and even the United States to annex the peninsula and suffocate the rebellion, but none was interested in inheriting such chaos. From its nearby colony in Belize, Britain was in fact selling arms to both sides in the war, perhaps hoping that the Mayas would eventually turn to the British Crown for protection. Finally, with order slowly being restored in the capital, an army was sent to the Yucatán, and after two years of vicious fighting the Mayas were again defeated and half their population killed. Some Indians fled into the jungle and held out for many more years—their last stronghold finally fell in 1901—but most of the survivors returned to a state of serfdom, punished and distrusted even more than before.

The War of the Castes lasted as long as three years because Mexico City was too weak and distant to stop it sooner. But by 1850, although stable government was still two decades away, national politics were at last being shaped by two clearly identified parties—the Liberals and Conservatives. The Liberals, who tended to be of urban middle-class extraction and whose leaders were intellectuals and professionals, believed that Mexico should turn its back on its Spanish, Indian and Catholic traditions and build a new nation modeled after the United States. The Conservatives were supported by the landed, Catholic and military hierarchy and believed that the Church should be all-powerful, a strong army should be maintained and a dictatorship installed. "We are lost beyond recall if Europe does not soon come to our aid," the Conservative leader Lucas Alamán wrote in his program.

The new disarray that followed bore witness to his words. While awaiting some European solution, Alamán astonishingly gave power anew to Santa Anna, who immediately began persecuting Liberals and provoked an uprising that led to his ouster and the installation of Ignacio Comonfort in August 1855. The Liberals called elections for an Assembly to approve a radical new constitution broadening individual freedoms and curbing the power of the Church. In 1857, Comonfort was elected President and an Indian lawyer from Oaxaca, Benito Juárez, his Vice-President. But Conservatives led by General Félix Zuloaga forced

Comonfort to repeal the 1857 Constitution and imprison Juárez. Gripped by remorse, Comonfort freed Juárez and went into exile, leaving Zuloaga and Juárez both claiming the presidency. Juárez, however, was forced to flee and a new civil war erupted. But his struggle over the next fifteen years won him a prominent role in Mexican history.

A pure-blooded Zapotec Indian, Juárez was born in 1806 in the mountain village of San Pedro Guelatao, forty miles outside Oaxaca. Orphaned at the age of three and brought up by an uncle, he spoke little Spanish until his teens, when he found work in the home of a Franciscan lay brother-cum-bookbinder in Oaxaca. In exchange for helping around the house, Juárez was sent to school and eventually he entered a seminary. But the study of law appealed to him more than the priesthood and he later switched courses and graduated at the age of twenty-five. As a lawyer, he helped the poor, often defending them against the Church and local landowners without fee and, in the process, becoming drawn into politics. In the mid-1840s he was a Liberal delegate to a National Congress and in 1847 was called home to become provisional governor of Oaxaca, being confirmed in his post in elections the following year. From there, he built up his power base and developed his own version of the Liberal philosophy.

Juárez was unable to return to Mexico City until 1860, when he at last implemented the controversial Reform Laws that had provoked the Conservative rebellion three years earlier. Their main target was the enormously powerful Church, and they brought nationalization of Church property, establishment of a civil registry, closure of monasteries and convents and suppression of many religious festivals. But the Conservatives again reacted, appealing to Europe for help. In December 1861, drawn by the opportunities offered by Mexico's internal conflict, Britain, Spain and France landed troops in Veracruz under the pretext of securing payment on pending debts. Britain and Spain were eventually repaid and withdrew, but France had different ambitions.

Dreaming of spreading his influence to the New World, Napoleon III responded to the appeal of the Conservatives. And despite a much-celebrated Mexican victory at Puebla on May 5, 1862, the French expeditionary force occupied Mexico City and installed an Assembly which offered the crown of Mexico to Maximilian of Hapsburg, brother of the emperor Franz Josef. Soon afterwards, Maximilian arrived, accompanied by his wife, Archduchess Carlota, and they were installed as emperor and empress.

A decent but weak man, Maximilian was unable to assert his authority over the country. He angered the Conservatives by refusing to revoke the

Liberal reforms. Finally, when the United States, its civil war at an end, began aiding the Liberals and Napoleon withdrew most of his troops to meet a new threat from Prussia, Maximilian's adventure was doomed. He contemplated abdication but, according to legend, was told by his mother that "Hapsburgs never abdicate." He was captured at Querétaro and was executed on June 19, 1867.

Once again, Juárez returned to the presidency and defeated General Porfirio Díaz, a mixed-blood *cacique* from Oaxaca, in elections. For the first time in decades, the country was at peace; but the government was close to bankruptcy and its authority evaporated within miles of Mexico City. Juárez nevertheless discharged two-thirds of the army, ordered completion of the Mexico City–Veracruz railroad and reorganized the educational system. Ironically, he showed no special concern for the Indian population, apparently believing they were best served by integration into national life rather than isolated preservation of their traditions. His land reform program, aimed essentially at Church property, thus decimated the communal Indian lands, leaving them more vulnerable than ever to large landowners. In 1871, Juárez again defeated General Díaz in elections, but in July of the following year he died of a heart attack and his Vice-President, Sebastián Lerdo de Tejada, assumed office.

Brooding in his hacienda in Oaxaca, Díaz planned a new bid for power. He had fallen into disgrace for leading an abortive revolt against Juárez in 1871, but after Lerdo won re-election in 1876, Díaz rebelled once more, and in new elections that followed, he at last became President at the age of forty-seven. Having used the principle of "effective suffrage, no re-election" against Lerdo, Díaz felt obliged to step down in 1880, allowing Manuel González to serve out a disastrous four-year term. By 1884, however, Díaz had come to believe in his "manifest destiny" to save Mexico, and he repeatedly won re-election, becoming steadily more conservative until, to the familiar cry of "effective suffrage, no re-election," the Revolution erupted in 1910.

Díaz nevertheless brought Mexico its first extended period of stability since the Colonial period. He developed the country, built up the economy, kept the rich happy, made peace with the Church and virtually abolished politics. His motto—"little politics, much administration"— in practice meant that he was the only politician. Press censorship was instituted and many journalists and editors jailed, and all criticism of the government disappeared, while every state governor, senator and deputy was chosen by the President. A 3,000-man federal force known as the *rurales*—well versed in the *ley fuga* by which escaping prisoners could be shot—ended sixty years of chaos in the countryside by controlling banditry. In urban areas, even intellectuals were coopted. Mexico, it seemed, had been tamed.

During the Porfiriato, as the dictatorship became known, mining boomed, new industries appeared and foreign trade expanded thanks to the construction of new ports on both oceans. Between 1877 and 1910, the railroad network grew from 287 to 12,000 miles, enormously helping the integration of the country. Foreign investment also poured into Mexico for the first time, particularly into agriculture and mining, while foreign bankers at last felt confident that the government would pay off any new debts incurred. Such was the bounty for foreigners, in fact, that one disenchanted nationalist described Mexico as "the mother of foreigners and the stepmother of Mexicans." After 1892, when José Limantour became Finance Minister, government revenue even began to exceed expenditure, while economic activity boomed. In 1896, Díaz again sought re-election "so that Mexican and foreign businessmen may continue to enjoy the guarantees which enable them to increase their respective capital."

But Limantour and his powerful group—known as the *científicos,* or the scientists, because of their determination to apply science to the art of politics—also introduced a new degree of economic injustice into the system. While Mexico City seemed to flourish, little of the wealth filtered down to the *mestizo* miners and factory workers who continued to live off the traditional diet of tortillas and beans. In the countryside, although food production grew slowly, land concentration intensified. Some 3,000 families owned half the country and lived in magnificent haciendas, while millions of Indian and *mestizo* peasants were virtual serfs, tied either by their debts to the local store or by unpaid back wages which they still hoped to receive. Of the total population of some 13 million, almost half were Indians still living in traditional communities, but the expansion of agriculture meant that their communal lands were constantly being stolen from them. They therefore faced the choice of working as peons on their own land or opening up less fertile undergrowth.

Given the fatalism of the Indians and the repression prevailing throughout the country, revolution could only begin in the middle classes. When Díaz sought his fifth re-election in 1904 there were few protests, despite his unpopular choice of the cruel and corrupt Ramón Corral as Vice-President. The vice-presidency was an unimportant post, except that its holder would become President should the aging Díaz die. In 1908, however, the dictator caused consternation by telling an American journalist that Mexico was now ready for democracy, that an opposition party would be tolerated and that he would leave the presidency at the end of his current term. But it soon became apparent that Díaz was merely saying what he thought an American audience wished to hear, and when he decided to remain in office and again picked Corral as his running mate for the 1910 elections, some middle-class intellectuals and professionals decided to react.

In 1908, Francisco I. Madero, a dreamy idealist of wealthy extraction, had written a daring and popular book entitled *The Presidential Succession of 1910,* in which he proposed that someone other than Corral become the next Vice-President. Soon Madero was traveling the country promoting his ideas and stirring peasants, workers and the middle classes with the promise of change. In January 1910, Madero finally met Díaz and offered himself as the ruler's next Vice-President. Díaz treated him patronizingly and rebuffed him, but the interview steeled Madero's determination to keep going. In April 1910, his Anti-Reeleccionista Party nominated him as its presidential candidate, and by late summer his popularity was so great that he was jailed in San Luis Potosí and released only after Díaz's re-election on June 26.

But dissatisfaction with the government continued to grow, and having slipped over the Texas border in early October, Madero published his Plan of San Luis Potosí, claiming he was the rightful President and calling for an uprising on November 20, 1910. The rebellion was a disaster and Madero was soon back in hiding in the United States. But it sparked unrest, and rebel bands led by Pascual Orozco and Francisco Villa began attacking government forces in Chihuahua, eventually seizing the small border town of Ciudad Juárez. Madero decided to join them, and by early 1911 the irregulars had grown into an army as government forces defected to the rebel cause. Madero then called for the resignation of Díaz and Limantour, and when opposition groups became active in Mexico City and nearby Morelos state, the eighty-year-old dictator finally agreed to leave, boarding a train on May 26, 1911, for Veracruz and exile in France, where he died four years later. Madero arrived triumphantly in Mexico City on June 7 and in October was elected President. The Revolution, it seemed, had triumphed with only minimal bloodshed. In reality, it had only just begun.

3

From Revolution to Institution

I

Morelos, just south of Mexico City, was the first valley colonized by the Spaniards in the sixteenth century. Cortés himself built a palace in Cuernavaca and many powerful Colonial families had estates in the area. By the end of the nineteenth century, Morelos was the richest cane-growing region of Mexico. Its haciendas were small, but the land was fertile and wealth was enormously concentrated: its thirty-seven haciendas and twenty-four mills were owned by just seventeen *criollo* families. (After Independence, *criollo* became synonymous with aristocratic Mexicans with no Indian blood.) The demand for land was such that Indian communal lands, or *ejidos,* were also constantly being taken over by private farmers. And when the Liberal reforms put all Church and communal lands up for sale, most Indian plots in Morelos were absorbed by haciendas. Those Indians who protested were either killed or deported as slaves to the Yucatán. But most had no choice but to work on the haciendas or migrate to Mexico City.

Resentment at the loss of communal lands ran deep. When a thirty-year-old *mestizo* peasant, Emiliano Zapata, was elected head of the council of Ananecuilco, a village of just 400 inhabitants, his uncle gave him the legal titles to the land stolen by the nearby Hospital and Cuahuiztla haciendas. It was more than a symbolic gesture. Despite their fear of the *rurales,* the villagers had been agitating for recovery of their land and they looked to Zapata for action. He was respected as a man of courage, honesty and idealism, and having worked as a horse trainer for the rich families of Mexico City, he was also angry at the injustices and inequalities suffered by Ananecuilco. Behind his sad eyes and quiet voice, he was determined to defend the community's existing land and water rights and to recuperate lost land.

When the Plan of San Luis Potosí finally sparked the Chihuahua uprising in early 1911, Zapata and other community leaders in Morelos sensed an opportunity. They organized a band of eighty armed men and pledged loyalty to Madero, although unsure what he represented. Within weeks, the Zapatistas had seized numerous haciendas as well as the towns of Cuautla and Yautepec, adding to the pressure on Díaz, just fifty miles away in Mexico City. But the rebels seemed less interested in "effective suffrage, no re-election" than in a solution to their local problems. Implicit in Zapata's support for Madero was his understanding that the Revolution would return the communal lands to the villages. The contrasting objectives of the two leaders therefore sowed the seeds for the first conflict among the revolutionaries: Madero was seeking a political revolution, Zapata an economic one.

Relations between Madero and Zapata deteriorated rapidly. Under pressure to crush the "bandits" of Morelos, Madero persuaded Zapata to lay down his arms in exchange for a promise of land reform, but this truce lasted only a few months. The Zapatistas held on to land they had seized, and in September 1911 the brutal General Victoriano Huerta was dispatched to deal with Zapata, carrying out atrocities against villages and forcing the revolutionary leader into hiding. Finally, on November 25, with his own army reorganized, Zapata issued his Plan of Ayala, denouncing Madero as a traitor and calling for a new Revolution. "In the same way that we took up arms to elevate him to power," the proclamation noted, "we again take them up against him for defaulting on the promises to the Mexican people and for betraying the Revolution initiated by him. We are not personalists; we are partisans of principles and not of men." With this, the Revolution had a new social testament.

Zapata was not alone in his disillusionment. Madero believed his election comprised the entire Revolution and he did nothing to satisfy the demands or expectations of the Liberal and Anarchist intellectuals who had supported him. Even more serious, Madero failed to consolidate his power by filling the vacuum left by the ousted dictatorship. The new Congress therefore became a forum for endless squabbling among different factions, including a vocal group representing Porfirista interests. Further, much of Díaz's army and bureaucracy remained intact, while the Church, business groups and the United States were openly hostile to the new government.

Early in 1912, Pascual Orozco led a rebellion in northern Mexico, but it was put down by Huerta. In October of that year, General Díaz's nephew, Félix Díaz, and a Porfirista general, Bernardo Reyes, organized a new uprising, but they were captured and jailed. From their cells they continued plotting against Madero and on February 9, 1913, were freed by supporters who began marching on the National Palace. Madero called on Huerta to help him, but after ten days of artillery exchanges during which Reyes died, Huerta and Félix Díaz were brought together in a pact sponsored by the ultraconservative United States ambassador, Henry Lane Wilson. Félix Díaz then apprehended Gustavo Madero, the President's brother, and ordered him murdered, while Huerta's men seized Madero himself and his Vice-President, José María Pino Suárez. In exchange for sparing their lives and allowing them to go into exile, Huerta persuaded them to resign. But the following night, February 19, they too were murdered and Huerta became President.

The Huerta government was a total disaster, almost a caricature of the worst years of the ousted dictatorship. Supported by much of Díaz's army, Huerta ran the country like a general and trampled on politicians: all liberals and revolutionaries were purged and not a few opposition spokesmen were murdered before Congress was dissolved. Soon the dispersed revolutionary forces were united against Huerta. The long-term impact of the regime, however, was still more important: by supporting Huerta, the Church, the business and landed classes, the foreign community and the United States—at least the Taft administration—all defined themselves as enemies of the Revolution and earned the permanent distrust of the governments that followed.

As with Madero's own revolution, rebellion came again from the north. Venustiano Carranza, the governor of Coahuila, proclaimed himself First Chief of the Constitutionalist Army of the North and found in three men from Sonora—Alvaro Obregón, Adolfo de la Huerta and Plutarco Elías Calles—the military leaders he needed. Francisco Villa in turn entered Mexico from Texas and, while pledging loyalty to Carranza, formed his own army and began advancing through central Mexico. His charisma served him well: he managed to recruit thousands of poor Indians and *mestizos* into his ranks and, although responsible for innumerable atrocities, not least against Chinese immigrants, he became a romantic hero to American newspapers.

The new United States President, Woodrow Wilson, was also anxious to be rid of Huerta. Claiming that the Mexican government had not apologized adequately for the brief arrest of some American sailors in Tampico the month before, Wilson ordered Marines to seize Veracruz in April 1914 in the hope of accelerating Huerta's departure. As things turned out, the move backfired: Huerta did not leave immediately and Carranza was forced to demand the withdrawal of the invading force.

Meanwhile, riding the railroad built by General Díaz thirty years earlier, Villa moved rapidly south, finally winning the crucial battle of Zacatecas in June. To the west, Obregón took Guadalajara and Querétaro, and by cutting off Villa's coal supplies at Zacatecas, Carranza ensured that Obregón reached Mexico City first. By July, Huerta had fled into exile, although the U.S. Marines did not leave Veracruz until November of that year.

The second Revolution, then, had been won, but the revolutionary forces were still deeply divided over the crucial question of land. Under the Huerta regime, Zapata had retained control over much of Morelos. Villa had also confiscated the vast Chihuahua estates of the Terrazas family and converted them into state enterprises. But Carranza, a political moderate and himself a landowner, emerged as a new Madero, intent on resisting the pressure for sweeping land reform. And when a new political convention incorporated Zapata's Plan of Ayala into its program, Carranza ordered his followers to walk out. Villa then took over, named General Eulalio Gutiérrez as President and marched on Mexico City. Ill prepared to fight, Carranza and Obregón withdrew to Veracruz, while some 50,000 Villista and Zapatista soldiers took over the capital. Briefly, the two peasant revolutionaries met, even posing for historic photographs together, but Villa was clearly in charge and Zapata soon returned to Morelos, leaving many of his soldiers scavenging for food in the city.

Villa's brief rule was disastrous. General Gutiérrez soon fled, while middle-class liberals turned away in despair. In January 1915, the government collapsed and Obregón retook the capital, immediately giving chase to Villa, who fled north, his army rapidly disintegrating. In October, when President Wilson recognized Carranza's government, Villa felt betrayed and, returning to his guerrilla activity of earlier times, declared open season on Americans. In March 1916, he raided Columbus, New Mexico, killing numerous Americans and destroying property. This in turn prompted Washington to dispatch a 10,000-man expeditionary force headed by General John J. Pershing into Mexico in pursuit of Villa. It never found him and finally withdrew eleven months later, but it resurrected Villa as a hero, remembered to this day as the leader of the only foreign "invasion" of the United States. Nonetheless, Villa's political days were over. He retired to a hacienda given to him by the government in 1920; three years later he was murdered.

Zapata, in contrast, had such deep roots in Morelos that he was more difficult to defeat. For years, he had dominated the region, extracting taxes and "protection" money from some surviving haciendas, expropriating others and destroying many more. The "stolen" communal lands were returned to the villages, which were in turn permitted a high degree of self-government. Disputes over boundaries plagued the Indian communities, but Zapata sent agrarian commissioners to mediate the quarrels. The general's own headquarters was in Tlaltizapán, a small town near Yautepec that seemed to epitomize the simplicity of rural life: the peasants wore large straw hats and rough white pajama-like costumes, drank beer, rode horses and gambled at cockfights. But failing to recognize that the Morelos experience could not survive unless repeated elsewhere in Mexico, Zapata never took his troops beyond the nearby states of México and Puebla. Instead, he continued to look to the central government to implement his Plan of Ayala. Carranza, though, had already disappointed him and Zapata pledged to keep on fighting.

In June 1916, having isolated Villa in the north, Carranza ordered General Pablo González to put down Zapata. The cost was high. Thousands of peasants were executed and hundreds more deported to the Yucatán "to become useful to society," while many towns and villages were badly damaged by artillery. The Zapatistas at first withdrew, but soon regrouped and retook Cuernavaca and Cuautla. Confident that Carranza would be overthrown, Zapata began issuing a stream of revolutionary proclamations. But in 1918 Morelos was ravaged by Spanish influenza and tens of thousands of people died. That winter, General González returned to the offensive, capturing Cuernavaca and forcing the Zapatistas to flee. The fighting was as bloody and bitter as any that took place during the Revolution: Carranza, angered by Zapata's survival and jealous of his greater popularity, was determined to eliminate the general; Zapata and his men waited in the hills for an opportunity for revenge.

In April 1919, González ordered one of his officers, Colonel Jesús Guajardo, to feign defection to Zapata's side with 500 men and, to give credibility to the ploy, he even allowed the "rebels" to attack a federal column and kill fifty-nine soldiers. On April 9, Zapata met with Guajardo and agreed to confer the following day at Guajardo's headquarters in the Chinameca hacienda. After waiting in the sun for hours outside the hacienda, Zapata finally accepted an invitation to beer and a meal inside. As he and a ten-man escort rode through the gates of the hacienda, he was shot down by a fusillade, dying instantly. His body, draped over a mule, was taken to González's headquarters in Cuautla that night. As poor peasants paraded past Zapata's coffin, many of them crying with grief and trembling with fear, Carranza and the "revolutionaries" in Mexico City raised glasses of champagne to celebrate the demise of the "gangster."

While fighting continued in Morelos, the new Mexican state was being shaped by the Constituent Assembly that met in Querétaro in November 1916. The drafting of the Constitution was difficult. In contrast to earlier conventions, the Assembly was not dominated by intellectuals or combatants, but by members of a rising urban *mestizo* class—professionals, teachers and bureaucrats whose social mobility had been blocked during the Porfiriato. They were not revolutionaries as such, but had strong dislikes, not least of the Church, foreigners, large landowners, industrialists and dictators of the ilk of Díaz and Huerta. They also envisioned a nation ruled by true Mexicans—that is, Indians and *mestizos*—rather than descendants of the conquistadors and other white foreigners. And through their pressure, Carranza was obliged to accept a liberal Labor Code as well as the basic tenets of Zapata's Plan of Ayala, including revival of the *ejido* land system.

Still more controversial was the federal structure to be adopted. The ideal appeared to be autonomy for individual states and separation of the powers of the executive, legislative and judiciary branches along the lines operating in the United States, but this also seemed to be a formula for chaos: Presidents would be paralyzed by Congress and states would be in a perpetual state of rebellion. Mexico's democratic dream and authoritarian tradition were therefore fused: a formal democracy was created in the Constitution, but the President was given disproportionately greater power than Congress. To prevent personal dictatorships, though, he was barred from seeking re-election after a single four-year term. Each President would personify the system and the system would provide the continuity.

With the Constitution in place, however, little improved. Open pressure and meddling by the United States, Britain and Germany continued, both to protect their local economic interests and to influence events in Europe.* The economy was devastated by years of warfare, with the

---

*The famous Zimmermann telegram that accelerated the United States' entry into World War I in 1917 revealed a German proposal that Mexico attack the United States, thereby tying down American troops who would otherwise be available for the European front. In exchange, following the supposed German victory over the Allies, Mexico would recover territories lost to the United States in 1848. The telegram was intercepted and decoded by British intelligence and made public by Washington before Mexico had a chance to respond.

haciendas no longer producing exportable food and the mines virtually shut down, although oil output and exports continued to grow in the peaceful Gulf coast area. The land reform soon lost its way in the emerging agrarian bureaucracy. Trade unions were formed, but were repressed when they called a strike to protest inflation. New political parties—from ultra-Catholic to Moscow-line Communist—appeared in hopes of seizing a share of power. And throughout the country there were young colonels and generals who had fought in the Revolution and were suddenly unemployed and restless. Some became state governors and pushed along reforms faster than the central government; others seemed more concerned with enriching themselves by defending business or landed interests.

Perhaps most critically, Carranza himself provided no leadership. A man of few words, his thoughts well hidden behind tiny round glasses and a long white beard, he was a patriarch at a time when a politician was needed. As the country drifted, Alvaro Obregón began to cast an ever-deeper shadow over the government. Supposedly retired in his home state of Sonora, Obregón remained a popular figure and, having single-handedly installed Carranza in the presidency in 1915 and backed his election in 1917, he expected to become his successor in 1921. But Carranza had different ideas. Perhaps because he would lose all power once Obregón became President or, as his defenders argue, perhaps because he hoped to lead the country away from militarism, he picked Ignacio Bonillas, at that time Mexico's ambassador in Washington, as the civilian candidate of the Constitutionalist Party.

Early in 1920, Carranza sent troops to smother a conflict over water rights in Sonora, but Obregón, supported by the civilian state governor, De la Huerta, and the local army commander, General Calles, rebelled and marched south. Carranza panicked, ordered that a convoy of trains be filled with archives, furniture, presses and whatever gold coins remained in the Treasury and headed for Veracruz, where he hoped to continue the government. But the lead train was derailed and Carranza had to make his way on foot toward Veracruz. Accompanied by General Rodolfo Herrero and a handful of soldiers, he spent the night of May 21 in the village of Tlaxcalantongo. The following morning, his body was found riddled with bullets and Herrero announced that the President had committed suicide. The Sonora generals—the Northern Dynasty, as it would become known—marched into Mexico City a few days later. De la Huerta became provisional President until elections in November 1920, which were overwhelmingly won by Obregón. The Revolution at last had a true *caudillo*.

II

In contemporary terms, Obregón was an authoritarian reformer: politically, he felt the country needed a dictator for some semblance of order to be restored; socially, he recognized the need for change, but along bourgeois and not Marxist lines. He nevertheless faced pressure from all sides. Conservatives—the wealthy, the Church and the United States government—considered him a dangerous radical. The trade unions were flexing their muscles, intellectuals demanded more rapid reforms and peasants waited impatiently for their promised land. Finally, there were the scores of revolutionary generals who were unaccustomed to a strong central authority.

Obregón therefore moved carefully, gradually establishing the state as the ultimate political arbiter. Trade unions were increasingly coopted by bribery, intimidation and the illusion of shared power, all of which helped to appease the private sector. Land reform was embraced as a firm political commitment, but many haciendas remained in the hands of their traditional *criollo* owners or revolutionary generals. Moreover, coming from the north, where arid land required large landholdings, the President had a strong personal aversion to the distribution of small plots.

Obregón showed particular skill in handling the United States. Following Carranza's murder, President Wilson refused to recognize the newly elected government. And when President Harding took office in 1921, he demanded confirmation of the rights of foreign oil companies, compensation for damage caused to American property during the Revolution and resumption of interest payments on the foreign debt. At the time, Obregón was under strong pressure to move against foreign companies that owned key sectors of the economy—oil, mines, railroads, electricity and banks—and were openly hostile to the revolutionary government. But in the Bucareli Agreements of 1923, a compromise was worked out: foreign-owned land would be protected from the agrarian reform, compensation claims would be studied by a special commission and foreign oil concessions were ratified, although a new production tax would be used to cover Mexico's foreign debt obligations. In August 1923 United States recognition was finally granted.

The revolutionary generals, however, remained a permanent source of trouble, attracting all sectors interested in subverting the established order. As in the past, the selection of the next President became a new excuse for rebellion. Obregón picked his right-hand man, Calles, to be his successor. But De la Huerta, another longtime associate, felt rebuffed and in December 1923 was joined by military commanders in Veracruz, Jalisco and Oaxaca in a rebellion. After three months of hostilities, during which the United States shipped armaments to Obregón, the uprising was defeated and all the mutinous generals were executed, although De la Huerta escaped to Los Angeles.

But if Obregón's main contribution was to pacify the country after the chaos of the Revolution, it was Calles who tamed the political forces that had been released, not only avoiding a clash with his mentor but also building on Obregón's achievements. He tightened controls and resorted increasingly to violence to eliminate his enemies, but he was also a skilled political negotiator. The Army, purged following the 1923 rebellion, was kept happy with payoffs and privileges, while the peasantry was rewarded for its loyalty with more land. Calles also began to modernize the country's economy, benefiting from oil production, which, although down from its 1921 peak, remained important. He founded the Bank of Mexico, instituted the first income tax and spent heavily on education, health and infrastructure. Some Porfirista wealth returned and was invested in banks and industry, although politics remained in the hands of the revolutionary elite.

Calles' ruthlessness was most apparent in his persecution of the Church. The traditional anticlericalism of Liberals had been reinforced by the Church's support for the Díaz and Huerta dictatorships. Still more crucial, the post-revolutionary regime viewed the Church as a permanent obstacle to consolidation of its power and modernization of the country. The 1917 Constitution had nationalized churches, established that only Mexican nationals could be priests, banned religious processions and forbade clergy from appearing in public in cassocks, from voting or discussing politics, from owning property and from involvement in education. But it was only under Calles that these articles were strictly enforced. When the government required additionally that all native-born priests be licensed in 1926, the Catholic hierarchy ordered a boycott of churches by the clergy. In the western states of Jalisco, Michoacán, Guanajuato, Colima and Zacatecas, fanaticized peasants led by conservative priests then launched a guerrilla war to the cry of "Viva Cristo Rey!"—"Long live Christ the King!"—which gained them the name Cristeros. And in the name of Christ, they carried out murder, arson and sabotage.

The government promptly responded in kind, unleashing a fierce wave of persecution throughout the provinces. Cristeros were massacred and priests hanged, while in other regions masses were held in secret. In the southeastern state of Tabasco, Governor Tomás Garrido Canabal organized bands of "red shirts" to attack priests and destroy churches. In Mexico City, it became fashionable to loot churches of their Colonial art. Even after 1929, when the dispute was formally settled and churches reopened, religious fanaticism and confrontations persisted. In 1932, the archbishop of Morelia was deported amid official warnings that renewed agitation would lead "churches to be turned into schools and workshops for the benefit of the proletariat." In 1935, there were still bloody clashes in Mexico City between Catholics and "red shirts." In the late 1930s, a new ultraconservative religious movement called Sinarquismo emerged among the peasants of the Bajío region. But the traditional power of the Catholic hierarchy had been broken.

The removal of the Church from politics consolidated the revolutionary leadership and centralized bureaucracy that had come to power a decade earlier. The country was still dominated by strong political personalities, but its two *caudillos*—Calles and Obregón—seemed able to share the limelight. When it came to selecting his successor, Calles amended the Constitution to enable Obregón to run again and extended the presidential term from four to six years. The strength of Calles and Obregón was such that only two generals rebelled, and they were quickly caught and executed. Many intellectuals, labor leaders and young politicians were dismayed at the prospect of indefinite alternation in power, but could do little.

Just days after his new election, however, Obregón was murdered by a newspaper cartoonist and fervent Catholic, José de León Toral, while celebrating his victory in a restaurant. Apparent links between the assassin and a nun fanned the terror campaign against the Church, although many suspected that Calles himself was behind the murder. In any event, with Obregón joining Madero, Zapata, Carranza and Villa as revolutionary martyrs, Calles became the sole ruler of the country. He announced pompously that the era of the *caudillos* was over, that the time had come "to pass from a country of one man to a nation of institutions and laws." To the astonishment of the nation, he stepped down from the presidency at the end of his term. But he had no intention of surrendering power. Between 1928 and 1935, running the country from his mansion in Cuernavaca, Calles was known as *Jefe Máximo* and his rule as the *maximato*.

Calles was not a dictator in the traditional mold. He brutalized the Church, repressed the Left, tolerated large landowners and wooed the United States. But he also saw the need to institutionalize the Revolution in a broad political party that would accommodate the ambitions and interests of normally competing sectors. Upon leaving the presidency, he virtually decreed the National Revolutionary Party (PNR) into existence. It incorporated assorted liberal, socialist and intellectual factions and it absorbed the growing bureaucracy and even the Army. Everyone in and around the government—ministers, governors, congressmen, army officers, judges, civil servants—was simply pronounced a member, as were the rank-and-file of the 400 or so parties and movements that emerged from the Revolution. The PNR was born with perpetual power virtually guaranteed. It adopted the national colors and became instantly synonymous with the state.

A left-leaning lawyer, Emilio Portes Gil, had been named provisional President in 1929, pending new elections in which the PNR would first make its appearance. But the perennial succession problem had still not been resolved. The first party convention favored nominating General Aaron Sáenz, but Calles imposed his choice, General Pascual Ortiz Rubio. Numerous generals led by Gonzalo Escobar then rebelled, but were crushed. The Communist Party, founded in 1919, stirred unrest among workers and peasants and was also repressed. PNR dissidents then backed Obregón's former Education Minister, José Vasconcelos, who attacked the authoritarianism and corruption of the *maximato*. But he was awarded just 105,000 of almost two million supposed votes and then chased out of the country.

Political problems continued. In 1932, Ortiz Rubio convinced himself he was in power as well as in office and dismissed several ministers without consulting Calles. Informed of this, the *Jefe Máximo* ordered an aide to draft the President's letter of resignation, which Ortiz Rubio lamely signed. Congress then replaced him with Calles' choice, General Abelardo Rodríguez. The mood of the country was agitated. Fascist influence from Italy and Germany was beginning to make itself felt. The depression had shattered the weak commodities-linked economy, while peasants, workers and younger politicians were creating pressure within the PNR for more rapid social change. The mood of disillusionment was echoed by Luis Cabrera, an influential figure at the time of the Revolution. "Freedom, equality, justice, effective suffrage, no re-election, separation of powers, free municipalities, sovereignty of the states, international independence . . . words, words, words," he wrote in *Twenty Years After*. "The Revolution has resolved none of the country's political problems."

When, therefore, the party met in December 1933 to pick its candidate for the 1934 elections, a clash seemed certain. Calles himself favored Manuel Pérez Treviño, the PNR's first president, but he followed the mood of the convention and accepted the thirty-nine-year-old governor of Michoacán, General Lázaro Cárdenas del Río. The choice seemed good to the *Jefe Máximo:* not only had Cárdenas always been loyal, but his image as an energetic reformer promised to revive popular faith in the new party. Although opposed only by two insignificant candidates —one from the Communist Party and the other from an anti-Calles coalition—Cárdenas campaigned untiringly throughout the country, visiting remote villages on horseback, reaching out to ordinary workers and illiterate peasants and in the process building a true popular base for himself. His election was a foregone conclusion, and by the time he took office, he already felt that his power came from the masses and not from Calles.

III

A *mestizo* with Tarascan Indian blood in his veins, Cárdenas had demonstrated his concern for the common man while governor of Michoacán. Once in the presidency, he continued to hear the complaints and problems of the poor as if his reformist fervor were kept alive by these contacts. He was austere in his personal life: he did not smoke or drink, he suppressed gambling and prostitution and he moved out of the opulent official residence in Chapultepec Castle. Jokes abounded that Cárdenas had no time to receive ministers or ambassadors, but would spend hours chatting with peasants in the countryside. But his style was not empty demagoguery, as Calles would soon discover.

Cárdenas first showed his hand by supporting workers in several strikes and then by committing himself to resuming expropriation and distribution of large haciendas. By mid-1935, a disgruntled Calles was sniping publicly at Cárdenas from Cuernavaca, at one point even suggesting that the situation resembled that existing under Ortiz Rubio, a clear call for Cárdenas' resignation. But the President took up the challenge and abruptly removed all military zone commanders, state governors, senators, deputies and ministers identified with Calles. And in April 1936, after new plotting by the Calles group, Cárdenas ordered the arrest of Calles and several aides, had them placed on a plane for exile in Texas and then announced to the nation that the epoch of revolutionary *caudillos* was truly over.

During his remaining four years in office, Cárdenas was to prove a daring and visionary leader whc succeeded in reviving some of the dreams of the Revolution. Until then, many promises had been made and some haciendas had been taken over, but no President had confronted the perennial problem of the landless. Between 1934 and 1940, however,

Cárdenas created some 180,000 *ejidos* covering 46 million acres and benefiting 750,000 families. He also formed the National Peasant Confederation (CNC), an attempt to give the peasantry a voice within the ruling party, and launched a campaign to integrate the country's Indian population.

In the labor movement, the power of the corrupt pro-Calles boss Luis Morones was undermined by that of Vicente Lombardo Toledano and his socialist General Worker and Peasant Confederation of Mexico (CGOCM), which in February 1936 was absorbed by the new Confederation of Mexican Workers (CTM). At first, this too was run by Lombardo, but its cabal, known as "the Five Little Wolves," also included Fidel Velázquez, an anti-Communist former milkman who would dominate the Mexican labor movement for the next five decades. Under Cárdenas, though, the role of labor was still being shaped. After nationalizing foreign railroad companies in 1937, for example, he handed over management to railroad workers. A disastrous year later, the government resumed direct control.

With enough agitation taking place at home, Cárdenas preferred to avoid disturbing the modus vivendi worked out with the foreign oil companies. Having once served as army commander in Tampico, the center of operations for these companies, his nationalist sensibilities had long been offended by the arrogance of the foreign oil executives and the discrimination suffered by their Mexican employees. Had the companies not displayed this same arrogance in challenging the government during a labor dispute, Cárdenas might not have carried out the act for which he is most remembered: the nationalization of the oil companies. On March 18, 1938, however, citing the "defamation, disobedience and challenge" of the American and British companies, the expropriation decree was signed.

Both Cárdenas' personal popularity and the popularity of the measure helped to avert a serious political crisis. But an acute economic slump followed, including a 66 percent currency devaluation, a wave of inflation and a freeze on investment. The nationalization also complicated Mexico's relations with the world. In exile, Calles had already complained about Cárdenas' "Communism," a charge that was now widely repeated. Further, Cárdenas had granted asylum to Leon Trotsky in January 1937 and had enthusiastically helped the Republican cause in the Spanish Civil War. (Trotsky was murdered by Stalinists in Mexico City in August 1940.) After the oil expropriation, he faced a boycott of Mexican oil exports and enormous pressure to restitute the companies' interests. In fact, only World War II saved the Mexican economy from total collapse.

Cárdenas' role in this drama alone earned him a prominent place in Mexican history. Yet, while the land expropriations, the labor agitation and the nationalization itself seemed to be pointing Mexico along a radical path, Cárdenas was essentially a transitional figure. Leftist intellectuals were influential in his administration, while his own popularity among peasants and workers frightened much of the new oligarchy. But Cárdenas was no Marxist; rather, his main objective seems to have been the strengthening of the emerging system. He made the last serious effort to carry out the agrarian promises of the Revolution, he prepared the country for its subsequent industrial takeoff and he turned the ruling party into a powerful instrument of the presidency.

When Cárdenas took over in 1934, he found that the PNR reflected Calles' personal power and lacked an internal structure capable of organizing the country's political forces along essentially corporativist lines. After creating the CNC peasant group and encouraging the emergence of the CTM over other labor organizations, he therefore sponsored the formation of a civil servants' union that could dominate a new white-collar National Confederation of Popular Organizations (CNOP). Finally, anxious to limit the political ambitions of the revolutionary generals but unable to eliminate their influence entirely, Cárdenas formed a military sector. Thus, organized into four groups—labor, peasant, popular and military—and guided by a National Executive Committee and a President named by Cárdenas himself, the party was ready to become a machine. In 1938, the PNR was renamed the Party of the Mexican Revolution (PRM).

Soon afterwards, the struggle for the succession began and once again the generals reached for power. In May 1938, General Saturnino Cedillo, a maverick *cacique* from San Luis Potosí, had rebelled, but the Army remained loyal to Cárdenas and Cedillo was defeated and killed. Several other generals, however, were seeking the PRM's nomination, among them Manuel Avila Camacho, the conservative Defense Minister, who eventually won Cárdenas' backing. Middle-class and Catholic groups disenchanted with Cárdenas' radicalism then formed the Revolutionary Party of National Unification and nominated General Juan Andreu Almazán, an influential figure during the Revolution who had grown rich and conservative. He did well at the polls, and after the government resorted to fraud to ensure his defeat, there were fears of a civil war. But the Army proved loyal to the system and in December 1940, like Calles before him and every President since then, Cárdenas was able to hand over power to his chosen successor.

More than any strategy of the Avila Camacho regime, it was World War II that marked the end of the agrarian revolution and the beginning of the industrial revolution. The United States, eager to buy all the raw materials available in Mexico, contributed capital and technology to stimulate production of minerals, metals, oil and food. The absence of imported consumer goods also stimulated the domestic manufacturing industry, which could live off a captive market. Employment possibilities multiplied in Mexican cities, provoking a massive exodus of peasants from the countryside. Tens of thousands also obtained well-paid temporary jobs in the United States under the 1942 Bracero Agreement. And while inflation rose sharply, corruption flourished and price and quality controls were nonexistent, the balance was positive, ending Mexico's role of supplier of raw materials and turning it toward industrialization. It was a precarious launching pad, but it nevertheless served as a platform for the takeoff that would follow.

The war also provided an excuse for the reversal of many of the policies instituted by Cárdenas. The land reform program was halted on the grounds that the breakup of large estates would affect production at a time when secure food supplies were essential. The local Communist Party's support for the Axis powers during the life of the Non-Aggression Pact between Germany and the Soviet Union was reason enough to purge the CTM of all leftist influence, including that of Lombardo Toledano. Relations with the United States were also patched up, and in 1943 Avila Camacho attended a border conference with President Roosevelt, the first encounter of U.S. and Mexican Presidents since Porfirio Díaz and William H. Taft met in 1909. Mexico had joined the Allies in April 1942 after a Mexican oil tanker was sunk off Florida by a German U-boat, and although thousands of Mexicans fought in the U.S. Army, Mexico's dispatch of an air squadron to the Philippines in 1945 became an important symbol of the end of its isolation.

Politically, the country was in sound shape. Although an uncharismatic bureaucrat, Avila Camacho was strong enough to drop the military sector from the PRM. He even celebrated Independence Day in 1942 by inviting all living ex-Presidents—including Cárdenas, who was serving as Defense Minister, and Calles, who returned home from exile —to stand with him in a display of national unity. Two capable men were also in charge of key ministries—Ezequiel Padilla managed relations with the Allies as Foreign Minister and Miguel Alemán Valdés oversaw domestic political security from the Interior Ministry. Alemán's control of the labor movement was crucial in the succession race. At the PRM's convention of January 1946, Alemán was not only nominated; he also changed its name to the Institutional Revolutionary Party (PRI), the name it still holds today. It was a fundamental reform. The concept of an "institutionalized" Revolution left no room for the romance and improvisation of a Zapata or a Villa. The Revolution was growing mature and respectable.

IV

Most historians identify Alemán as the architect of modern Mexico. A series of phenomena that continue to shape the country today—massive industrialization, chaotic urbanization, high economic growth rates, emergence of a big-spending middle class and neglect of social problems —first made their appearance in the late 1940s. A crucial transfer of power also took place from those who had fought the Revolution to a much younger generation of civilian university-trained *técnicos,* as they described themselves. In the process, control of the highly centralized regime passed increasingly to the political bureaucracy.

Once in office, Alemán moved the government sharply to the right. Although still only forty-two years old, he had already proved himself a good businessman, building up a fortune while governor of Veracruz and Interior Minister. He firmly believed that wealth must be formed before it can be distributed, or, as his critics put it, growth first and justice later. With the war over and Mexico's coffers full, Alemán also felt the competitive advantages enjoyed during the war years would soon be whittled away. The country had to grow rapidly if it was not to fall back into the stagnation that dominated the prewar era. Development thus replaced nationalism as the guiding principle of the regime.

An extraordinary boom followed. The government spent heavily on construction of roads, dams and irrigation canals and, through fiscal incentives, encouraged local and foreign private investment. Alemán also protected commercial farmers from expropriation and stimulated cultivation of new export crops. It was a formula for concentration of wealth and corruption. Public works in particular enriched many officials and Alemán himself bought up much of Acapulco before building a new airport and oceanfront boulevard in the resort as well as a new road linking it to Mexico City. But with the Army no longer a threat, officials could safely turn their attention away from politics toward business. "Government is business and business is government," Valentín Campa, a Communist railroad workers' leader, remarked at the time.

In 1952, Alemán chose as his successor Adolfo Ruiz Cortines, a soft-spoken bureaucrat who, although twelve years his senior, had succeeded him as governor of Veracruz and Interior Minister. The new government was unspectacular. Ruiz Cortines eliminated some of the worst graft and tried to consolidate the wild growth of the late 1940s, devaluing the peso in 1954 and slowing the expansion of public expenditure. Foreign investment continued to increase, attracted by tax breaks, a captive market and a growing middle class. In politics, Ruiz Cortines gave women the vote, but was otherwise cautious. His decision to pick his Labor Minister, Adolfo López Mateos, as the PRI's candidate for the 1958 elections therefore seemed out of character. López Mateos was young and energetic and would bring a new verve and style to Mexican politics. After three successive conservative administrations, Ruiz Cortines clearly recognized the system's need for an injection of populism.

López Mateos was no leftist. Soon after taking office in 1959, he used the Army to break a strike organized by the Communist-led Railroad Workers' Union and jailed its leaders. During his administration, Rubén Jaramillo, perhaps the most important peasant leader to emerge since Zapata, was also murdered. Yet López Mateos was undoubtedly a populist. The middle classes seemed charmed by his good looks and Don Juan reputation. He stepped up the distribution of plots to peasants, handing out almost as much land as Cárdenas, albeit of inferior quality. He also expanded the social security system to incorporate more urban workers and launched an ambitious school-building program in rural areas. He even upset the private sector with his rhetoric. But his main obsession was foreign policy, and he became the first Mexican President to travel extensively abroad. He refused to join other Latin American countries in breaking ties with Cuba's new revolutionary government, demonstrating Mexico's independence from Washington. But the impact of the Cuban Revolution was also felt among Mexican youths and intellectuals, and the resulting mood of restlessness prompted a flight of nervous private capital.

The leftist unrest affecting much of Latin America contributed to the selection of the Interior Minister, Gustavo Díaz Ordaz, as successor to López Mateos in 1964. Díaz Ordaz was known to be pro-American and a political conservative, the qualities sought by the domestic and foreign private sectors. In fact, soon after taking office, Díaz Ordaz sent troops against striking doctors and nurses and put students on notice that the new government had little sympathy with their noisy activism. Even the idea of adding a fourth sector—business—to the PRI was mooted, and dropped only when it was realized that the private sector was in power without having to seek office. Some land continued to be distributed pro forma to the peasantry, but living conditions in the countryside deteriorated. A population growth rate of 3.5 percent added to tensions and forced more peasants to migrate to urban slums. But abroad, Mexico's political stability and "economic miracle"—annual growth rates averaging over 6 percent—were cited as models for other developing countries.

The decision to invite the 1968 Olympics to Mexico City had in fact been made by López Mateos, but Díaz Ordaz was no less proud that Mexico should become the first developing nation to host the Games. The political mood of students, intellectuals and much of the middle classes, however, had soured under Díaz Ordaz's unsubtle version of authoritarianism, and the huge expenditure on preparations for the Olympics became a further irritant. The protests that erupted in the summer of 1968 nevertheless came as a surprise. The ingredients for widespread unrest had long existed, yet the fatalism of the masses, disarray among the opposition and an efficient security apparatus had helped to preserve stability. But the system proved ill prepared to deal with a seemingly spontaneous movement.

The first clashes between students and police in Mexico City on July 22 went almost unnoticed. Four days later, leftist demonstrators marked the fifteenth anniversary of the start of the Cuban Revolution and were attacked by police when they headed for the National Palace. Leftist leaders from the Autonomous National University (UNAM) and the National Polytechnic Institute (IPN) then began planning a protest strike, while senior high school students barricaded themselves in the Preparatoria No. 1 in the former Convent of San Idelfonso. But soldiers fired a bazooka at the school door, beat up numerous students and arrested many more. In charge of the government's response were the Interior Minister, Luis Echeverría Alvarez; the Defense Minister, General Marcelino García Barragán; and the mayor of Mexico City, General Alfonso Corona del Rosal. They congratulated themselves on their victory over "agitation."

But the repression only mobilized the disenchanted middle classes to join the protests. The issue became freedom, not for peasants and workers, but for the educated and affluent, including many bureaucrats. And the rallying cry was opposition to the regime rather than support for any specific alternative. On August 13, 150,000 people marched to the Zócalo, and two weeks later even housewives and office workers were among the 300,000 protesters. On September 1, with the Olympics only six weeks away, Díaz Ordaz warned that unrest would be stopped "to avoid any further loss of prestige." But on September 13, huge crowds again marched down the central Paseo de la Reforma toward the Zócalo, this time in dramatic silence. Despite its size, the movement was more cathartic than expectant of change. When the Army occupied the UNAM and shot its way into the IPN, secret negotiations between the government and student leaders began and the protests appeared to lose momentum. A new meeting was nevertheless called for the afternoon of October 2 in the Plaza de Tlatelolco.

There was not a huge turnout: many people felt intimidated by the government's growing toughness, others had heard that the real political debate was taking place behind closed doors. At around 5:30 P.M., there were only some 10,000 people in the plaza, many of them women and children sitting on the ground. Two helicopters circled above, but the crowd was accustomed to such surveillance. Even the speeches sounded familiar. Then suddenly one helicopter flew low over the crowd and dropped a flare. Immediately, hundreds of soldiers hidden among the Aztec ruins of the square opened fire with automatic weapons, while hundreds of secret police agents drew pistols and began making arrests. For thirty minutes, there was total confusion. Students who fled into the adjacent Church of San Francisco were chased and beaten and some were murdered. Journalists were allowed to escape, but then banned from re-entering the area when the shooting stopped. That night, army vehicles carried away the bodies, while firetrucks washed away the blood. By morning, the plaza was empty except for a dozen armored cars and several hundred soldiers. The government conceded that thirty-two people had died, but a more probable number was between two and three hundred.

The massacre achieved its immediate objective. With more than a thousand people under arrest and the remaining student leaders in hiding, the protest movement disintegrated. Before dawn on October 3, Díaz Ordaz's spokesman told correspondents that "the focus of agitation has been eliminated." And on October 12, as the Olympic flame was lit and white doves were released into the air, television viewers around the world saw no shots of the thousands of heavily armed soldiers guarding Aztec Stadium. As host nation, Mexico could control the television images being fed to the world. But the government could not save its image at home.

In reality, the system had not been threatened, because neither organized labor nor peasants had identified with the movement, while the private sector and the Army never doubted that Mexico was the target of an international Communist conspiracy. But the regime's response shattered the concept of rule by consensus and undermined the legitimacy of the entire system. During the remaining twenty-six months of Díaz Ordaz's term, the country lived in fear. The President assumed ·sponsibility for the Tlatelolco massacre, but rarely appeared in public. O1ganized opposition was impossible and critics of the regime spoke in whispers. The 1968 prisoners were sentenced to jail terms ranging from th1ee to seventeen years on an assortment of spurious charges. In November 1969, convinced that Mexico was still threatened by the Left, Díaz Ordaz picked his hard-line Interior Minister, Luis Echeverría, to be his successor.

V

Post-revolutionary Mexico has been marked by a series of critical turning points—Carranza's murder in 1920, Calles' deportation in 1936 and Alemán's takeover in 1946. Since 1970, a different Mexico has emerged. It too is deeply rooted in the past, yet many of the dominating traits of contemporary Mexico have appeared since then: a more liberal political system, the rising power of technocrats, growing foreign indebtedness, massive oil finds, a huge rise in public spending and corruption, destabilizing cycles of boom and bust, a restive middle class and an activist foreign policy. In the process, Mexico has become more complex and less predictable. The public record since 1970 traces the varied fortunes of three administrations, yet less visible political, economic, social and cultural forces have also transformed the country.

Echeverría seemed an unlikely innovator. Balding, unsmiling, with metallic spectacles hiding narrow eyes, he personified the political bureaucracy that had grown up since Alemán. Born into a middle-class family in Mexico City's Colonia del Valle, he attended private school and then studied law at the UNAM, where he was remembered as serious, hardworking, disciplined and discreet. From an early age, he was attracted to politics, climbing patiently up the ladder until in 1958 he was appointed Deputy Interior Minister by López Mateos, a post that made him responsible for all intelligence activities. Six years later, Díaz Ordaz promoted him to be Interior Minister and, as such, the country's chief political operator. But during his career, he rarely left his office: his contact with the world was by telephone and his perception of Mexico came from intelligence reports. He was the perfect apparatchik: he obeyed all orders from above and revealed no thoughts or ideology of his own. He was conservative because Díaz Ordaz was conservative.

As outgoing Interior Minister, however, he recognized the system's political failure in 1968. During his electoral campaign, he saw that the crisis was even deeper: the "economic miracle" had brought industrial growth but had left millions of Mexicans in deep poverty. He therefore began to offer the promise of change. Once in office, he released the 1968 political prisoners, encouraged the media to question the myths of the Revolution and announced a "democratic opening." Echeverría himself replaced the tired revolutionary slogans of the past with a more modern rhetoric markedly similar to that used by leftists in 1968. And if his intent was to sow confusion within the Left, it served him well during his first government crisis.

On the afternoon of June 10, 1971, about 8,000 students gathered for the first protest march since Tlatelolco. The official purpose was to support a student strike in Monterrey, but newly released 1968 leaders were also anxious to test Echeverría's word. While still gathering, however, the demonstration was attacked by a paramilitary band known as the *halcones,* or hawks. As police stood by, at least thirty people were killed and many more wounded by gunfire. Although the repression could not have taken place without Echeverría's authorization, he condemned it and skillfully convinced leftists that rightist politicians were trying to sabotage the "democratic opening." After presiding over a mass gathering of support in the Zócalo on June 15, he fired the capital's mayor, Alfonso Martínez Domínguez, and its police chief, Colonel Rogelio Flores Curiel, implicitly blaming them for the killings.

Having used the crisis to consolidate his political power, Echeverría then tried to rejuvenate the system, bringing younger technocrats into the administration, encouraging new independent unions, injecting militancy into the official peasant movement and even retiring hundreds of aging revolutionary generals to make room for younger officers. Within a matter of months, in fact, Echeverría placed an entirely new generation in power, which, he presumed, would remain loyal to him for years to come. Liberal and leftist intellectuals were particularly pleased by Echeverría's new activist foreign policy, which involved flaunting Mexico's independence from the United States by taking up Third World causes and seeking closer ties with Chile's socialist government and Cuba.

Not everyone was won over. While Washington grew irritated with Echeverría's rhetoric, leftist guerrillas appeared in Mexico for the first time, prompting a new—though less visible—wave of repression. But the most serious opposition came from the private sector, which viewed Echeverría as an enemy of business intent on increasing the state's role in the economy. As a result, private investment slowed down, while the government began borrowing heavily abroad to finance rising and inflationary public expenditure. Finally, on August 31, 1976, with large amounts of capital leaving the country, the Mexican currency was devalued for the first time since 1954. Then, just eleven days before leaving office, Echeverría expropriated rich private farmlands in the northwestern state of Sonora. Wild rumors shook the country; some feared an imminent military coup. Confidence in the entire system was shaken.

Echeverría was unorthodox even in his choice of his Finance Minister, José López Portillo, to be his successor. Four of five predecessors had served as Interior Ministers, while the fifth, López Mateos, had held the no less political post of Labor Minister. López Portillo, in contrast, had minimal political experience and showed little passion or ambition for politics. His interests were more intellectual: he gave classes in political theory and public administration at the UNAM, he had published two books and he enjoyed painting. He was a keen sportsman and proud of his athletic physique, but his political career was almost accidental. A lawyer by training, he entered government at the late age of thirty-nine, rising to Under Secretary of the Presidency under Díaz Ordaz. Echeverría, a childhood friend, then named him to a succession of posts, first Under Secretary of National Patrimony, subsequently head of the Federal Electricity Commission and, in May 1973, Finance Minister. His selection for the presidency therefore seemed to reflect Echeverría's desire to perpetuate his own influence after leaving office.

But López Portillo was able to restore private sector confidence by delivering a powerful inaugural address that suggested he would not be manipulated by Echeverría. He also appeased foreign creditors by imposing an austerity program worked out with the International Monetary Fund. When this brought a sharp drop in living standards, he opted for greater political freedom as a way of channeling disaffection along institutional lines. Protest marches, which had been consistently broken up under Echeverría, were permitted, and Congress approved a political reform that facilitated the registration of new parties, including the Communist Party. It was a skillful performance for a man thought not to be a politician.

By 1978, huge oil finds had begun to change the mood of the country, and increased government spending as well as foreign and domestic private investment fed an economic boom that would bring 8 percent growth rates through 1981. Companies that only two years earlier seemed close to bankruptcy recorded unprecedented profits. The value of the Mexican peso stabilized, allowing even the middle classes to buy imported luxury goods and take their vacations abroad. Inflation inevitably grew, but the government decided that only by creating permanent jobs in industry could the country's nonrenewable oil wealth be converted into renewable prosperity. And when neglect of the countryside resulted in enormous food imports from the United States, the government poured money into the agricultural sector. Even the fact that expenditure was far outstripping oil revenues seemed to be no obstacle to growth: foreign bankers were battling for the chance to lend to Mexico.

Oil also changed the world's view of Mexico and Mexico's perception of itself. Mexico found itself being courted for its energy resources, but also began to exude a new self-confidence that verged on arrogance. Like his predecessor, López Portillo began concentrating on foreign affairs, clashing with the Carter administration on a number of issues and incessantly traveling abroad. After the 1979 Nicaraguan Revolution, his attention became focused increasingly on Central America. At first, Mexico provided the new Sandinista regime with financial and technical assistance, but after the Reagan administration began an anti-Communist crusade in the region in January 1981, López Portillo assumed the defense of Cuba, Nicaragua and even El Salvador's guerrilla-led opposition while advocating negotiated solutions to the region's conflicts.

In June 1981, a sudden drop in world oil prices exposed the vulnerability of Mexico's economic strategy. Rather than seeing this as the time for a slowdown in its own growth rate and even a devaluation of its overvalued currency, however, Mexico opted to make up for lost revenues by borrowing abroad. Yet continuing doubts about the peso's stability fed a massive flight of capital, and in February 1982, just days after he pledged to defend the peso "like a dog," López Portillo devalued the currency by 40 percent. In August, a new devaluation was followed by a suspension of principal payments on the country's $80 billion foreign debt. In his final State of the Union address on September 1, López Portillo ordered exchange controls and decreed nationalization of the country's private banks, somehow blaming them for the debacle. Meanwhile, terrified that Mexico might declare a moratorium on all foreign debt payments, Washington, the IMF and foreign banks organized an emergency rescue package to keep the Mexican economy afloat.

In the midst of this crisis, faith in Mexico's political system was badly bruised. López Portillo, who had enjoyed extraordinary popularity during the boom years, became the target of widespread hostility. The President himself seemed a defeated figure, at one point even referring to himself as a "devalued President." In the absence of strong leadership, the vacuum was filled by uncertainty and rumors. Even the chosen successor, the former Budget and Planning Minister, Miguel de la Madrid Hurtado, could do little to restore equanimity. Between his selection in September 1981 and his inauguration on December 1, 1982, Mexico's profile had changed unrecognizably: having expected to administer prosperity, De la Madrid could offer only a period of stiff austerity accompanied by tumbling living standards.

As the first Mexican President to come to office with a strong economic background, De la Madrid was in a sense the right man for the job. After joining the government from the UNAM, he obtained a master's degree in public administration from Harvard University and held a succession of key financial jobs in the Bank of Mexico, Petróleos Mexicanos and the Finance Ministry before joining the Cabinet in 1979. Only forty-seven years old when he assumed the presidency, he personified the generation of young technocrats that now came of political age. No less important, he seemed convinced that a less corrupt and inefficient system could be forged from the crisis.

A tough, unemotional decision-maker harshly critical of traditional populism, De la Madrid immediately set about slashing government spending, controlling imports, reducing subsidies and raising the price of myriad public services. The resulting contraction decimated both industrial production and purchasing power, but improvement of the country's financial indicators won praise abroad. At home, despite somber predictions of political instability, serious unrest was somehow avoided, even after De la Madrid ignored strong pressure from the labor movement to decree emergency wage increases. Middle-class discontent was expressed in support for the main conservative opposition party in municipal elections, but the regime was able to "fix" several results without provoking violent protests. Instead, De la Madrid tried to appease leftists by maintaining the broad lines of López Portillo's foreign policy and conservatives by launching an anti-corruption campaign that landed the former head of the state oil monopoly, Jorge Díaz Serrano, in jail.

But it was also apparent that, even if the stunned economy were to recover consciousness during the De la Madrid administration, Mexico could not return to the spending and growth rates that had long held the system together and sustained the legitimacy of the regime. Ideally, during his six-year term, De la Madrid hoped to design a less vulnerable and more self-sufficient economy and to permit greater democracy without surrendering authority. But he faced the task of managing a more complicated Mexico with fewer resources than any of his predecessors. New political challenges seemed certain to follow.

4

The System: Myths and Rewards

I

Mexico's political stability has rested on the myth that the President is all-powerful. It is itself a powerful myth, believed by most Mexicans and sustained by those who know it to be untrue. Like the Divine Right of Kings and the infallibility of the Pope, it maintains the mystery of the office. The President is, after all, the heir to a pre-Hispanic tradition of theocratic authoritarianism that was enormously reinforced by the political centralism and religious dogmatism of the Spanish Colony. Submission to each President therefore provides continuity to the system. And because the myth reflects the traditional need of Mexicans to believe in some unifying symbol of power, the incumbent is largely above public criticism: he is too important a focus of security and stability to be openly challenged.

During his six-year term, then, the President dominates not only the state but also the public life of the nation: he controls Congress, the judiciary and state governors as well as the ruling party and the huge bureaucracy, he determines economic policy and foreign affairs and he is treated with solemn reverence by the media. The projection of this power in turn wraps each President in an almost imperial aura. He travels everywhere surrounded by a court of acolytes and an army of bodyguards, he is bombarded constantly with flattery and his personal whims become indistinguishable from public policy. "What time is it?" asks the President, according to an old joke that has the ring of truth. "Whatever time you say it is, Mr. President." Hardly surprisingly, several Mexican Presidents have become intoxicated by power while in office and greatly disturbed when it evaporated on the day they stepped down.

But the President is merely the temporary personification of a political system which itself is a product of Mexican society. The presidential system has survived, not because it has subjected a passive Mexico to decades of dictatorial rule, but because it mirrors the strengths and weaknesses, virtues and defects, of the Mexicans themselves: it combines a ritualistic sense of hierarchy with an enormous capacity to negotiate. The system is therefore not an automatic and permanent political formula for Mexico. It requires constant servicing to maintain its flexibility and frequent renewal to preserve its sensitivity. When, as increasingly since 1970, the system has ignored its own rules of pragmatism, reflecting the caprices of the President rather than the natural dynamics of society, the country has become less stable. Presidential power has undoubtedly increased, yet the costs of exercising it have also mounted.

For the system to work, then, the President can enjoy absolute power so long as he does not wield it absolutely. He is part of a much broader and complex equation of interests, traditions, principles and superstitions that places him in office and sustains his authority. Even at the height of his power, he cannot seek re-election and, above all, he cannot change society. He could not, for example, reverse the nationalization of the oil industry, revoke the land reform or even adopt a blatantly pro-American foreign policy. Rather, behind a monolithic façade, he must share power with the country's key interest groups—the bureaucracy, traditional *políticos,* the media, organized labor, the private sector, the Army, the intellectual Left and the Church. For the arrangement to work, political bargains must be constantly reviewed and renewed, conflicting interests must be conciliated and internal squabbles settled.

The President sits atop the pyramid, but his real job is to balance what he perceives to be the "national interest" with the need to maintain strong supporting pillars beneath him. He is the powerful referee who can interpret the rules, but he must make sure that the teams keep playing the game. His effectiveness as a negotiator, persuader and arbiter is therefore more important than his popularity as a politician. Even as a symbol, he could be replaced. But he is the focal point of an intricate system of loyalties which, if he were to die suddenly, would likely disintegrate, creating enormous political uncertainty.* The secret, then, lies in the President's ability to manage those economic lobbies and political factions that could threaten the system if they no longer benefited from its survival.

*Under the Constitution, the Chamber of Deputies would name an interim President. If the President died during his first three years in office, new elections would be called; otherwise, the interim President would complete the six-year term. In practice, however, the resulting struggle for power could undermine the entire system.

In the constant juggling that characterizes the art of government, different interest groups may provoke crises when they feel neglected or mistreated. But they are either quickly appeased or dissuaded from mounting any serious challenge to the regime by their confidence that the equilibrium will eventually be restored. Similarly, a President can turn against a key interest group, as when López Portillo nationalized the country's private banks, but he cannot safely alienate all the system's allies at the same time. Further, the system traditionally rewards patience and discipline by redistributing power and privilege with each change of administration, because not to do so would be to risk destabilization. Peace is therefore best preserved through the avoidance of confrontation and unwavering respect for the political rules.

Like everything else in Mexico, real politics takes place behind masks, far from the view or influence of the great majority of citizens. Even the mask of presidential absolutism is covered by a veil of republican democracy. In theory, Congress and the judiciary are independent of the executive branch, and the 1917 Constitution guarantees the autonomy of the country's thirty-one states as well as an impressive body of individual and social rights. Elections are held every six years for the presidency, the Senate and state governorships, and every three years for the Chamber of Deputies and municipal posts. In these elections, candidates of registered opposition parties are free to challenge those of the Institutional Revolutionary Party. All parties are then given free time on television for their propaganda, while the government spends heavily on public service advertising urging the electorate to vote.

But this is all political theater, an elaborate ritual. Mexicans know that the President in fact picks his own successor as well as all PRI candidates for key posts. The PRI has won every election for President, senator and state governor since its formation in 1929 and has frequently resorted to fraud to avoid defeat in elections for the Chamber of Deputies and municipal mayoralties. Similarly, the Supreme Court has never overturned any key government decision, and despite the presence of opposition deputies, the PRI's huge majority guarantees the obedience of Congress. To suit the whims of a succession of Presidents, for example, Congress amended the Constitution on 369 occasions between 1917 and 1984. Moreover, the ban on immediate re-election to Congress prevents deputies from seeking independent parliamentary careers and forces them to depend on the bureaucracy for future employment. Even the PRI's congressmen recognize, in the words of one senator, that "we're paid to applaud": the same Congress that hailed López Portillo's bank nationalization in September 1982 dutifully endorsed De la Madrid's decision to sell off 34 percent ownership of the banks three months later.

Nonetheless, the ritual is considered vital because, like most authoritarian regimes, Mexico's ruling elite is obsessed with the need to justify the perpetuation of its power. It defends the overwhelming weight of the government in society as a function of the state's historical role in creating and defending the nation. It explains its own juridical inconsistencies by arguing that, in contrast to the case in the Anglo-Saxon world, the purpose of the Constitution is not to establish the working rules of society—those are provided by the exercise of power—but rather the sociopolitical objectives toward which the system is working. Thus, by preserving the ideals of the 1910 Revolution in rhetoric and law, the regime obtains its "popular" legitimacy. Even though power has never passed peacefully from one party to another in Mexico, regular elections provide the system's "democratic" legitimacy.

The climax to the ritual is the presidential election campaign. From the moment the outgoing President picks his successor, usually some nine months before polling day, the outcome is already known. But even if the PRI's candidate is unopposed, as was López Portillo in 1976, he embarks on a grueling—and expensive—tour of the country, anxious to legitimize his administration by piling up a record number of votes. In the months preceding De la Madrid's election in July 1982, for example, he made some 1,800 speeches, ending each with a request that his audience vote for him. At the same time, the campaign takes on the trappings of a triumphal march, with the PRI machine trucking in workers and peasants to become acquainted with the name, face and voice of the man who will rule for the next six years. Unable to criticize the outgoing President directly, the candidate must limit his public discourse to vague promises and "revolutionary" generalities. Tradition requires little more of him until he takes office: only then can he remove his mask of subservience and show his true face.

The campaign has a more hidden level as well. The PRI's last three presidential candidates, each seeking elective office for the first time, were career bureaucrats based in Mexico City whose knowledge of the country came more from speeches and reports than direct personal experience. For the first and probably the only time, therefore, the campaign enables the incoming President to get a feel for the real mood of the country: before his nomination, the candidate is intent on proclaiming the success of the incumbent's programs, and once in office, the new President will be shown only the positive things being carried out by his ministers. The campaign thus serves as a crash course in the poverty and injustice still endemic to Mexico. Significantly, both López Portillo and De la Madrid spent as much time attending round-table discussions of these problems as they did public meetings. Although the PRI invariably publishes an electoral platform at the beginning of the campaign, this on-the-road experience is more influential in shaping the new government's policies.

No less important, it is during the campaign that the incoming President begins hard bargaining with the country's key interest groups. His experience as a minister was probably limited to isolated areas and sectorial lobbies, but now he must deal with the entire range of *influyentes*—above all, those that felt ignored by the outgoing administration. Since Mexican politics is dominated by pragmatism rather than ideology, however, these adjustments come easily.* Mexican Presidents may eventually be tagged as "leftist" or "rightist," but such definitions are more the result of style than substance: Echeverría was considered a radical, yet he tamed the domestic Left and did nothing to hurt the private sector; López Portillo was seen as pro-business, but he took over the country's banks at the end of his term; and De la Madrid began conservatively but did not reduce the state's role in the economy. Thus, the pendulum does swing—not to left and right, but in all directions— and its purpose is to correct a political imbalance even if in the process a new imbalance is created.

By adopting the democratic mechanism of elections, Mexico, alone among the world's authoritarian regimes, has also resolved the critical question of succession: no President has been re-elected since the Porfirio Díaz dictatorship, no President has been assassinated in office since Carranza in 1920 and every President since Cárdenas has completed a six-year term. At first, in the years following the Revolution, the selection of the official presidential candidate provoked uprisings by regional generals. Even as late as 1940, the government was forced to resort to fraud to guarantee Avila Camacho's "victory" over General Almazán. But after civilians assumed full control of politics in the late 1940s, the system has always fallen into line behind the chosen official candidate. Various myths were created to disguise the process of selection—not least, that the incumbent polled ex-Presidents and other key members of the "revolutionary family"—but it remained the exclusive prerogative of

*Even the PRI has studiously avoided defining its ideology. Asked by reporters in the early 1960s to clarify whether the PRI was leftist, centrist or rightist, one party president, General Alfonso Corona del Rosal, said in reply, "Look, boys, the PRI is socialist, but we can't say so."

the outgoing President to name his successor: only in this way could the transfer of loyalties take place smoothly.

The real, though disguised, campaign therefore occurs before the *destape*, or unveiling, of the PRI's candidate, with leading aspirants spending heavily in the media as they try to show their best face—and their competitors' worst faces—to the public and the President. At the same time, with the outgoing President himself anxious to prevent the emergence of any strong favorite who could undermine his own power and even force his decision, all aspirants must deny they are "pre-candidates." The President himself may even inform several contenders that they are front-runners, yet they must maintain utmost loyalty and discretion and refrain from displaying too much enthusiasm.

After he left office, Echeverría disclosed that he had been told of his selection by Díaz Ordaz one year before the announcement, but the "phantom" campaign nevertheless proceeded, with the Minister of the Presidency, Emilio Martínez Manatou, favored by many politicians. When Echeverría himself came to pick a successor, he was still more Machiavellian. Since the Interior Minister, the key political figure after the President, had been chosen on four of five previous occasions, Echeverría's Interior Minister, Mario Moya Palencia, was automatically the front-runner. But both in private and through the media, Echeverría led several other ministers to believe they would be *el bueno*—"the good one." By thus creating disarray within the political bureaucracy, Echeverría was able to impose the unlikely candidacy of his Finance Minister, José López Portillo. Moya Palencia's stunned followers, who had already prepared his campaign posters, even urged their leader to run as an independent candidate. But the minister wisely opted for a disciplined response—"López Portillo is the best man available to the Mexican Revolution," he said—and the system united behind the official candidate.

Prior to the 1982 succession, López Portillo also kept the issue open as long as politically feasible. His friend and disciple, Miguel de la Madrid, at the time Budget and Planning Minister, was well placed, but the country's politicians were pressing for the consideration of others. The Labor Minister, Pedro Ojeda Paullada, seemed a possible choice, but the president of the PRI, Javier García Paniagua, the son of a former Defense Minister with strong ties to the Army, gradually became convinced he would be picked. And when, on September 25, 1981, López Portillo invited the labor leader Fidel Velázquez to announce that the PRI had chosen De la Madrid, García Paniagua was unable to contain his fury. Asked by a television reporter whether the PRI had chosen the right man, he mumbled an injudicious "We'll see." After López Portillo saw the videotape of this remark, he ordered that García Paniagua and Ojeda Paullada switch jobs. At first, García Paniagua resisted, claiming that only the PRI convention could remove him, but his erstwhile allies had abandoned him. He lasted three months as Labor Minister and then resigned, his political credentials badly tattered.

Yet, while successors have been chosen and elected without major difficulty, the last three changes of administration have been marked by crises of such severity that public credibility in the entire system has been badly eroded. Paradoxically, this is in part a function of the system's own fear of instability: it has largely tolerated the idiosyncratic vanities and abuses of power of successive Presidents rather than break ranks. But it is also a product of the difficult fourteen-month period between the *destape* and the inauguration when power and political loyalties are gradually moving from outgoing to incoming Presidents, when both political bureaucracy and private sector are nervously awaiting the appointments and policies of the new President, when economic activity slows down and the system is at its most vulnerable, floating between two pillars of stability like a trapeze artist in midair.

By changing the date of the 1988 presidential elections from the first Sunday in July to September 1 and delaying the *destape* of his own successor, De la Madrid hopes to reduce this dangerous interregnum. Yet Mexican politics is unavoidably based on a powerful six-year cycle. For the system to work, the President must be strong, and for his authority to be recognized, he must turn—at least symbolically—against his predecessor. By sacrificing the officials and policies of the past in an Aztec ritual, pent-up frustrations are thus released and loyalties renewed. At the same time, unwilling to accept that the ritual will eventually demand his own destruction, the incumbent struggles to project his power and influence beyond his own administration. (Having reached the top of the pyramid, his political career in fact climaxes on a predestined day, when he is sacrificed to permit the system to live on.) Once he picks his successor, the President therefore becomes obsessed with his own place in history and, to judge by the last three regimes, the waning power of his final months in office creates a sense of despair. Concerned more about himself than the nation, and increasingly resigned to "betrayal" at the hands of his own personally chosen successor, he may then act irrationally.

Convinced that he had "saved" the nation by crushing the 1968 student movement, Díaz Ordaz was infuriated to find Echeverría courting his leftist critics during the 1970 election campaign. At one point, after Echeverría joined a group of students in Morelia in one minute's silence for victims of the Tlatelolco massacre, the Presidential Military Staff that accompanied him informed Díaz Ordaz that they were withdrawing from the campaign because of the "insult." Warning that the PRI could still change its candidate, Díaz Ordaz ordered Echeverría to present all his speeches for prior review by the PRI's president, Alfonso Martínez Domínguez. But the campaign had its own dynamics and, in the end, Díaz Ordaz dropped out of view and then watched silently as the new administration turned against his followers and abandoned his policies. When Echeverría left office, Díaz Ordaz remarked bitterly: "Echeverría was a better President than I. He knew how to pick his successor."

In contrast, six years later, Echeverría refused to surrender power gracefully. He appointed his own aides to run López Portillo's electoral campaign, insisted on holding the spotlight of public attention and created a mood of great agitation in the country by stepping up his attacks on the private sector. His own actions, however, ineluctably accelerated the destruction of his image. A massive flight of capital forced the first currency devaluation in twenty-two years, for which he was blamed. And just eleven days before stepping down, amid wild rumors of a possible coup d'état, Echeverría "punished" his business foes by expropriating private landholdings in Sonora state, yet in so doing created sympathy for his successor. Even after he left office, in fact, Echeverría tried to remain influential, but his entire group was gradually removed from the government and the former President himself was dispatched into diplomatic exile, first to Paris as ambassador to UNESCO and later as ambassador to Australia. By the time he returned in 1980, López Portillo's own power was consolidated.

The psychological dimension of the political crisis was even more evident during López Portillo's last year in office. Always an emotional and temperamental man, López Portillo sank into a depression when the currency devaluation of February 1982 eroded Mexico's new grandeur. The following month, he even seemed to recognize his failure by appointing followers of De la Madrid to run the economy. But the power vacuum created new uncertainty, and in August, one month after the elections, a new devaluation produced a wave of hysteria. Clearly desperate to rescue his place in history, López Portillo then ordered the expropriation of the country's banks. For a few days, he wrapped himself in the flag of nationalism and savored the cheers of leftists. But by then he seemed to have lost touch with reality: despised and even hated by many Mexicans, he traveled through the country inaugurating projects—many of them still unfinished—and receiving the "thanks" of trucked-in crowds.

Such was the avalanche of anger and bitterness that burst over López Portillo once he stepped down that De la Madrid found himself with a problem that none of his predecessors had faced. López Portillo's vanished power offered him no front wind to fly against. Moreover, to encourage the popular cry for public bloodletting would further weaken the office of the presidency. Thus, although the media were allowed to pick through the remains of the previous administration, De la Madrid avoided personal attacks on his predecessor. López Portillo was urged to leave the country, not because he was competing for power, but because his very presence kept alive the demand for revenge.

Yet ritual still required an "enemy," and Echeverría now conveniently cast himself in this role, first by appearing to mobilize groups of out-of-favor politicians and then by publicly defending "populism" and "nationalism," qualities seemingly lacking in the new administration. Angered by this challenge, De la Madrid cancelled a $2 million annual subsidy for the former President's Third World Studies Center. López Portillo had financed the center as a way of buying his predecessor's silence, but early in 1984 Echeverría also chose to excoriate López Portillo's performance as President, even to the point of mocking his emotionalism. From Rome, López Portillo sent orders for publication of a full-page advertisement in a Mexico City daily that said simply: "You Too, Luis??!!—Jose López Portillo." The sight of the President and his two predecessors wrestling in public suggested that the system was tearing itself apart. Antonio Ortiz Mena, the Mexican president of the Inter-American Development Bank and Finance Minister under Díaz Ordaz, then joined the fray, describing both Echeverría and López Portillo as no less than "traitors" to the Revolution. But tradition at last won out: within two years of his taking office, full power had passed to De la Madrid and the succession crisis had passed.

Whether this destructive cycle can be broken in 1988, however, will depend largely on De la Madrid's personal reaction to the power he will gradually accumulate during his term. The cost to the political system of the last three changes of administration has been enormous. The economy has also been badly bruised by the stop-go cycles that have resulted. Further, the country as a whole has become both too sophisticated and too vulnerable to live without the continuity of a senior civil service and long-term planning. Early in De la Madrid's administration, there was some reason for hope.* Unlike Echeverría, he is considered a straightforward player of the political game; and unlike López Portillo, he has a reputation for making decisions in a cold and unemotional manner. Yet his predecessors had also seemed rational before they became powerful. And it seems worthy of note that De la Madrid looked far enough ahead when entering office to set up a bureau whose sole task is to chronicle his administration.

II

One party has ruled Mexico without interruption since 1929, yet it is wrong to describe Mexico as a country with one-party rule: unlike in the Soviet Union, in Mexico it is the government that runs the party. Decreed into existence by General Calles, the National Revolutionary Party (PNR)—the forerunner of today's PRI—was in fact born as an instrument of a small ruling elite. It had already achieved the main purpose of any new political party, since its leaders were in power, but they needed to order and discipline the ranks below them. When General Obregón ran for office in 1920, for example, he was supported by some 3,000 different parties, movements and factions. And when the PNR was founded by Calles, it immediately embraced over 1,000 different groups willing to concede that sharing was better than fighting over the fruits of power. But, organized along essentially corporativist lines—into labor, peasant, popular and, until 1940, military sectors—the party has not been allowed to become independent of the state. In fact, every six years it has been the incumbent President who makes the party's only truly important decision—that of picking a successor.

The party nevertheless has served as a useful forum where different political and even ideological currents can struggle for influence. For a long time, it was also the most attractive vehicle for political mobility. Politicians were lifted by the power they accumulated beneath them and they bargained on the basis of the peasant, worker, student, bureaucratic or other organizations that they controlled. Through the process of negotiation, these *caciques*—most of them *mestizos* of humble origins who were thrust into public life by the convulsion of the Revolution—then provided a natural chain of command from the narrow top of the pyramid to the rest of society. Many eventually found themselves enjoying sinecures in Congress and a few even reached top positions in govern-

---

*Soon after his inauguration, one aide told De la Madrid that he was the first President in recent years who did not play God. "Thank you," he reportedly replied, "but please keep reminding me."

ment. So long as loyalty was rewarded with economic and political privilege, so long as this was the main path to power, the traditional system worked.

Even today, in the provinces, the PRI retains some of its appeal and effectiveness: it still draws ambitious young *políticos* into its ranks, it can mobilize big crowds during election campaigns and its local leaders remain *influyentes*. And even though state governors are invariably native sons who made their political name in Mexico City and are chosen by the President, they must come to terms with regional party interests in order to succeed. Small-town *caciques* can make their influence felt through the PRI, frequently monopolizing local mayoralties in exchange for political loyalty, while peasant and labor leaders can use the party to pressure for public works or wage increases. At the grass-roots level, then, through its peasant and labor sectors, the PRI is still the only political option available.

But when both the economy and government expenditure began to grow rapidly after World War II, the federal bureaucracy also expanded dramatically, gradually providing the pyramidal system with a new base. Whereas thousands of top political positions change hands every six years, continuity is provided by the 3 million bureaucrats, whose loyalty must be continually serviced. Most Mexicans view the bureaucracy as lazy, inefficient, self-serving and corrupt, and incoming officials are often shocked by its conservative resistance to change. But those on the inside rightly recognize that they belong to an exclusive club. At medium and lower levels, not only is there job security, but strong unions also campaign effectively for assorted privileges. Some ministries pay an annual bonus equivalent to three months' salary or purchase uniforms for their secretarial staff; most operate department stores for their employees where food, clothes and consumer goods are available at reduced prices. Working hours are short and vacations generous for junior civil servants, and dismissal of unionized employees is difficult.

Still more important, as more and better-educated professionals were needed to manage the increasingly complex affairs of state, the bureaucracy replaced the PRI as the main ladder to power. Thus, between 1946 and 1982, 60 percent of Cabinet officers never held party or electoral posts. The change was even sharper after 1970. Before reaching the presidency, Ruiz Cortines and Alemán had served as governors, and Díaz Ordaz and López Mateos as senators, but Echeverría, López Portillo and De la Madrid had never run for office. Except during elections, in fact, the party was disdained by aspiring young politicians, who no longer felt the need to work among the grass roots. To rise within the bureaucracy required not power from below but approval from above.

In this new forum, however, the system's golden rules still apply: loyalty and discipline are rewarded with power and privilege. An ambitious young *licenciado*—traditionally, most pass through the Law Faculty of the National University—begins his career by attaching himself to some official who can offer him a job. The son of a politician or senior bureaucrat is assured of being looked after as a favor to Father, but he too must learn to be dedicated and discreet. "You'll always get in trouble for something you say, never for something you don't say," he is counseled. His boss in turn owes his job and allegiance to a more senior benefactor whose political fortunes are linked to someone above him, successively up to the President. Conversely, every President must name some 700 top officeholders, each of whom fills hundreds of jobs below him. Myriad pyramids of power are thus superimposed on the larger hierarchical pyramid: everyone except the President is both boss and servant.

This process spawns political cliques—known as "mafias"—that are loyal to the President but compete fiercely with each other. Without them, the system of loyalties could not work. At an early stage of his career, a politician must begin collecting a retinue, starting with a chauffeur and a personal secretary, then gathering around him those friends and acolytes whom he employs or can place in jobs. Through their loyalty and deference, these "dependents" create an aura of authority and influence around the politician, but they also gain a measure of security. It is their *jefe* who must do the thinking and fighting in the political arena: if he does well, they too will prosper; if he does poorly, he must still look after them.

Each change of administration brings a major shake-up. As the selection of the new President approaches, the young *licenciado* finds that, through his own patron's commitments, his political fate is linked to that of one or another minister's luck. A strange ritual nonetheless follows, in which supporters of various "pre-candidates" hold a series of informal meetings, usually over meals, at which they express their support for their leader and try to woo political neutrals to join them. With the exception of a handful of politicians too well established to assume the risk, most top bureaucrats must define (none of this is visible to the public or covered by the media) their preference so the crucial lines of loyalty can be established. Ideological questions are rarely relevant, since the commitment is to persons and not policies. A successful gamble virtually guarantees a job, first in the electoral campaign and then in the new administration.

But the system also has room for those temporarily out of favor. Career bureaucrats who back the wrong pre-candidate and must accept a demotion will invariably find a job through some better-placed friend or relative. If lucky, they may resume their climb within the system attached to a new boss. Outgoing Presidents also routinely ask their successor to "look after" close aides, some of whom then appear in the new President's first Cabinet. When replaced, they may still be assured an embassy abroad. For example, Porfirio Muñoz Ledo, Labor Minister and PRI president under Echeverría, first switched to Education Minister under López Portillo and was then appointed ambassador to the United Nations, a post he retained under De la Madrid. Even Mario Moya Palencia, front-runner to succeed Echeverría, managed a government tourist development fund under López Portillo and an obscure state-owned seafood export company under De la Madrid. Similarly, López Portillo's controversial economic adviser, José Andrés de Oteyza, was named ambassador to Canada by De la Madrid, while Pedro Ojeda Paullada, Labor Minister and PRI president under López Portillo, became Minister of Fishing.

The system's ability to recycle ostracized politicians helps to preserve a good-mannered formality. Díaz Ordaz once remarked that in politics "all friends are false and all enemies are real," reason enough to be cautious. But Cárdenas' maxim is also remembered: "In politics, no one is fully alive or completely dead." And because an enemy's career cannot be permanently buried, politicians must temper their desire for revenge with their instinct for self-preservation: like favors, acts of malice also become debts. In reality, as one deposed governor remarked, "in Mexico you can be pardoned for theft, assault and murder, everything except a political mistake." (Oscar Flores Tapia was ousted as governor of Coahuila in 1981 for "inexplicable enrichment," but he always claimed he was a political scapegoat.) The capital mistakes are disloyalty and indiscipline. Those humiliated or fired by one government must therefore remain patiently silent in the hope of being reincorporated by the next.

Martínez Manatou, the losing pre-candidate for the presidency in 1970, vanished under Echeverría but returned as Health Minister and then governor of Tamaulipas under López Portillo. Jesús Reyes Heroles, who fell out successively with Echeverría and López Portillo, became Education Minister under De la Madrid. Even the two Mexico City officials publicly blamed by Echeverría for a student massacre in 1971 were back in key posts a few years later—former mayor Martínez Domínguez as governor of Nuevo León and former police chief Flores Curiel as governor of Nayarit. In all cases, confident that the wheel of fortune would turn again, they resisted the temptation to answer the orchestrated press attacks that accompanied their fall from favor. In private, for example, Martínez Domínguez denounced Echeverría as a "miserable traitor," but even after he was resurrected politically, he never publicly defended his own performance in 1971. Conversely, those whose loyalty to the system proves weaker than their hate for a person are never trusted again. Without this discipline, the system would tear itself apart.

Political management of the system has nevertheless lost much of its smoothness, because new fast tracks to the top of the government have appeared. In the past, even without passing through the PRI, a steady career up the bureaucracy involved the accumulation of political experience and canniness. While attaching their fortunes to some *jefe*, "politicrats" owed their principal allegiance to the system. But in order to incorporate the post-1968 generation and to build his own new political class, Echeverría began bringing young, talented, but politically immature figures into positions of influence. Old *políticos* were still present in his administration, but their weight was counterbalanced by that of the new technocrats, who owed their power entirely to their proximity to the President. Through the system of appointment known as *por dedazo*—by pointing a finger—administrative power began to overshadow political power.

Under López Portillo and De la Madrid, this trend has accelerated. Both also brought in veteran politicians to compensate for the newcomers' lack of political experience, but the key decision makers in their administration were young technocrats and old friends—as well as family members under López Portillo—rather than party faithful. Economic policy in particular became the preserve of foreign-educated academics. In López Portillo's Cabinet, two Cambridge graduates, José Andrés de Oteyza and Carlos Tello Macías, were enormously influential. And De la Madrid, himself a fluent English-speaker with a master's degree from Harvard, parachuted so many bright young technocrats into senior positions that a degree from a foreign university seemed a better passport to power than the traditional credentials of political savvy and loyalty. (Such was the refinement of this "government by curriculum" that Mexicans studying at Harvard and Yale were assured better jobs than those attending the universities of, say, Wisconsin and Texas.) His economic team was headed by Yale's Jesús Silva Herzog as Finance Minister and Harvard's Carlos Salinas de Gortari as Budget and Planning Minister.

Since a President's personal power grows and the institutional controls weaken during the six-year cycle, he tends to govern increasingly through an inner circle. By the end of their administrations, relying for advice on a small cabal of "idea men," both Echeverría and López Portillo were not only screened from a political reality unfamiliar to their advisers and obliged to choose from a limited range of policy alternatives; they were also unrestrained by the minimal checks and balances that experienced politicians could provide. Full Cabinet meetings became rare and many major decisions were made during informal gatherings of key aides. (López Portillo did not inform his Cabinet of his plan to nationalize the country's private banks until the decree was actually signed, just two hours before the public announcement.) In contrast, De la Madrid tried to resist the temptation to build a parallel administration inside the Palace, but this seemed hardly necessary, since his closest aides had been appointed directly to the Cabinet—not only Silva Herzog and Salinas, but also Manuel Bartlett as Interior Minister, Francisco Rojas as Comptroller General and Bernardo Sepúlveda as Foreign Minister. Yet within two years of his taking office, complaints were already heard that the President was being shielded from bad news by his immediate circle.

By the mid-1980s, however, the split between technocrats and politicians was feeding tension throughout the system. In part, it was simply a problem of cliques: the political clique was unhappy because it was no longer enjoying its traditional influence and privileges, while the technocratic clique was greedy to consolidate its new grip on power. But the problem also involved a clash between two different visions of the country which became symbolized by two new political epithets: "populism" and "technocracy." It was not an ideological division as such, although the old politicians were more traditionally nationalist, whereas the new technocrats were more Western. Yet in a pragmatic world even a change in style becomes substantive. Ominously for the system, the infighting spilled into public view.

De la Madrid and his followers blamed the "populism" of the past for the state of the country and favored a more sober scientific approach. For them, the enemy was not the Left or the Right, but mismanagement, corruption and deficit spending, all of which were synonymous with populism. And when Echeverría, the personification of this style, defended populism as "nationalism and contact with the people," he was immediately attacked by the new team. Politicians, on the other hand, mocked the technocrats as the products of wealthier and less *mestizo* families, young men who had attended private schools and foreign universities and had scorned the dirty work of party politics and who, above all, were intellectually arrogant and therefore politically less reliable.

Certainly, by ignoring the traditional political interlocutors with society, the government has become more isolated from the population. Strong on theory and weak on pragmatism, it seems more inclined to adopt policies ill suited to Mexico's idiosyncrasies. "The ruling class can no longer hear the grass grow," one worried politician put it. In the past, the system's social mobility enabled schoolteachers, union leaders and small landowners to become politicians of influence as well as transmission belts of popular sentiments. But now, natural political leaders who once climbed through the party or the bureaucracy lack the academic preparation and social contacts required for promotion to the bureaucracy's upper reaches. Further, they are not even courted by the new technocrats. "This new lot doesn't understand the importance of having breakfast, lunch and dinner," one veteran politician complained, recalling the traditional settings for political negotiations. As a result, the commitment of old-style politicians to the system is wavering: access to the top and sensitivity to the bottom are no longer assured.

Nowhere is this political crisis more apparent than in the PRI itself. From the time of Calles, the leader of the party has always been chosen by the President, with first generals and later experienced *políticos* invariably picked. But since 1975, the only requirement has been loyalty to the President. Similarly, state governors as well as federal senators and deputies are increasingly chosen from among friends, further disturbing the tradition of political rewards. The new technocracy in particular regards the PRI as little more than a Ministry of Elections, to be used every six years and ignored in the interim. When he campaigned for office, De la Madrid showed little interest in trying to rejuvenate the party, seemingly content to let the old party machine steamroll its way through the country.

But the weakness of the PRI soon came to plague the new administration: in 1983, the PRI lost several northern state capitals in municipal elections and the "democratic" legitimacy of the system began to be questioned. In part this reflected middle-class discontent with the economic crisis, but it also exposed the low morale within the PRI. The provincial ranks of the party could not disguise their scorn for the technocrats suddenly thrown into the maze of political management: the soldiers in the trenches had lost confidence in their generals. In some cases influential local *políticos,* as a sign of their disaffection, even refused to run as candidates in municipal elections. When the worried government resorted to fraud to "win" several provincial elections, its maneuvers were, owing to inexperience, clumsily—and too publicly—executed.

Instinctively, De la Madrid preferred greater democracy to more efficient frauds, but his administration seemed paralyzed by indecision—reluctant either to give the PRI some independence and credibility or to recall the old *políticos* to run it—as the crucial test of the July 1985 mid-term congressional elections approached. Two state governors, General Graciliano Alpuche Pinzón of the Yucatán and Enrique Velasco Ibarra of Guanajuato, were unceremoniously forced to resign in 1984 in the name of improving party effectiveness, but De la Madrid nevertheless sustained Adolfo Lugo Verduzco as president of the PRI for no better reason than friendship and loyalty. In March 1984, Lugo Verduzco briefly tested a system of primaries to enable the party to pick popular local candidates, but after an inauspicious start in Nayarit the experiment was abandoned. Earlier efforts to reform the PRI in the 1960s and '70s had also failed because, on balance, a less democratic party was considered more useful to the government. But the crowds that continually surrounded the former PRI president, García Paniagua, during the party's twelfth convention in August 1984 well illustrated the vacuum of political leadership under Lugo Verduzco. At a time of widespread discontent with conditions in the country, the risks posed by a weakened and demoralized party were great: the government faced the choice of recognizing significant opposition gains or further alienating public opinion with frauds.

III

Without tight interdependence between the government and other key pressure groups, the traditional system cannot survive: somehow, all must be willingly tied to the center. But the political and economic turbulence since 1970 has subjected these alliances—with the media, labor, business, Church and Army—to new strains. The negotiating process that was long invisible to the public is now giving way to more open competition and collaboration. The government remains the final arbiter but, less generous with its patronage during times of economic crisis, it is also less sure of the loyalty of its allies. More than ever, then, the separate components of the system can be seen juggling for position and privilege through the cracks in its once monolithic façade.

In a sense, the media remain the least of the government's concerns. Many journalists are coopted by corruption and favors, and the press as a whole depends on the state not only for newsprint but also for much of its advertising and other revenue. Operating under government concessions and earning income from the state, television and radio stations are particularly vulnerable to government pressure. The media therefore devote an enormous amount of coverage daily to promoting the President and his administration, while discreet telephone calls from the Interior Ministry guarantee either omission or softer treatment of the less welcome news items. Since combative and independent media would be incompatible with the system as it currently functions, recent governments have adjusted the boundaries of press freedom to suit their particular needs.

With occasional interruptions, however, freedom of expression has grown steadily since 1970, not only opening up many issues to public debate but also complicating the business of government. For example, both Echeverría and López Portillo welcomed the support given by left-leaning publications to their foreign policies, but were angered by these periodicals' criticism of their domestic performance. Similarly, De la Madrid sought to reinstitute tighter controls over the press, but discovered that any vacuum of information was immediately filled by rumors. The tensions between a changing society and an antiquated system were once again apparent. The press retained its traditional role in the system—read by politicians for its hidden messages, used by the government to float controversial ideas and exploited as a forum for infighting between different political mafias. But the urban middle classes were now more articulate and critical and demanded more information than before.

The government's continuing obsession with the written press reflected its poor understanding of modern communications. Whereas the circulation of all the country's dailies is less than 1 million, between 15 and 20 million people watch television news every night, and of these more than 90 percent watch "24 Hours," broadcast by the giant corporation Televisa. This program and its presenter, Jacobo Zabludovsky, are thus shaping the political thinking of much of the nation. Televisa readily accepts official guidelines on how specific news items are to be handled and rarely criticizes the government directly. Yet its treatment and selection of news are consistently slanted to the right. On home affairs, a leftist position on any issue rarely makes the air, while strikes and demonstrations will be mentioned only if accompanied by a hostile editorial remark. On foreign affairs, the slant is even sharper, with Televisa effectively endorsing Washington's anti-Communist view of the world. Thus, while supporting each President, Televisa is in fact undermining the system by subtly leading the viewing public to the right.

In contrast, successive governments have been able to rely on organized labor. In many ways, in fact, it was the regime's success in controlling labor after the Revolution that created the foundations for the entire system. At first, socialists and anarchists competed for influence, but in the late 1930s the Confederation of Mexican Workers (CTM) was formed and subsequently integrated into the official party. And when the CTM's founding secretary-general, Vicente Lombardo Toledano, proved too independent, the regime had no difficulty ousting him. Since then, the rules have been clear: the government supports the union leaders in exchange for political loyalty, and it channels wage and other benefits to unionized workers, themselves a privileged elite comprising only one-third of the 20 million work force, in exchange for labor tranquillity. As the only mass organization within the system, the labor movement also permits the government to counterbalance pressure from the private sector and to maintain its revolutionary credentials. Further, unlike the peasant and white-collar sectors of the PRI, whose leaders are changed at the whim of the President, the labor movement has been controlled by the same group over four decades and during eight administrations. This continuity has brought stability.

But the strength of this arrangement was also its vulnerability, since it leaned heavily on one man, Fidel Velázquez. Born into a poor family in 1900, he began work as a milk delivery boy and was soon attracted by union activities. He was one of the infamous "Five Little Wolves" that founded the CTM and by 1941 had emerged as its undisputed boss. He established close ties with the American Federation of Labor (AFL) and worked with George Meany to combat Communist union activities elsewhere in Latin America. But his main role was domestic, backing every President and PRI candidate, who in turn would reward his loyalty. "In politics," he once noted, "there are no commitments, only discipline." Typically, in 1968 his opposition to the anti-government protest movement torpedoed any possible alliance between students and workers. Díaz Ordaz responded by decreeing a new Labor Code.

Velázquez's relations with the government, however, were not always smooth, a reflection of the CTM's relative independence within the system. Part of the price of labor peace was that the leaders of CTM unions often became corrupt *caciques,* using their own thugs to suppress dissidence in the ranks and enriching themselves by selling out to factory managers. But in the early 1970s, in the name of creating more democratic unions, Echeverría promoted a new labor movement that would be more answerable to him. He therefore encouraged the press to attack Velázquez and allowed new left-leaning independent unions to emerge. But he failed to dislodge Don Fidel, as the CTM boss is known, and as his deteriorating relations with the private sector threatened political instability, the President once again turned to Velázquez for support, repaying him by decreeing emergency wage increases for CTM members. When Echeverría picked López Portillo as his surprise successor, he chose Velázquez to make the announcement to forestall any schism in the party.

Inheriting an acute economic crisis, López Portillo immediately made a deal with Don Fidel: in exchange for accepting a 10 percent wage hike at a time of 45 percent inflation, independent unions were persecuted, a new Workers' Bank was created and control of the state housing fund, INFONAVIT, passed to the CTM. Ritual required Velázquez to lash out verbally against the private sector, but he also made sure that when the economy began to boom, most new jobs were controlled by the CTM. Velázquez was therefore well placed to support the government when the crisis erupted early in 1982. Because of the CTM's strong position in industry, fewer new jobs were subsequently lost. Duly appreciative, López Portillo noted two days before leaving office: "The history of Mexico cannot be understood without Fidel Velázquez. He is an extraordinary and exceptional leader as well as an exemplary patriot and magnificent Mexican."

Under De la Madrid, the familiar figure of Velázquez once again emerged as pivotal to the country's stability, struggling to maintain control over urban workers as their purchasing power shrank. In this, Don Fidel received little help from the technocrats in the Cabinet, who at times seemed more jealous of his power than conscious of his role in keeping them in office. When, for example, Velázquez threatened a general strike to press for an emergency wage increase in 1983, even De la Madrid sniped back that he would not be pressured by "old styles of negotiation," as if ignoring the need to preserve Don Fidel's credibility. Similarly, in June 1984, after a 20 percent wage increase was immediately followed by sharp rises in the price of corn tortillas and bread, a protest from Velázquez seemed like a political necessity, but the President again lashed out at the labor leader and gratuitously fed tensions through the entire system. The fact that Don Fidel preserved labor peace while the government imposed an austerity program worked out with the International Monetary Fund reflected how much he felt that he—rather than recent Presidents—truly personified the system.

Velázquez does not control all labor in Mexico. A majority of workers are either peasants or underemployed; many also belong to company-controlled associations or to unions that are too weak, divided or corrupt to defend their members' interests. The construction industry, for example, has over a hundred different unions, all of them vehicles for the racketeering of individual bosses. Some left-leaning independent unions still survive, notably among university workers, while a number of other labor groupings—the General Workers' Confederation (CGT), the Revolutionary Workers' Confederation (COR), the Mexican Regional Workers' Confederation (CROM) and the Revolutionary Confederation of Workers and Peasants (CROC)—are linked to the CTM through the pro-government Labor Congress. There are also two powerful union bosses—Joaquín Hernández Galicia of the Oil Workers' Union and Carlos Jonguitud Barrios of the Teachers' Union—with whom the government must deal directly. The price of their loyalty to the system became so high that De la Madrid sought to undermine their fiefdoms.

But such is Velázquez's control over the 11,000 CTM-affiliated unions and his personal stature within the PRI that his death will create a vacuum in the entire political system. He has prepared no heir apparent —his day-to-day deputy, Blas Chumacero, is only five years his junior —and has shown no inclination to step down voluntarily, arranging re-election to an eighth six-year term as Secretary-General in 1980. He was in fact infuriated when the De la Madrid administration began courting the CROC leader, Alberto Juárez Blancas, as if preparing a successor. And the mere suggestion of his mortality stirred Don Fidel again into action, renewing attacks on the private sector, calling for reforms in the PRI and warning opposition parties that they will never reach power "as long as I am head of the CTM." He even announced that the CTM would start buying textile, food-processing and soft-drink factories to combat "extortionist businessmen" on their own terms.

But when—Mexican politicians prefer to say "if"—Don Fidel dies, the government will nevertheless be forced to create a new *supremo* in the hope of perpetuating traditional arrangements. A massive power struggle within organized labor, though, is unavoidable and has in fact already begun. Velázquez's successor in the CTM will lack the experience and authority to counter the influence of such semi-autonomous groups as the Oil Workers' and Teachers' unions, while leftist and independent labor leaders will seek to expand their constituencies. Even in the past, labor unrest in Mexico was frequently the result of union warfare, and the most immediate consequence of disintegration of the Labor Congress and weakening of the CTM could be a wave of violent strikes. Faced with the erosion of one of the principal pillars of the party and government, the regime will have little choice but to intervene forcefully. Clearly, for the government to be strong, it needs strong allies elsewhere in the system.

The political role of the private sector has been less consistent. After the traditional alliance between government and landed aristocracy was broken by the Revolution, a new urban industrial, financial and commercial class began to emerge in the 1920s. But only during the quarter-

century of industrial expansion and concentrated enrichment that followed World War II was the private sector effectively incorporated into
the system. In 1946, President Alemán marked this change by naming
three businessmen to his Cabinet. Bargaining took place on an assortment of specific issues and some squabbles even went public during the
López Mateos administration, but there was no fundamental philosophical disagreement between government and business, no change in the
rules of the game. The "revolutionary" regime had concluded that it was
helping the country's development by controlling the labor movement,
stimulating foreign investment, protecting industry from foreign competition and providing fiscal and other incentives. Business naturally agreed.

The dramatic change came in 1970. Echeverría not only turned against
the "reactionary" private sector, but also began expanding the state's
role in the economy. Soon alarmed businessmen stopped investing. Having taken their privileges largely for granted during the four previous
administrations, however, they suddenly discovered the limits on their
political power. The Confederation of Industrial Chambers (CONCAMIN)
and other sectorial organizations were unaccustomed to playing politics,
and on numerous occasions their leaders were pressured into making
pro-government statements that angered their members. Ordinary businessmen also felt abandoned by the country's thirty or so top industrial,
commercial and financial moguls, all members of a little-known Mexican
Businessmen's Council,* who negotiated directly with the President and
his ministers. When Echeverría tried to court the private sector, he made
the mistake of believing it was sufficient to deal with the top. He met
almost weekly with the council and even required pre-candidates for the
1976 succession to address the group. But business hostility toward the
government still spread through the country.

By the time Echeverría left office, the private sector had discovered
that its principal political weapon was economic: by refusing to invest
and by shipping capital out of the country, it could throw the country
into disarray. Further, although surface tensions with the government
evaporated quickly when the economy flourished under López Portillo,
business now recognized its essentially competitive relationship with the
state. The private sector therefore maintained a more combative stance,
using the newly formed Business Coordinating Council (CCE) to criticize the government's inflationary spending, even when these policies
were bringing larger business profits than ever. López Portillo continued

*The Council has no statute, no office, no secretariat and no budget, it seeks to avoid
any media reference to its very existence and its sessions are held in the privacy of its
members' homes, but its collective influence is enormous.

to meet privately with the Mexican Businessmen's Council and he too paraded his possible successors before the group. But as the administration drew to a close, many businessmen—as well as politicians—again began shipping money abroad, accelerating the financial collapse of early 1982, which they then blamed on the government.

López Portillo's decision to nationalize the country's private banks on September 1, 1982, therefore included a strong element of vindictiveness. By denouncing bankers as usurers who had long exploited the population and had now betrayed the nation, he won the easy support of leftist parties and labor groups. But while the action demonstrated the extent of his power, he in fact weakened the system. The country needed a strong economy, which the state alone could not provide. By seizing the banks, the government not only politicized the delicate financial sector, but also convinced many businessmen of the state's hunger to control the rest of the economy. Moreover, since top bankers had come to represent all regions and economic areas of the country, an important channel of communication between the government and the private sector was eliminated.

De la Madrid, it seemed, understood this. He made clear his disapproval of the bank nationalization, and although the measure was politically irreversible, he ordered that 34 percent of bank shares as well as bank-owned companies be sold and negotiated the compensation for the expropriated bankers. The government also helped the private sector to reschedule its foreign debt and insisted that the state's role in the economy would not expand. He invited several expropriated bankers to join other business leaders at a televised breakfast in his residence of Los Pinos, and he also began meeting without publicity with the multimillionaires of the Businessmen's Council. But after the experience of the two previous administrations, the private sector was not easily wooed. With the banks in government hands and even large corporations struggling to stay afloat, the business chambers, particularly the Mexican Managers' Confederation (COPARMEX), assumed a more militant role that reflected the anger and distrust of many smaller entrepreneurs. The bank nationalization had marked the final psychological break between the government and business, and every government promise was now viewed with skepticism. "The private sector accepts the government but no longer believes it," one business leader remarked. Some businessmen moved closer to the conservative National Action Party, but their options remained limited, not least because they still depended on the government for subsidies, incentives and a vast array of permits: they could decide whether or not to play, but they could not lay down the rules.

The government has also been forced to learn to live with the Roman Catholic Church. As the effective heir to the Spanish Colony and an outspoken opponent of change during the Revolution, the Church is viewed as a permanent threat to the hegemony of the political bureaucracy. But while it must limit the political power of the clergy in order to survive, the state must also move carefully. With 93 percent of Mexicans baptized as Catholics and strong strains of religious fanaticism bequeathed by the past, a less-than-tolerant official attitude toward the Church would be a recipe for instability. Politicians and clergy have therefore worked out a complex modus vivendi, taking place on many hidden levels, occasionally disturbed by confrontations, but held together by the stark consequences that would ensue on its collapse.

The separation of Church and State was achieved by Juárez in the mid-nineteenth century, and the political power of the Church was broken in the Revolution, but the anticlerical campaigns of the 1920s merely helped to keep alive Catholic fervor. In 1929, churches finally reopened for the first time in three years, but it was still more than a decade before peace was restored by President Avila Camacho's simple phrase: "I am a believer." Even then, strong anticlerical sentiments survived within the system, just as the Church's distrust of the government continued. But the two sides gradually learned to coexist. The Catholic hierarchy had strongly opposed the "socialist" education of the 1930s, but it later backed government health and literacy programs and avoided sensitive political subjects. In exchange, the government ignored violation of the constitutional ban on Church involvement in education, permitting clergy to run private schools for children of the wealthy.

Today, the Church remains a powerful force, working not only at grass-roots levels through some 10,000 priests in fifty-three dioceses, but also through Church-related organizations as varied as Catholic Action, the Christian Family Movement and the National Parents' Union. Over the past two decades, the conservative Opus Dei movement has become influential in business circles, while two opposition parties, the National Action Party and the Mexican Democratic Party, are openly Catholic. In 1972, the country's bishops found a way of not opposing the government's new family-planning program by endorsing the vaguer formula of "responsible parenthood." But when the idea of legalizing abortion was mooted in 1983, rapid mobilization of Catholic lay organizations quickly prompted the government to withdraw its proposal.

Within the government the Church still stirs strong—often contradictory—feelings. Many veteran politicians regard it as a dangerous rightist force and in 1979 campaigned strongly, but unsuccessfully, against Pope

John Paul II's visit to Mexico, arguing that it would stir fanaticism and encourage renewed political meddling by the Church. Certainly since then, the Catholic hierarchy has been more assertive in its political statements and activities, benefiting from the government's unpopularity and the relative absence of anticlerical feeling among the new technocratic class. Mexican Presidents studiously avoid any public association with clergy, but many officials now distinguish between the Church as an institution and religious beliefs. López Portillo even allowed his mother to install a small chapel in his official residence of Los Pinos, which was personally blessed by the Pope, and De la Madrid's wife, Paloma, regularly attends mass and is widely rumored to sympathize with Opus Dei.*

Politicians involved with security matters, on the other hand, worry more about a relatively small number of left-leaning priests working in urban slums or impoverished peasant communities. Until his retirement in 1983, the bishop of Cuernavaca, Sergio Méndez Arceo, was the most controversial Mexican advocate of the theology of liberation. His political association with Echeverría protected him from reprisals, but several other bishops, among them Samuel Ruiz García of San Cristóbal and Arturo Lona Reyes of Tehuantepec, are frequently criticized when their pastoral letters touch on social and political issues. Theirs are minority voices within the Catholic hierarchy, yet some of their thinking was reflected in a 1983–85 Pastoral Program issued by the Mexican Bishops' Conference, which took note of the failure of Mexico's economic model, the general mood of discontent and the "unmeasured" concentration of power in the state. But having said this, it quickly praised the efforts of the De la Madrid government and reiterated that its own mission was entirely pastoral.

But while the Church remains a potentially divisive force politically, religion in fact contributes to Mexico's social stability. At one level, the authority of local priests helps to maintain the cohesion of rural communities and urban slums. The Church also controls many of the festivals and symbols around which the nation unites. None is more powerful than the cult of the Virgin of Guadalupe, the *madre* of all Mexicans, under whose banner wars have been fought and in whose name enormous energy can be mobilized. In recognition of this, the government even financed construction of a new Basilica of Guadalupe in 1976, and it counts on the Church to keep alive *Guadalupanismo* without turning it

---

*Señora de De la Madrid's conservative sense of morality prompted her to request the removal of numerous statues of nude figures from Mexico City streets and parks.

against the state. Thus, more than five decades after the system was forged by anticlericalism, the Church has become part of the system. On a day-to-day basis, the government has struggled to contain—and the Church to extend—its sphere of influence, but their bargaining is governed by rules which neither seems interested in changing fundamentally.

Perhaps more remarkable than the informal cooptation of the Church is the system's success in removing the Army from the center of power. Alone in Latin America, Mexico can boast no military coup d'état since 1920. Today, the Army's peripheral role is taken for granted by the population. The depoliticizing of the Army was initiated, ironically, by Mexico's last three military Presidents—Calles, Cárdenas and Avila Camacho—who established the principle that military threats would be brutally suppressed and military loyalty would be richly rewarded. As the first civilian President since Carranza, Alemán then refined the rules. To reduce the danger of provincial uprisings, not only were the fuel* and food supplies of the thirty-three military zones† controlled by civilians, but zone commanders were rotated every three or four years to prevent their building a local power base. At the same time, since Mexico was unlikely to become involved in a conventional war with either of its neighbors, the Army's share of the federal budget was steadily reduced —to under 2 percent today—the purchase of new weapons was discouraged and military service for male eighteen-year-olds, which at first involved rudimentary training every Saturday morning for one year, later amounted to merely inscription on a reserve list.

Still more important, it became government policy to corrupt the Army. Senior officers were encouraged to enrich themselves with assorted business opportunities, sinecures and favors, and even illicit activities, such as contraband, drug trafficking and prostitution, were tolerated. Corruption also helped maintain tensions between the Army and the Presidential Military Staff: promotions were more rapid in the Army, but the opportunities for contraband, influence peddling and other rackets were greater on the Staff. At the same time, the government protected the armed forces from media criticism, and even when files on the rackets of several top generals were presented to the De la Madrid administration, no action was taken. To preserve the Army's self-respect, on a half dozen ceremonial occasions each year the President pays tribute to its dubious historical record as a defender of the nation.

---

*The Army is normally allowed to store fuel for two weeks of normal activities and for just three days of mobilization.
†Owing to a recent reorganization, the number is now thirty-six.

One factor working in the system's favor is that, unlike other military institutions on the continent, Mexico's post-revolutionary Army has no aristocratic tradition. Its troops are drawn from the poorest sectors of the peasantry and are duly grateful for the food, clothes and social security they receive from the state, although they rarely stay in uniform longer than one year. Officers come from the lower middle classes and, through military education, often become engineers, doctors, dentists and even lawyers, thereby attaining professions that they can later practice privately. More affluent sectors of the population would never place their children in military schools.

Politically, while firmly anti-Communist, the Army is also a stronghold of nationalism and, as such, less vulnerable to outside manipulation. Some officers have attended General Staff courses in the United States, but almost none are sent to the U.S. Army's School of the Americas in Panama because of its association with American military involvement in the region. Mexico has refused to sign a military assistance agreement with the United States, and the simmering xenophobia of Mexico's military establishment has prevented American defense attachés from establishing the cozy personal-cum-political relationships with local officers that are so common elsewhere in Latin America. Mexican officers may admire their American counterparts, but the two countries have different strategic concerns: for the United States, the principal enemy is the Soviet Union; for Mexico, the only possible threat is the United States.

Domestically, the Army remains an important part of the system's security apparatus. But except as a rural police force, controlling the narcotics traffic, banditry and peasant agitation, the civilian authorities have preferred not to use it, aware of the political cost involved. When Díaz Ordaz called on the Army to suppress the 1968 student movement, for example, there were immediate rumors of an imminent coup. In the early 1970s, Echeverría sought to secure the Army's loyalty by retiring dozens of octogenarian and septuagenarian officers—there were some 400 old generals in a 50,000-strong force—and promoting younger, more professional soldiers. In exchange for the Army's role in wiping out a rural guerrilla movement, Echeverría ordered construction of a luxurious military college. "It's better to give them concrete than guns," a presidential spokesman explained at the time.

Under López Portillo, however, the armed forces—the Air Force is part of the Army, whereas the Navy is autonomous—became even more visible. At the time, Mexico's military hardware still comprised a museum collection of thirty-year-old aircraft, tanks and artillery, a handful of patrol boats and some 20,000 horses. With oil wealth giving Mexico a more prominent diplomatic and economic role in the world, the Defense Minister, General Félix Galván López, was eager to share in the national pride. López Portillo therefore approved purchase of Mexico's first-ever supersonic fighters—a squadron of U.S.-made F-5Es—and a fleet of naval patrol boats. Galván also gave the Army a more modern image, selling off most of the horses and replacing them with freshly painted jeeps, providing soldiers with a variety of new uniforms and colored berets, requiring that the 1981 Independence Day parade be carried out at a trot and even increasing the armed forces to about 120,000 by the end of López Portillo's term.

Unlike his immediate predecessors, López Portillo did not need the Army to combat internal subversion. Yet with little knowledge of the inner workings of the armed forces, many politicians continue to view the institution with nervous suspicion, only reluctantly accepting retired generals in such senior posts as state governors. They fear, for example, that the wild coup rumors in 1968, 1976 and 1982 could sow ideas among the officer corps, and they point to the growing sophistication of military education as evidence that the Army might be preparing to return to government. In private, senior officers express dismay and impatience at the mismanagement of recent civilian administrations. But there are no signs that the Army has any interest in seizing power. The problems that have plagued recent military governments in Argentina, Uruguay, Chile and Brazil have led some officers to applaud their wisdom in keeping out of politics. In fact, only massive unrest might induce the Army to act independently. But so long as the government can coopt generals with political ambitions, enrich others and indulge the Army's institutional vanity, the carefully nurtured alliance is likely to be preserved.

In its constant bargaining with the system's key lobbies, the government must therefore ensure that these groups—the media, labor, business, Church and Army—develop no common interests other than a selfish commitment to the system's survival. The temporary disenchantment of any specific group can then be handled in isolation. But this also requires political skills and sensitivity that are less in evidence than in the past. Within the system, there is the feeling that the new technocrats do not understand—and certainly do not respect—the traditional way of doing things, yet any sudden unilateral effort by the government to impose new rules on the system could be dangerous. The system's credibility must be preserved in almost schizophrenic fashion: those on the outside must believe in its authoritarianism, with those on the inside convinced of its flexibility.

5

The (Generally) Loyal
Opposition

I

Without a formal opposition, elections would be meaningless. And without elections, the system would lose its mask of democratic legitimacy. The existence of an opposition therefore enables the system to monopolize the political center, with rightist parties serving to underline its "revolutionary" qualities and leftist parties to distinguish it from socialism. Through elections, those opposed to the government can express their dissent, all the while indirectly perpetuating the system.

Over the years, then, out of necessity rather than principle, the Mexican state has gone out of its way to keep alive a formal opposition. It has encouraged its critics to work through parties. It has provided them with the funds needed to run candidates in elections, and it has promoted "political reforms" to guarantee them a voice in Congress. Today, as evidence of its success, two rightist and four leftist parties run candidates against the PRI and its two satellite parties in elections, while innumerable lobbies and factions serve as channels for protest. The only danger is that the democratic theater might become too real: economic problems could eventually spawn a level of electoral opposition which the government could not tolerate.

Traditionally, opposition parties have served as tiny cogs in the system's broader survival mechanism. The governments of the 1920s and 1930s considered their legitimacy to be rooted in the Revolution itself, while more recently popular representation has come through negotiations among key interest groups within the system rather than through the electoral process. Moreover, since the state has sought the modernization of the country through economic, social and cultural—rather than political—development, crude pragmatism has invariably proved stronger than democratic principle. Thus formal opposition is permitted, but it can only play its assigned role in the system. As a former Interior Minister, Mario Moya Palencia, once put it: "A vote against the PRI is a vote for the system." And as his successor, Jesús Reyes Heroles, noted of the opposition: "What resists also supports."

The government has the means to ensure that no opposition party comes close to threatening its monopoly of power. Almost instinctively, for example, it coopts emergent opposition leaders, either giving them influential jobs in government or neutralizing them with money. It works quietly to sow dissension among opposition groups to forestall formation of powerful coalitions. And it writes its own electoral laws. The government can gerrymander to attach middle-class neighborhoods to poorer districts where the PRI is assured a strong majority. Only the PRI is in a position to place representatives at all voting booths—50,438 during the 1982 elections—and therefore it enjoys an advantage during ballot counting. Since, by law, official results are announced one week after polling, the government has ample time to arrange the outcome or negotiate deals with the opposition. Even on the rare occasions when opposition victories in municipal elections are recognized, the government may withhold the locality's share of federal and state funds in the hope of stirring disaffection against the new mayor.

Opposition groups that stray outside this context are more vulnerable to direct repression. Spontaneous peasant movements, independent labor organizations and militant squatter groupings must negotiate with the government in order to survive, and the students who challenged the system in 1968 soon reached the limits of its tolerance. And just as the government was willing to shoot down students in 1968 and 1971, when leftist guerrilla groups appeared in the early 1970s, the regime resorted to torture and "disappearances" to eliminate them. But the government also considers resort to such tactics a poor reflection on its bargaining talents: it should be the fear—and not the fact—of unrest and repression that makes negotiation possible.

The Interior Ministry, with its broad responsibility for preserving the country's political stability, is in charge of managing the political arena where both the opposition and the PRI perform. It runs the highly effective Federal Security Directorate, which does everything from tapping the telephones of senior officials and monitoring the activities of legal opposition parties to infiltrating extremist factions and eradicating guerrillas. The ministry dominates the Federal Electoral Commission, and through its sophisticated intelligence network around the country, can decide where the opposition is strong and when electoral frauds are called for. It is also its job to "service" the opposition, both politically and economically. It alone can gauge the political mood of the country and design strategies to relieve tensions. It is best placed to determine if recognition of an opposition victory over the PRI is the wisest course of action. And when, as occasionally occurs, the government decides to support an opposition party in a dispute with a state governor, such deals are negotiated in the ministry's offices.

The government's need to promote a formal opposition first arose in the 1950s, when the system no longer felt threatened by internal dissension. The last uprising by a revolutionary general—Saturnino Cedillo in San Luis Potosí—had been crushed in 1939, the last presidential election to be decided by fraud was in 1940, the last independent candidate to emerge from government ranks and challenge the official nominee did so in 1952* and the real struggle for the presidency was by then being fought before the PRI nominated its candidate rather than at the polls. In addition, the Left was badly divided and the private sector had been coopted by pro-business policies. As the system became more efficiently authoritarian, then, the need to maintain democratic appearances grew. Increasingly over the past three decades, the system came to spend more energy supporting rather than suppressing the opposition.

Opposition parties had long existed—even General Porfirio Díaz would insist on a challenger when he sought re-election—but there was now a need to give them greater visibility, above all in Congress. As a result, in 1963, the law was changed to create opposition party deputies who were elected to the Chamber of Deputies through a scheme of proportional representation. Parties that won a minimum of 2.5 percent of the congressional vote were given a deputy for every 0.5 percent of their vote up to a maximum of twenty seats. Three parties benefited—the conservative National Action Party (PAN), the pro-government Popular Socialist Party (PPS) and the Authentic Party of the Mexican Revolution (PARM)—but although they offered candidates for most elections, the events of 1968 demonstrated that they were ineffective channels of anti-government sentiments.

Fresh valves were therefore opened. In 1970, the minimum voting age was lowered from twenty-one to eighteen years. In 1973, the Echeverría administration reduced the minimum age for election as senator from thirty-five to thirty and as deputy from twenty-five to twenty-one years. More significantly, it also established that opposition parties winning just

---

*General Miguel Henríquez Guzmán, who was "awarded" 19 percent of the vote.

1.5 percent of the congressional votes would get five deputies, with an extra deputy for every additional 0.5 percent of the vote to a maximum of twenty-five seats. But it was still enormously difficult for new parties to obtain registration, and as a result, the reforms were unconvincing and abstentionism continued to grow.

In 1976, with the PPS and the PARM supporting the PRI's presidential nominee and the PAN unable to agree on a candidate, López Portillo was unchallenged at the polls except for the write-in candidacy of a Communist Party veteran, Valentín Campa Salazar. (It was rumored—though never confirmed—that he won close to a million votes.) López Portillo therefore opted for yet another political reform to inject credibility into the country's democracy. During months of negotiations between his experienced Interior Minister, Reyes Heroles, and existing and prospective political parties, new rules were drawn up. Coinciding with an economic crisis, the negotiations themselves were useful since the government threatened to deny official recognition to those parties—notably the Communist Party—that were tempted to stir unrest. But the regime was in fact more interested in strengthening the Left to counterbalance the much greater weight of the Right within the system.

The result, in 1978, was a new law expanding the size of the Chamber of Deputies to 400 seats, 100 of which would be filled by the opposition under a complicated scheme of proportional representation and parallel elections. Further, political groupings could request permanent or conditional registration as parties or recognition as political associations. Parties seeking permanent registration were required to prove they had at least 65,000 members spread over half the country's states or electoral districts, with a notarized list of supporters presented to the Electoral Commission. Those opting for conditional registration had merely to demonstrate four years of political activity under a recognized name, but they needed to win at least 1.5 percent of the vote in a national election in order to obtain permanent status. Registration could be lost if a party received less than 1.5 percent of the vote in three successive elections.

Under the law, all registered parties were given free—and equal—time on radio and television for regular political broadcasts, and the Electoral Commission would offer equipment and advice to those that lacked resources of their own. The state was to provide political parties with resources to run election campaigns, to publish and print a newspaper and to cover postal and telegraphic costs. The Chamber of Deputies itself would give each represented party free office space. Thus, new parties were assured relative financial security. And for not a few young leftists, a deputy's salary gave democracy an additional appeal.

Not surprisingly, considering the obstacles involved, no group sought permanent registration. But prior to the 1979 mid-term elections for the Chamber of Deputies, conditional registration was given to the Mexican Communist Party (PCM), the Socialist Workers' Party (PST) and the conservative Mexican Democratic Party (PDM), all three of which won more than the 1.5 percent minimum of votes. For the first time in many years the rate of abstentionism fell. After the results were in, the breakdown in the new Chamber was: PRI 296 seats,* PAN 43, PCM 18, PARM 12, PPS 11, PDM 10 and PST 10. The PRI's dictatorial majority was unaffected, but the increased opposition presence enlivened congressional debates and even temporarily prompted outside groups to lobby Congress as if it enjoyed true independence.

Before the 1982 elections, a new bevy of political movements, most of them minuscule leftist factions with no significant following, applied for conditional registration, but only two were recognized—the Trotskyist Revolutionary Workers' Party (PRT) and the centrist Social Democratic Party (PSD). A third, the Mexican Workers' Party (PMT), seemed to merit registration, but its leader, Heberto Castillo, was "punished" for having previously denounced the political reform as meaningless. For the presidential and congressional elections, then, nine parties were in the running: the PRI's fellow travelers, the PPS and the PARM, followed tradition by endorsing the official nominee, Miguel de la Madrid, but the six other parties ran their own candidates. All presented candidates for congressional seats, while the government launched a massive publicity campaign urging people to vote. It was easily the biggest democratic show in the country's history.

With the outcome of the presidential election known before the campaign began, however, the unprecedented array of opposition candidates failed to generate much excitement: according to one poll, 95 percent of the voters already knew the PRI would win, no matter how they voted. The electorate's indifference to the process was evidenced by its ignorance of the names or political positions of the opposition nominees. Predictably, De la Madrid's own campaign overshadowed all the others in size, publicity and cost† as it moved methodically around the country, and with the worst of the mounting economic crisis artificially held back until after the election, the opposition offered him few worries.

In ideological terms, the clearest alternatives were provided by the candidates of the conservative PAN and the Unified Socialist Party of

*That is, in the direct election, the PRI lost in only four of the 300 electoral districts.
†According to reliable estimates, the government provided close to $100 million to be spent on the PRI campaign.

Mexico (PSUM), a leftist coalition built around the old Communist Party. Arguing that the ideals of the 1910 Revolution had been betrayed, the PAN nominated Pablo Emilio Madero, a prominent businessman and, more pointedly, a nephew of Francisco I. Madero, whose rebellion had initiated the Revolution more than seven decades earlier. The PSUM picked Arnoldo Martínez Verdugo, the Communist Party leader, who had led the PCM toward a more "Eurocommunist" view of the world. The opposition candidate who stirred most interest, however, was the PRT's Rosario Ibarra de Piedra. An apolitical middle-class housewife from Monterrey until her activist son was "disappeared" by police in 1975, Ibarra gained fame as organizer of the National Committee to Defend Political Prisoners, Fugitives, Exiles and Disappeared Persons. Feisty and charismatic, though not herself a Trotskyist, she gave life to the PRT's campaign.

The "transparency" of Mexican democracy, however, faded after the polls closed on July 4, 1982. Long before any detailed results were disclosed, the Interior Ministry announced that De la Madrid had won with a record number of votes in a record turnout, which, coincidentally, were the two objectives he had set for himself. But it was weeks before the full results were available. Out of a registered electorate of 31.5 million, 69 percent had cast ballots. In the presidential race, 70.9 percent went to De la Madrid, 15.7 percent to Madero, 4.5 percent to Martínez Verdugo and the balance to the remaining candidates. The PRI also won all 64 Senate seats and lost only one of the 300 seats up for direct election in the Chamber of Deputies. Combining the elections for the 100 opposition seats, the new breakdown in the Chamber was: PRI 299 seats, PAN 51, PSUM 17, PDM 12, PST 11 and PPS 10.

The detailed results, however, strongly suggested some vote-fixing. The PSD and the PARM did badly and lost their registration. While Ibarra won 1.7 percent of the vote as the PRT's presidential candidate, the party itself was attributed only 1.3 percent in the congressional elections. As a result, it retained its registration but was excluded from the Chamber, where Ibarra's ebullient style might have given the government cause for alarm. Even more suspect was the dramatic contrast in the number of ballots annulled in the various polls: for the presidency, 4.47 percent—an extraordinary 1 million of 23.5 million ballots cast— were annulled; for the Senate, 7.94 percent; for the direct Chamber elections, a mere 0.04 percent; and for the "plurinominal" race, 4.9 percent. Moreover, the number of votes cast in each election varied inexplicably, with 1.7 million more people voting for senators than for deputies, even though all ballots were marked at the same time. The overwhelming impression left by the 1982 polls was that the government had adjusted the results to suit its political needs.

But once the electoral process was over, just as the PRI immediately lost importance within the system, opposition parties also found their forum for expression largely reduced to the surrealism of congressional debates. Even in the midst of the country's worst economic crisis in memory, no opposition party seemed able to tap effectively into the popular discontent: the PSUM remained isolated from its natural constituency of peasants and workers, and even the PAN was unable to translate its 3.7 million—mainly middle-class—votes into a powerful political voice. Instead, opposition parties preferred to continue looking inward toward the center of power, trying to win the recognition and respect of the system rather than organizing the grass roots of society. Prior to the 1985 congressional elections, eleven new political groupings sought conditional registration as parties, eager to join the game. The government restored the PARM's legal status in order to retain its majority on the Federal Electoral Commission, while the PMT was finally recognized, but the other groups merely mirrored the fragmentation of opinion among the politically literate.

The government was not entirely reassured by this passivity. The 1978 political reform had created a much greater sense of freedom in society, evident in a more open press and a new official tolerance of strikes, demonstrations and verbal dissent. But at a time of economic hardship, the opposition parties failed to provide a channel for the inevitable anger and frustration. What was even more worrisome, the political reform resulted in a strengthening of the Right rather than the Left and disturbed the traditional asymmetry of extremes that held the PRI in the Center. Mounting support for the PAN in local elections—votes that were still more anti-PRI than pro-PAN—reflected the growing conservatism of the country as a whole. Not for the first time, Mexico seemed to be changing faster than its formal democracy.

II

The chaotic history of the Mexican Left is accurately mirrored in the literally dozens of Marxist parties, movements and factions that exist in the country today. It is a history of dogmatic squabbles over ideological minutiae, intense personality clashes, violent purges and rebellions, intellectual elitism, even corruption and betrayal. When it has felt the need, the government has repressed the Left, but for most of this century the

Left has been too weakened by internal disarray to pose any threat to the system.

Founded in 1919, the Mexican Communist Party (PCM) grew steadily in the 1920s and 1930s, controlling several trade unions and some peasant cooperatives as well as embracing many influential writers and artists, not least among them the muralists Diego Rivera and David Alfaro Siqueiros. It was, however, a stolidly pro-Soviet party, and while it suffered persecution under Calles and lost influence over organized labor under Cárdenas, it was its loyalty to Moscow that eventually proved most damaging. Not only did it defend the Moscow Trials, assist in planning the murder of Trotsky in Mexico City in August 1940 and seek to justify Stalin's non-aggression pact with Hitler, but it also embarked on a series of internal purges that shattered the concept of leftist unity. In 1940, the party's secretary-general, Hernán Laborde, and the railroad union leader, Valentín Campa, were themselves expelled for opposing Trotsky's murder and resisting Moscow's dictates. Laborde was replaced by Dionisio Encinas, a dogmatic Stalinist who succeeded in reducing party membership from 30,000 to just 3,000 during his twenty-year rule.

Not surprisingly, many leftists looked elsewhere. Some were drawn toward the Popular Party, formed in 1948 by the Marxist intellectual and labor leader Vicente Lombardo Toledano. Lombardo even ran for the presidency in 1952, but his movement, which survives today as the Popular Socialist Party (PPS), was gradually absorbed by the PRI and lost all credibility. In the early 1960s, a number of independent leftists, many of them disciples of Cárdenas, founded the National Liberation Movement to support the Cuban Revolution, but it too failed to grow as a leftist alternative. When student demonstrations suddenly escalated into a major anti-government protest movement in the summer of 1968, the old Left was totally unprepared. The Communist Party tried unsuccessfully to take over the movement, but during the ten weeks of activities that preceded the Tlatelolco massacre and the long prison terms that followed, an entirely new generation of leftist leaders emerged, most of them markedly nationalist and scornful of the Moscow-line PCM.

But the Left was to re-emerge no less divided than before. When Echeverría freed jailed student leaders in 1971 and opened the doors of the system to leftist intellectuals, many were willingly coopted under the age-old maxim that progressive influence can be exercised more effectively from the inside. Echeverría himself liked to boast that many youths who were on the streets in the late 1960s were in the government in the early 1970s. Other leftist leaders saw the "democratic opening" as an opportunity to organize new parties and movements, and even the PCM launched its own recruitment campaign in the country's universities, pointing to its condemnation of the Soviet invasion of Czechoslovakia as evidence of its new independence from Moscow. But some student groups, particularly in provincial universities, felt the events of 1968 had proved the need for "armed struggle." Coincidentally, a wave of repression in the state of Guerrero spawned a rural insurgency movement: one decade later than most other Latin American countries, guerrilla activities finally reached Mexico.

The guerrillas themselves never won a sufficient following to pose a direct challenge to the government. In Guerrero, first the Nationalist Revolutionary Civic Association led by Genaro Vázquez Rojas and later the Party of the Poor under Lucio Cabañas Barrientos, both rural teachers forced to flee by local *pistoleros,* organized small bands of armed peasants in the mountains above the town of Atoyac and occasionally carried out kidnappings in the nearby resort of Acapulco. The two soon became popular legends in Guerrero and folk heroes elsewhere in Mexico, but probably fewer than 200 people were ever willing to follow them.

In urban areas, the Armed Revolutionary Movement (MAR) first gained prominence when twenty activists were arrested soon after their return from training in North Korea in March 1971. Although this and other small bands of radical students operating in Guadalajara and Monterrey as well as Mexico City probably numbered less than 1,000 activists and collaborators, they caused considerable disarray by carrying out numerous kidnappings of officials, wealthy businessmen and one United States diplomat. Subsequently, another group, known as the Communist League 23rd of September, was blamed for a wave of bank assaults and assassinations of police. By then, the rest of the Left, enjoying its honeymoon under Echeverría, was anxious to disassociate itself from the guerrillas.

Long before they were wiped out, however, the guerrillas were to have a major, if indirect, political impact. First, the insurgency led the government to adopt the tactics of a "dirty war." On the Guerrero front, Vázquez purportedly died in a car crash in 1972 and Cabañas was killed in combat in 1974. But in the process of defeating the rural guerrillas, the Army adopted terror tactics, detaining and torturing suspected sympathizers—several of Cabañas' relatives were held incommunicado in the First Military Camp in Mexico City for months on end—and deepening hate for the government. The Federal Security Directorate was charged with dismantling the urban guerrilla bands, and it too resorted routinely to torture, assassinations and "disappearances" of young leftists. Finally,

in 1977, to improve coordination among police forces involved in counterinsurgency, the government formed a secret unit known as the White
Brigade, comprising agents from military, security and judicial police
forces, which, using largely illegal tactics, eventually eliminated the
guerrillas.

The price of this victory was a serious blemish on the government's
image. Between 1971 and 1978, over 400 people "disappeared," and while
political freedoms increased during the López Portillo administration,
the government refused to accept responsibility for the "disappearances"
and did not dismantle the White Brigade until 1980. As a gesture to
human-rights groups, López Portillo proclaimed an amnesty for most
imprisoned rebels, but he insisted that all those listed as missing had
either been killed in combat, died of natural causes or simply gone into
hiding. But even now, the occasional release of someone who has "disappeared" for several weeks or months serves to confirm the continued use
of the old tactics by the Security Directorate. (In 1983 and 1984, there
were several brief incidents of "kidnappings" of political activists, including three journalists, two Chilean exiles and a human rights worker.
In each case, the government denied responsibility.) And the interroga-
tion of suspected terrorists still routinely includes beatings and torture.

Perhaps the guerrillas' greatest success in the early 1970s was to damage the government's relations with domestic conservatives. The private
sector argued that Echeverría's leftist rhetoric had served to encourage
terrorism, and after a prominent Monterrey industrialist, Eugenio Garza
Sada, was murdered during a kidnap attempt in 1973, business leaders
began suggesting that the government itself was behind the guerrillas.
When Echeverría's father-in-law, José Guadalupe Zuno, was supposedly
snatched by guerrillas in 1974, there were rumors in official circles that
the entire "kidnapping" had been invented by the government to maintain political tensions. And when López Portillo's sister Margarita was
the target of a murder attempt shortly before the change of administrations in 1976, even aides to the incoming President suspected Echeverría
was somehow responsible. Indirectly, then, the guerrillas helped to shatter business confidence and accelerate the economic crisis that erupted
in 1976 and, in the process, caused more damage to the system than they
could ever have imagined.

The nonviolent Left sought to grow in the narrow space between the
"armed struggle" and cooptation by the government. In September
1971, Heberto Castillo, a university professor who was jailed for his
involvement in the 1968 protest movement, brought together a group of
independent leftists with the idea of forming a new party. But once again

disputes over strategy and leadership soon surfaced, and one group broke away to found the Socialist Workers' Party (PST), while Castillo himself formed the Mexican Workers' Party (PMT). Arguing that the extreme Right posed a greater threat to the country than the government, the PST decided to support "nationalist" elements within the regime and was rewarded with Echeverría's protection. To give the new party credibility, the government frequently acceded to demands brought by the PST on behalf of peasant groups. Castillo, in contrast, was more outspoken in his criticism of the government and was frequently harassed, above all in the provinces, where the "democratic opening" was slow to arrive.

The most effective leftist opposition in the early 1970s was provided through the press, but even here the limits on freedom also became apparent. Echeverría at first encouraged self-criticism of the system, but in practice this meant sharp attacks on his predecessors and warm praise for his administration. A small weekly, ¿Por Que?, which reported on— and thereby appeared to endorse—the new guerrilla movements, soon found itself struggling to survive. After its editor, Mario Menéndez, was jailed in 1974, police broke into its offices, destroyed machinery and closed down the publication. The case of the liberal daily Excelsior was even more illustrative. Under its longtime editor, Julio Scherer García, Excelsior gradually became disillusioned with the emptiness of Echeverría's leftist rhetoric and began questioning his policies and performance. Echeverría himself was infuriated, and in July 1976, using a combination of threats and bribes, he orchestrated a "rebellion" among the members of the Excelsior cooperative and Scherer and his team were ousted.

Internal divisions within the Left, however, continued to stunt its growth. Even with the opportunities offered by López Portillo's political reform, every leftist leader of renown or ambition insisted on leading his own group rather than agreeing to surrender some authority to the idea of unity. In other cases, personality or ideological clashes led to new splits in existing parties. One collection of leftist intellectuals, including Rolando Cordera and Arnoldo Córdova, resigned from the group that published the political monthly Punto Crítico and formed the Political Action Movement (MAP). As early as 1975, Alejandro Gascón Mercado had left the PPS and created the Mexican People's Party (PPM), but he insisted on maintaining his autonomy. Two veteran Communists also led their own tiny parties—Roberto Jaramillo's Revolutionary Socialist Party (PSR) and Miguel Angel Velasco's Movement for Socialist Action and Unity (MAUS). The alphabet soup was endless. Each time applications for registration as legal parties were presented to the Interior Ministry, another dozen initials appeared.

One major effort at unity was made in 1981 when the Communist Party agreed to join forces with several smaller parties—among them, the MAP, PPM, PSR and MAUS—to form the new Unified Socialist Party of Mexico (PSUM). The more influential PMT, however, withdrew from unification talks after personal and ideological disagreements between Heberto Castillo and the PCM's Martínez Verdugo, who then became the new PSUM's presidential candidate in July 1982. But while the PSUM emerged in the elections as the country's third political force, numerous other leftist parties continued competing for the support of a relatively small number of students and middle-class liberals. Even the Left's influence over the labor movement was limited to some of the country's university, steel and auto workers. With the exception of the young Trotskyists of the PRT, in fact, no leftist party tried to use the economic crisis to build a base among poor peasants and urban slum dwellers. Even when spontaneous popular movements did appear and leftist parties rushed to offer advice in the hope of seizing control, their opportunism was invariably rejected. And when two Molotov cocktails were thrown at senior officials watching the May Day workers' march in 1984, the President blamed "foreign interference" and leftist parties accused the United States, when radical students from a Preparatoria Popular were in fact responsible. For the loyal Left, angry protests were considered "provocation."

The PSUM, which won over 900,000 votes in the 1982 elections and claims some 40,000 registered members, seemed particularly uncertain how to function, with different factions dedicated to arguing over tactics instead of agreeing on strategy. One current favored a more critical and confrontational approach to the government. But at the party's Second Congress in September 1983, apparently fearful of provoking repression,* a moderate majority opted for informal alliances with progressive sectors of the system. The party secretary-general, Pablo Gómez, spoke hopefully of building "a great socialist force of the masses" and strengthening "popular resistance" to the government's economic austerity program. But with a new name and new members, the old Communist Party seemed to become an even more conservative and more intellectual bureaucracy, with neither the interest nor the capacity to organize the masses.

---

*One month earlier, the government had shown its hand by ousting the Communist-backed mayor of Juchitán in Oaxaca after local police killed a PRI member in a clash.

The question, then, is not whether the Left poses a threat to Mexico's stability, but rather why it has been unable over the past fifty years to mount a significant opposition to the government. It has been subject to sporadic repression, but the Left in Spain, Portugal and many other countries emerged from long dictatorships with powerful organizations. Internal bickering has clearly contributed to its weakness, yet leftists traditionally turn on each other in frustration over their ineffectiveness in the rest of society. Perhaps more important, the post-revolutionary governments considered themselves leftists—they even boasted that the Bolshevik Revolution followed the Mexican Revolution—and therefore easily coopted leftists in their struggle against the Right. At the same time, positions to the left of the government smack of extremism to many ordinary—Catholic—Mexicans: secret government studies show that use of the words "Communism" and "socialism" and of red flags and the hammer-and-sickle emblem are politically counterproductive.

In contrast, Marxism has a strong appeal among middle-class students and intellectuals in Mexico, as elsewhere in Latin America. As a result, limited to these circles, a nationalist—rather than Moscow-run—current of leftist thought has emerged since the 1970s. The PSUM, for example, pointedly criticized the Soviet occupation of Afghanistan and called for a "democratic solution" in Poland. The country's cultural and academic worlds are largely dominated by leftist thought. Many writers and painters belong to leftist parties and, appropriately, the centenary of the death of Karl Marx on March 14, 1983, was celebrated in the government's Palace of Fine Arts. Through trade unions and radical professors, the PSUM also exercises considerable influence in the Autonomous National University and in the state universities of Sinaloa, Puebla and Guerrero, where it is considered heresy not to profess Marxism. Books on Marxism, revolution and an assortment of other topics of leftist interest are readily available, even sold on a sidewalk in front of the Interior Ministry, while leftist groups control numerous publications which, paradoxically, depend mainly on government financing. Conversely, by using the printed word as its main weapon the Left automatically excludes the illiterate and semiliterate from its embrace.

The main media outlets for the Left today were born out of Echeverría's 1976 "coup" against *Excelsior*—the former editor, Scherer García, launched the political weekly *Proceso* in late 1976, his deputy, Manuel Becerra Acosta, founded the daily *Uno más Uno* one year later and, in 1984, dissidents from *Uno más Uno* formed a new daily, *La Jornada*. Although their joint circulation is under 100,000, their readers include much of the political elite: government officials, who ignore speeches by PSUM deputies in Congress, regularly read the opinions of leftist politicians and intellectuals in the columns of *Proceso* and *Uno más Uno*. The publications also enjoy considerable freedom—so angered was López Portillo by *Proceso*'s coverage in 1982 that all government advertising was withdrawn—but with so many leftist factions wanting to be heard through these periodicals, they also become forums for fierce personal and ideological disputes. *Uno más Uno,* for example, was for several years strongly influenced by the dominant faction of the PSUM, while the PMT and other leftist parties received more space in *Proceso.*

A handful of columnists have also emerged as important leftist spokesmen, although in recent years few have exercised as much influence as Manuel Buendía in *Excelsior.* He avoided identification with any party and in fact maintained good relations with many officials, but he also campaigned daily against ultra-rightist factions, corruption in powerful sectors of the government and U.S. policy toward Central America. On May 30, 1984, Buendía was murdered, shot in the back by a paid assassin before he could draw the weapon that he always carried in his belt. The shocked reaction to his death—De la Madrid even attended his wake— reflected the important role played by Buendía in the system's broader balancing act.

Through its columnists and publications, the Left is expected to lobby and pressure the government. Official repression can be denounced and restrained, and *Proceso* in particular has a good record in exposing corruption within the government and the labor movement. In foreign affairs, the Left exercises an almost disproportionate influence, not only because United States imperialism is the one issue on which all leftist parties can agree, but also because recent governments have themselves supported leftist causes abroad, at least in part to appease leftist opinion at home. At times, the Left even tries to take credit for government actions. After the nationalization of private banks in 1982, the hearty support of the Left enabled López Portillo to cloak himself in a revolutionary banner. But in practice, the government was using—rather than being used by—the Left.

III

Since the Revolution, Mexican governments have taken right-wing opposition more seriously. It is regarded as the natural successor to the unpatriotic conservatives who welcomed a French occupation force in the mid-nineteenth century, and as synonymous with the three traditional foes of the revolutionary regime—the Catholic Church, the private sector and the United States. Even more worrisome, the Right has attached little importance to working through opposition parties, preferring to exercise its influence more directly on the government and, not infrequently, infiltrating its ranks. Unlike the Left, it does not accept the PRI's rules of the game.

In the early decades of this century, the revolutionary process itself fed resistance. In the 1920s persecution of the Catholic Church provoked the populist Cristero uprising in western Mexico, and in the 1930s President Cárdenas' acceleration of land reform, "socialization" of education and expansion of the state's role in the economy upset many conservatives. The economic crisis that followed the nationalization of foreign oil companies in 1938 further alienated business, while in the western state of Guanajuato a neo-fascist ultra-Catholic peasant movement appeared under the Sinarquista banner. Much of the support for General Almazán's powerful but unsuccessful bid for the presidency in 1940 also came from sectors disenchanted with the populist socialism of Cárdenas.

The National Action Party (PAN) was founded in 1939 in direct response to the Cárdenas experience. Through its dominant leaders, Manuel Gómez Morín and Efraín González Luna, it brought together conservative businessmen and Catholics around a doctrine that stressed individual over state rights. By the late 1940s, however, the Alemán administration had given the private sector a prominent place in the system. Because powerful bankers and industrialists preferred to deal directly with the government and felt no compunctions about proclaiming themselves members of the PRI, the PAN grew slowly, running a presidential candidate for the first time only in 1952. But the more conservative the government became, the more it needed an electoral Right to preserve the myth of its "revolutionary" alliance with the country's peasants and workers. Unlike the PPS and the PARM, the PAN therefore retained its identity as an opposition party and as such became the main recipient of protest votes. Between 1952 and 1970, its share of the vote in presidential elections increased from 7.8 to 13.8 percent.

Even more significant, the PAN built up a solid following among the urban middle classes that emerged during this period of rapid economic growth. When local problems combined with the nomination of an unpopular PRI candidate, the PAN often did well in municipal elections. In 1964, for example, the PAN won the mayoralty of Mérida, the capital of the strategic state of Yucatán. Five years later it took the mayoralty of Hermosillo, the capital of Sonora, and was prevented only by fraud from winning the governorship of Yucatán. Similarly, even though it made no attempt to offer itself as an authentic alternative at a national level, growing electoral support for the PAN in Mexico City reflected the demand for greater democracy among the more educated and affluent.

During the mid-1970s, however, the PAN demonstrated that it was no less vulnerable to ideological and personality disputes than the Left: the mood of the country had soured and the private sector and Echeverría were barely on speaking terms, yet the PAN failed to exploit the situation. A younger generation of PAN leaders had come to the fore, and as Echeverría moved leftward in his rhetoric, the party's new president, José Angel Conchello, adopted an aggressively anti-Communist tone in his pronouncements. While Conchello gave the PAN a higher profile, it was not the image favored by more traditional party members. And when he lost his bid for re-election in 1975, party ranks were further split. He nevertheless tried to impose Pablo Emilio Madero as the PAN's nominee for the upcoming presidential elections. But after dozens of ballots during two highly charged nominating conventions, Madero failed to win the required 80 percent of the votes. Amid widespread disenchantment with the government, the PAN thus ran no candidate in 1976, and without a flag-bearer, its share of the congressional vote fell from 16.3 percent in 1973 to just 8.9 percent three years later.

Although the PAN was always associated with the Catholic Church and has at times flirted with the ideas of both Christian democracy and the Opus Dei movement, religious conservatism has in practice found diverse expression. During the late 1960s, ultrarightist Catholic paramilitary bands were formed in Puebla and Guadalajara to combat leftist students and progressive priests. One group, known by its Spanish acronym MURO, which was infamous for disrupting leftist and liberal conferences and meetings, still exists today as a fascist university clique. Similarly, Opus Dei, although not a political party, remains an important center of conservative political thought and action. Most recently, a well-financed group known as *los tecos* in Guadalajara has emerged as the most extremist right-wing force in the country.

The Cristero uprising has also left a legacy of Catholic fanaticism among the peasants of several western states, while in the Bajío area around Guanajuato the National Sinarquista Union has survived as a powerful regional lobby since the late 1930s. After the 1978 political reform, the Union gave birth to the Mexican Democratic Party (PDM), which obtained its registration and ran candidates in the 1979 and 1982 elections, winning only about 2 percent of the total vote. Although the PDM and the PAN are both rightist Catholic-inspired parties, however, their links are tenuous: whereas the PDM appeals mainly to peasants in specific regions of Mexico, the PAN today gathers votes principally among the urban middle classes.

Owing to both the rapid growth of the middle classes and its long resistance to cooptation by the PRI, the PAN remained the dominant opposition force even after the appearance of new parties. When the financial crisis of 1982 provoked deep resentment against the government, the PAN was the natural beneficiary. With its internal problems largely resolved, its presidential candidate, Pablo Emilio Madero, won more than twice as many votes as all four leftist candidates combined. Moreover, while De la Madrid's 16.7 million votes came largely from "organized" peasants and workers, Madero's 3.7 million supporters included the more prosperous, literate and demanding middle-class heart of the country. Within a year, PAN candidates had captured the mayoralties of the northern industrial city of Monclova and the state capitals of San Luis Potosí, Hermosillo, Durango and Chihuahua, as well as of the border city of Ciudad Juárez and six other Chihuahua municipalities.

While the government continued to regard the private sector as the "real" Right and to deal with it outside the context of party politics, for the first time it found the voting behavior of the middle classes giving cause for concern. In the 1982 elections, the PAN won 39.7 percent of the votes in Monterrey, 35.1 percent in Guadalajara and 27.3 percent in Mexico City. (By contrast, in its best performance nationwide, the PSUM won 13.2 percent in Guadalajara.) Then, in the municipal elections in Chihuahua in early 1983, the first ominous signs of an alliance among the economic, religious and political Right appeared: Eloy Vallina's Chihuahua Group—angered by the expropriation of its bank, Multibanco Comermex—helped finance the successful PAN candidates, while Catholic prelates criticized the management of the country from pulpits. PRI officials tried to cover up the electoral disaster by charging the Roman Catholic Church and United States diplomats with campaigning on behalf of the PAN, but they suddenly feared they were losing control of "democracy."

The principal problem lay in the more modern and developed north of Mexico. Unable to woo back voters in the midst of the economic crisis, the De la Madrid administration resorted to the old-fashioned tactics of fraud. The President himself took the rare step of personally campaigning for local candidates before the September 1983 Northern Baja California elections, but the results had been decided before the polls opened. After the setback in Ciudad Juárez, the government was determined not to lose another city on the U.S. border. It therefore "won" both Tijuana and Mexicali—where the PAN victory was blatant—and allowed a dissident PRI member running on a PST ticket to take Ensenada. In the months that followed, there was also strong evidence that PAN candidates were the real winners of municipal elections in the border town of Matamoros as well as Mazatlán, Culiacán, Zamora and Puebla, all important provincial cities which the PRI claimed to have held.

In reality, the PAN as such posed no serious threat since it is organized more as a loyal opposition than a true party, with neither charismatic leadership nor a powerful political machine. In the poorest rural states of Mexico, where peasants are still trucked in by officials to vote, the PRI continues to win around 90 percent of the ballots. And even when the PRI is weak in urban areas, its rural control has so far prevented the PAN from winning any election for federal senator or state governor. In all but a handful of provincial cities, the PRI is still assured of a majority, while in Mexico City, where the PRI took all 40 congressional seats but won only 48.3 percent of the total vote in 1982, the absence of municipal elections eliminates the danger of an embarrassing confrontation.

Yet the growing turnouts for the PAN were warning signals of the changing mood of the country and signs that the democratic ritual could turn complicated. Gubernatorial elections in the key states of San Luis Potosí, Sonora and Nuevo León, as well as mid-term congressional elections in 1985, posed the risks of political violence if PAN victories were overturned by fraud. Moreover, there was evidence that provincial businessmen were beginning to pick and support local PAN candidates as a new way of pressuring the government. At a national level, major industrialists and private-sector spokesmen still preferred to deal directly with the administration, yet disenchantment at a prolonged economic slump could also lead them to participate more openly in partisan politics. Already for gubernatorial elections in 1985 and 1986, two business leaders prominent during the López Portillo administration were chosen as PAN candidates—José Luis Coindreau in Nuevo León and Manuel Clouthier in Sinaloa.

While the Left exerts pressure through unions and the media, then, the political Right is doing so through elections as well as the economy. Any clear alliance between the private sector, conservative clergy and the PAN would therefore test the system's commitment to democracy. In theory, so long as its formal legitimacy and political control were unaffected, the government could simply recognize opposition victories and live with a higher degree of political pluralism. Yet the political managers, while accepting the principle of power-sharing within the system, resent surrendering any control to an opposition party. In 1978, traditional sectors of the PRI objected to "giving" even one-quarter of the congressional seats to the opposition under the political reform. After the party's defeats in Chihuahua's municipal elections in 1983, local PRI leaders shouted fraud as their way of complaining that the government had not in fact used fraud. Resort to fraud and repression, however, could have two dangerous effects: it would create regional foci of tension and it would eliminate a vital escape valve for popular discontent.

But the system is not without options. It can fragment the opposition vote by legalizing more parties with middle-class appeal and secretly financing their campaigns. It can pour public investment into regions where support for the opposition is growing. It could introduce genuine primary elections to improve the quality of its candidates and to create new transmission belts to carry grass-roots sentiments up the bureaucratic pyramid. Given the heterogeneous electorate it must embrace, the PRI could even borrow from the experience of the Democratic and Republican parties in the United States and project a different image in different parts of the country—"one PRI for the north, one PRI for the center and another PRI for the south," as one politician put it. If it does not show flexibility or imagination, however, the system may find in the 1980s that democracy has become both too important a myth to dismantle and too dangerous a reality to tolerate.

6

Corruption: Oil and Glue

I

Mexican officials find difficulty in admitting—above all to foreigners—
that corruption is essential to the operation and survival of the political
system. But the system has in fact never lived without corruption and
it would disintegrate or change beyond recognition if it tried to do so.
In theory, the rule of law would have to replace the exercise of power,
privilege, influence and favors as well as their supporting pillars of loyalty, discipline, discretion and silence. In practice, the mere attempt to
redefine the rules could shatter the entire system of alliances. Thus, even
good intentions are crushed by reality: the pledges of incoming administrations to clean up corruption invariably look naïve or cynical six years
later.

The problem starts with the very word "corruption," which inserts the
custom into a moral context that many Mexicans do not recognize: for
them, economic crimes do not carry the same weight as human or
spiritual offenses. What the Protestant ethic might consider corruption
emerged as a practical way of bridging the gap between idealistic legislation and the management of day-to-day living. Rigid laws have always
been adopted, but they were promulgated in an environment where they
could not be applied. Corruption was therefore an aberration of the law,
but not of society. And in a traditional Mexico, it provided a parallel
system of operating rules. If corruption has become a political problem
today, it is because Mexico's new "Westernized" middle classes now
measure it with alien yardsticks. But even they focus only on government
corruption, unwilling to look for its deeper roots in society itself.

The phenomenon is not easy to explain. Some Mexicans blame the
system of favors and patronage that flourished in pre-Hispanic times,
even noting that the emperor Moctezuma tried to "buy off" the God

Quetzalcóatl—his initial identification of Cortés—with gold. Nationalists in turn insist that corruption was brought from Spain, pointing out that the conquistadors viewed Mexico as booty to be ransacked, while government jobs were routinely sold by viceroys and the Colonial court: "ointment of Mexico" became a Spanish euphemism for a bribe. Independence from Spain, though, brought no change of customs, with governments invariably in the hands of cliques seeking individual or class benefit unrestrained by constitutional or legal precepts. By the late nineteenth century, public life could be defined as the abuse of power to achieve wealth and the abuse of wealth to achieve power.

The lines between honesty and dishonesty, then, were blurred by entrenched traditions. Any position of authority implied an opportunity for self-improvement; conversely, ordinary citizens learned to petition for favors rather than to demand rights. Government, in particular, was a prize to be exploited, but no sector—from business to Church—was excluded from this modus operandi. It was not thought of as corruption: it was the way things had always been done. The system that emerged in the twentieth century merely institutionalized this praxis: the government exercised power with authoritarianism and rewarded loyalty with patronage.

Today, corruption enables the system to function, providing the "oil" that makes the wheels of the bureaucratic machine turn and the "glue" that seals political alliances. Without the continuity afforded by a senior civil service, officials are almost obliged to enrich themselves in order to enjoy security and protection when out of power. It is argued that Mexico's political system is still young, perhaps at the stage reached by Europe in the eighteenth century, when corruption was rife. The United States is said to contribute to the situation simply through the "demonstration effect" of a materialistic society on Mexico's northern border. Marxists blame the capitalist model imposed during the Alemán administration, whereas businessmen claim that dishonesty was stimulated by the populist excesses of the Echeverría and López Portillo governments. Even officials find a way of blaming the system without sharing responsibility as individuals.

Yet the problem is not exclusive to the political system; nor was it born in 1946 with Alemán or in 1970 with Echeverría. Writing in 1916 of the system that he hoped would emerge from the Revolution, the anthropologist Manuel Gamio noted: "Politics has always been the greenhouse of corruption. Before the new politics emerge, it is necessary to disinfect the environment, to demand of politicians credentials legitimized by moral sanity, personal efficiency and effective representation."

After the Revolution, however, most generals were bought off with expropriated haciendas, while Obregón himself used to boast: "There is no general who can resist a cannonade of 50,000 pesos." Since then, the permanence of corruption could be measured by the frequency of promises to deal with it. As early as 1924, General Calles came into office offering "moralization," a concept that has been religiously repeated in successive inaugural addresses. Even as he took over from the supposedly honest Cárdenas administration in 1940, Avila Camacho noted: "We must strengthen public morals."

Corruption grew dramatically in the late 1940s under Alemán, who had nonetheless declared that "public moralization" would be a norm of his government and that "public works and other contracts with the administration are not the privilege of favored people." For the first time, in fact, indignation was stirred by the problem, even prompting Alemán's successor, Ruiz Cortines, to point at the outgoing President when he criticized "venal public servants" during his inaugural address. The subsequent reduction of blatant corruption did in fact contribute to his popularity. During the 1960s, however, illicit wealth continued to be harvested, and in 1970 Echeverría warned: "People who seek administrative or elective office must be conscious that these jobs are not just another way of accumulating a fortune." After taking office, he added: "The presidency of the Republic is not booty." Then, in 1976, it was López Portillo's turn to note that "corruption is a cancer eating away at our society" and to promise that "any official who deceives or steals will be punished by the law."

Yet, despite this deeply entrenched tradition, by the time De la Madrid took office in 1982, corruption had become a major point of contention between government and key sectors of the population. Many ordinary Mexicans still regarded officials as the same *bola de rateros*—gang of thieves—as ever, but the urban middle classes for the first time blamed corruption for the economic crisis and, specifically, for their falling living standards. Conservative businessmen, accused by the government of bringing on the financial disarray of 1976 and 1982, also jumped at the chance to escape the spotlight, using the media to create the impression that all would be well if the government were honest. In offering a "moral renovation" of society, De la Madrid himself warned that corruption had become a threat to the system and rejected a familiar justification: "We will not accept corruption as the cost of our system's stability or efficiency in the management of the affairs of state."

Yet even this change in attitudes had less to do with morality than with politics and economics: corruption—rather than society—had changed. Many Mexicans saw the problem as one of quantity rather than quality. The government's role in an expanding economy had grown dramatically, multiplying both the opportunities for corruption and the amounts available to be stolen. Huge foreign indebtedness and rising oil revenues financed public-sector contracts on a scale unimaginable only a few years earlier. As a result, the complaint was often voiced: "We know government officials steal, but why so much?" Further, the dishonesty of some officials was so brazen—and their lifestyle so outrageous—that it suggested an almost insulting degree of impunity. The demand for punishment of a handful of key politicians therefore reflected as much a desire for vengeance as any faith that future corruption could be avoided.

Perhaps more important, the changing nature of the system had also affected the "quality" of corruption. When the country was governed mainly by politicians sustained by their own power bases, corruption was passed down through the system in exchange for loyalty. It was a way of redistributing wealth within the pyramid of power and, as such, corruption contributed to political stability. But with the growth of presidential authority, particularly since the 1970s, power came increasingly from above rather than below and, consequently, the fruits of corruption began to move upward rather than downward. With top officials taking more for themselves and their bosses and sharing less with their political supporters, not only were larger illicit fortunes accumulated but this new wealth was also concentrated in fewer hands. Corruption was therefore working less as a system than as a racket and many of the traditional beneficiaries began to object.

In a sense, the fact that corruption continues to flourish in myriad forms elsewhere in society confirms that the problem is cultural rather than moral. Even now, many old habits, such as conflict of interest, nepotism and influence-peddling, are not considered wrong, and since power rather than law dominates society, honesty itself is seemingly negotiable. As one politician put it, "corruption has been corrupted." Overcharging by a top industrialist or a shoeshine boy is considered normal, while tax evasion is justified on the grounds that the government would steal the money. Still more illustrative, those who pay bribes to officials, union leaders or traffic cops believe they are victims of—rather than contributors to—corruption. But even though most Mexicans play by the same rules, the government is considered the principal culprit. It is at the center of wealth and power and everyone in some way or other depends on it.

II

The most visible form of official corruption, *la mordida*—"the bite" of the traffic cop—is almost part of the way of life, and it takes place thousands of times daily. The cop stops trucks, taxis or ordinary cars and, depending on their purported offense, extracts a bribe in lieu of a fine. This is not difficult, because most drivers prefer to pay the *mordida* rather than a more expensive fine. A ritual is nevertheless required to avoid the suggestion of corruption: while the bribe is being negotiated, it must be referred to as a fine; or if the cop does the "favor" of pardoning the offense, he expects the "favor" of a tip in return; or if a driver has credentials suggesting influence, he must show them without humiliating the policeman. The variations in the battle of wits, however, are endless: some policemen are charmed by a pretty woman, others will agree to take a check; some drivers stubbornly insist on going to the precinct until the cop is bored, others appeal to sentimentality by claiming to be rushing to visit a sick mother.

In practice, however, the traffic cop has no choice but to "bite." His wages are low on the understanding that he will supplement it. Not only must he "buy" his job, including his uniform and bullets for his pistol; he must also pass a daily "rent" to his immediate superior. The "rent" in turn depends on his beat: a policeman stationed near a traffic light or a "No Right Turn" sign partly obscured by trees must pay a premium, whereas a motorcycle cop who can roam like a shark, "biting" at will, earns and must pass on still more. Between cities, the rules of the Federal Highway Patrol are so institutionalized that officers merely park their cars at regular intervals and truck drivers automatically stop to pay them off. The ordinary Mexican's most regular contact with government is through the police, and he hates them with a passion: during the annual Independence Day parade, while the Army is cheered, passing police cars switch on their sirens to drown out the abusive heckling and whistles.

Police corruption, however, has traditionally extended far beyond traffic matters. Police provide protection for drug, contraband and prostitution rings, they release petty criminals and drunken drivers only after extorting a bribe and they demand a "tip" before investigating a crime. Even when an arrest is ordered by a judge, police units often compete to arrive first in order to take a bribe and allow the person to escape. "We only pay attention to cases that make the papers," a detective once explained, "then everyone looks efficient until the case blows over." Detainees unprotected by money or influence are routinely mistreated or tortured until "confessions" are extracted: in one case, twenty-two men "confessed" to murdering someone who had actually committed suicide. Certainly, in their dealings with the urban poor, many police seem confident that their abuses will go unpunished. A Center for Raped Women in Mexico City reported that half the women who sought assistance had been raped by policemen. Many of the assaults and kidnappings that take place in the capital are also attributable to policemen, present or former.

Part of the problem stems from the proliferation of different police forces within the country. Mexico City, for example, has a dozen police and security bodies, while citizens in the provinces are exposed to municipal and state police as well as an array of federal forces, all of which may be competing for control of business opportunities. The Migration Police, for example, are infamous for their abuse and extortion of Central Americans who are either seeking refuge from political violence or simply trying to cross Mexico in order to enter the United States illegally. At municipal and state levels, police forces may be changed entirely by each new mayor or governor; as a result, policemen not only are lacking in adequate professional training but are also eager to exploit the chance for enrichment while they still have it. Similarly, the number of people who at one time or other have worked as policemen is very large and many of them are quite willing to be employed as bodyguards or paramilitary thugs.

Probably no greater symbol of police corruption has appeared in recent years than Arturo Durazo Moreno, the Mexico City police chief under López Portillo. A childhood friend of the President who had worked in the Federal Judicial Police, "El Negro," as he was nicknamed, had already earned a grand jury indictment in the United States as a narcotics trafficker—information that was conveyed to López Portillo—at the time of his appointment in 1976. Protected by his friend in the National Palace, Durazo converted the police into a racketeering empire that made his predecessors' performances seem positively innocuous.

Until the 1982 change of government, only his public excesses were evident: he appointed himself "General," his security convoy would seal off highways before he passed along them, he gave exorbitant presents to influential politicians, he invited American and European police chiefs to visit him with all expenses paid and he built multimillion-dollar homes in Mexico City and the Pacific resort of Zihuatanejo. But in 1983, with Durazo safely ensconced in yet another retreat in Los Angeles, his former personal aide, José González, began revealing details of police abuses during the previous administration. (González published a short book, *Lo Negro del Negro Durazo*, which became the biggest best-seller in Mexican history.) These ranged from kickbacks on the purchase of police vehicles and concentration of the fruits of *la mordida* in Durazo's hands to the marketing of cocaine and the elimination of a Colombian gang, whose bodies were found in the Tula River. Much of the dirtiest work was carried out by the Department for the Prevention of Delinquency, a much-feared body of plainclothes "detectives" dedicated to myriad forms of extortion.

The judiciary, on the other hand, rarely provides justice. Even the Supreme Court, which has a reputation for not taking bribes, is susceptible to political pressure, with cases challenging the legality of administrative decisions or the constitutionality of government decrees invariably dismissed. Although new judges are appointed by the Court itself, some have left to become PRI senators, reinforcing the popular belief that they too are government functionaries. Lower ranks of the judiciary are more vulnerable to economic pressure. Because the legal system is slow and bureaucratic and the judges are poorly paid, bribes serve a double function. A payoff can "convince" the court clerk to bring a case to a judge's attention. Some judges then try to combine a fair decision with a fair reward, offering the party in the right the first chance to contribute, but others simply "auction" off their verdict. Similarly, in criminal cases, money can buy innocence and freedom unless politics or publicity interferes.

As in many countries, Mexico's penitentiaries house mainly the poor, yet money can still be made. Prison authorities frequently steal and resell food and other supplies destined for the institution, while drugs, liquor and other banned products can be routinely bought by prisoners from the wardens. Wealthy detainees—occasional politicians, professionals and union leaders—can in fact live in relative comfort, renting a suite of two or three adjoining cells equipped with television, refrigerator and occasionally even a telephone, obtaining food daily from the outside, receiving regular visitors, including wives or mistresses, and hiring other prisoners to carry out their assigned chores, to clean their cells, to cook their meals and to provide protection from intramural assailants. Poor prisoners, in contrast, may spend years awaiting trial and are condemned to overcrowding, violence and inadequate food.

It is the bureaucracy, which includes such huge decentralized agencies and public utilities as Petróleos Mexicanos and the Federal Electricity Commission, that provides the most familiar path to wealth, not only because internal controls have traditionally been lax, but also because the sexennial recycling of top posts imposes haste on the process of enrichment. Even here a distinction can be made between lower-level officials who provide a service and more senior officials with authority to assign multibillion-dollar contracts.

Most small-scale corruption involves bribes to expedite paperwork, be it a driver's license or a construction or import permit. Although the bribes may be small, the turnover is huge and modest fortunes can be made. For example, one middle-aged woman clerk in the Mexico City government, who received documents from the public and could therefore misplace them or give them priority, proudly drove a late-model Ford sedan on the minimum wage. The surest guarantee that this kind of corruption will continue is the bureaucratic maze that awaits anyone dealing with the government. A businessman wanting to build a factory, to import or export goods, even to embark on a new line of production, must confront dozens of rules and regulations and obtain a handful of permits and licenses. At each stage he must choose between the long, frustrating honest route or the short, efficient corrupt route. In some cases, an entire assembly line is halted pending importation of a vital spare part: the industrialist will have no compunction about bribing an official for an import license or bringing in the spare part as contraband. The cliché is based on reality: the bureaucratic machine indeed does not turn without "oil."

Corruption in the agrarian bureaucracy is more scandalous since it involves exploiting the poorest sector of the country. Private farmers with landholdings larger than the legal maximum can easily purchase protection from expropriation. If a presidential decree is to be signed, agrarian officials will "sell" the information in good time for the property owner to obtain an *amparo agrario* injunction freezing the order. And should peasants "invade" this land, local police or private *pistoleros* can be hired to evict them, not infrequently with loss of life. But peasants in possession of land plots are dependent on the government's Rural Development Bank for the credit needed for seeds, fertilizer and machinery. Not only must they pay bribes in order to obtain credits, but the bank has been so repeatedly looted by officials that its resources have been seriously depleted. On one occasion, the manager of a bank branch in the Yucatán was stoned to death and the building burned to the ground by infuriated peasants.

The truly impressive fortunes, however, are made at the top of the government, where the major contractual decisions are made. A contract for public works or for goods made in Mexico will often be granted to a company owned by the official with responsibility for making the decision. If he has no such company, one will often be formed merely to act as intermediary. In either case, price or quality competition is overlooked: conflict of interest has long been considered one of the perquisites of power. Frequently, major industrial works—say, in oil, steel or electricity—must be contracted abroad, and here a direct commission is involved. When the Las Truchas Steel complex was built in the early 1970s, a consultant from British Steel estimated that 15 percent of the $1 billion cost was attributable to corruption. During the oil boom, when billions of dollars of borrowed money was spent on a crash expansion program, almost every purchase by Petróleos Mexicanos involved a kickback of between 10 and 15 percent.

In a handful of departments where something of a career civil service exists, notably the Foreign Ministry, the Bank of Mexico and parts of the Finance Ministry, officials enjoy a solid reputation for honesty and professionalism. But myriad opportunities for illicit enrichment exist in almost every other sector of government. In some cases, corruption involves no more than abuse of privilege, such as the assignment of cars and chauffeurs to friends and relatives or the use of government executive jets for weekend jaunts. More frequently, the profit motive is awakened. Officials involved in public works, for example, may purchase land at a reduced price before a major investment is announced. Others will contract with their own consulting companies to carry out studies that their departments should complete. In fact, wherever money flows, there is an opportunity to be tapped. "The problem with corruption," one official explained, "is that a hundred pesos may be spent unnecessarily in order to steal ten pesos."

The concept of corruption often becomes indistinguishable from that of influence, which flourishes among the family and friends of leading politicians and blends naturally into the old tradition of favor and patronage. The children of key officials or wealthy businessmen, known disparagingly as "juniors," are infamous for their wild and occasionally illicit antics, carried on behind the vague but well-recognized shield of influence. Similarly, senior police officers will distribute the credentials of a police commander to friends to protect them from the authorities, while many middle-class men will feel undressed unless carrying some —perhaps counterfeit—press, police or government pass. Nepotism naturally thrives in this environment: officials may turn to members of their extended family as the only people they can trust, just as less fortunate relatives will expect to be looked after by a well-placed cousin.

This network is also serviced by the exchange of favors: the sight of a well-dressed woman passing a half dozen suitcases through airport customs without prior inspection is evidence of influence. But every favor granted is a political debt incurred, thus prompting those with administrative authority to look for chances to offer favors. Because of the complexity of most bureaucratic procedures, even "rights" are respected as favors: the law thus only works for *influyentes* who are in a position to violate it. Yet few Mexicans would regard this as corruption. Similarly, the practice of giving presents as a way of reaffirming friendship, expressing thanks or gaining attention is considered normal, part of a centuries-old tradition of tribute: the present is given in exchange for nothing specific, but it serves as a point of communication.

Officials involved in blatant embezzlement or fraud, however, will avoid direct involvement by using lawyers or intermediaries or simply more junior officials to negotiate the deals. In some cases, the private secretaries of ministers have become known as their "bagmen," while businessmen seeking contracts with the government invariably know which back channel to use. But the fingerprints of corruption are often left in the lifestyle of officials: they can hide the hand that steals but not the hand that spends. It is almost a cliché in Mexico that, after a couple of years in office, many nouveaux riches officials move to larger homes and begin surrounding themselves with such trappings of wealth and power as expensive cars and bodyguards. Some have shown a particular weakness for collecting imported cars; in one case, an official kept a dozen autos, including Rolls-Royces and Ferraris, behind windows surrounding his sitting room. Others can suddenly afford to invite movie starlets for weekends at Las Vegas. Mexican bureaucrats also prefer to invest their new wealth in real estate at home and abroad rather than in productive ventures that would serve to recycle their takings.

Since a revolution in living standards takes place for many officials every six years, Mexicans are thoroughly accustomed to the phenomenon. Every wealthy family, the saying goes, has a thief in its past. Yet the lines between friendship and favoritism, between authority and influence, between commissions and bribes, between tips and payoffs, remain nebulous. Traditionally, discussion of new fortunes is tinged with a mixture of jealousy and admiration: few Mexicans would claim they would behave differently if given the opportunity for illicit enrichment; and few respect those who ignore such an opportunity. *La Revolución le hizo justicia*—the Revolution brought him justice—is still the cynical euphemism for appointment to a government job with perks. By definition, no chance should be missed.

III

"Wherever you put your finger," an Attorney General once noted darkly, "pus comes out." Though it is an exaggeration to say that all of Mexican society is corrupt, corruption is nevertheless present in every region and sector of the country. While it is a function of the pyramidal power structure that exists even in nongovernmental areas, there is also a common attitude, almost a pattern of behavior, that seemingly permits many Mexicans to accept practices of questionable honesty. Although the government is the target of most criticism, corruption is no less likely to be found at different levels in the worlds of sports, academia, culture and religion as well as in business, labor and the media.

Probably no group complains more about government corruption than business, but it too is riddled with illegal habits aimed at economic advantage. There are, of course, examples of internal corruption, such as purchasing managers who, like their government counterparts, routinely accept kickbacks from suppliers. But much of it occurs in the private sector's institutional dealings with either the government or the public. Tax evasion by doctors and architects as well as companies is widespread, while price gouging and speculative hoarding by the commercial sector is frequent. The poor quality of products sold to the public or to the government is an additional way of profiteering. On one occasion, a pharmaceutical company sold millions of pills to the Social Security Institute at less than their official strength, causing serious problems for ailing patients.

Businessmen complain bitterly at having to pay commissions for government contracts or bribes for court decisions, yet they pay up when it is to their advantage. Many factory managers happily pay off government inspectors to overlook violations of health, labor and environmental standards since adherence to regulations would prove more costly. Similarly, the cost of kickbacks on public works contracts is passed on to either the taxpayer or the consumer. Corruption is in fact such an ingredient of doing business that, after the U.S. Foreign Corrupt Practices Act of 1978 prohibited U.S. companies from paying bribes abroad, American subsidiaries in Mexico insisted that they lost business to European and Japanese competitors who were not subject to similar restraints. Through intermediaries and agents, some American companies therefore continued to offer commissions, and as of 1983 only one had been caught and prosecuted by U.S. authorities.

The private sector's collusion with corruption is perhaps most evident in its relationship with the labor movement, with many companies preferring to "buy" a union leader at contract time rather than agree to a higher wage scale for workers. Most union leaders, though, are just as anxious to be "bought," seeing this as one of the privileges of their position. Not surprisingly, the principal motivation for the formation of independent unions is the corruption of the old bosses. In some industries, such is the power of the union that its leaders are guided entirely by personal and political interests. Nowhere are labor bosses stronger or wealthier than in the Oil Workers' Union: there, the union decides who fills most vacancies and sells off jobs to the highest bidders. As elsewhere, power means money, and money means power.

With all key players in the system embraced by corruption, the country's media could be no exception. Although able to apply pressure directly, the government in fact prefers to exercise its control through money. Most publishers are willing collaborators, more interested in obtaining advertising and favors from the government than in criticizing its performance. The scores of privately owned newspapers in Mexico City and hundreds more in the provinces obtain between 60 and 80 percent of revenues from government advertising or official handouts published under the guise of editorial content. Some newspapers—such as *El Heraldo* and *Novedades*—are owned by family business groups that use their publications to support their activities in other areas of the economy. Similarly, the huge Televisa television company protects its commercial interests by supporting the government. The relationship is subtle and flexible. Newspapers—though not the broadcast media—can reflect political pluralism and report the shortcomings of the administration so long as they support the system as such.

Some smaller publications are involved in direct extortion. With the private sector, they will threaten to publish devastatingly adverse articles unless advertising is forthcoming. Or they will turn against the bureaucracy, publishing vicious attacks on ministers, state governors or other vulnerable officials until the price of their silence is found. Many of these newspapers and magazines are not even sold on the streets, since they have no takers, but they are distributed in government offices in order to maintain their power of blackmail. Some survive only during the life of a single government because they are sustained by a friend or relative in a government press office. Others merely appear prior to the selection of the official candidate for the presidency, promoting one pre-candidate, attacking others and making money from the illusion that they can affect the outcome.

Perhaps the most institutionalized aspect of media corruption involves editors, columnists and journalists. There are notable exceptions to this rule—for example, Manuel Buendía, the respected *Excelsior* columnist murdered in 1984, died poor—but all wield a degree of power, either as individuals or through their newspapers, that can be converted into money. Most publishers condone the arrangement, since it obviates any need on their part to pay adequate salaries to their editorial staff. The usual practice is for reporters covering a regular beat to receive a monthly stipend, known as an *embute,* which varies depending on the importance of the assignment, the prestige of the newspaper and the reputation of the journalist. When reporters travel with prominent officials, their expenses are covered by the government, which also provides them with additional "pocket money." Other extras are available, such as a commission on advertising placed by "their" government department and access to the world of influence and favoritism. Those assigned to the presidency are traditionally best placed, often earning several thousands of extra dollars per month. The political ambitions of key officials can often be measured by the amount they spend on their journalistic entourage.

The ritual is well established in the euphemisms used for *el embute,* among them *el sobre, el chayo, la raya* and *la talis.* None is easily translatable: *talis,* for example, is simply a reordering of the word *lista,* meaning the "list" of favored reporters, but it includes a play on the word *listo,* meaning "clever." In an essay on press corruption written in the late 1960s but no less applicable today, Renato Leduc described the scene in an expensive restaurant when a government press chief invites reporters to meet his boss: "There are French wines, the host has hired a violinist, everyone arrives punctually, their cars double-parked with the word 'Press' visible on their windshields. The press chief organizes. 'You on the right of the *licenciado,* you on the left, the rest where you like.' The *licenciado* arrives and all stand up. He pats each on the shoulder and remarks to some: 'I always read you, I never miss one of your articles,' etc. Then the meal starts and there are jokes, dirty stories, gossip, general euphoria. A crystal glass is tapped with a knife and there is silence. The *licenciado* speaks: 'I have wanted to meet with you . . .' and then parades out all the sacred phrases of the regime: the Revolution, the poor, political and monetary stability, progress with social justice, order, but with freedom. The speaker is applauded as he leaves. The press chief then calls the reporters one by one to the bathroom and each returns smiling and whispers to his colleague, 'It's your turn now,' until the *talis* is complete."

Editors receive a share of the bounty since they can decide which reporter covers a story and how it is displayed in the newspaper. They also receive *embutes* from an array of ministries since they take the telephone calls suggesting which stories should be emphasized or ignored. On rare occasions when a reporter refuses to take his *embute,* press chiefs call up editors and ask for the assignment of a different journalist. A handful of respected political columnists resist cooptation in this way, but others devote their widely read columns to either lavish praise or character assassination of officials. Some officials feel they must win over these columnists by providing them with lucrative sinecures as advisers, others donate cars or houses, a few will invite them on all-expenses-paid trips to Europe. Under López Portillo, dozens of leading editors and columnists were given cars and drivers by the Mexico City police chief. Many outsiders, both politicians and intellectuals, also write weekly columns in the country's dailies, less for the pitifully small honoraria than to establish a position from which to bargain.

Willing to exploit the power that the system has assigned to them, many journalists have become wealthy. Some own gas-station concessions donated by grateful directors general of Petróleos Mexicanos, others own shops with goods imported duty-free as favors from officials, many collect cars provided by friends in government. One well-known television reporter acquired a luxury yacht thanks to the "sale" of the content of his daily commentaries. Another journalist obtained protection from the authorities for the prostitution ring that he operated in a Mexico City neighborhood. In reality, while the opportunities are endless, even some reporters who resist the temptation of massive corruption concede that they cannot survive on the low salaries paid by their newspapers and have little choice but to accept the *embute.*

The government, on the other hand, is too sophisticated to establish a direct relationship between payoffs and stories. In moments of crisis, it can stop publication of any story with one telephone call. But while the government does not want a hostile press, it also recognizes the need to maintain the escape valve of a seemingly free press. It therefore sees corruption simply as a way of tying the press to the system. The public's opinion of most newspapers reflects understanding of the rules: during protest marches by leftist students, a favorite chant as they pass by some newspaper offices is: *"Prensa Vendida,"* or "Sold-out Press."

IV

During the Echeverría administration, corruption blossomed as at no time since the Alemán years. Barely audited government spending on massive industrial projects and rural public works reached record levels, but Echeverría also used corruption as a political weapon, concentrating his favors on journalists and intellectuals whose political approval he coveted. By 1976, when the mood of the country was soured by a currency devaluation, Echeverría himself was rumored to have used ill-gotten gains to buy a chain of newspapers as well as extensive real estate in the Caribbean resort of Cancún and in Morelos state near Mexico City. And even though the story was untrue, middle-class Mexicans avidly passed on the word that the French magazine *Paris-Match* had named him as one of the richest men in the world. In reality, no strong evidence was ever presented against Echeverría; but, more significantly, middle-class Mexicans for the first time began to identify corruption as a principal cause of bad government.

López Portillo recognized this sentiment in his campaign by promising to combat corruption, and he then raised expectations of a thorough cleanup by jailing several senior officials of the Echeverría government. Félix Barra García, when Agrarian Reform Minister, had allegedly extorted money from a large landowner under threat of expropriating his property. Eugenio Méndez Docurro reportedly took a kickback on the purchase of telecommunications equipment when he was Minister of Communications. And Fausto Cantú Peña, as head of the Mexican Coffee Institute, was accused of speculating with government-owned coffee supplies on the New York Commodity Exchange and in the process embezzling $80 million. But when several other renowned racketeers remained free and some even became members of the new administration, Mexicans soon concluded that the arrests were motivated by politics rather than morality: they served as a warning to Echeverría not to meddle in politics now that he was out of office. All three jailed officials were released before the end of López Portillo's term.

By the time massive oil discoveries had fired the Mexican economy back to life in 1978, it was apparent that corruption under López Portillo would surpass that of the Echeverría years. The government embarked on unprecedented public spending, not only on the oil, natural gas and petrochemical industries but also on steel, aviation, fishing and urban development. Three men in particular came to symbolize the benefits of public office. Durazo's handling of the Mexico City police was clearly the most vulgar. In contrast, Carlos Hank González had already built an impressive business empire while head of the CONASUPO basic goods corporation and governor of México state before becoming mayor of Mexico City. In his new job, however, his fortune multiplied as he speculated in real estate and contracted his own companies to provide vehicles and construct highways for the city government. A multimillionaire whose son collected luxury cars, Hank González owned numerous homes, but it was his purchase of a $1-million mansion in New Canaan, Connecticut, that stirred the greatest indignation. The director general of Petróleos Mexicanos, Jorge Díaz Serrano, already a wealthy man when he took office, assigned massive drilling contracts to a company he had founded, while little effort was made to hide the fact that huge commissions were being paid inside the corporation for the purchase of billions of dollars' worth of exploration, production and industrial equipment.

By the end of the administration, however, attention and irritation were focused squarely on López Portillo and the blatant nepotism of his government: he named his son, José Ramón, to be Deputy Minister for Budget and Planning; his mistress, Rosa Luz Alegría, was made Tourism Minister; one sister, Margarita, was given the powerful post of Director General of Radio, Television and Cinematography; another sister, Alicia, handled his personal affairs as private secretary; his cousin Guillermo was placed in charge of the National Sports Institute; another cousin, Manuel, was Deputy Health Minister; and his wife, Carmen Romano, took over the Guanajuato Cultural Festival and a cultural promotion fund known as FONAPAS, as well as the Family Welfare Department traditionally assigned to the First Lady.

In addition, the extravagant lifestyle of the López Portillo clique suggested—even if it did not prove—corruption. Señora López Portillo, for example, traveled on government aircraft with an entourage of aides for shopping trips in New York and Paris, meditation sessions in India and voodoo séances in Haiti. She became well known along New York's Fifth Avenue for her lavish spending. Her tense relations with her husband were public knowledge, and after he bought a $2-million villa in Acapulco for his mistress, the First Lady took it over and forced the President to buy yet another for Señorita Alegría. Margarita López Portillo, whose principal offense was her administrative incompetence, also provoked indignation when she built a grand mansion on federal property in the residential area of Lomas Altas. Neighbors watched as government equipment filled in 36,000 square feet of ravine for her garden: at one point, an earth mover fell to the bottom and was buried. Finally, in an extraordinary display of political insensitivity, López Portillo himself constructed a five-mansion complex, with tennis courts, swimming pools, stables and gymnasium, on a hillside outside the capital in full view of a highway used by thousands of commuters. After he promised to defend the peso "like a dog" in early 1982, the complex became known as "Dog's Hill."

What perhaps aroused the greatest anger at López Portillo, however, was his performance following the nationalization of the country's banks on September 1, 1982. Even though it was not previously illegal to remit dollars abroad, he blamed the banks for the collapse of the peso and pledged dramatically to unmask the unpatriotic *sacadólares*—the "dollar-looters"—who had taken some $15 to $25 billion out of Mexico during the previous three years. It seemed a daring threat, since many senior officials and politicians were known to own property in the United States, and most Mexicans waited with morbid fascination for the results. Fearing that the exposures would include only the names of businessmen, some bankers who had been expropriated drew up their own lists of political *sacadólares* and prepared to leak them to the foreign press. In the end, mocking the nationalist sentiments stirred up in the media, nothing happened, no names were publicized and the great *sacadólares* scandal fizzled out. During his final days in office, aware of his disintegrating image, López Portillo took to defending himself, telling his Cabinet that he had received not one "ill-gotten" peso and praising his close collaborators, including his son, whom he described as "the pride of my nepotism."

Prior to López Portillo's chaotic and scandalous final months, De la Madrid addressed the corruption issue in his campaign for the presidency, even converting "moral renovation" into one of the key planks of his electoral platform. By the time he took office, inheriting a bankrupt government, his credibility rested largely on that single promise. He therefore issued a stream of orders and decrees to tighten controls on the use of public funds. For the first time, "conflict of interest" and "nepotism" were defined as punishable offenses. Officials were required to declare their financial worth upon entering and leaving government. Loopholes were closed in the Law of Public Responsibilities to prevent corrupt officials from being released from jail after returning embezzled money. Guidelines were issued prohibiting the use of government cars, drivers and bodyguards for personal or family purposes. Even the salaries of the President and several hundred top officials were announced, while other traditional sources of income, such as honoraria for attending board meetings of state companies, open-ended expense accounts and institutional slush funds, were discontinued. An Office of the Comptroller General, headed by Francisco Rojas, an accountant and close aide to the President, was created to oversee the new rules.

In his inaugural address, De la Madrid also pointedly stressed the need to "moralize" the country's police forces, and in the capital he named an army general, Ramón Mota Sánchez, to head the police department with a mandate to sweep it clean. General Mota immediately fired dozens of top commanders—"I urge you not to pass on bribes to your superiors," he told police cadets—and the President himself ordered the disbanding of the infamous Department for the Prevention of Delinquency. Resistance, though, was strong. The police's press office was found to be working with reporters in an assortment of illicit activities, ranging from contraband to the "sale" of freedom for petty criminals. When the ring was broken, the reporters responded with a fierce campaign against the new police chief, suggesting that the city was being overrun by criminals and calling—unsuccessfully—for the replacement of General Mota. Conversely, at the level of the traffic cop, fear of reprimand led to an initial reduction of *la mordida,* but within weeks the old tradition was restored, with some policemen even noting apologetically that their wages were so low they needed to "bite" in order to survive.

De la Madrid's hopes of changing the government's corrupt relationship with the press also soon encountered obstacles. During his own electoral campaign, the PRI had routinely paid all expenses for the press entourage, and even as De la Madrid preached "moral renovation," party aides were distributing *embutes* to reporters. But the new President was determined to rationalize government advertising, to prevent public funds from sustaining dozens of phantom "political extortion" publications and to end the *embute.* He convened a group of publishers to explain his plan and urged them to pay adequate salaries to their reporters, and his aides predicted that at least half of the capital's thirty daily newspapers would disappear. Yet when government advertising dropped sharply, prompted as much by economic austerity as by moral concerns, there was an outcry from publishers. Within a few months, both the presidency and the Interior Ministry were again paying *embutes*—albeit reduced—to key reporters, arguing privately that an old habit could only be broken slowly.

De la Madrid's principal objective was to preside over an honest administration, to clean up the corruption of the future. But he was soon being pressed to punish dishonest members of the López Portillo administration, to clean up the past. It was a difficult political dilemma. On the one hand, businessmen, politicians and journalists argued that De la Madrid could only assert his personal authority by moving directly against López Portillo himself. On the other hand, the precedent of bringing charges against a former President would damage the system by puncturing the aura surrounding the presidency. Within a few weeks, a well-known conservative lawyer initiated a formal action of "embezzlement" against López Portillo, but the Attorney General's office dismissed the case. Rumors began circulating that De la Madrid was protecting his old mentor. Finally, De la Madrid met with his Cabinet and decided that no action would be taken against López Portillo—he was effectively pardoned and left the country to live in Rome—but no other member of his government would enjoy impunity.

Slowly then, amid a great deal of public skepticism, the new government began looking over the books: Lydia Camarena, a former congresswoman, Everardo Espino, once chief of the Rural Development Bank, and Leopoldo Ramírez Limón, the former head of the Monte de Piedad, the huge government pawnshop, were among the first to be jailed for fraud. But the principal inspection effort was reserved for Petróleos Mexicanos, where some of the largest fortunes had bloomed under López Portillo. When the first arrest warrants were issued for former oil officials, however, the accused escaped into hiding. Soon cartoons appeared showing the Comptroller General proudly holding a tiny fish as sharks swam undisturbed behind him. De la Madrid insisted that he would embark on no witch-hunt to appease the public demand for sacrificial "blood." Yet until he was able to move against some symbolic figure of the past, the credibility of his entire "moral renovation" and even the strength of his government were in doubt.

On June 29, 1983, just six months after the change of administration, formal charges were brought against Díaz Serrano for embezzling $34 million on the purchase of two oil tankers while director general of Petróleos Mexicanos. At the time, Díaz Serrano was serving as a federal senator and enjoyed immunity. In the weeks before Congress removed his shield against prosecution, Díaz Serrano spent heavily among journalists to promote the idea that he was being victimized in lieu of the real culprit, López Portillo. In public, however, while insisting on his innocence, he behaved like a true product of the system, expressing his faith in the judiciary and resisting the temptation to use his vast knowledge of the inner workings of Petróleos Mexicanos to involve other officials. Finally, in late July, Díaz Serrano was jailed to await trial.

With Díaz Serrano, the necessary big fish had been caught and the "moral renovation" campaign could look ahead. But even after several junior officials in the new administration—including two inspectors from the Comptroller General's office—were arrested, public opinion seemed unconvinced. Some critics argued that Díaz Serrano had been chosen because, in contrast to former mayor Hank González, he headed no powerful political mafia and was therefore vulnerable. When new charges were brought against Díaz Serrano in late 1983, ensuring his imprisonment for at least one more year, reports circulated that the judge had informed the government that its original case involving the two oil tankers was weak.*

Revelations about Durazo's outrageous behavior as the capital's police chief also kept the past alive. The government was anxious to exorcise his ghost, yet every new detail of his crimes served to ratify the opinion most Mexicans already had of their rulers. Finally, in January 1984, Durazo was charged *in absentia* with tax evasion—"like Al Capone," Mexicans quickly recalled—and two months later his extradition was sought on charges that also included extortion, contraband and possession of illegal weapons. His bank accounts and homes were seized and his $2.5-million mansion in Mexico City, with its racetrack, discothèque, heliport and casino, was opened to the public as a unique Museum of Corruption, visited by thousands every weekend. Few Mexicans in fact expected Durazo to be caught, but he was arrested on June 29, 1984, by U.S. authorities when he arrived at San Juan Airport in Puerto Rico, and was transferred to Los Angeles to await extradition hearings. Soon afterward, charges were brought against twenty-four former DIPD members for the "Tula River" murders.

Durazo's detention breathed much-needed life into the "moral renovation" campaign. Six weeks earlier, De la Madrid had arrived in Washington for talks with President Reagan and had been met by a Jack Anderson column in the *Washington Post* quoting U.S. intelligence sources as putting "the total of De la Madrid's 'take' during his presidency at $162 million—minimum." De la Madrid was outraged, and obtained a cautious denial of the story from the State Department: "Information available to all U.S. government agencies leads us to the firm conclusion that President de la Madrid has set both a high personal and official standard in keeping with [his] commitment . . . to addressing the issue of honesty in government." Political and intellectual circles also rushed to defend the President, arguing that he was the victim of character

*In July 1984, when the trial for the oil tankers fraud was already overdue, Díaz Serrano charged that his son, also named Jorge, had been "kidnapped" and tortured by secret police and "disappeared" for five days in an effort to force him to confess to the murder of Manuel Buendía, the newspaper columnist, six weeks earlier. Buendía had indeed frequently attacked Díaz Serrano, but this incident was read in political circles as a warning to the jailed politician not to agitate over his trial date. The government denied all responsibility for the "kidnapping."

assassination by American rightists opposed to his policy in Central America. But the problem was that ordinary Mexicans were inclined to believe the story. If, according to Jack Anderson's purported sources in the CIA, Echeverría had pocketed between $300 million and $1 billion and López Portillo between $1 billion and $3 billion, the popular expectation at least was that De la Madrid would eventually behave likewise.

In reality, as the new administration settled into place, there were already signs that internal regulations were being relaxed: cars packed with bodyguards reappeared on the streets of Mexico City, relatives of many *políticos* found government jobs, and salaries at senior levels were raised unannounced much faster than the official minimum wage, with special "bonds" worth some $3,000 each distributed among top officials over Christmas 1983. The practice of newly promoted politicians moving to larger homes resumed. Even optimists withheld judgment on the "new morality" until an economic recovery could finance government investment projects and offer the first real temptations to the new generation of officials.

The perennial need for "oil" and "glue" remained. At middle levels of the bureaucracy, fear of arrest had a paralyzing effect, with officials insisting on following complex new regulations before spending any money. Since action suddenly involved risks, new excuses for inaction appeared. Within the system itself, the "moral renovation" campaign created uncertainty and many politicians warned privately that an inquisitorial atmosphere would seriously damage relationships of trust and loyalty. To end corruption, one politician argued, would be "to saw off one leg of the system": the system could not survive unless some new support was found.

De la Madrid himself appeared to harbor no illusions that centuries-old habits and traditions could be broken. He also recognized the limits of his power, not only "pardoning" López Portillo and overlooking corruption within the Army, but also seemingly renouncing his dream of cleaning up the powerful Oil Workers' and Teachers' unions. But he needed to reduce corruption to the point where it neither aroused public opinion nor disturbed the government's relations with its allies in the system. In essence, the problem was political rather than moral. A system that had never worked smoothly without corruption was no longer working smoothly because of excessive corruption. It was simply the system's refined instinct for self-preservation that was now mobilized.

7

Economic Models, Miracles and Mistakes

I

For four decades Mexico's economy generated enough wealth to hold the political system together. The social cost of this strategy was high, and even before the crisis of the early 1980s, the economic "miracle" had failed to protect tens of millions of Mexicans from malnutrition, underemployment, illiteracy and slum housing conditions. But the model was an economic success because annual growth rates averaged over 6 percent, an impressive industrial sector emerged, millions of jobs were created and a big-spending middle class appeared. It was a political success because it not only enriched key government, business and labor elites, but also sustained a huge system of subsidies that cushioned ordinary Mexicans against the harshest blows of poverty. Thus, while the majority of the population patiently awaited redistribution of this new wealth, harmony between the economic and political systems helped to preserve stability.

The real significance of the post-1982 crisis to Mexico, then, was not that a shaken foreign banking community faced the specter of defaults by major Third World debtor nations, nor even that Mexico's poor masses were subjected to greater hardship than at any time since the Depression. Rather, it was that Mexico's economy could no longer finance the traditionally profligate ways of the political system. In the short term, as the price of recovering international confidence, economic activity contracted, public spending was slashed, the country's workers resiliently accepted sharply reduced real wages and businessmen struggled to live with huge debts and falling sales. But, more ominously, the resources needed to recover "historical growth rates," as officials put it, were not available. Without long-term growth—without high salaries and profits for the few as well as jobs and subsidies for the many—the entire system of political alliances would have to change.

Throughout Mexico's history political stability and economic growth have leaned on each other: one was rarely possible without the other. In the first fifty years after Independence, both were absent. But during the Díaz dictatorship, Mexico grew rapidly as foreign investment and credit helped build railroads and to develop export-oriented mining and oil industries, while large haciendas gobbled up communal land in the name of more efficient production. But the political system collapsed and the economy soon followed. After the 1910 Revolution, a more nationalist— and inward-looking—economic policy was attempted as a new political system took shape. But only in the late 1930s, when President Cárdenas revived the land reform program and expropriated foreign-owned rail- road and oil companies, did this strategy appear to work. Growth rates were low and businessmen unhappy, but the government's role in the economy was consolidated and real social development took place.

With the outbreak of World War II, Mexico's isolationism was broken and for the first time its economy became dependent on developments outside its borders. Social expenditure and land reform faltered, but there was a great demand for Mexican commodity exports, while new indus- tries appeared locally to meet needs no longer satisfied by scarce im- ported goods. The growth was unplanned, the profits exorbitant and the products often shoddy, yet an industrial boom of sorts nevertheless began. Then, under Alemán between 1946 and 1952, the accident of growth became a strategy of growth, with economic nationalism re- placed by greater liberalism. The government remained an important catalyst of growth by providing a basic infrastructure and assorted fiscal incentives, although the state's share of economic activity in fact fell from around 50 percent to 40 percent over this period. The central idea was to use the private sector to industrialize a largely rural economy through a program of "import substitution." (Between 1940 and 1970, agriculture's share in the economy fell from 21 percent to 11 percent, while industry's grew from 25 percent to 34 percent.) Everything was done to encourage foreign and domestic investors.

Through high import tariffs and, later, through a complex system of import licenses, manufacturers were protected from competition by im- ported goods—theoretically, for a "reasonable" time, although in prac- tice indefinitely. The rule that foreign investment be restricted to 49 percent of share capital was ignored as large transnational corporations formed wholly owned subsidiaries in Mexico. New investors were able to negotiate tax holidays of five to ten years, although taxes on profits for existing industries remained among the lowest in the world. Energy —oil and electricity—and railroad transportation were often provided by state-owned entities at subsidized rates, while even cheap credit was available from Nacional Financiera, the state development bank. Finally, through its control of the trade union movement, the government could guarantee labor peace.

Alemán also embarked on the modernization of agriculture. He personally had little time for land reform—peasant migrants could provide industry with cheap labor—and instead invested heavily in irrigation to open up the fertile coastal plains of Sonora and Sinaloa in northwestern Mexico to private farming modeled after the capital-intensive agriculture of the United States. The resulting produce—mainly cotton and winter vegetables—was destined either for export or for processing by U.S. companies that were busily opening plants in Mexico. Finally, always conscious of the need to save or earn foreign exchange, Alemán discovered Mexico's tourist potential, "creating" Acapulco as an international resort and establishing a pattern that would be followed by his successors. In subsequent years, employment and foreign exchange would be repeatedly used to justify construction of "new Acapulcos" in Cancún, Ixtapa and other locations.

Built into Alemán's economic "miracle," however, were both short-term and long-term weaknesses. Massive government spending fed inflation, which brought on currency devaluations in 1948 and, after Alemán left office, in 1954. Further, corruption blossomed, with the "entrepreneur President" himself acquiring extensive real estate in Acapulco in anticipation of government investment and building a business empire that assured him of influence until his death in 1983. Alemán's narrow expansionist view of the economy also sowed seeds that bore problems years later. Neglect of the peasantry stimulated the uncontrolled growth of Mexico City. Import substitution fed the consumerism of an emerging middle class. Trade protection would prevent industry from developing the necessary strength to compete abroad. The private sector became accustomed to quick profits and low taxes, and while it accepted state participation in the economy when infrastructural investment and subsidized inputs were involved, it resisted any move to strengthen the government's own finances.

Mexico's population boom—the result of reduced infant mortality and unchanging birth rates—increased demands on the state. In the past, domestic savings, foreign investment and modest foreign credits provided the necessary resources for steady growth. But as the population rate rose steadily between 1945 and 1975, when it peaked at 3.6 percent a year, the government was obliged, first, to invest heavily in educational and health facilities and, later, to assume the responsibility for creating jobs for millions of new Mexicans. The population itself jumped from 20 million in 1940 to 51 million in 1970 and 77 million in 1984. In the subsidized areas of food and transportation, the government was looking after more and more people, while the economically active share of the population was falling. To maintain political stability, then, the government had to move ever deeper into the breach.

Yet when Alemán stepped down, no thought was given to changing a strategy that was being held up as a model for other developing nations. In reality, most African and Asian nations were still more consumed by their struggle for political independence, and the intense contemporary debate about economic underdevelopment had not begun. But Latin America, comprising the majority of independent developing nations at the time, took note of Mexico's lunge for industrialization and started competing for foreign capital.

Offering enviable political stability, exceptional fiscal incentives and a convenient location, Mexico remained the favorite of investors. With Western Europe and Japan still struggling to recover from the war, United States investors soon gained a predominant position in the new manufacturing sector. Some areas, such as banking, oil, electricity, steel, basic petrochemicals and communications, were reserved for the state or Mexican nationals and even today foreign investment accounts for only 2.2 percent of total fixed capital. But the new middle-class market and the big profits were to be found in the import substitution of consumer goods, an area wide open to foreigners.

American investors concentrated on satisfying fast-growing demand in several obvious industries—automobiles, rubber tires, electrical appliances, food processing, chemicals and pharmaceuticals—and in each, well-established American firms soon controlled the market. Ford, General Motors, Chrysler and American Motors all built assembly plants and later, under pressure from the government, manufactured auto parts in Mexico. Uniroyal, Firestone and Goodyear, in turn, opened factories that supplied most tires in the country, while General Electric was the first to introduce refrigerators, toasters, hair dryers, irons and even television sets to the average Mexican household. Nowhere, though, was American economic penetration more visible than in food processing, where a new world of Kellogg's Corn Flakes, Campbell's soup, H. J. Heinz's tomato ketchup and Coca-Cola was created for all to share. Finally, in both medicines and cosmetics, Procter & Gamble, Colgate-

Palmolive, Johnson & Johnson and Bristol-Myers were only the first of dozens of pharmaceutical companies that installed themselves in Mexico. In fact, almost without exception, all the names and initials familiar to Americans—from Eastman Kodak and Sherwin Williams to ITT and IBM—made their appearance in Mexico.

During this period, the American Chamber of Commerce in Mexico grew into the largest such chamber in the world, representing not only the transnational corporations, which in practice could deal directly with the highest levels of government, but also the dozens of smaller companies, many of them from the American Southwest, that saw Mexico as their natural—and closest—foreign market. Not until the 1960s did Western European and Japanese investors arrive to challenge the near-monopoly of the American companies. Volkswagen, Renault and Nissan then began making cars in Mexico, while similarly experienced companies from Japan, West Germany, Sweden and Switzerland entered electrical, pharmaceutical and other manufacturing fields. Between 1960 and 1970, the U.S. share of total investment fell from 83 percent to 79 percent and would continue to fall in the 1970s, reaching 69 percent in 1980.

The surge of foreign investment was evident in statistics. As a result of the expropriation of the oil and railroad companies, direct foreign investment in Mexico fell by almost $1 billion to $449 million in 1940, climbing slowly to $566 million by 1950 as confidence in Mexico returned. But it reached $1 billion in 1960 and $2.8 billion in 1970. Still more dramatic, foreign investment in manufacturing jumped from $147 million in 1950 to over $2 billion in 1970, with more than half of this total in chemicals, electrical goods, food processing and automobiles. Yet while foreigners were undoubtedly developing "Mexican" industry, they were also making good profits: according to Bank of Mexico statistics, between 1960 and 1970, new foreign investment worth $2.06 billion contrasted with profit and royalty remittances of $2.99 billion, leaving Mexico with a net exchange loss of $931 million, of which $839 million returned to the United States.

Coincidentally, the postwar boom created an entirely new class of Mexican magnates—energetic and ambitious industrialists and bankers who would become known as the Rockefellers, Mellons and Paleys of Mexico. The private sector as a whole still seemed plagued by the "fast buck" mentality, looking for easy profits under the protectionist umbrella of the state. But the dominating figures were self-made men who, while intent on making fortunes, were also "nation builders" who helped to integrate the country. Names like Carlos Trouyet, Bruno Pagliai, Antonio Ruiz Galindo, Enrique Ballesteros came to symbolize the emerging industrial class. A powerful financial elite also appeared, led by Manuel Espinosa Yglesias, who founded the Banco de Comercio and built it into the country's largest bank, and by the Legorreta family, which had traditionally run the older Banco Nacional de México. Many regional banks were founded, some by existing entrepreneurial groups, others by businessmen, shopkeepers and farmers interested in stimulating local development.

It was a time in which initiative was rewarded. At the age of twenty-eight, Bernardo Quintana pulled together a group of fellow civil engineers to form the ICA construction company, which eventually grew into a powerful conglomerate responsible for projects as varied as hydroelectric dams and soccer stadiums, subway systems and hotels. The ICA Group in fact became Mexico's first multinational corporation, winning contracts in competition with American and European companies in several countries of Latin America. Its principal client, though, was the Mexican government and much of Quintana's success was attributed by competitors to his ability to maintain good—and presumably mutually convenient—relationships with a succession of administrations.

Several large provincial cities served as springboards for the appearance of new entrepreneurs on the national scene. The O'Farrill and Alarcón families, both involved in newspapers, real estate and other businesses, had their first base in Puebla. Eloy Vallina owned a huge timber industry in Chihuahua as well as a local bank that later grew into the Multibanco Comermex, the country's fourth largest. Guadalajara, Saltillo, Toluca and Hermosillo also witnessed the arrival of modern industry and new business groups. But the most dramatic industrial growth took place in Monterrey, where the Garza and Sada families had joined forces at the turn of the century and had gradually diversified from a brewery into glass, steel, banking and television. During the postwar "miracle," under the leadership of Eugenio Garza Sada, the Monterrey Group expanded rapidly. At times, Monterrey seemed almost like a company town, but the Group also began constructing factories in other regions of the country. Perhaps more than any other industrialist of his generation, Garza Sada himself personified the new breed of imaginative, daring and profit-hungry businessmen who were transforming the Mexican economy.

Emilio Azcárraga, another extraordinary figure of enterprise, virtually created mass entertainment in Mexico. He began by traveling through northern Mexico in the 1920s selling imported records, and then opened one of Mexico's earliest radio stations. His talent was to turn his XEW station into a nationwide network, and in so doing he initiated a process of cultural integration. In the 1940s Azcárraga moved into the world of cinema and constructed the Churubusco Studios, which in turn gave birth to a "Golden Age" of Mexican movies. And when television appeared in the 1950s, Azcárraga naturally moved into the new medium, first opening his own channel and later merging with stations owned by the Alemán and O'Farrill families to create Telesistema Mexicano. Azcárraga was its driving force, always looking for new areas to develop. He entered publishing. He built the Aztec Stadium in Mexico City and bought a soccer team, América, to play in it. He developed a new kind of Latin soap opera and sold it across Latin America. Later, his son, also called Emilio and no less dynamic, continued the family tradition, setting up the Spanish International Network (SIN) in the United States as well as expanding Telesistema—now Televisa—in Mexico.

The Azcárragas, like other leaders of the private sector, depended for their success on maintaining good relations with each government. Television, radio and banking were all state concessions and, as such, directly vulnerable to outside pressure. In practice, powerful industrialists had no reason to argue with a regime that was buying their products, controlling labor and providing them with assorted tax breaks and indirect subsidies. Under the three Presidents—Ruiz Cortines, López Mateos and Díaz Ordaz—who succeeded Alemán, relations were only occasionally disturbed: the private sector left politics to politicians, while the government governed largely for the private sector, and with per capita income growing by an average of 2.8 percent each year, enough trickled down to organized labor and the bureaucracy to preserve political stability.

II

By 1970, however, serious cracks in the model of "stabilizing development" were visible. The 1968 anti-government movement, although essentially a middle-class political phenomenon, had drawn attention to rural poverty, massive urban underemployment and the skewed distribution of wealth in the country, but the process of rapid growth had also created new economic problems. While the government's share of total investment had fallen over the previous two decades, its expenditures in such areas as health, education, public works and food, energy and transportation subsidies had struggled to keep up with the population boom. Instead of financing this through higher taxes, however, the government had begun covering its budget deficit with foreign credits. (In 1970, taxes accounted for an extremely low 9.9 percent of the Gross

Domestic Product.) Similarly, despite a slowdown of domestic consumer demand, Mexico's import-substituting industry still refused to be weaned away from its captive domestic market. Without compensating exports, imports of machinery and raw materials spawned a chronic trade deficit. Thus, the model was failing to provide the government with sufficient revenue to cover current expenditures and the private sector with a market able to sustain its expansion.

The incoming Echeverría administration began looking for an alternative. Concluding that many of the obstacles to Mexico's development were in fact functions of the world economic structure, Mexico joined the vociferous Third World campaign for higher and more stable commodity prices, new market opportunities in richer nations for its semi-manufactured goods and a major transfer of capital resources. Mexico's dependence on trade with the United States had fallen from 80 percent in the late 1930s to 65 percent in the late 1960s, but Echeverría argued that it could be reduced further only if the state assumed a stronger role in shaping the economy. To justify this, Echeverría took to blaming the Mexican private sector for conditions in the country and promising sweeping economic and social reforms. Identification of scapegoats at home and abroad, however, would prove easier than finding an alternative strategy. Almost fatalistically, six years later, he bequeathed his successor the same model, but in ruins.

The economic failure cannot be explained outside the political climate that accompanied it. As early as 1971, much of the private sector concluded that Echeverría was a dangerous radical, and while it blocked some of his key reforms and benefited from others, it continued to view his administration with deep distrust. In December 1972, for example, pressure from the business sector dissuaded Echeverría from signing into law a sweeping tax reform that had already been approved by the Cabinet. Similarly, Mexican manufacturers argued successfully that reduction of protectionist barriers would destroy local industry, but they nevertheless took advantage of an assortment of export incentives. Even the regime's decision to decree a new Foreign Investment Law in 1973, limiting foreign ownership to 49 percent of share capital, seemed aimed essentially at protecting local businessmen. But the law was perceived as a leftward lurch and, until it was interpreted with flexibility, served to discourage new investment.

Echeverría nevertheless seemed determined to address the country's acute social problems and he embarked on a program to build roads, schools and health clinics in depressed rural zones. The spending, however, was poorly planned. Echeverría would tour the countryside and, in response to petitions brought by local communities, simply order his bureaucracy into action, forcing ministries to shift men, equipment and funds from other programs. The result was administrative chaos. If peasants complained about accumulated debts to government banks, Echeverría would often cancel them. And because money seemed to be no object, large amounts fell between the cracks into private pockets. When, in May 1973, the Finance Minister, Hugo B. Margáin, announced that the Treasury was empty, he was abruptly fired, to the words: "I'll name someone who can find the money." The new minister, José López Portillo, found the money by borrowing abroad, and forty-two months later, as President, he inherited the economic mess this policy had produced.

Echeverría was eager to preside over a period of economic growth and industrial expansion. When the private sector, dismayed by the state's growing meddling in the economy, slowed down its investment, Echeverría further expanded public expenditure. No major nationalizations actually took place, but the number of companies with government participation more than doubled to 845 between 1970 and 1976. Echeverría was particularly drawn by big projects, inevitably financed from abroad. In Cancún and Ixtapa-Zihuatanejo, for example, entirely new tourist resorts were constructed. The government also formed joint ventures with foreign mining corporations and expanded the country's electrical generating capacity. But planning was often inadequate, above all when political considerations were involved.

Nowhere was this more apparent than in Echeverría's principal industrial project, the Sicartsa steel complex on the Pacific coast of Michoacán. Former President Cárdenas, himself a native of Michoacán, had promoted this idea before his death in 1970. Anxious to emulate Cárdenas, Echeverría ordered construction of the $1 billion plant at a town he renamed Lázaro Cárdenas. It became, however, a monument to the perils of government involvement in the economy: migrant construction workers immediately built a slum city; equipment came from numerous countries, with the accompanying problems of maintenance and spare parts; it produced steel wire when the country's main need was for flat products; nearby iron ore reserves were smaller than anticipated; numerous illicit fortunes were made; and because there was no railroad link to the rest of the country, coal had to be imported from Colombia and initial steel production was exported. The plant was "completed"—that is, it produced a puff of smoke—before Echeverría left office, but it was in every way a disaster, and three more years were spent ironing out its problems.

By 1974, government spending and the sudden rise in world oil prices had brought serious inflation to Mexico for the first time in memory. (The average rise in consumer prices between 1957 and 1970 was just 3.5 percent per year.) The world oil price hike proved fortuitous since it forced the government to raise domestic prices and thereby provided Petróleos Mexicanos with the resources necessary to step up exploration and exploitation. The aim was to eliminate imports of 100,000 barrels daily from Venezuela, but in the process new hydrocarbon reserves were discovered in southeastern Mexico. The government ignored other warning signs, not only maintaining expenditure levels and stepping up foreign borrowing but also decreeing annual rather than biennial review of wages and ordering an immediate 20 percent wage increase. Inflation, which averaged 10 percent over the previous three years, reached 20 percent in 1974, 11 percent in 1975 and 27 percent in 1976, introducing double-digit price hikes as a permanent feature of the economy.

One result was to undermine the real value of the peso. This stimulated imports and foreign vacations by Mexicans, but discouraged exports. As speculation against the peso mounted, both politicians and businessmen began shipping money out of the country. Reflecting these trends, the country's current account payments deficit jumped from $945 million in 1970 to $3.1 billion in 1976. But Echeverría was determined not to preside over the first devaluation since 1954, and both to cover the government's deficit spending and to finance the flight of capital, he simply borrowed more abroad. Astonishingly, perhaps a function of the flood of petrodollars that followed the 1973 oil price hike, foreign banks ignored the mounting evidence of an imminent financial debacle and provided the requested funds. As a result, the public sector's foreign debt jumped over 450 percent, to $19.6 billion, between 1970 and 1976. In contrast, the private sector's foreign debt rose by "only" 100 percent to $4.9 billion over the same period, evidence of its distrust of the Echeverría administration.

Finally, on the evening of August 31, 1976, just hours before Echeverría's final State of the Union address, with López Portillo already President-elect, the government could no longer sustain the currency against the flight of capital. It immediately sank from 12.50 to 19 pesos to the dollar, but the measure merely aggravated the mood of crisis. Anxious to preserve his populist image, Echeverría decreed an emergency wage hike, but prices quickly followed. The U.S. Federal Reserve Board stepped in with an emergency $800 million credit, but with confidence in the government in shreds, the run on the peso continued. Three weeks before he left office, Echeverría privately suggested to López Portillo that all foreign exchange markets remain closed until inauguration day, but the incoming President angrily opposed the move. When Echeverría expropriated private farms in Sonora on November 19, the peso slumped again, to 29 to the dollar. But by then the political and economic crises were virtually indistinguishable.

In reality, buoyed by public spending, economic activity had grown by an annual average of 5.4 percent during the Echeverría years. Per capita income had risen by only 1.8 percent annually, but many new jobs had been created. The economy's essential stability, however, was undermined by inflation, exchange uncertainty, chronic public-sector deficits and a growing foreign debt. Confidence, the invisible cord that had linked government and private sector since the 1940s, was shattered by Echeverría's political demagoguery and economic mismanagement. López Portillo's economic options were therefore largely defined by the crisis he inherited: either he strengthened the government's finances and persuaded the private sector to resume investment or he faced the prospect of a prolonged slump with its accompanying political risks.

In exchange for a $1.5 billion credit, the new government agreed to apply an orthodox austerity program worked out with the International Monetary Fund, cutting public spending, holding down wages and limiting new foreign borrowing to $3 billion a year for three years, compared to $5.5 billion in 1976. Having reawakened business confidence with a stirring inaugural address, López Portillo signed a so-called Alliance for Production with key industrial and commercial sectors involving $8 billion worth of private investment and the creation of 300,000 new jobs per year. In political terms, pro-government labor leaders were able to control the situation, while militant peasant groups were coaxed off private lands seized during the final months of the Echeverría administration. As if confirming the new mood of tranquillity, the peso even recovered some lost ground and stabilized at around 23 to the dollar.

The year 1977 was nevertheless a difficult one. Many firms struggled to renegotiate their dollar debts and the government took over management of the Fundidora de Monterrey steel company in exchange for guaranteeing a new $50 million rescue loan. For the majority of Mexicans, the year also brought increased hardship, with real wages falling and unemployment rising. In strictly monetarist terms, though, the "cooling off" strategy was successful. Gross Domestic Product (GDP) growth fell from 4.2 percent in 1976 to 3.4 percent in 1977, but inflation and the public-sector deficit also dropped sharply. López Portillo saw his administration as comprising two years of recovery, two years of consolidation and a final two years of rapid growth, while adherence to the

IMF's three-year program would ensure the public sector's financial good health. There was renewed talk of a major tax reform, ending trade protectionism and stimulating nontraditional exports. Then oil arrived to disrupt the situation.

The administration had announced a sharp increase in proven hydrocarbon reserves—from 6.3 billion to 11.1 billion barrels—just three weeks after taking office and seemed confident that a bonanza was imminent. But businessmen and bankers had received the news with skepticism, believing it a ploy to reinflate confidence. By 1978, however, American oil actuaries as well as the Central Intelligence Agency had confirmed Mexico's new oil wealth and the economy began to respond accordingly. Oil revenues as such were still small, but the sheer optimism created by the oil finds led both government and the private sector to resume investing. Foreign bankers began returning to Mexico and the IMF's domestic spending restrictions were quietly forgotten. The government concentrated on the energy sector, but every other area of industry also came alive. After just one year of severe recession, the economy grew again by 8.2 percent in 1978 and the government made no attempt to control it.

A veritable fiesta of borrowing and spending then followed. Petróleos Mexicanos' budget grew in real terms by 50 percent in 1978, by 55 percent in 1979 and by 88 percent in 1980, while in 1981 alone it borrowed $15.7 billion, although much of this was on behalf of the federal government. The giant corporation responded by discovering extraordinary new oil fields that raised proven reserves to 72 billion barrels by 1980 and by increasing both production and exports. Construction of a natural gas pipeline, new oil refineries and huge petrochemical plants accelerated, reviving Mexico's steel industry and sharing the fruits of the boom with foreign suppliers of capital goods. From fishing to electricity, from transportation to tourism, no area seemed to escape expansion. Even the agricultural sector, neglected during the first years of the administration, received billions of dollars in additional subsidies beginning in 1980 in order to achieve national self-sufficiency in basic grains under a much-vaunted program known as the Mexican Food System, or SAM.

The private sector responded with equal enthusiasm, and most existing foreign-owned companies embarked on expansion programs. Led by automobile companies that invested in engine factories, new foreign moneys were available: total foreign investment, which grew from $3.7 billion to $5.3 billion between 1970 and 1976, jumped to $10.7 billion by 1982. With domestic credit unable to finance the investment needed to satisfy seemingly insatiable domestic demand, many Mexican companies also became major dollar borrowers, the private sector's foreign debt increasing from $4.9 billion in 1976 to $20 billion in mid-1982. Floating in new petrodollars following the 1979 oil price rise, foreign banks were more than happy to lend to manufacturing companies whose production, sales and profits were rising. Such were the opportunities that several large companies, among them VISA, Protexa, ICA and Vitro, embarked on diversification programs that soon converted them into major conglomerates.

None was more active than the Alfa Group. Formed in 1974, Alfa inherited the HYLSA steel company from the Monterrey Group, which split up into Alfa and VISA following the murder of its chairman, Eugenio Garza Sada, in 1973. Financed from abroad and encouraged by tax breaks at home, Alfa grew into Latin America's largest private corporation, taking over existing companies or founding new firms involved in food processing, electrical appliances, tourist development, real estate and automobile parts. Every year its assets and profits increased by over 50 percent: its chairman, Bernardo Garza Sada, enjoyed a direct line to the President, its top executives flew around the world in private jets and its young foreign-educated managers earned exorbitant salaries. Indeed, if Petróleos Mexicanos was the government's symbol of success, the Alfa Group carried the flag for the private sector.

In both government and business circles there was a feeling that Mexico had at last turned the corner in its long march toward modernization. Looking toward the end of the century, López Portillo sponsored a series of ambitious sectorial plans, for the first time defining aims beyond his own administration. Although it preceded the Global Development Plan, with its target of 8 percent annual growth between 1982 and 1990, the Industrial Development Plan was the more influential, committing Mexico to 10 percent annual growth rates and providing tax rebates and subsidized energy for companies that invested in one or more of seventeen designated provincial priority zones. The concept was important because it aimed to dissuade industry from further clogging Mexico City, Guadalajara and Monterrey and to focus future urban development in coastal areas of the country. New multibillion-dollar industrial ports, where export-oriented industries could concentrate near a deep-water harbor, were also ordered built near Coatzacoalcos, Tampico and Lázaro Cárdenas.

But this boom began to generate problems. When the extent of Mexico's oil wealth first became apparent in 1977, the government solemnly pledged to avoid the economic and political problems that oil booms had brought to Iran, Nigeria, Venezuela and the like. It even placed a 1.5

million daily barrel "ceiling" on oil exports to prevent either "financial indigestion" or the re-export of surplus capital to industrialized nations. Yet by 1980 there were signs that the economy had become "petrolized," that the "oil syndrome" was at work, that Mexico would irrevocably commit most of the mistakes it had vowed not to repeat.

In essence, the economy grew too fast and the government spent too much. Since oil revenues were insufficient to finance the boom, the government resorted to printing pesos and borrowing dollars to finance its swelling public-sector deficit. In the absence of adequate controls, both corruption and waste proliferated, typical signs of "financial indigestion." Such was domestic demand for consumer goods and raw materials that soon little but oil was available for export, with its share of total exports rising from 10 percent in 1976 to 75 percent in 1982. Growth in turn required massive imports of capital equipment and raw materials—although highly visible, luxury imports were unimportant in the broader trade picture—for the oil, petrochemical, steel and manufacturing sectors. Between 1976 and 1981, exports rose from $3.6 billion to $19.4 billion, while imports increased from $6.2 billion to $23.9 billion. And when the government succumbed to combined business and labor pressure and opted not to join the General Agreement on Tariffs and Trade, it also chose to perpetuate the chronic inefficiency and uncompetitive nature of Mexican industry.

Perhaps most ominously, prices began to rise sharply again. Inflation had fallen to 20 percent in 1977 and 17 percent in 1978, but then it began climbing and reached 30 percent in 1981. López Portillo ignored the warning signs, arguing that the choice was "inflation or destruction." Stated differently, he believed that the solution to the country's economic and social ills lay in the creation of employment and that inflation was the price that had to be paid. At the time the creation of some 4 million new jobs between 1978 and 1981 seemed to support his case. Growth at any cost had become the official motto.

But inflation once again undermined the real value of the Mexican currency. The peso "floated" for three years at 23 pesos to the dollar, and even when allowed to go downward, it moved so slowly that it failed to compensate for inflation. Neither Mexican exports nor tourist resorts could therefore compete, while the government's policy in effect encouraged Mexicans to purchase imported goods, to travel abroad, to acquire real estate in the United States and, eventually, to speculate against a devaluation by buying dollars. The dollar was the cheapest item in Mexico. And no less than other large oil producers, Mexico had become an exporter of capital, albeit unofficially.

López Portillo lost one final chance to avoid the disaster that followed. Soon after the Reagan administration took office in January 1981, its tight money policies began to strengthen the dollar and push up world interest rates. In June of that year, a $4 per barrel drop in world oil prices further altered the international environment: Mexico would earn less from its oil exports and fewer surplus petrodollars would be recycled through international financial markets, resulting in still higher interest rates. Able to blame external forces, then, López Portillo had an ideal opportunity to adjust his strategy—to cut public expenditures, to hold down imports, to reduce foreign borrowing and, most crucially, to devalue the peso.

But domestic politics stood in the way. Just eighteen months from leaving office, López Portillo had presided over Mexico's most dramatic economic surge in its history and he refused to believe it was over. Further, with the "campaign" for the presidential succession in its final stages, none of López Portillo's key advisers, including De la Madrid, seemed willing to proffer unwelcome advice. His closest aide, José Andrés de Oteyza, the Industrial Development Minister, even believed that inflationary growth and fixed exchange rates could still somehow coexist. As a result, despite the loss of some $6 billion from lower oil, coffee and silver prices, the economy in 1981 grew for the fourth successive year by over 8 percent. Only in late November did the Finance Minister, David Ibarra, reveal how this had been possible. In one year, he told Congress, the Mexican government borrowed $14.7 billion abroad, much of it to cover an unprecedented $12.5 billion current account payments deficit. The truth was even worse: the public sector's foreign debt in fact jumped by $19.7 billion in 1981, of which some $12 billion was in previously unannounced short-term credits.

The situation was clearly no longer tenable. The price index of the Mexican Stock Exchange, which had jumped from 338 to 1,488 points between 1978 and 1980, was tumbling daily. Even more dramatically, the Alfa Group, the shining success symbol of the private sector, was in trouble, with many of its newly acquired companies unable to generate the resources necessary to service a $2.3 billion foreign debt. In October 1981, Alfa persuaded López Portillo to approve a $400 million credit from the government's Public Works Bank, but even this was insufficient and the Group was eventually forced to suspend payments on its foreign debt and start divesting itself of many losing subsidiaries.

Still more alarming, some $8 billion had already in 1981 left the country in anticipation of a devaluation and early the next year the flight continued. On February 5, López Portillo made his impassioned pledge to defend the peso "like a dog," but the hemorrhaging of the country's foreign exchange reserves continued in a mood of growing political uncertainty. Businessmen were unhappy about an announced trip by López Portillo to Nicaragua and had heard rumors that the President had secretly loaned Cuba $100 million to help it meet its own debt obligations. And outside Mexico's immediate control, six-month credits acquired following the oil price drop in August 1981 were due to be repaid or rolled over. Finally, on the evening of February 17, the Bank of Mexico announced its withdrawal from exchange markets and the peso slumped from 26 to 45 to the dollar.

Domestic politics once again intervened. De la Madrid was already campaigning for the presidency, and anxious for a smooth transition of power, López Portillo refused to turn to the International Monetary Fund before the July 4 polling day, even approving scaled emergency wage increases of 10, 20 and 30 percent. He named two of De la Madrid's trusted aides to assume control of the crisis—Jesús Silva Herzog as Finance Minister and Miguel Mancera as head of the Bank of Mexico —but their efforts to control public spending were unsuccessful. Finally, on August 1, four weeks after De la Madrid's election, the government ordered across-the-board price hikes to reduce the public-sector deficit. But this merely provoked a new flight of capital—as much as $300 million per day—and on August 5 partial exchange controls were imposed. Still worse was to follow. Many foreign banks that were once again due to roll over Mexico's short-term debt panicked and demanded repayment. Another $12 billion in dollar-denominated accounts in Mexican banks were no longer backed by reserves. On the evening of August 12, the government therefore closed all foreign exchange markets indefinitely, suspended principal payments on the country's $80 billion foreign debt and announced that local "Mex-dollar" accounts would be convertible only to pesos.

In strictly financial terms, this was the worst moment of the crisis. The following day, Silva Herzog and several other ministers flew to Washington for talks with the U.S. Treasury and the IMF. Treasury officials balked at involving themselves until reminded that the top thirteen American banks were owed $16.5 billion—or the equivalent of 48 percent of their capital—by Mexico. The repercussions of a Mexican default on the U.S. and international banking system suddenly seemed obvious. On August 17, the Finance Minister was able to announce details of a major rescue package that included $1 billion in advance payment for oil sales to the United States, another $1 billion guarantee from the U.S. Commodity Credit Corporation for food imports, $1.85 billion provided by leading Western central banks through the Bank of International Settlements and plans to negotiate a $3.9 billion "extended fund facility" with the IMF. Exchange markets then reopened—the dollar immediately jumped to over 120 pesos—and a few days later in New York, Silva Herzog obtained the agreement of Mexico's private creditors for a three-month suspension of all principal payments. The country, it seemed, had obtained a breathing space.

Since February, López Portillo had been studying various radical options to "save" his economic strategy and rescue his badly battered image. Finally, around August 20, he ordered a group of left-leaning economists, including Oteyza and a former Budget and Planning Minister, Carlos Tello, to draft decrees nationalizing the country's private banks and imposing total exchange controls. On August 31, just hours before announcing these measures during his final State of the Union address, López Portillo informed De la Madrid, Silva Herzog and Mancera of his plans. All three were shocked, believing the measures politically motivated and economically unwise. Mancera, who months earlier had published a booklet entitled "The Disadvantages of Exchange Controls," resigned and was immediately replaced by Tello. The following morning the full fifty-member Cabinet was asked to initial the decree, and only one official, Adrián Lajous, head of the government's Foreign Trade Bank, refused to do so and resigned. López Portillo, convinced that he was about to enter history, then drove to Congress and, in an emotional speech, ordered the most drastic economic reform since the expropriation of foreign oil companies forty-four years earlier.

It was clearly unrealistic for the President to attempt to impose a new economic model—a kind of "fortress economy" involving tight import and exchange controls—just three months before leaving office. The results merely aggravated the crisis. On September 4, Tello, who suddenly replaced Silva Herzog as the government's financial spokesman, announced a two-tier exchange rate of 50 pesos to the dollar for "essential" transactions and 70 pesos to the dollar for ordinary trade. But in practice, almost no foreign exchange was available at either rate and both travelers and businessmen were forced to turn to a new black market where the dollar rate rose from 95 pesos in September to 135 pesos in November. Tello also announced a series of populist banking measures, including a lowering of interest rates to less than half the prevailing inflation rate, but in the process discouraged savings and fed inflation. In fact, it was only under pressure from De la Madrid that López Portillo permitted Silva Herzog to sign a letter of intent with the IMF on November 9, and even then, Tello was allowed to preserve the myth that exchange controls would be maintained.

López Portillo's handling of both the boom and the bust produced the worst economic crisis in more than fifty years. In 1982, Mexico registered minus 0.2 percent growth and 100 percent inflation, hard-core unemployment doubled to 8 percent, the public-sector budget deficit reached an unprecedented 18 percent of GDP and the country had declared a partial moratorium on its foreign debt, at the time the largest in the Third World. (Brazil's external debt would surpass that of Mexico during 1983.) The virtual suspension of imports in the second half of 1982 had reduced the current account payments deficit to $2.6 billion, but it had also accelerated the economy's downward drive. Further, unlike the crisis that López Portillo inherited in 1976, the situation he bequeathed could not be alleviated by an inspired inaugural address or even the discovery of new oil fields. He had raised expectations and then smashed them. He had shattered the confidence of foreign bankers, Mexican businessmen and the broad middle classes in the state's ability to run the country. Most dangerous of all, he had allowed the economic model to weaken the political system.

III

When De la Madrid took office on December 1, 1982, his political options were defined by the economy and his economic options were defined abroad. Facing a similar crisis at a later stage of his administration, he might have responded differently, distributing the burden of the crisis more equitably and standing up to the IMF and foreign bankers more defiantly. But the domestic political situation was precarious and could only be stabilized by an incoming President who behaved in an orthodox manner. Given the vulnerability of the Mexican economy, confidence had first to be rebuilt among bankers abroad and businessmen at home and only later among the middle and poorer classes. During the first two years of the new government, if not longer, Mexico was governed by its debt problem.

In his inaugural speech, De la Madrid warned that hard times lay ahead. They began the following day when domestic oil prices doubled and continued over the next three weeks with government-ordered hikes in the price of numerous other goods and services provided by the state, among them corn tortillas, electricity, telephones and water. It was an unenviable way to begin an administration, guaranteed to convince many

Mexicans that "this President is worse than the last." But under the agreement ratified in late December by the IMF, the government pledged to reduce the public-sector budget deficit from 18 percent of GDP in 1982 to just 8.5 percent of GDP in 1983, to 5.5 percent in 1984 and to 3.5 percent in 1985. Further, to survive with only $5 billion per year in new commercial credit between 1983 and 1985, the government agreed to limit imports and gradually remove all exchange controls. It was a classic IMF prescription, "a monetarist counterrevolution," in the words of one Mexican economist, which dealt with the problems of growth by smothering growth. Mexico was given the money needed to prevent its financial collapse, but not to ensure its economic recovery.

While economic activity contracted by 4.7 percent in 1983, the country's worst performance since the 1910 Revolution, the government struggled to put its affairs in order. Its budget deficit was reduced by steadily raising the price of its goods and services to keep up with inflation, by cutting some subsidies, by postponing all major investments and by raising some taxes. It then negotiated postponement until 1987 of principal payments on $23 billion worth of foreign debt which had matured between August 1982 and December 1984, although interest payments on this and other debt absorbed 70 percent of Mexico's oil revenues. The government also pressured foreign banks and private Mexican corporations to renegotiate their $14 billion debt, offering to guarantee foreign exchange if principal payments were also postponed until 1987.

Projecting an image of tough realism, De la Madrid stressed repeatedly that recovery would bring hardship. "We cannot fight inflation through magic," he noted in June 1983, responding to the labor movement's demand for stricter price controls. "We cannot rationally think of freezing prices and wages. This would be self-deceit. Lies cannot be used as political instruments. We leave that to demagogic and irresponsible minorities." The burden of 80 percent inflation, however, was carried mainly by the poor majority, whose wages rose by only 45 percent. But unemployment grew less than expected because the wage proportion of production costs was reduced by inflation, while the "informal economy"—family enterprises and a great variety of improvised forms of self-employment, none of which are recorded in the government's fiscal or welfare records—absorbed many into the job market. The middle classes were forced to reduce their consumption and foreign travels, although crowded restaurants, tourist resorts and shopping centers over the year-end vacations of 1983 and 1984 suggested little change in their expectations.

The productive apparatus was more seriously bruised. With foreign credit restricted, the government's new ownership of the country's banks enabled it to absorb most domestic savings, leaving little available for the hard-pressed private sector. A special effort was made to provide resources to small labor-intensive operations at negative real interest rates, but many large factories were working at between 30 and 50 percent capacity, in a few cases forced to close or to operate for less than the normal workweek, in other cases simply running up new debts. Import controls or delays in obtaining foreign exchange frequently contributed to the slump by blocking essential raw materials from entering the country. New construction projections were canceled and many large buildings were left half-finished.

But the government was soon winning accolades abroad for its success in cutting spending and deflating the economy without provoking widespread political unrest. At the end of 1983, De la Madrid could claim that the worst of the financial crisis was over. Cutbacks in the budget deficit conformed to the IMF's guidelines, exchange controls were limited and a "sliding" exchange rate aimed to prevent the reappearance of an overvalued peso, hard currency reserves had tripled to $4.9 billion, an unprecedented trade surplus of $13.6 billion was recorded and inflation had been reduced by 20 points. Looking for new sources of foreign capital, the government also sought to attract new foreign investors by promising to waive the 49 percent "minority rule" in 34 priority sectors of the economy, including industrial machinery, telecommunications and computers, chemicals, high-technology equipment and hotels. The predictable protests of the Left were ignored. Although fresh foreign investment in 1983 was only about $350 million, compared to well over $1 billion in 1980 and 1981, the government registered its first success in January 1984 when the Ford Motor Company announced plans to build a $500 million auto factory in the northwestern city of Hermosillo. Compensation was also paid to the former owners of the nationalized banking system, while their shares in 339 companies—out of a total of 467 firms in which banks held equity—were placed on the market for re-purchase.

But the future still did not look bright. In 1984, while continuing to restrict spending and imports, the government struggled to keep inflation to 60 percent and saw a modest economic reactivation in a 1 percent growth rate. A National Development Plan in June 1983 had optimistically forecast average growth rates of 5 to 6 percent between 1985 and 1988, but this began to look overoptimistic. The recession remained deep, and the resources necessary for a resumption of growth were unavailable. Foreign credit was restricted and an outflow of private capital continued, with the perception growing that the peso was once again overvalued. Foreign investment was an important factor in rebuilding confidence, but its impact on the economy as a whole was limited. The financial cushion bequeathed by the 1978–81 boom was disappearing along with domestic savings, while tax revenues could not grow in a stagnant economy. Import controls and steady oil exports ensured another trade surplus of around $13 billion in 1984, but this was dedicated to interest payments and rebuilding foreign exchange reserves, which exceeded $7 billion by September 1984.

As he entered his third year in office, De la Madrid's economic policies remained hostage to the debt crisis. No thought was given to repaying Mexico's foreign debt—which was in fact expected to rise to about $120 billion by 1991—although the government achieved a major success in rescheduling some $48.5 billion in public-sector debt maturing between 1985 and 1990 for periods of between ten and fourteen years. But continuing annual interest payments of $12–16 billion through the rest of the decade were enough just by themselves to forestall domestic growth. In April 1984, Mexico's loyalty to the IMF had been rewarded with improved terms for a $3.8-billion commercial loan, but these did not compensate for the continuing rise in world interest rates during the year, each percentage point costing the country an additional $700 million. Further, with interest payments far exceeding "new money," Mexico had become an exporter of capital, an impossible status for any developing nation.

De la Madrid was aware that in the eyes of the world Mexico's financial problems were inseparable from the broader Latin American debt crisis, and he therefore worked to prevent defaults elsewhere in the region that might affect Mexico's renegotiating position. In March 1984, for example, he persuaded Venezuela, Colombia and Brazil to join Mexico in an emergency $500-million "bridge loan" to cover Argentina's past-due interest. Similarly, he discouraged the idea that a "debtors' cartel" could provide an answer by declaring a unilateral regional debt moratorium. But De la Madrid nevertheless felt trapped by the interest burden, and insisted more and more loudly that some relief was necessary for Latin America. Mexico was beginning to pay an intolerable price at home for its image of financial responsibility abroad.

Thus, as the short-term crisis appeared to ease, new long-term problems came into sharper focus: the traditional foreign credit solution to many of the economy's structural weaknesses—the chronic depression of the agricultural sector, low industrial productivity, an inability to export nontraditional products, insufficient domestic savings, a new but profound dependence on oil and a vast maze of subsidies—had now become the principal obstacle to dealing with them. An austerity program that attacked the symptoms of crisis could do little to eliminate its root causes. Although De la Madrid declared during his second State of the Union address, on September 1, 1984, that "we will not lower our guard prematurely," there was a growing consensus that the IMF approach had little left to offer.

There was, in the words of López Portillo's former adviser, Carlos Tello, "a crisis of ideas." Leftist economists claimed that De la Madrid was offering the country a choice between "Argentinization or Canadization"—that is, between prolonged stagflation or near-total foreign control of local industry. Others warned that a successful monetarist policy required political authoritarianism and that economic repression would be followed by a political crackdown. Many analysts also worried about Mexico's vulnerability to external forces and argued that slower growth was preferable to increased foreign investment and indebtedness, while others insisted that only more state control of the economy could prevent recurrence of the 1976 and 1982 crises.

Yet, just as its critics proved more adept at assailing monetarism than at offering a viable alternative, the government was also more effective in blaming the big-spending populism of the 1970s than in designing its own new strategy. Many key questions were left unanswered: Would import substitution remain the main objective of industry? Would food continue to be imported from the United States? Would oil exports be increased to provide additional foreign exchange? Would protectionism be reduced to stimulate competitive exports? Would a genuine effort be made to encourage labor-intensive activities? Would the government live up to its promise to dismantle part of the state's economic apparatus and return non-strategic production to the private sector? The administration did offer for sale industrial shares owned by private banks at the time of the bank nationalization, but it did so in packages of "good" and "bad" companies that discouraged takers. The broadcasting magnate Emilio Azcárraga even gathered together a group of wealthy businessmen who offered to take over other state enterprises, but the government was quickly intimidated by protests from the Left.

Short of carrying out a new economic revolution involving state takeovers and a total reordering of development priorities along socialist lines, a course that De la Madrid showed no interest in pursuing, an export drive offered the only immediate option. But even this was fraught with problems. Apart from oil, traditional commodities and the semi-manufactured products of transnational corporations, Mexico had little to export. Few businessmen displayed the necessary drive to pursue new markets abroad, while the adventurous minority encountered extraordinary obstacles to their efforts: twenty-seven bureaucratic steps were required for exporting. In fact, while captive markets were well protected, the private sector preferred to await the next cyclical boom at home. Only through the shock treatment of joining GATT and liberalizing the economy could the government hope to change these attitudes.

Behind every discussion of economic strategy remained the fear of political unrest. Even De la Madrid felt no need to apologize to monetarist purists when he maintained $1 billion per year in subsidies for corn, beans and cooking oil. But the economy has traditionally sustained political stability with a great deal more than this. It has absorbed enough of the 800,000 new faces on the job market each year to prevent a deterioration of the situation. It has allowed the middle classes, comprising perhaps 20 percent of the population, to expect a steady rise in their living standards. And it has provided the key components of the political system—bureaucracy, private sector and organized labor—with a share of an ever-expanding economic pie. The government therefore faced a disturbing dilemma: it could begin a gradual transformation of the economy and accept the risks of slow growth; or it could stimulate an artificial burst of growth, consumer spending and profit-making and assume the greater risks of a new financial crisis. In either case, the economic pillar of political stability could no longer be taken for granted.

8

"The Oil Is Ours!"

I

Mexico's highly emotional relationship with oil can only be understood if viewed through the prism of its endless struggle for independence. Since the turn of the century, when first discovered, oil has been inseparable from the concept of nation, more vulnerable to political passion than economic logic. Initially, it was a symbol of foreign domination and interference as foreign oil companies, protected by the United States and British governments, were seen to be perniciously draining away Mexico's future. Then, after a long political struggle climaxed in the nationalization of foreign companies in 1938, oil became a symbol of pride, self-respect and independence. Even the idea of exporting oil was instinctively resisted, as if this sovereign resource should benefit only Mexicans.

The discovery of large hydrocarbon reserves in the mid-1970s therefore stirred deep sentiments and ambivalent reactions: many nationalists warned of the dangers of both sudden wealth and overexploitation and called for conservation; other officials saw a development opportunity that a poor country could not responsibly ignore. In the end, oil proved a more dangerous temptress than anyone had imagined, absorbing vast resources as it hypnotized the country with the illusion of greatness, then betraying the dream when falling oil prices tumbled the economy into crisis. The resentment that many Mexicans feel toward Petróleos Mexicanos today is as much a function of their bruised national pride as it is a rational response to the corporation's corruption and mismanagement.

The stage was set for this extended drama in 1884, some seventeen years before the first oil strike in Mexico, when the government of Porfirio Díaz surrendered the state's ownership of the subsoil. Díaz's purpose was to attract investment by foreign mining companies, but the law cleared the way for foreign involvement in oil. Appropriately, it was an American, Edward L. Doheny, who first found oil in Mexico on private land near Tampico in 1901. Five years later, a highly successful British engineer, Weetman D. Pearson, who had built the railroad across the Isthmus of Tehuantepec, struck oil farther south on the Gulf coast. As Doheny's Huasteca Petroleum Company and Pearson's Eagle Petroleum Company expanded production and initiated exports, established oil companies—Gulf, Standard Oil, Texaco, Sinclair and Royal Dutch among them—soon joined the oil rush.

Remarkably, the biggest jump in production took place during and immediately following the Revolution: through accident of geography, the main oil fields in the *Faja de Oro,* or Golden Lane, along the Gulf coast were far from combat areas. In 1910, production was still only 10,000 barrels a day, but it reached 530,000 barrels a day by 1921, equivalent at the time to 25 percent of world output. It was a period of extraordinary profit making for the foreign companies,* with all top management posts occupied by foreigners and only a handful of independent Mexican producers involved in the industry. Mexico was also assuming strategic importance: over 80 percent of its oil was being exported during this period. During World War I, the first major oil-fueled war, Mexican crude accounted for 95 percent of oil imported by the United States, which was in turn the principal supplier of Britain. Almost exclusively, then, Mexican oil served foreign interests.

But by 1915, with the chaos of the Revolution giving way to some order, attention began turning toward the oil industry and the foreign enclaves it had spawned. Appointment by Carranza of a Petroleum Technical Commission led to new decrees raising export taxes and revising the rules for concessions and production. Soon afterward, Article 27 of the 1917 Constitution reasserted the state's ownership of the subsoil. This was in turn viewed as a hostile act by the oil companies, which mobilized their governments to protest against retroactive application of the law. Some American oilmen even provided Manuel Peláez, a powerful Veracruz *cacique* who controlled the oil region, with the money, weapons and munitions he needed to oppose Carranza. In public, they argued that they risked sabotage of their wells if they rebuffed Peláez, but in private they welcomed the opportunity to weaken an increasingly threatening central government.

*Pearson subsequently founded a financial and publishing empire in Britain, and after he was given the title of Lord Cowdray in 1911, he became known to his colleagues as "the member for Mexico." He sold Eagle Petroleum to Royal Dutch Shell in 1923 and thus escaped nationalization.

Over the next two decades, the quarrel between successive governments and the foreign oil companies became a permanent feature of public life in Mexico, and because the United States adopted the cause of the companies, the dispute increasingly took on the appearance of a clash of sovereignties. After Carranza was assassinated and succeeded by Obregón in 1920, Washington withheld recognition of the new government until the oil situation was settled. Finally relations were restored under the 1923 Bucareli Agreements, which converted the property rights of the oil companies into almost indefinite concessions, while a new production tax was levied, purportedly to finance war reparations. This was then reversed by a new law in 1925, implementing Article 27 of the Constitution, which noted that the nation's ownership of the subsoil was "inalienable" and limited concessions to fifty years. But there were so many protests, including calls for U.S. military intervention, that a 1928 decree revised the law once again, permitting open-ended concessions.

As the 1920s advanced, however, Mexico's bargaining position gradually weakened. Once World War I ended, there was a world oil glut that was later aggravated by the depression. With the cost of production suddenly decisive, many overexploited Mexican wells were no longer commercially viable. Further, the agitated political debate in Mexico persuaded many companies to start investing in the less troublesome environments of Venezuela and the Middle East. Production dropped precipitously to just 108,000 barrels a day by 1930. Yet the end of the country's first oil boom only intensified political pressure on the government to "do something" about the oil companies.

In 1931, the government decreed a new Labor Code, requiring that 90 percent of all company employees be Mexican nationals, that Mexicans be trained to replace foreign technicians and that trade unions be allowed to inspect the accounts of any commercial enterprise. Then, in the wave of union activism that followed Cárdenas' takeover in 1934, the oil workers were particularly prominent, not only because they were among the oldest, best-paid and largest organized groups in the country, but also because a nationalist government would be naturally inclined to support them against such a visible foreign presence. In December 1935, Cárdenas himself encouraged formation of the Mexican Oil Workers' Union (STPRM), pulling together two dozen independent unions under a single —and, at the time, radical—leadership. Through 1936 and early 1937, the new union tried to negotiate its first collective contract with the oil companies.

Finally, in May 1937, the STPRM struck over the new contract and specifically over the companies' refusal to allow the union to inspect their books. To the dismay of the companies, the government recognized the strike as a "conflict of economic order" and, for the first time, referred it to compulsory arbitration. In December, the Arbitration Board reported that the companies were earning higher profits and paying lower salaries in Mexico than anywhere else in the world—the government later calculated that they earned ten times more than they invested between 1901 and 1938—and ordered a 27 percent wage increase plus such additional benefits as a pension plan, medical care, sick leaves and vacation pay. When the companies appealed to the Mexican Supreme Court, the ruling was confirmed on March 1, 1938.

Cárdenas still had no intention of exercising his constitutional right to withdraw the concessions. Anxious to compromise, he called the foreign oil executives to the National Palace and reassured them that the cost of the wage hikes would not exceed $7.2 million, approximately half the companies' estimated profits. The executives claimed that the settlement would cost much more and that their profits were much less than was assumed, but Cárdenas reportedly told them: "You are unduly disturbed, gentlemen. The sum won't be more than $7.2 million because my experts say so. I guarantee that you won't have any problems." Whereupon one company representative is recorded as replying: "Mr. President, those are your words. Who guarantees for you?" The implication that Cárdenas' word was insufficient served to seal the companies' fate. On March 18, Cárdenas broadcast to the nation that the seventeen American and British oil companies were to be expropriated for their "arrogant and rebellious attitude." Stunned and disbelieving, the companies quickly agreed to the wage increase, but the nationalization decree was already law.

The measure was received with an immediate explosion of emotional support. Cárdenas was hailed by workers, peasants and students as the architect of Mexico's economic independence, while even wealthy women were seen donating jewelry to the National Solidarity Fund that would be used to compensate the expropriated companies. A severe economic slump also followed, forcing the devaluation of the Mexican peso and prompting rumors that the companies were plotting military uprisings against the regime. But for both ordinary oil workers and revolutionary politicians, who had long felt humiliated by the power of the oil companies, it was a moment of vindication. (Years earlier, Cárdenas had been stationed in Tampico and had personally experienced the "gringo" oilmen's disdain for Mexicans.) In an October 1938 article entitled "Mexico in Revolution," *Fortune* magazine noted: "General

Cárdenas is undisputably the most popular President that Mexico has ever had."

The reaction abroad further stirred domestic nationalism. President Roosevelt, who was himself wrestling with the American oil companies, was reportedly pleased to see them weakened by the Mexican nationalization. But Cárdenas was denounced as a Communist by numerous U.S. congressmen and newspapers, while the oil companies organized a punitive boycott of Mexican oil products which eventually forced the export of crude to the Axis Powers. British oil companies suffered most, since they lost the new Poza Rica fields discovered by Royal Dutch Shell in 1930, whereas the Golden Lane under mainly American control was by then seriously depleted. Britain sent several sharp diplomatic protest notes which Cárdenas regarded as insulting and which prompted a severing of diplomatic relations with London. Once World War II broke out, Mexico's relations with Britain were restored, ties with the United States patched up and compensation for the expropriation worked out and duly paid. By then Cárdenas was enshrined as a nationalist hero comparable only to Cuauhtémoc and Juárez: oil had graduated from resource to symbol.

II

Mexico was not entirely unprepared to take over the companies. As early as 1925, the government had established an Office of National Petroleum Management, which controlled domestic oil prices and operated a small number of wells. In 1935, Mexican Petroleum, or Petromex, took over these functions and began training Mexican technicians. The following year, the General Administration of National Petroleum was created by Cárdenas. When Petróleos Mexicanos, or Pemex, was founded on June 7, 1938, however, it inherited an array of different companies that could not be easily integrated. Much of the expropriated machinery was also outdated, evidence of the companies' preference for investing in Venezuela. But a corps of Mexican engineers and a few independent American contractors were able to keep the fields in operation, and although production immediately fell off, it recovered within a year. Average output of 126,250 barrels a day in 1937 dropped to 106,350 in 1938, but bounced back to 118,600 in 1939.

Born of a political decision, however, Pemex was soon caught in a dilemma that plagues the corporation to this day: should the oil industry be run as a public utility or as a profitable concern, as a sociopolitical instrument of the state or as a private company that happens to be government-owned? As the catalyst for the expropriation, the Oil Workers' Union seemed to take literally the nationalist cry of *"El petróleo es nuestro!"*—"The oil is ours!"—and successfully demanded a role in the management of Pemex. The resulting anarchy soon persuaded the government of its mistake. In 1942, after lengthy negotiations during which oil workers were granted wage increases, social benefits and numerous other privileges, the union finally recognized the absolute authority of Pemex's board of directors. Efficiency and profit motivation became the corporation's new mottoes, and over the next decade output doubled. Under President Alemán, the union was further tamed when the Army was used to break a strike, some foreign contractors were allowed back and there were even occasional rumors of a possible reversal of the nationalization.

In the 1950s, however, the criteria changed yet again. The government's direct control over Pemex grew, thus increasing its vulnerability to political interference and corruption. But despite a wave of inflation followed by a 60 percent devaluation of the peso in 1954, the government refused to approve an oil price hike, arguing, in the words of President Ruiz Cortines, that "the role of Pemex was not one of profit but of social service." The logic rang true: since the foreign companies had been concerned only with profits and exports, oil should now be consumed internally for the profit of the nation. In practice, through the "social service" of subsidized energy, cheap fuel played a crucial role in building Mexico's emerging industrial sector.

The cost of this policy to Pemex was high. Unable to generate sufficient income to pay its taxes, to finance expansion or, eventually, even to maintain day-to-day operations, Pemex could not grow. Domestic oil prices were raised in 1959 for the first time since 1946, with the director general of Pemex, Antonio Bermúdez, arguing that the corporation "ought to increase its capital and profits." But the benefits were quickly consumed by inflation and the decapitalization of the corporation continued: in many years, it paid no taxes to the federal government and was already in debt abroad. Ambitious plans were drawn up for the construction of new refineries and petrochemical plants, but exploration and exploitation of oil began to lag and proven reserves to stagnate. The essential equilibrium between reserves, production and demand was lost.

Meanwhile, Pemex was expected to employ friends and relatives of politicians, and with all efforts to run it along strict entrepreneurial lines abandoned, contracts were handed out on the basis of influence rather than price or quality. Lucrative gasoline station concessions were granted as political favors or rewards, while Pemex contracted private truckers, themselves invariably politicians, to deliver fuel around the country. The Oil Workers' Union, as corrupt and nepotistic as the rest of the corporation, had by the mid-1950s made peace with management, but the price of this arrangement was high. Not only was Pemex obliged to finance the corruption of labor leaders and the welfare structure of oil workers, but featherbedding was rife at all levels, earning the corporation the reputation of being the most inefficient of major world oil companies. Only in 1972 did Mexico finally surpass its 1921 production level, but by then domestic demand was so high that the country was importing 100,000 barrels a day from Venezuela, where output per worker was four times higher.

When the Organization of Petroleum Exporting Countries suddenly raised world oil prices in late 1973, however, Mexico's new dependence on imported oil became a political issue. The government therefore decreed the first domestic price increase in fourteen years, at last providing Pemex with more funds for exploration. Mexico, though, was not ready for what would follow. In May 1972, Pemex had quietly disclosed the discovery of oil at a marshy site called Reforma near the southeastern city of Villahermosa, but the announcement received little publicity. Following the Middle East oil embargo during the winter of 1973, the United States government as well as major oil companies began looking for both new non-Arab sources of oil and ways of weakening OPEC. In October 1974, a memorandum, written on an ordinary sheet of paper without any company letterhead and circulated among officials, congressmen and journalists in Washington, estimated that Mexico had found at least 20 billion barrels of new oil reserves, twice that of Alaska's North Slope and "comparable to the Persian Gulf." Soon afterward, without any attribution, the story surfaced in the American press. Later the report was traced to an American geophysical survey company that had been contracted by Pemex and had apparently shared its findings with American officials.

The Mexican government immediately responded with nationalistic instincts. The fact that an American company appeared better informed than the Mexican authorities raised suspicions of industrial espionage. Moreover, coming just days before President Echeverría was to meet President Ford at the border, the "leak" suggested an American maneuver to use Mexico against OPEC, which seemed all the more offensive given Mexico's new alliance with Third World causes. As a result, rather than celebrating the country's unexpected new wealth, Echeverría felt obliged to deny the story. When he met Ford, he referred only informally to the topic, noting vaguely that any new deposits had not been quantified and avoiding any mention of oil in their joint communiqué. In fact, rather than bolstering Mexico's independence, history warned Echeverría that the new oil finds could simply make the nation more vulnerable to American pressure.

Over the next two years, Echeverría's posture became more puzzling. Continuing oil strikes and rising production in the Villahermosa region confirmed the mounting speculation about Mexico's bonanza. Imports of oil had ended in 1973 and exports were now growing steadily. The government was channeling 17 percent of public investment into the industry. Foreign equipment suppliers were crowding the Pemex offices in Mexico City, while new hotels were being rapidly built in Villahermosa to house the influx of Mexican and foreign oilmen. Further, by 1975, the Mexican economy was moving into crisis, with business insecurity feeding a growing flight of capital. Official recognition of the new oil reserves might even have changed the economic climate and released fresh foreign credit. But Echeverría and his Pemex chief, Antonio Dovalí Jaime, stubbornly ignored the situation. Oil, it seemed, was too sensitive a political issue to be used for short-term economic gain. It was a maxim, however, that Echeverría's successor would take years to learn.

III

Jorge Díaz Serrano, a wealthy private oil contractor with investments in both Mexico and the United States, had received secret technical reports from friends inside Pemex that convinced him that Mexico had indeed struck oil in abundance. When in late 1975 he joined the presidential electoral campaign of his longtime friend José López Portillo, Díaz Serrano began arguing his case with Pemex's top managers. "It was really easier to show we had a lot of oil," he later recalled, "but they insisted we didn't." About to inherit a severe financial crisis, López Portillo was happy to be convinced. Upon taking office he named Díaz Serrano as director general of Pemex. It would prove to be the most important appointment of his administration.

A man with no previous political experience, Díaz Serrano brought instead the entrepreneurial talents and engineering expertise that had turned his drilling, dredging and transport companies into highly profitable concerns. For the first time in twenty-five years, he introduced private-sector management techniques to Pemex. "We had a bureaucracy in which everything was done in writing, memoranda galore, with copies to all departments and communications very slow," he recounted soon after taking up his post. "So instead of sending memos, I'd sit down with everyone, explain what I wanted and demand an immediate reply. We cut through all the bureaucracy." Aware of Pemex's exorbitantly high production costs, he also held down new employment as output began to expand, and between 1976 and 1980 production per worker grew from 14.9 to 26.1 barrels a day. For a time, at least, business rather than political criteria had returned.

Díaz Serrano's first move in Pemex was dramatic: he abruptly announced that Mexico's proven hydrocarbon reserves—roughly two-thirds crude oil and one-third natural gas—had increased from 6.3 billion to 11.1 billion barrels. Yet despite the bonanza visible around Villahermosa, the announcement was received with skepticism; foreign bankers suspected a ploy to raise new credits at a time of economic difficulties. To gain credibility, Díaz Serrano hired the American oil actuaries DeGolyer and MacNaughton to verify the reserves. By the time they endorsed an estimate of 11 billion barrels, Pemex had raised its figure to 14.7 billion barrels and was encouraging semi-official reports of up to 60 billion barrels. Díaz Serrano took it upon himself to travel the world spreading the news of Mexico's finds, while at home Pemex embarked on a $15.5 billion investment program with the target of raising production from 800,000 barrels a day in 1976 to 2.25 million by the end of López Portillo's six-year term in 1982.

Gambling that oil could revive the prostrate economy, López Portillo channeled 28 percent of total public investment into Pemex between 1978 and 1980. Drilling along the Tabasco-Chiapas border south of Villahermosa revealed that some wells miles apart belonged to the same geophysical structure, while entirely new deposits were discovered in other areas. To the north in Veracruz state, a vast field of heavy oil was found in the Chicontepec region, which added 17 billion to total reserves. Close to the U.S. border in the so-called Sabinas basin of Coahuila state, dry gas was also struck, although no immediate move was made to develop these deposits since natural gas was still being flared on the oil fields. With Pemex claiming that it had only explored 10 percent of the national territory with hydrocarbon potential, it also began prospecting offshore from Nayarit state and found a dry gas field off Baja California.

The most dramatic discoveries occurred almost accidentally offshore in Campeche Sound, just fifty miles north of the fishing port of Ciudad del Carmen, after a local fisherman drew Pemex's attention to oil leaking into the sea. Finally, in May 1977, the Akal I well, the first exploratory drilling in the area, revealed deposits several times larger than onshore in the Tabasco-Chiapas area. Construction of a pipeline to Tres Bocas delayed commercial production, but oil began to flow in June 1979, and within two years offshore production rose to 1.5 million barrels a day, with wells averaging a stunning 30,000 barrels. Offshore reserves were subsequently estimated at 34.4 billion barrels, but many experts believed the deposits extended far beyond the 800-square-mile zone chosen for initial exploration and might stretch west toward Tabasco-Chiapas and east around the Yucatán Peninsula.

The mood of euphoria in the country was fed by the 1979 oil price hike, which doubled Pemex's export earnings and stimulated further exploration. By March 1981, proven hydrocarbon reserves had jumped to 72 billion barrels, comprising 57 billion barrels of crude oil and the oil equivalent of 75 trillion cubic feet of natural gas. Subsequently, probable reserves were raised from 58 billion to 90 billion barrels and, with proven deposits, were included in an estimated 250 billion barrels of potential reserves. Mexico was said to possess the fifth-largest oil and seventh-largest gas reserves in the world. The production target of 2.25 million barrels a day was reached two years earlier than expected and the ceiling raised to 2.75 million, while exports had increased from 200,000 to 1.5 million barrels a day by 1982. Winning less attention but equally important, natural gas production rose sharply, satisfying 23 percent of the nation's energy demand by 1982.

Spending by Pemex—on exploration and production equipment, oil tankers and tugs, port facilities, new refineries, primary petrochemical complexes and the new 52-floor headquarters in Mexico City—was running far ahead of schedule, but money was no problem. Foreign bankers would literally line up outside Díaz Serrano's office for an opportunity to lend money. Some was spent on subsidizing the domestic price of gasoline, at the time less than half the price charged in the United States. Foreign oil companies competed to sign up the country's future production, while many Western governments, among them Sweden, Canada and France, desirous of a non-Middle Eastern supplier, were persuaded to make major investments in Mexico in exchange for contracts with Pemex.

No less important, oil gave Mexico a new pride and confidence in its dealings with the world. López Portillo ignored invitations to join OPEC, arguing publicly that, as the owner of its oil, Mexico had no place in a cartel that was created to protect oil-exporting nations against the transnational giants. Eager to raise a responsible voice in a chaotic market, however, he presented an idealistic World Energy Plan to the UN General Assembly in 1979, and the following year Mexico joined Venezuela in a scheme to provide cheap oil to the tiny economies of the Caribbean region, a strategy that would cost each around $180 million per year. Moreover, it took pride in helping Cuba, Nicaragua and Costa Rica look for their own deposits. Oil also reinforced Mexico's ambivalent feelings about the United States: it gave the country the self-assurance to stand up to the Carter administration on a number of issues, but excessive dependence on the U.S. market and the United States' increased reliance on Mexican oil created a new feeling of vulnerability. In 1980, López Portillo ordered that no more than 50 percent of Mexico's crude exports should go to any single client.

The oil boom was not without problems. In 1977, after construction of an 800-mile pipeline to export natural gas to the United States had begun, a deal worked out with American gas importers was suddenly blocked by the Carter administration in a bitter dispute over pricing. Mexico was not harmed since it used the gas domestically and avoided the problems provoked by gas deregulation in the United States several years later, but at the time it stirred a wave of nationalism and served as a reminder of the pressures that energy wealth attracted. In June 1979, a new well being drilled in Campeche Sound, Ixtoc I, went out of control, spilling 30,000 barrels a day of crude into the sea. When some oil floated across the Gulf onto Texas beaches, a diplomatic row over compensation ensued with Washington. Even with expensive foreign equipment and advice, Pemex spent $50 million over nine months before the blowout was capped.

More serious was the impact of Pemex's activities on the rural environment surrounding Villahermosa. Mexican industry in general—and Pemex in particular—had traditionally showed little concern for pollution, but exploration and exploitation in the swampy Tabasco-Chiapas area soon brought protests from local peasants. Water holes were poisoned by oil leaks, while sulphur emissions into the atmosphere damaged crops. After farmers began blocking roads to oil wells, the governor of Tabasco took up their case and pressured Pemex to pay compensation and improve its pollution controls. But the problem persisted, with Campeche fishermen joining a chorus of complaints that extended beyond pollution to include the high inflation, uncontrolled urban migration and disruption of provincial life brought by Pemex. After a new wave of protests in 1983, Pemex paid out more compensation in Tabasco and launched a nationwide advertising campaign to demonstrate its concern for nature, yet in many areas it had already caused irreversible damage.

The rush to raise production at any cost also caused disarray within the corporation itself. Some of Pemex's headaches came simply from trying to manage the simultaneous expansion of exploration, exploitation, refining and petrochemical facilities. With much of the new equipment coming from abroad, there were delivery delays and bottlenecks, while expensive rented tugs and storage vessels were at times left idle for weeks. The need to complete construction jobs as rapidly as possible meant that quality and costs were often inadequately monitored. Official accounting procedures were seemingly ignored in the name of speedy execution of priority projects. A study by the Ministry of Budget and Planning estimated that 85 percent of contracts awarded by Pemex in 1979 and 1980 were not subject to proper competition.

Encouraged by the absence of central government controls, this bureaucratic chaos in turn fed massive corruption at all levels of the monopoly, with many top officials in the oil industry widely known to be willing to exchange contracts for commissions. A selective auditing by the Finance Ministry of just 1.3 percent of Pemex's 1980 accounts revealed $130 million in "unexplained irregularities" ranging from payments without receipts to unrecorded exports. Some of this was attributed to mismanagement, yet during the López Portillo administration the cost of Pemex's corruption to the country probably ran into billions of dollars. The purchase of equipment routinely brought kickbacks of between 10 and 15 percent, while a share of export revenues was rumored to have been siphoned off and kept in foreign bank accounts. Millions of barrels of oil were sold on spot markets in Europe without being registered as exports by Pemex. Further, because of a legal prohibition on direct foreign involvement in the oil industry, foreign oil rigs were contracted through Mexican intermediaries, many of them companies—like the Permargo Company, which Díaz Serrano had founded years earlier—owned by politicians.

But while the scandalous level of corruption within Pemex gradually became known, it seemed a small price to pay for the corporation's dramatic success in raising reserves, production and exports. Díaz Serrano himself weathered several storms of criticism. The fact that he came from the private sector and had once been a business partner of U.S. Vice-President George Bush had made leftists suspect his nationalist credentials, but Díaz Serrano spent heavily in the media to counter this image. As a professional oilman, he was also faulted by conservation-minded nationalists for wanting to produce and export as much oil as possible. But López Portillo stood behind his friend. The President appeased conservationists by placing a 2.25-million-barrel-a-day "ceiling" on production, but this was raised to 2.75 million when the target was reached, and by late 1982 output occasionally exceeded 3 million. The reality was that Pemex was producing and exporting as much as it could.

An even more controversial circumstance was that the oil boom gave Díaz Serrano political power that won him enemies within the government. José Andrés de Oteyza, who as Industrial Development Minister was ex officio chairman of Pemex, particularly resented that Díaz Serrano dealt directly with the President on oil matters. Other key figures, including Finance Minister David Ibarra and Budget and Planning Minister Miguel de la Madrid, also complained that Pemex had become a mismanaged and corrupt state within a state. More than that, although a latecomer to politics, Díaz Serrano used the power and wealth of Pemex to promote himself as a successor to López Portillo. Abroad, many large oil companies and several governments courted him as if his designation were assured. After López Portillo himself appeared to be encouraging Díaz Serrano, choosing him to speak on behalf of the entire government on an important political occasion in February 1981, the other pre-candidates joined forces against him: it seemed inconceivable that, because of the accident of oil, a politically inexperienced friend of the incumbent should attain the presidency.

In the spring of 1981, the world recession resulted in the first oil glut in almost a decade. OPEC oil ministers met in Geneva in May but were unable to agree on either a price reduction or a production cutback. The initiative had nevertheless passed from sellers to buyers, and on June 1 Díaz Serrano recommended to López Portillo that Pemex lower its export price to retain its commercial clients in the United States. His logic was sound: other oil exporters were already selling at a discount and Mexico had to adjust to market forces. The following day, Pemex's clients were informed by telex that the price of light Istmo crude would drop from $38.50 to $34.50 per barrel and heavier Maya oil from $32 to $28 per barrel. In the same week, several OPEC members followed suit.

Despite the economic wisdom of the move, Díaz Serrano committed several crucial political mistakes. He neither consulted the economic ministers who had been gunning for him nor warned the President of the likely repercussions of a price drop. As the first nation to announce a lower price publicly, Mexico appeared to be violating Third World solidarity and undermining OPEC. The fact that word of the move first came from New York seemed to imply that Díaz Serrano had succumbed to American pressure. Living a dream of imminent prosperity, the Mexican people were ill prepared for this dose of realism. Díaz Serrano's enemies saw their chance: they orchestrated a media campaign portraying the price drop as a betrayal of Mexican nationalism and forced the President to fire his Pemex chief.

In the month that followed, all of Mexico's irrational passions about oil seemed to surface. Julio R. Moctezuma Cid, a former Finance Minister, succeeded Díaz Serrano, but Oteyza was able at last to assert his authority over Pemex. To the delight of nationalists and the dismay of realists, he announced that Mexico's oil prices would be raised $2 per barrel for July. It was presented to the public as a victory over the world: in the name of pride, Mexico would go against the market trend. Almost immediately, Pemex began receiving telex messages canceling commercial contracts. When France's Compagnie Française des Pétroles suspended 100,000-barrel-a-day imports, Oteyza threatened to cancel contracts with French companies for subway construction in Mexico. Mexican officials then tried to rescue existing government-to-government contracts. But exports fell from 1 million to 460,000 barrels a day during June, and though the figure was disguised by announcing CIF rather than traditional FOB prices, Mexico's export price rose only 10 cents per barrel in July. In one month, misplaced patriotism had cost Mexico $1 billion.

But the government still could not accept the idea that the bubble of hope inflated by steadily rising oil prices could suddenly burst. Pemex therefore continued to increase production and in August 1981 signed a long-term agreement to supply the U.S. Strategic Reserve. But to cover a $6 billion shortfall in anticipated oil and other revenues without reducing economic growth, the government borrowed heavily abroad in the second half of 1981—much of this was done in Pemex's name, raising the corporation's own foreign debt to some $22 billion by the end of 1982—and prepared the ingredients for the financial collapse that followed. Oil production and exports reached 3 million and 1.6 million barrels a day, respectively, by the time López Portillo left office in December 1982, but Pemex was by then a tamed giant.

Barely four months earlier, during an intense weekend of negotiations in Washington at the height of the financial crisis, Pemex had accepted an offer of $1 billion in advance payment for additional Mexican oil sales to the U.S. Strategic Reserve. Oteyza, the fiery nationalist of mid-1981, had approved terms—a price varying between $25 and $30 per barrel, but at a stunning 20 percent interest rate—that were so humiliating the government banned any mention of them in local newspapers. Word of the deal nevertheless spread in oil circles and deepened OPEC's distrust of Mexico. "We are sitting on a sea of oil," Díaz Serrano had boasted in 1977, yet the economy had managed to sink in it. Having been led by oil into its worst crisis in memory, Mexico now had no choice but to depend on oil for its continued economic survival.

IV

The real sheikhs of Mexican oil are the Pemex union leaders. Staying at their posts for years on end as Mexican Presidents and Pemex directors general come and go, these quintessential *caciques* have accumulated great power and wealth, controlling all but a handful of Pemex's employees, resorting to threats and violence to crush internal opposition movements and "buying" politicians who stand in their way. Rather than risk labor unrest and possible sabotage of oil installations by confronting them, however, successive governments have preferred to appease the bosses in exchange for their support for the system and their control over oil workers. As a result, if Pemex has become a state within a state, the union now operates as a company within a company. In the process it has become the strongest union in Mexico and the richest union in Latin America.

The power of the newly formed Oil Workers' Union was already apparent in the months leading up to the nationalization of 1938. Although the government quickly eliminated the union's direct role in management and established that a leftist leadership would not be permitted, the STPRM was allowed to grow into a privileged elite within the official labor movement. As early as 1946, the union was granted 2 percent of the value of all contracts between Pemex and private companies. Pemex also recognized that it was a closed shop and not only agreed to withhold 2.5 percent of wages as union dues but also surrendered the right to select all except senior personnel. Later, as the STPRM and its leaders became entrepreneurs in their own right, the monopoly gave the union the power to carry out or assign a share of all Pemex contracts; this share gradually increased over the years and today amounts to more than 40 percent of drilling contracts and 50 percent of other contracts. Not surprisingly, many of the companies awarded these contracts are owned by the union leaders themselves.

As a veritable treasure of medical, educational and housing benefits as well as lucrative business opportunities flowed from Pemex, competition to control this arena intensified. The STPRM has twenty-nine locals, each able to hand out jobs and receive a share of Pemex's expenditures in its jurisdiction and each dominated by a local *cacique*. Depending on the size of the locals, they are variously represented on the National Executive Committee. But the key post of secretary-general has traditionally rotated only among the nominees of Local 1, headquartered in Ciudad

Madero near Tampico, Local 30 in Poza Rica near Veracruz, and Local 10 in Minatitlán in southern Veracruz state. One or another local has invariably sought to dominate the entire union, but at no time has power been so centralized as it is today.

Since the early 1960s, the story of the STPRM has revolved around one *cacique,* Joaquín Hernández Galicia, a slightly built man in his early sixties who is known everywhere as La Quina. Born into an oil family in the Gulf coast town of Ciudad Madero in 1922 and trained as a welder, he fought his way up union ranks until his political ties to President López Mateos helped win him the job of secretary-general of Local 1 in 1959. At the time, the government was trying to break the power of Jaime J. Merino, who, while serving for sixteen years as Pemex's Area Superintendent in Poza Rica, had managed to control Local 30 and install a loyal aide, Pedro Vivanco García, as national secretary-general. López Mateos therefore abruptly dispatched Merino to Pemex's office in Los Angeles, and in 1962, with the aim of eliminating the autonomous power of the union, he approved La Quina's election as the new national secretary-general for a three-year term.

The battle to control the STPRM continued through the 1960s. In 1965, La Quina was succeeded by Rafael Cárdenas Lomeli of Local 10, and Cárdenas in 1968 by Samuel Terrazas Zozaya of Local 30; both men were encouraged by the then head of Pemex, Jesús Reyes Heroles, to resist La Quina's empire-building. La Quina nevertheless maintained close ties with Díaz Ordaz's Interior Minister, Echeverría, and after the latter became President in 1970, the union boss recovered his power, nominating Salvador Barragán Camacho to be the union's new secretary-general on behalf of Local 1.

The rotation of the post led Sergio Martínez Mendoza from Local 10 to take over in 1974. But when his successor, Heriberto Kehoe Vincent of Local 30, began building his own power base, purportedly encouraged by the new López Portillo government, he was murdered in Poza Rica in February 1977 and replaced by La Quina's nominee, Oscar Torres Pancardo. In 1980 Barragán Camacho once again took over, this time for an unprecedented five-year term. La Quina held the post of Director of Social and Revolutionary Works within the union, but by then his nationwide power was undisputed.

Open opposition to La Quina and his clique is considered unwise. Two small dissident groups do exist—the Lázaro Cárdenas Movement and the National Petroleum Movement—but they are kept alive largely by the media, and their occasional efforts to organize oil workers are disrupted by the STPRM's paramilitary thugs. Since any threat to La

Quina's position would more likely come from within the system, he spends much time and money servicing his political contacts elsewhere in the country. In 1981, he provided most of the financing for a new headquarters building for the Confederation of Mexican Workers (CTM). Following the first devaluation of the Mexican currency in February 1982, he ordered the union to donate 30 million pesos—worth $650,000 at the time—to the government to help repay the $80 billion foreign debt. Governors and politicians from oil states also soon become indebted politically to La Quina and shy away from any effort to destabilize him. More recently, dreaming of succeeding Fidel Velázquez as the country's top union leader, La Quina has tried to improve his image by financing several left-leaning unions.

La Quina is a true godfather, rewarding those supporters who display blind loyalty to him and in this way building up a massive network of personal relationships and commitments. In a country where almost all power is centered in Mexico City, it is all the more remarkable that La Quina rules the union from Ciudad Madero, capital of a traditional oil region that has lost importance today. Occasionally, he travels to Mexico City for the day to meet the President or the head of Pemex or to attend a major political ceremony, but most of the time he holds court at his home, where several dozen petitioners are invariably waiting to see him. Many are ordinary oil workers or their families hoping for a chance to ask a favor, but oil contractors, real estate developers, politicians, foreign ambassadors and even foreign political activists are no less likely to be in his waiting room. La Quina's personal austerity—he does not smoke or drink, is a vegetarian and has been "faithful" to one mistress for many years—also contributes to his mystique, while his command of details and his memory for names and faces give him an important edge over all his aides.

Money is nevertheless at the heart of his power. The leaders of all the union locals are allowed to enrich themselves by "selling" jobs in Pemex and by winning or auctioning off construction contracts in their areas. Kept informed by his own secret agents, La Quina establishes clearly that all rackets take place with his permission. The union itself is immensely wealthy as an institution, owning oil-drilling companies, two oil tankers, a chain of supermarkets, a small fleet of aircraft, thousands of acres of farming land, urban real estate in many oil towns and the Alameda Hotel in Mexico City. In 1983, La Quina estimated the STPRM's assets at 10 billion pesos, or $670 million at the prevailing exchange rate, although no independent auditing of the union's accounts has ever taken place. Apart from the profits obtained by controlling 40 percent of all contracts, just the 2 percent commission paid to the union for Pemex's investments between 1977 and 1981 would total over $450 million.

During the oil boom, the union's economic and political power grew dramatically. The number of permanent employees in Pemex increased more slowly than production, reaching some 80,000 by 1982, but between 60,000 and 90,000 temporary workers engaged in construction, contract drilling and other projects were also subject to union controls. Typically, foreign oil rigs were permitted to operate only if an entire Mexican crew was paid for doing nothing. The high wages being paid by Pemex meant that jobs could be sold for as much as $4,000 each, while even temporary workers were required to rent their jobs for fees ranging from $15 per month for an office cleaner to $100 per month for a skilled welder.

López Portillo and Díaz Serrano soon went out of their way to embrace La Quina and his secretary-general, Barragán Camacho, giving them expensive presents on their birthdays and surrealistically praising their patriotism. "If any group of workers in recent times has shown efficiency," López Portillo told them in July 1981, "it has been you, the workers of Pemex. You are the cornerstone of the country's development and I am deeply grateful to you." No less grateful, the union in turn promoted Díaz Serrano's dream of becoming President. But even after Díaz Serrano was replaced by Moctezuma Cid, La Quina's influence within Pemex was undiminished. One visitor to Ciudad Madero recounted hearing La Quina order Barragán Camacho to inform Moctezuma Cid that a particular businessman should be awarded a contract to supply a California refinery. Moctezuma himself refused in interviews even to discuss the corruption of the STPRM. To run Pemex successfully, the new director general soon concluded, meant accepting the power of the union.

As the López Portillo administration drew to a close, however, complaints about the union began to be voiced publicly. La Quina himself appeared to use money principally to sustain his political power, but the ostentatious and extravagant ways of Barragán Camacho and other union leaders won the attention of the country's newspapers. Barragán Camacho, a heavily built, bombastic man given to wearing jewelry and surrounding himself with armed guards, had become a familiar figure in the casinos of Las Vegas and Atlantic City, on one occasion boasting of having lost $300,000. Other regional leaders were no more modest, using union funds to pay for lavish parties, with food, entertainment and guests often brought from Mexico City. One Coatzacoalcos boss even flew in hundreds of tuxedos so that guests at his daughter's fifteenth birthday party would be well dressed. Bombarded with such stories during his electoral campaign, De la Madrid pledged in private to move against STPRM corruption. But, like his predecessors, he too would conclude that it was a small price to pay for more than four decades of labor tranquillity in the oil fields. As a pillar of the system, the STPRM had also to be supported by the system.

V

When President de la Madrid took office in December 1982, he inherited an oil industry that, in the irritated eyes of public opinion, had contributed to the country's financial collapse. Pemex and its union therefore seemed the obvious place for De la Madrid to initiate his much-vaunted "moral renovation" of society. At the same time, Mexico's economy depended more than ever on oil, which accounted for almost 75 percent of Mexico's exports and would provide $16 billion in foreign exchange in 1983, enough to cover the country's immediate debt obligations. Not for the first time, then, an incoming President faced a dilemma when dealing with oil: he had to balance the risks of appearing to condone disagreeable practices against the perhaps greater risks of changing a deeply rooted modus operandi.

Mario Ramón Beteta, a former Finance Minister with a reputation for personal honesty, was named director general of Pemex with instructions to "moralize" the corporation. He started by proclaiming, in an apparent reference to Díaz Serrano, that "while I am director of Pemex, no private business will be done in the office of the director general." He warned that the years of "easy spending and abundance" were over, that a "new Pemex" would be built through "very efficient and scrupulous management." To prevent Pemex from re-emerging as a semi-autonomous center of political power, a new Ministry of Energy, Mines and State Industry was charged with defining oil policy. And to put an end to private racketeering within the monopoly, tight new controls were imposed on all spending, which, in any event, was far lower in 1983 and 1984 than in the recent past.

Having dismissed or retired Pemex's top management, the new government also embarked on the enormously difficult task of going through the books of the López Portillo years. (A fire in Pemex headquarters in September 1982 destroyed many files and raised suspicions of arson.) Soon embezzlement charges were brought against former Pemex officials, climaxing with the arrest and indictment of Díaz Serrano himself in June 1983, accused of a $34 million fraud in the purchase of two oil tankers for Pemex. Having set this powerful precedent, however, the government opted not to publicize the full story of Pemex for fear of damaging the political system as a whole. Many of the strong rumors of the past, including the alleged involvement of members of the López Portillo family in unregistered spot-market sales of oil in Rotterdam, were left unconfirmed and undenied. But enough had seemingly been done to prevent the new generation of Pemex officials from following the same path of corruption. Some foreign contractors even confirmed that kickbacks were no longer being demanded by Pemex officials.

The problem of the STPRM involved more hazards. The union leadership was disturbed by official rhetoric and the orchestrated press attacks, prompting a sharp response from La Quina. "President de la Madrid will have to become a friend of the oil workers whether he likes it or not," he said in February 1982. "What does it matter if our friends the Presidents start in opposition to us and finish up being our friends?" He then praised the oil policy of López Portillo and Díaz Serrano at a time when both men were immensely unpopular and, sniping at the "inexperienced" technocrats now running Pemex, ordered Barragán Camacho to threaten strike action if union wage demands were not met. (Before he left office, López Portillo made sure that both Díaz Serrano and Barragán Camacho would serve as federal senators, posts that gave them immunity from prosecution. Although Díaz Serrano's immunity was lifted prior to his arrest in mid-1983, Barragán Camacho found the additional protection useful.)

With La Quina raising the stakes, the new administration's will seemed to waver. While most workers were being given a 15 percent emergency wage increase, for example, Pemex awarded a 28 percent raise and assorted new benefits to its employees in June 1983. Moreover, De la Madrid and Beteta were photographed with La Quina and Barragán Camacho while visiting one of the STPRM's model farms in what appeared to be a public reconciliation. "If the management of Pemex has decided to improve the efficiency, honesty and rationality of this corporation's operation," Beteta said, "it counts on the ever-growing support of the union." In private, administration officials were already trying to explain why the STPRM could not be touched.

After Díaz Serrano's arrest, however, pressure mounted from the private sector, opposition parties and much of the media for the cleanup to reach into the union. This in turn created new tensions within the STPRM, and in September 1983 Barragán Camacho brought fraud charges against the union's Secretary for Education, Hector García Hernández, in an effort to demonstrate a commitment to "moral renovation." The events that followed revealed still more about the STPRM.

García fled to his apartment in McAllen, Texas, but days later was kidnapped by union gunmen, smuggled back into Mexico and taken before La Quina in Ciudad Madero. The government was reluctant to arrest García in these circumstances, but was forced to do so by La Quina. García was then formally charged with embezzling 958 million pesos—$6.4 million at the going exchange rate—of union funds and jailed, appropriately a few cells away from Díaz Serrano.

In reality, García was no different from other wealthy regional bosses. He operated out of the port city of Coatzacoalcos, where he had bought a local newspaper, *La Tribuna,* and owned a number of businesses. At first, there were even suggestions that he was a voluntary scapegoat to relieve the pressure on La Quina. But once in custody, he wrote to the President claiming that he had handed over all union funds received from Pemex to La Quina and Barragán Camacho, who, he added, had failed to account for 20 billion pesos—then the equivalent of $1.35 billion —over the previous ten years. In the midst of this squabble, Oscar Torres Pancardo, the former STPRM secretary-general and still secretary-general of Local 30 as well as mayor of Poza Rica, was killed when his car purportedly crashed into a truck. His driver was found with a bullet wound in the head, and Torres Pancardo's family claimed that he too had been murdered. Amid rumors that Torres Pancardo had begun collaborating with the government against La Quina, the union boss installed his own loyal successor. Government officials privately concluded that Torres Pancardo had indeed been murdered, but federal authorities never pursued the case.

This public exhibition of union gangsterism, however, strengthened the government's hand in attacking the problem of subcontracting in the oil industry. New regulations announced in January 1984 banned the resale of all government contracts to third parties, but their obvious target was the STPRM and the lucrative commissions received by its leaders. The union was allowed to hold on to the 2 percent for "social works" collected on all outside contracts awarded by Pemex, but it would now have to bid for contracts like any other company and execute all those it won. With troops placed on the alert to discourage any retaliation against the measure, La Quina was served notice that times were changing. He responded with disciplined silence, and soon afterward was rewarded with a visit from De la Madrid to Ciudad Madero.

The best opportunity for peaceful change was offered in late 1984, when Local 10 in Minatitlán was to name the new STPRM secretary-general to replace Barragán Camacho. Aware of this, La Quina moved to control Local 10 almost two years before the national elections. But the perception that La Quina's political power was waning encouraged mutinous rumblings against his authoritarian rule in other locals. If a union boss not entirely subservient to La Quina were guided into the national leadership, the government would have six years in which to carry out a slow-motion coup before Local 1 in Ciudad Madero once again assumed control. The issue was not labor democracy, but power: the government still needed strong, even corrupt, union bosses to preserve the peace in the oil industry, but over the long run it could not tolerate the survival of an independent *cacique* who had begun to believe he was stronger than the system and had successfully blackmailed at least two administrations. In the short run, however, it seemed unsure how best to remove him.

The government's caution reflected its acute awareness that Mexico had no choice but to earn as much as possible from oil. Even without a clash with the union, there were reasons for concern. A drop in production from onshore oil wells in Tabasco and Chiapas suggested they had been carelessly overexploited in the late 1970s: by 1984, they accounted for only 19 percent of total reserves. There were also disturbing indications that natural gas and oil reserves had been inflated by Díaz Serrano. In October 1983, Pemex reduced its estimate of the Sabinas dry gas deposits from 3.5 trillion to 1.1 trillion cubic feet, while the 17 billion barrels in Chicontepec were privately recognized as being too costly to develop. Only the offshore fields offered new promise, already representing 48 percent of total reserves. In March 1984, in the hope of burying rumors, Pemex announced a new rise, albeit of only 500 million barrels, in its total proven hydrocarbon reserves to 72.5 billion barrels, comprising 50 billion barrels of crude oil and the equivalent of 22.5 billion barrels in natural gas and liquids. The economic slump and a sharp hike in domestic gasoline prices, however, did reduce local consumption and release more oil for export.

But market conditions abroad were not favorable. Soon after the change of government, a new oil glut prompted several oil exporters to lower their price. In contrast to June 1981, when Mexico unilaterally dropped its price, the government consulted at length with both OPEC and non-OPEC exporters before its reduction of $2 a barrel—to $29 per barrel for Istmo and $23 per barrel for Maya—and agreed to limit exports to 1.5 million barrels a day. This time, no contracts were canceled, less than $1 billion in anticipated revenue for 1983 was lost and Mexico for the first time demonstrated its willingness to work in concert with other producers in stabilizing the international energy market. Yet the new government was also abruptly reminded that the key instrument for rebuilding the economy was vulnerable to market forces outside the country's control.

Unlike López Portillo, then, De la Madrid did not enjoy the option of simply raising oil exports. Government experts estimated that Mexico could double exports to 3 million barrels a day within eighteen months at a cost of some $10 billion. But without a dramatic recovery of the world economy or a lengthy disruption of Middle East oil supplies, market conditions did not justify the investment. Mexico's economy was likely to remain as "petrolized" as before, but, in theory at least, a more nationalist thesis seemed relevant: growth of the oil industry should not be a substitute for more solid development. Plans were announced to reduce oil's share of Mexico's total energy generation from 93 percent to 70 percent by the year 2000. Certainly, if the country's objective remained that of strengthening its economic independence, scarce resources would be more wisely channeled toward other sectors of industry, with Pemex playing a supportive rather than dominant role in the economy. The "new Pemex" proclaimed by De la Madrid was to be a tamed Pemex.

9

Land Sí, Liberty No

I

On April 10 each year, the Agrarian Reform Minister marks the anniversary of the murder of Emiliano Zapata by laying a wreath at a statue of the revolutionary hero in Cuautla and ritualistically renewing the government's promise to bring "justice" to the peasantry. Hundreds of aging peasants are always trucked in to hear his words, many of them distinguishable by their white Indian costumes and huge mustaches as octogenarian survivors of the Revolution in Morelos. The mood is always somber. Only teenagers when they joined the Zapatista fight for "Land and Liberty," the old men still remember the hopes that inspired them and the disappointments that ensued. They had dreamed that expropriation of the huge private estates in the valley would bring them prosperity, but instead they were given tiny plots on *ejido* farms without the means to work them efficiently. And as new industrial oligarchies grew up in the cities, their rural revolution was forgotten and their families remained trapped by poverty.

Repeated in thousands of rural communities across Mexico, the hopeless backwardness of the villages of Morelos bears witness to the failure of the agrarian model sustained by successive "revolutionary" governments. It promised to transfer "land to those who work it," and although some 2.7 million peasant families have benefited from the agrarian reform program, 3 million to 4 million adult peasants are still awaiting their plots. It claimed that all large private landholdings would be expropriated, yet much of the best-irrigated land is still in the hands of *latifundistas,* many of them government party politicians. It pledged to improve the welfare of the rural poor, but most of the 30 million or so peasants and their families still live below the poverty line defined by the government itself. Finally, it established the nationalist objective of food self-sufficiency, but billions of dollars have been spent since 1970 on imported grains.

Yet in a crucial political sense, agrarian policies have been a success: where peasants farm *ejido* or communal land, political unrest is rare; and where landless peasants are still demanding expropriation of surviving estates or *latifundios,* patience is somehow kept alive by the expectation of a tiny plot. Thus, reality or myth, the land reform has effectively demobilized the peasantry and maintained relative peace in the country-side since 1920. Even at a time of acute national crisis, the peasants lack the economic weight and the political organization to pose any threat to the ruling system.

That this should be the case can only be explained historically, and perhaps also psychologically. It was the discovery of corn some 6,000 years ago that enabled the nomadic tribes of Meso-America to settle down and eventually to build great civilizations. Corn therefore became synonymous with life—most pre-Hispanic legends had man himself being born of corn—while religion revolved around worshipping those gods that could protect the corn crop and appeasing those that could destroy the harvest. Similarly, because corn was born of the earth, land also took on sacred significance. As a result, since long before the Spanish Conquest, the *milpa*—the corn field—has been at the heart of Mexico's rural society. To this day, corn accounts for at least half the food con-sumed by the peasant family, while even time itself is defined by the cycles of planting and harvesting the grain. By growing his own corn on his own land, then, the peasant secures his survival and renews his communion with nature.

Conversely, when this relationship has been disturbed, peasant unrest has followed. In the War of the Castes of the mid-nineteenth century, for example, the Mayas fought with almost religious zeal to recover their communal lands. When the seizure of peasant plots by the sugar *latifun-distas* of Morelos in the late nineteenth century caused a sharp drop in local corn production, the seeds of the Zapatista rebellion were sown. The distribution of land after the Revolution therefore restored some-thing of the internal harmony of the countryside. Living conditions rarely improved—educational, health, nutritional and housing standards are still dramatically worse in rural than in urban areas—but the peas-ants were willing to tolerate enormous hardship before abandoning the land of their forefathers.

In reality, millions of landless peasants have moved permanently to urban areas in recent decades, but much of the migratory movement is seasonal: poverty forces them out to supplement their income and the land draws them back. Jobs will be found as laborers—*peones*—on construction sites or harvesting fruit, vegetables, sugar and coffee, but most peasants return punctually to their *milpa* in time to plant and harvest their corn and beans. Most of the hundreds of thousands who cross illegally into the United States each year also have the intention of returning: in myriad communities of central and northern Mexico, wives and children look after the livestock and farm the *milpas* while awaiting the money orders sent from the farming valleys of the American Southwest. But these are merely survival strategies: there was never enough land to go around or the political need to make the agrarian reform work.

The stage was set for this endless battle between principle and reality by Article 27 of the 1917 Constitution, which established the peasant's right to a piece of land. Yet as soon as Zapata was killed and the countryside pacified, the pressure to implement this commitment abated. The first distribution of land in fact involved the seizure of attractive haciendas by leaders of revolutionary armies or bands. In Morelos, President Carranza even reversed Zapata's improvised land reform by rewarding loyal officers with many of the best estates. Further, Carranza and his two successors, Obregón and Calles, were landowners from the dry underpopulated north where no tradition of communal farming existed and where control of water and agricultural commerce are still more important than possession of land. Some land was distributed to appease restive peasants during the depression, but the new "revolutionary" elite gave little priority to the program. In 1930, Calles proclaimed that "agrarianism is a failure," yet no real effort had been made to test it: some 2.3 million peasants were still without land, while hundreds of pre-Revolution haciendas survived.

Campaigning in the provinces for the 1934 presidential elections, General Cárdenas sensed mounting frustration among the rural poor and was moved to adopt the agrarian cause as his own. During his six-year term, he therefore gave enormous impetus to land reform, not only distributing some 18 million hectares*—12 percent of the entire country—among 810,000 peasants, but also creating the Ejido Credit Bank and integrating the rural sector into the ruling party through the new National Peasant Confederation (CNC). Resistance from surviving *latifundistas* was strong, but Cárdenas himself felt a powerful affinity with the Indians and peasants and would frequently travel in the *campo* to receive peasant

---

*This was three times more than had been distributed between 1917 and 1934, and it included more irrigated land—976,866 hectares—than has been handed out before or since.

petitions, even prompting complaints that he was neglecting administration of the central government.

But while Cárdenas romantically envisioned the emergence of a more affluent and educated rural proletariat, the *ejido,* his chosen political instrument, condemned the peasants to the perennial poverty of *minifundismo,* or tiny plots. Adapting the Indian tradition of communal farming, the state retained ownership of the *ejido* and granted peasants the right to usufruct the land. The intent was that, by allowing this right to pass only from father to sons and by banning the renting and/or sale of *ejidos,* large landholdings would not reappear. But in practice, not only were *ejidos* routinely rented and "sold" outside the law, but *ejidatarios* were also unable to mortgage their land in exchange for private bank credits. Cárdenas himself encouraged collective or cooperative farming of *ejidos* to achieve economies of scale and better management, but *ejidatarios* generally preferred to subdivide property into plots to be farmed individually. Built into the political solution, then, were the seeds of social and economic disaster. Only in the Yaqui, Mayo and Laguna regions of northern Mexico did collective *ejidos* work well, but subsequent governments viewed them as dangerously socialist and effectively sabotaged them.

Not surprisingly, the conservative opposition stirred by Cárdenas' program slowed the land reform after he left office. In 1947, the "counter-reform" in agriculture took place when President Alemán amended Article 27 of the Constitution to introduce the *amparo agrario,* an injunction that served to postpone execution of expropriation decrees. Alemán's objective was to increase food production, which, he believed, could only be carried out by commercial farmers using capital-intensive techniques. He therefore ignored the *ejidos* and provided private landowners with additional security by expanding the definition of *pequeñas propiedades,* or small landholdings, to mean 100 hectares of irrigated land, 200 hectares of rain-fed land, 300 hectares of orchards, 400 hectares of good-quality grazing land, 800 hectares of scrub and, in desert regions, the amount of land necessary to keep 500 head of cattle, which might be as much as 50,000 hectares.

The principal effect of these reforms was to protect existing estates from expropriation and to create *neo-latifundios.* Since individual members of a single family were regarded as separate small landholders, large estates could exist within the law. Similarly, a landowner could put various sections of his property in the names of his farm hands. In some regions, it became customary for *ejidos* to be rented out illegally to private farmers who then hired the *ejidatarios* to work their own land. Powerful *latifundistas* in league with local politicians took to occupying and fencing off communal lands owned by Indian communities. Where these lands contained important forests, timber companies obtained ten- to twenty-year concessions in exchange for small fees. In every state, there survived or emerged landed *caciques* who controlled much of production and commerce in their regions. But the lack of democracy within the *ejidos* also frequently converted the elected leader—or *comisario ejidal*—into a smaller *cacique* who might run the local store, rent out the *ejido* and strike deals with local politicians.

Perhaps most significant, the slowdown of land reform coincided with a population explosion which created new generations of landless peasants, increased social hardship in the *campo* and eventually provoked a mass exodus to urban areas. Over this period, it was government policy to stimulate industrial development, with the result that urban wages were allowed to rise while rural prices were held down. The *ejidos* came to be viewed merely as "parking lots" for the peasantry until their cheap labor could be incorporated into the new urban and industrial nation.

The agrarian myth was nevertheless kept alive by Cárdenas' successors through fiery rhetoric as well as expropriation and distribution of some private farms: even Alemán handed out some 3 million hectares during his administration. But the entire procedure took on an air of surrealism. Increasingly, *ejidos* were formed on infertile semi-arid land where only goats could survive or on forested mountainsides where the peasants were denied lumbering concessions but nevertheless cut down trees to make way for their *milpas*. Between 1952 and 1982, 85 percent of land distributed to the peasantry was unsuitable for arable farming. There was also frequently little relationship between the amount of land that each government claimed to have expropriated and the area that was in fact handed out to the peasants. López Mateos signed decrees expropriating 11.3 million hectares, but barely a quarter of this was distributed. Similarly, Díaz Ordaz formally expropriated 14 million hectares, but peasants actually received only 4 million hectares. Thus, a group of peasants might campaign successfully for a presidential decree expropriating a *latifundio*, only to find execution of the order blocked by an old-fashioned bribe or a new *amparo agrario*.

On any day of the week, pathetic groups of ragged peasants can be found in the dusty corridors of the Agrarian Reform Ministry, holding faded copies of expropriation orders, hoping to press their claim with officials who invariably counsel patience and renew those well-versed promises of "justice." Some of the groups make the journey two or three times a year at great cost to the community, only to return to their distant villages with the same message of failure. The average time between expropriation and distribution is over fourteen years. Not infrequently, organized by some outside political movement or simply driven by despair, peasants "invade" property that they have been assigned, and occasionally this is sufficient to extract a distribution order from local authorities. More often, however, police or the Army is called in to intimidate the peasants into leaving and, if necessary, to evict them by force. No year goes by without some peasants being killed in such confrontations.

Perpetuated by violence and injustice, a deep sense of hopelessness runs through the countryside. After their local leader was murdered by the *pistoleros* of local landowners in August 1983, for example, a community of Chinanteco Indians from southern Veracruz wrote to the President. "In Veracruz, to kill the cow of a landowner just with your thoughts is paid for by peasants with years in jail even if they prove their innocence," recounted the letter, which was reprinted in a Mexico City newspaper. "That's why one of our leaders has said that a cow has more rights than a peasant. Not that we have anything against these animals, but the contrast is ironic when it comes to applying justice to a man of the *campo* who has no greater patrimony than his honor and modesty but who in the end is ready to work so that others can eat." Two months later, the leader of *ejidos* near Huejutla in Hidalgo state, Benito Hernández, was murdered by two gunmen: the peasants of the region had won a long struggle for land in 1980, but the affected landowners seemed unwilling to accept their defeat. As so often the case, no one was charged with Hernández's murder.

Successive governments have themselves used corruption, coercion and repression to prevent the emergence of any truly representative independent peasant organizations. Since Cárdenas pulled together assorted peasant leagues under the National Peasant Confederation, the CNC has been run entirely from Mexico City, invariably by *licenciados* appointed by the President. It remains a useful instrument for controlling the countryside and for wheeling out peasants to vote for the PRI at election time. (The biggest turnouts for the PRI are in the poorest rural districts.) But its leaders owe their loyalty to the system rather than to the members, and even at the level of individual *ejidos,* local CNC officials frequently interfere to force an "elected" leader on the community.

Several other peasant organizations, among them the Union of Peasants and Workers of Mexico (UGOCM), the Independent Peasant

Confederation (CCI) and the Mexican Agrarian Council (CAM), have emerged around individual leaders who work out their own deals with the government, but they too form part of the system of control. In the early 1970s, Echeverría tied all the peasant groups together under the so-called Ocampo Pact, which survived until he left office. Similarly, in 1983, a loose National Peasant Alliance was formed, officially to campaign for revocation of the *amparo agrario,* but in practice to preserve a single line of command from government to peasant masses. For example, the government still refuses to authorize a union of migrant workers and it has watched warily as *ejidos* in Puebla, Oaxaca, Michoacán, Veracruz and Chiapas have organized a so-called National Coordinating Committee Plan de Ayala, taking their name from Zapata's land reform proclamation.

A traditional way of advancing politically is to emerge as an independent peasant agitator. Having gathered a group of landless peasants under the banner of "the fight for justice," the aspiring leader can then negotiate with—and, it seems, invariably sell out to—the authorities. But the system will normally try to coopt him without destroying his appeal, thereby enabling him to continue living off "his" peasants and, when deemed necessary by officials, to divide other groups of militant peasants.

The alternative to collaborating with the system is permanent harassment, frequent jailings and possible assassination. In some regions, local authorities seem happy to allow landowners to deal with peasant troublemakers. In the 1950s, Jacinto and Maximiliano López, two brothers who had organized peasants of the Yaqui Valley, were murdered by hired gunmen. In other areas, the Army's principal function is to serve as a rural police force, controlling agitators and evicting peasants squatting on private or disputed land. Should a leader become known nationwide, his fate will be decided in Mexico City. In the 1940s and 1950s in Morelos and nearby states, Rubén Jaramillo emerged as the most influential peasant leader since Zapata, with whom he had fought as a young man. But in March 1962, he and several family members were kidnapped and killed by soldiers. Danzos Palomino, a Communist organizer of the Independent Peasant Confederation, was jailed for five years in the 1970s and, when freed, found his group badly divided, with one faction coopted by the government. Francisco Medrano, on the other hand, tried to organize massive land takeovers in Oaxaca in the late 1970s and, when unsuccessful, took to the hills with a band of armed men and was killed by soldiers within weeks.

Ironically, the most serious peasant unrest in recent memory was orchestrated by the government itself. From the moment he took office in 1970, President Echeverría sought to emulate Cárdenas by speaking out on behalf of the country's rural poor and against powerful *latifundistas* who had escaped expropriation. The President's rhetoric soon provoked a slowdown of investment by worried private farmers, but Echeverría ordered his Agrarian Reform Minister, Augusto Gómez Villanueva, to mobilize the peasants to campaign for their rights. In some areas, peasants felt encouraged to seize private farms, and new violence erupted. Echeverría also expropriated 11.5 million hectares and distributed 6.5 million hectares, more than any President since Cárdenas. But in practice, he seemed more interested in weakening the political power of private farmers and their business allies than in strengthening that of the peasants.

In 1976, Echeverría set his sights on the wealthy *latifundistas* of Ciudad Obregón in Sonora state. Not only were they among his sharpest political critics, but one of Cárdenas' best-remembered agrarian actions had taken place in the same region. Echeverría instructed Gómez Villanueva to organize a grass-roots demand for land expropriations, and in the weeks that followed thousands of peasants camped out beside the irrigated farms of the Yaqui Valley. Since at first Echeverría's hand was not visible, the mobilization provoked rumors of peasant uprisings and even of armed bands terrorizing the countryside. In reality, it was carefully controlled, with the peasants themselves unable to understand why they were being fed by the CNC and "protected" by the Army. In other regions, notably Sinaloa, some "invasions" occurred, but they merely helped to justify Echeverría's decision to expropriate 90,000 acres of the Yaqui Valley on November 19, just eleven days before he left office.

Since the peasant agitation came from above, the incoming López Portillo administration had no difficulty in ending illegal land seizures and restoring calm to the countryside. In the hope of encouraging new investment by private farmers, López Portillo jailed Félix Barra García, who had succeeded Gómez Villanueva as Agrarian Reform Minister during the final months of the previous administration, on a charge of corruption. Further, while voicing concern about the social condition of the peasantry, he disputed the logic of continuing to hand out small plots of arid land. Rather, López Portillo's rhetoric focused on the need to increase and redistribute agricultural production, and to this end a new Agricultural Development Law was adopted encouraging association between *ejidos* and small landholders.

But this reform was strongly criticized by peasant organizations and leftist parties as increasing the private sector's control over the *campo*. Thus, no new formula to increase *ejido* productivity appeared, while pressure for land distribution continued. Having announced at the beginning of his term that there was no land left to distribute, that "land is not elastic," López Portillo too opted for the easy route, handing out 15.7 million hectares—91 percent of it unsuitable for agriculture—to some 300,000 peasant families with the expressed aim of clearing the backlog of unexecuted expropriation decrees. Rather than address the land tenure system, he preferred to buy peace in the countryside through massive subsidies and social welfare programs.

When President de la Madrid took office in December 1982, he inherited the agrarian myth. He reiterated the government's commitment to hand out all "affectable" land, but conceded that the situation was chaotic. "Half the national territory has been distributed and almost 27,000 *ejidos* have benefited some three million families," he noted in March 1983. "Nevertheless, half the land has not been regularized for lack of documents guaranteeing the right of possession, which in turn has generated uncertainty and insecurity, lack of interest in working the land and even simulation, illegal renting and abandonment of property." ("Simulation" refers to *latifundios* disguised as small landholdings.) In his State of the Union address on September 1, 1983, De la Madrid returned to the theme, noting even more soberly that the land area subject to expropriation is "steadily smaller and more difficult to locate." He warned: "We will promote agrarian rights but will not raise hopes demagogically. And still less will we tolerate violation of legitimate rights." Whether or not by government design, several dozen peasant leaders were killed in different parts of the country in 1984 alone.

The new government's priority, then, was to clear up the legal disorder in the *campo*, providing proper titles for communal lands and official documents to all *ejidos*, reviewing the membership of *ejidos* to see if new peasant families could be accommodated, reducing the bureaucratic steps involved in agrarian petitions from forty-three to just eight and granting formal recognition to genuine small landowners. But, it claimed, all but 4.7 million hectares of the 101 million hectares subject to expropriation had already been handed out. Only this balance would therefore now be distributed: some 20,000 peasants formed into new "rural production units"—rather than *minifundios*—would receive 600,000 hectares in 1983, with the rest benefiting 100,000 more peasants over the following five years. By the time De la Madrid left office in 1988, the *reparto agrario*, or agrarian distribution, would be over.

Immediately, peasant organizations and agrarian experts disputed the official statistics, although disagreeing among themselves over the true amount of land subject to expropriation. One academic study claimed that 7.6 million hectares of expropriated land had yet to be distributed, 8.7 million hectares of cattle-ranching concessions on state-owned land had expired and 1.5 million hectares of private land fell outside legal limits. In some cases, recognized cattle land was also suitable for growing grain and, if reclassified, would become *latifundios*. The CNC argued that 14 million hectares were protected by *amparos agrarios* and should be confiscated, while the new Agrarian Reform Minister, Luis Martínez Villicana, conceded that 10.5 million hectares of government land might be available for distribution. Such was the sensitivity of the issue that adoption by Congress of an amended Land Reform Law in December 1983, passing responsibility for expropriations and distributions to state governors, provoked a walkout by all opposition parties and strong protests in private from PRI deputies representing the CNC. Part of the complaint was that the reform was rammed through Congress in one day —before many deputies had even read it—but it was also perceived to be aiding private farmers and doing nothing to protect peasant producers or those without land.

The reality remained that seizure of the 96 million hectares of territory —some 25 million hectares of "small landholdings" plus desert and mountains—not currently organized into *ejidos* or communal farms would still not accommodate the 3 to 4 million peasants who have petitioned for land. But like his predecessors, De la Madrid was also hesitant about dispelling the illusion that kept millions of *jornaleros,* or migrant workers, in the countryside. The government had become a prisoner of the agrarian myth that it invented: land handouts were not the answer, but officials dared not say so because the peasants would not believe them.

II

Mexico is highly unsuitable for agriculture. Much of the north is desert, two mountain ranges run the length of the country, tropical jungles cover the southern region of Chiapas, while the topsoil in the Yucatán Penin-sula is so thin that little can grow. The shortage of water is particularly acute: the runoff from the Mississippi River alone is greater than that of all of Mexico's rivers. Put differently, 52 percent of Mexican territory is arid, 32.5 percent is semi-arid, 10.5 percent is semi-humid and 7 percent is humid, while about 50 percent is too steep for cultivation and only 15 percent is considered ideal arable land. "Water," De la Madrid once noted, "is one of the principal limitations on our development." This is dramatically evident in agriculture: rich farmers are rich principally because they have water, while plots distributed under the agrarian reform are usually too dry, too rocky or too eroded to farm well.

But this is only one of the problems faced by peasant farmers. Most are functional illiterates, with neither schooling nor training to help them break out of their cycle of poverty. They therefore resist efforts to collectivize their *minifundios,* opting for security over the alien concept of efficiency. (An exception is the Yaqui Valley, where both the old *ejidos* formed by Cárdenas and the new ones created by Echeverría work communally and cultivate wheat and soya, borrowing the techniques of private farmers in the region.) Further, they remain obsessed with corn and beans. These crops have the advantage of growing on a great variety of often infertile soils, being stored easily and providing consumers with a minimum of protein, fats and carbohydrates. But while vegetables, fruits and flowers could draw the peasant farmers into the money economy, corn and beans merely enable them to survive: around 80 percent of *ejidos* consume almost all their food production. And when, as occurs with devastating frequency, the spring rains arrive late and the harvest is poor, the *ejidatarios* are forced to migrate to make ends meet.

Unlike private farmers, who can mortgage their property as collateral for bank loans, *ejidatarios* and communal farmers must depend overwhelmingly on the government. In theory, they are well attended, but they have learned to expect little. Innumerable official studies have properly identified the lack of credit, seeds, fertilizer and machinery—as well as of adequate health and education services—as reasons for the low productivity of peasant plots. But these reports appear to go unread by policy makers. A huge agrarian bureaucracy has grown up since the Revolution: even after a recent streamlining, there were some 180 commissions, offices and funds aimed at promoting products as varied as candle wax and sisal. Most are monuments to past populism, more effective at benefiting political appointees than providing peasants with advice or assistance.

The government's Rural Credit Bank carries the main responsibility for servicing the *ejidos.* But, with its 38,000 employees, it is a bloated and inefficient bureaucracy racked by corruption. Because it must write off 15 to 25 percent of credits as bad debts each year, it has also become seriously decapitalized. In practice, it claims to look after only some 19,000 of the 27,000 *ejidos,* supplying the credit necessary for the purchase of seeds, pesticides, fertilizer and machinery. Yet each spring when these *ejidos* turn to the BANRURAL, as it is known, only about 40 percent come away satisfied.

Similarly, the government agricultural research and extension services contribute little to the *ejidos*. Thousands of agronomists and extension agents in fact graduate every year, but most prefer to work in offices rather than in the field. Such research stations as do exist frequently ignore the local needs of farmers; the result is minimal communication between the researcher, the extension agent and the peasant. Without a continuing system of support, major agricultural experiments of one administration, such as the tropical farming effort known as the Plan Chontalpa under Echeverría, frequently falter under the next.

After the crop is harvested, marketing of any surplus becomes an additional odyssey. The government's basic food agency, CONASUPO, is required to purchase all staple foods that it is offered. But remote *ejidos* without their own means of transport must frequently sell at unfavorable prices to middlemen. One motive for creating the Mexican Coffee Institute in 1971 was to eliminate intermediaries or force them to pay official prices. But government purchasing agents are themselves often accused of demanding a bribe to accept products that purportedly do not meet quality standards, or of underweighing crops brought in by farmers. Even producers of fruits and vegetables who can transport their products to Mexico City find themselves at the mercy of federal highway police, urban buyers and distributors. With the exception of corn and beans, where every stage is subsidized by the government, the vast differential between the cost of production and the retail price sustains a large commercial network.

Perhaps the greatest obstacle to higher productivity, though, is the country's land tenure system itself. Soon after taking office, De la Madrid offered to organize the 27,000 *ejidos* and 400,000 or so "small landholdings"—those where individual plots average less than five hectares—into "efficient and productive units that can absorb modern technology and infrastructural investment." But these were the phrases of urban technocrats, economic answers to political problems. The political risks of tampering with the *ejido* system still outweighed the advantages of addressing its built-in inequities and inefficiencies. Any move to modernize the sector by replacing the *ejido* with a more efficient unit of production would be strongly—and probably violently—opposed by the peasants themselves. In addition, capital-intensive agriculture would force millions more peasants to leave the *campo* and add to population and political pressures in urban areas. As a result, successive governments have opted to sacrifice *ejido* productivity in order to maintain social peace.

There is a profitable side to Mexican agriculture, but it has little to do with peasants or *ejidos,* corn or beans. Most private farmers—the large "small landholders"—concentrate on crops that are either exportable or aimed at more affluent domestic consumers. Even this enterprise is not without risks. Exporters are vulnerable not only to domestic exchange rate policies but also to the vagaries of protectionism and world commodity prices. Producers for the home market may find their products subject to price controls or, conversely, affected by sudden slumps in demand. And all commercial farmers—even those not regarded as *latifundistas*—have at different times feared expropriation by governments seeking to appease peasant unrest.

Yet most private farmers have traditionally done well. They have access to modern agricultural techniques at the same time as they benefit from cheap labor and subsidized fuel, credit and fertilizer. They can choose between selling in the world's richest market north of the border or in the rapidly growing urban zones of Mexico itself. Their wealth and political influence invariably protect them from the embrace of land reform. Outside the country's principal industrial centers, private farmers—the coffee growers in Chiapas, the cattle ranchers of Tabasco, the tomato exporters of Sinaloa and the strawberry producers of Guanajuato among them—comprise the most powerful local lobbies. It is rare, for example, to find a provincial governor who is not also an important landowner. Compared to these commercial farmers, the CNC and other peasant organizations carry little weight.

Private landowners naturally attribute their success to their greater efficiency. With access to all the vital inputs, such as seeds, fertilizer and water, as well as to modern technology, their productivity is unavoidably higher than that of the *ejidos.* (Significantly, in the Yaqui and Mayo valleys of Sonora, where collective *ejidos* use the same land, irrigation and technology as commercial farmers, comparable yields are obtained.) Further, they control much of the best land in the country, including 50 percent of all irrigated land. Producing 70 percent of all the marketable food on just 20 percent of the land, they have made themselves indispensable to the country, probably contributing more to political stability as aberrations of the agrarian reform than they would as victims of arbitrary expropriations.

Many privately owned cattle ranches as well as sugarcane and coffee plantations survived the Revolution, but President Alemán safeguarded them from expropriation when he redefined the limits of small landholdings and created the *amparo agrario.* He also gave enormous impetus to agro-exports, principally cotton and winter fruits and vegetables, by channeling government investment into reservoirs and irrigation canals in the arid coastal plains of northwestern Mexico. Coincidentally, many large American farm equipment, seed, insecticide and food companies established operations in Mexico, able to work well with the new class of commercial farmers in developing, processing and marketing their products.

Since the 1950s, assured of domestic irrigation supplies and credit and of imported machinery and fertilizer, Sinaloa and Sonora enjoyed an unprecedented agricultural boom. Both states benefited from outside political developments: the U.S. trade boycott of China in the late 1940s stimulated cotton production in Sonora, while the U.S. embargo that followed the 1959 Cuban Revolution enabled Sinaloa to take over the market for such winter products as tomatoes, cucumbers, melons and peppers. Sonora would later diversify into soya beans, while, only occasionally disturbed by "tomato wars" with Florida producers, Sinaloa's exports of winter vegetables to the United States grew steadily, with Mexican producers diversifying into distribution to California. Profits were high and many of the wealthy families expanded into industry, banking and commerce, frequently controlling lucrative distributorships for American fertilizer and pesticide products. The example of Sinaloa was soon followed in Guanajuato, where cultivation of winter strawberries for the American market began in the 1960s.

Traditionally, Mexico's principal agricultural exports were coffee, sugar and cotton, but this profile began to change. Government price controls eventually drove the sugar industry into crisis—and into the arms of the state—in the early 1970s and today Mexico is a major importer of sugar. Cotton and coffee exports, while still important, remain dependent on world commodity prices and fixed quotas and have not expanded. In contrast, exports of winter fruits and vegetables, growing from a mere $26 million in 1962 to over $300 million in 1983, came to provide Mexico with vital foreign exchange at a time of rising grain imports. Mexico's proximity to the United States was crucial: the United States was its principal market for all agricultural products except cotton, while Mexico was the United States' main foreign supplier of oranges, strawberries, melons, cucumbers and tomatoes.

The dramatic growth of the urban middle classes since the 1940s also fed demand for higher-quality food within Mexico itself. Although millions of Mexicans still suffer from undernourishment, consumption of meat, fruit, vegetables, eggs and milk has risen faster than the population. Particularly in the central states surrounding Mexico City, commercial farmers have learned to take advantage of an almost captive market. Many experimental programs with *ejidos* also aim to teach them to cultivate nontraditional products demanded by urban areas.

But the largest profits from this new agricultural experience have accrued to food companies, in the main American and European transnational corporations. These companies buy Mexican products, add foreign processing, packaging and marketing technology and then resell them to Mexican consumers. Domination of the Mexican processed food market by these companies is visible in any supermarket, where breakfast cereals, baby foods, fruit preserves, canned fruits and vegetables, assorted sodas and myriad other foods all carry familiar trademarks. By serving as a bridge between farmers and shoppers, these companies have stimulated both production and consumption. Their economic weight and cultural influence have nevertheless converted them into a perennial target of the Mexican Left, which has long demanded the nationalization of the food industry.

III

The chronic depression affecting Mexico's rural sector is a natural product of the political system and the economic model, accurately mirroring the extremes of wealth and poverty to be found elsewhere in society. A partial political solution was provided by land reform and a partial economic solution by the new generation of commercial farmers, but since the 1940s no regime has given priority to developing an all-embracing strategy for the rural sector. Emphasis was on industrialization and urbanization, while agriculture's share of both the Gross Domestic Product and total new investment fell steadily. Further, reflecting the emergence of commercial farming, even the government's share of total agricultural investment dropped sharply in the 1950s and 1960s.

Thus, while the Mexican economy as a whole grew impressively, agriculture gradually lagged further behind. With the exception of such freak years as 1981, per capita food production has declined continually since the early 1960s. Between 1965 and 1976, while GDP growth averaged 5.5 percent and the population increased by over 3.5 percent annually, agricultural growth averaged only 1.2 percent. Similarly, since 1970, despite unprecedented government expenditure in the rural sector, including expansion of basic grain subsidies for both production and consumption, Mexico has been forced to import food to meet steadily growing domestic demand. This slump, though, was attributable not only to neglect: by holding down guaranteed support prices, successive governments consciously protected urban consumers and discouraged production. The government thus subsidized agriculture and the *campo* subsidized the cities.

When López Portillo took office in 1976, he defined the priorities of his administration as the development of energy and food. But in practice government resources poured into the oil industry and little remained for agriculture. In 1979, after a chronically weak rural sector was struck by a severe drought, Mexico was forced to import an unprecedented 12 million tons of basic grains from the United States. Transportation bottlenecks appeared, with thousands of railroad cars stuck for weeks at the border and importation of equipment for the oil industry often delayed by the need to unload ships carrying corn, wheat and beans. While the imported food eventually reached the country's cities and was sold at highly subsidized prices, little filtered down to the peasants, who were unable to meet even their own immediate needs. Not for the first time, the government faced the tragic irony that the worst malnutrition was to be found among the country's food producers.

Yet it was politics—the belief that Mexico's vulnerability in agriculture threatened its independence—that prompted López Portillo to react. Just as Mexico was contracting for large food imports from the United States, the Carter administration imposed an embargo on grain sales to the Soviet Union in reprisal for its invasion of Afghanistan in December 1979. Following the new rise in world oil prices in 1979, there was a perception in Mexico that its oil wealth was coveted by the United States. Now Washington's use of food as a weapon against the Soviet Union awakened Mexico to the danger that its energy resources could become hostage to its food dependence. As a result, on March 18, 1980, using the symbolic occasion of the anniversary of Mexico's oil nationalization, López Portillo announced creation of the Mexican Food System —christened the SAM—and established the patriotic objective of self-sufficiency in corn and beans by 1982 and most other grains and oilseeds by 1985.

If the SAM's inspiration was political, however, its main instrument was economic. Rather than tackling the agricultural crisis at its peasant and bureaucratic roots, the government decided to smother the crisis with money on the premise that it was better to enrich Mexican than American farmers. In essence, the strategy involved raising the "guaranteed" price paid to grain producers while holding down the retail price paid by consumers, increasing technical assistance and other support for peasant farmers and subsidizing the cost of improved seeds, fertilizer, transportation, crop insurance and credit. Aware of the inclemency of

Mexican weather, the government also created a "shared risk" mechanism by which peasants would be protected financially against a bad harvest. In theory, the production, productivity and income of small farmers would in this way increase, improving their living standards and gradually integrating them into the money economy.

Innumerable obstacles to this metamorphosis soon became apparent. Before the SAM was announced by the President, neither the government's top agrarian officials nor state governors were consulted. Administration of the program was then placed in the hands of a general coordinator, Cassio Luiselli Fernández, a Wisconsin-trained economist who surrounded himself with advisers with impressive academic credentials and little practical experience. They drew up grandiose plans but, being neither peasants nor *latifundistas,* they knew little about—and therefore paid scant attention to—the operational details. Moreover, while Luiselli enjoyed the power of any senior official with direct access to the President, the federal agencies and state governments charged with executing the SAM seemed unconvinced of its viability and proved less than fully cooperative. Also, an important part of the money thrown at the program found its way into the pockets of lower-level bureaucrats. Yet even had these administrative problems not existed, with 1980 spent preparing the program, the idea of transforming a backward and disorganized rural sector before López Portillo left office in December 1982 was clearly unreal.

Blessed with the best rainy season in six years, however, the government could proclaim the success of the SAM in late 1981. Basic food production, just 18.2 million tons during the disastrous harvest of 1979, rose from 23.4 million tons in 1980 to a record 28.6 million tons in 1981. This included a 19 percent jump in corn output to 14.7 million tons and a 57 percent rise in bean production to 1.5 million tons, which, although still insufficient to cover domestic demand, convinced the government that self-sufficiency was within reach. The fact that it was the most expensive corn in the world seemed of little political importance.

But in 1982 the SAM's two key variables—weather and money—both failed. Although more land was prepared for planting than in the previous spring, late rains brought a 20 percent drop in the harvested area. Further, in February 1982, the economic boom that permitted the government such luxuries as the SAM ended abruptly with the devaluation of the peso. As a result, grain production for the year fell by 12 percent to 25 million tons, with corn output down to 12.2 million tons. In 1983, grain imports from the United States once again rose to around 8.5 million tons.

After De la Madrid took office, the SAM was immediately dismantled, its staff scattered among other ministries or universities and the controversial acronym quietly forgotten. Not only did the government lack the resources necessary to finance such a program, but it was fashionable to blame irrational subsidies for most of the economy's troubles: even the expenditure of an additional $6 billion by the SAM in 1982 had failed to protect peasant farmers from the effects of bad weather. Instead, farmers would be encouraged to produce by more attractive support prices and, with lower subsidies available for basic grains, urban consumers would simply have to pay more for food. Exports of winter fruits and vegetables would be stimulated, and any shortfall in basic grains would be covered by imports from the United States and guaranteed by its Commodity Credit Corporation. After the failure of the SAM, even the suggestion of grain self-sufficiency seemed demagogic.

It soon became apparent that this approach, too, was inadequate. A major debacle was avoided because of exceptionally good summer rains in 1983 and 1984, which not only filled the country's reservoirs but also ensured bumper corn and bean crops that reduced the need for imported foods in 1984 and 1985. Yet the problem of managing food prices at a time of economic crisis and high inflation proved overwhelming: put simply, the government needed to raise support prices to stimulate production and thereby eventually ease inflation; and it needed to hold down retail prices to control inflation and appease angry urban consumers. The result satisfied no one. Support prices were raised, but not sufficiently to encourage peasants to plant much beyond their immediate needs, to dissuade farmers from slaughtering cattle and chickens or, indeed, to eliminate the $1-billion annual subsidy on the market price of tortillas, bread, beans and cooking oil. Yet consumers were nevertheless outraged.

Still more revealing, De la Madrid moved in October 1983 to resurrect the SAM strategy that had been unceremoniously buried just months earlier. The new National Food Program, or PRONAL, typically made no reference to the SAM and promised "to work out new strategies, policies and actions" in agriculture, as if such an approach were fresh. While officials privately recognized that Mexico would still be importing 8 to 10 million tons of food per year from the United States by the time De la Madrid left office in 1988, the President revived the concept of self-sufficiency by referring vaguely to "food sovereignty" and warning of the dangers of food dependency. This can only be achieved, he said, through a massive production effort supported by "energy, clarity, creativity, efficiency and honesty." Specifically, it required changing the "terms of trade" between rural and urban sectors. "If we do not pay a just price to the food producer," De la Madrid went on, "the risks are that production will fall, scarce foreign exchange will be spent on imports or shortages will appear."

Definition of the problem, however, was a far cry from finding a solution. The unveiling of PRONAL, for example, coincided with further deterioration in the "terms of trade" between *campo* and city. In strictly political terms, it still seemed preferable to import grain and subsidize consumer prices rather than risk provoking the urban working and middle classes with new inflation. PRONAL in fact emerged as a SAM without money, concentrating on improving food distribution but doing little to stimulate production. The argument was even made that increased support prices would benefit only efficient private farmers and would bring greater hardship to the 3 million or more landless peasants who were forced to buy their corn on the market.

Inheriting a crisis that affected all areas of the Mexican economy, then, De la Madrid was in no position—economically or politically—to initiate a fundamental reform of the rural sector. As with so many of his predecessors, his principal priorities remained those of maintaining peace in the countryside and providing food for the cities. The "agrarian distribution" would be completed, but the land tenure system would not be changed. Both peasant and commercial farming would be encouraged, above all by reducing corruption and wastage in the government's agrarian bureaucracy, but urban consumers would still require the protection of subsidized food. Like the SAM and so many other official plans, PRONAL was a worthy ideal, but it seemed unlikely that the 1980s could bring either improvement in the lot of the peasantry or food self-sufficiency for the country as a whole.

10

Indians Body and Soul

I

Proud of its Indian past, Mexico seems ashamed of its Indian present. Government buildings are covered with murals and sculptures extolling the heroism of the Aztecs, while museums house the exquisite jewelry, pottery and artifacts found in pre-Hispanic ruins. But the Indians themselves, the direct descendants of that "glorious past," remain a conquered race, victims of the worst poverty and discrimination to be found in Mexico today. They have lost most of their communal lands, their culture has been besieged and eroded by "civilization" and even their past has been stolen from them. The modern Mexico that has unearthed its Indian roots and elevated Indianism to a symbol of nationhood has little room for the Indians of today.

Yet the strength and resilience of their religious and cultural vision of the world have helped preserve a separate Indian identity. Mexico still has between 8 and 10 million Indians divided into fifty-six recognized ethnic and language groups and speaking over a hundred different dialects. Some of the groups, such as the Nahuas, Mayas, Zapotecs and Mixtecs, number in the hundreds of thousands and dominate the population of entire regions of the country, though often fragmented into small communities. Others, like the Lacandones, Kiliwas, Cucapas and Paispais, have been reduced to a few dozen families. Some still live in almost total isolation and have retained the "purity" of their religious world, although most have gradually absorbed features of the wider *mestizo* environment into their lives. Since the Conquest, all have been waging a battle against assimilation and disappearance. Their very existence is a tribute to their determination to survive.

From the sixteenth century, they suffered virtual enslavement, forced conversion to Christianity and a ravaging of their population by new diseases imported by the conquerors. Many Indian tribes sought refuge in mountains, jungles and deserts, but the larger Indian communities were gradually absorbed by the Colonial economy, providing free or cheap labor on haciendas, in mines and later in small factories. There were occasional Indian rebellions, always put down with great loss of life, but the language and cultural differences among the Indian groupings prevented any nationwide movement from appearing. Indians were officially regarded as minors and protected by legislation, but in practice they were treated—and became accustomed to being treated—as inferiors. (The thoroughly ineffectual decision to order the extinction of Indian languages in 1770 was aimed at accelerating the integration of the Indians, although an estimated 93 Indian languages have in fact disappeared since the Conquest.) Their acceptance of the Virgin of Guadalupe as an Indian deity not only established their formal Christianity but also gave the Spanish Church an additional instrument of control over its remote subjects.

After Independence, the lot of the Indians deteriorated. Many fought —and died—in the War of Independence and in the constant upheavals and conflicts that followed, but they had no voice in the affairs of the state. They comprised a necessary labor force, but few nineteenth-century Mexicans considered that the new nation should find a special place for the Indians. The most progressive concept was to view them as an obstacle to the country's modernization and to seek their integration by destroying their "backward" culture. When Benito Juárez, the only full-blooded Indian ever to rule Mexico, dismantled the traditional system of communal lands to accelerate the incorporation of the Indians, he simply made them more vulnerable to exploitation. "Of the whites who determined the history of the country," one Mexican historian wrote, "Juárez was the whitest of them all."

During the 1910 Revolution, Indians once again provided most of the combatants and casualties. In many areas, they were not even sure why they were fighting: decisions would be made in their name, but they would not be consulted. A recent Tzotzil account of the Revolution in the Chiapas highlands recalled how the Indians were manipulated. "The Bishop of San Cristóbal, Señor Orozco y Jiménez, got the politicians all excited," according to the version now taught in Tzotzil village schools. "But neither the Bishop nor the politicians went to fight. They only handed out guns. Those who went to suffer were the Indians of Jacinto Pérez Pajarito. And to encourage them, the people with money promised the Indians land and the Bishop gave them medals and flags of the Virgin of Guadalupe." In reality, since Indians still comprised almost half the population, their demands were often indistinguishable from those of other peasants. Even the Zapatistas of Morelos and Guerrero, who in the main spoke Nahuatl and wore Indian costumes, were fighting for their communal lands rather than their ethnic identity.

After the Revolution, however, Mexico's ambivalence toward its Indian past and present began to emerge. An intensified search for a national identity led to idealization of the Indian, first through the murals of José Clemente Orozco, Diego Rivera and David Siqueiros and later in museums and folk art. Other intellectuals addressed the question of Indianism within the context of the emerging *mestizo* race. Manuel Gamio, an anthropologist who was the first to excavate the pre-Hispanic ruins of Teotihuacan, considered that the arrival of "other men, other blood and other ideas" from Spain in the sixteenth century had shattered racial unity. José Vasconcelos, a leading philosopher-politician of the period, was consumed by the concept of a "cosmic race"—*la Raza*— emerging in Mexico. "We are Indian, blood and soul," he wrote. "The language and civilization are Spanish."

But while the Indians had gained a certain recognition, their conservative agrarian view of social change was interpreted as an ethnocentric aberration within the new concept of national unity. In 1915, the "revolutionary" novelist Martín Luis Guzmán wrote with outright disdain: "Since the Conquest or even from pre-Hispanic times, the Indian has been prostrate, submissive, indifferent to good or ill, without conscience, his soul reduced to a rudimentary grain, incapable even of hope. To judge by what we see now, the Indian has not taken a step forward in centuries. Without idealism, hope or aspirations, feeling no pride in its race, overcome by some mortal and irritating docility, the Indian mass is for Mexico a weight and a burden." The new revolutionary elite therefore saw no alternative to integrating Indians into the rest of Mexico. As Education Minister in the early 1920s, Vasconcelos felt Spanish-language education was the only instrument for preparing Indian children to enter a Western environment. The idea of Mexico as a multi-ethnic nation had still to be born. The objective was to make the Indian, in Vasconcelos' words, "a civilized member of a modern community."

In the late 1930s, President Cárdenas recognized that Indians required special attention and, being of Tarascan Indian extraction himself, he felt a protective and paternalistic concern for their social welfare. By accelerating the land reform, he indirectly strengthened the territorial base and cultural identity of many groups. But the regime's long-term objective remained that of integration. "The program to emancipate the Indian is, in essence, the same as that of emancipating the proletariat in any country, but one cannot ignore that the special circumstances of his climate, his antecedents and his needs give him a peculiar social physiognomy," Cárdenas once explained. "Our indigenous problem is not to maintain the Indian as an Indian nor of 'Indianizing' Mexico, but it lies in how to 'Mexicanize' the Indian [while] respecting his blood, preserving his emotion, his love for the land and his unbreakable tenacity."

A Department of Indian Affairs was formed in 1936 to oversee this process. The first Inter-American Indian Congress, held in Pátzcuaro in Cárdenas' home state of Michoacán in 1940, also enabled Mexico to promote the idea of giving special attention to Indians elsewhere in Latin America. Then, in 1948, the National Indian Institute (INI) was created to serve as a transmission belt from the rest of society to the Indian communities. During the 1950s and 1960s, the INI established twelve coordinating centers in Indian regions, mainly Chiapas and Oaxaca, through which it promoted Spanish-language education, vaccination programs, more modern farming techniques and closer economic ties with nearby *mestizo* towns. "For a long time," an INI publication recalled with penitence in 1981, "this was seen as beneficial in that it stimulated the modernization of the Indians who were presumed to be poor because they were backward or because their culture prevented them from advancing. It was thought that contact with modern society would help them, but it was not to be the case."

In practice, rather than being strengthened through assimilation, the Indians were simply exposed to what became known as "internal colonialism"—the renewed loss of their communal lands, their exploitation as cheap labor at harvest time and the construction of roads that facilitated both migration by restless young Indians and penetration by the more consumerist *mestizo* lifestyle. A crude process of integration did take place in that, while the country's population grew sixfold in the seven decades following the Revolution, migration and higher mortality ensured that the number of Indians grew more slowly and their share of the total population shrank from 45 percent to 10 percent. But in the process neither the cultural nor the physical welfare of the Indians was safeguarded.

Under President Echeverría in the early 1970s, the Indian question was swept up by a new wave of populism. Not only was he eager to emulate Cárdenas' example in this as well as other areas, but he also felt new pressure to incorporate the Indians into the life of the country. As the poorest of the poor, however, the Indians were still regarded as victims of the country's socioeconomic system rather than heirs to a distinct cultural identity. "As long as Mexico's Indians do not participate in the civic, intellectual and productive life of the country, they will be foreigners in their own land, exposed to the abuse of those who possess most and excluded from the benefits of civilization," Echeverría once noted. Echoing Cárdenas, he said: "We talk of Mexicanizing our natural resources without realizing that it is also necessary to Mexicanize our human resources."

New investment therefore went into building schools, health clinics and roads in Indian areas, while the INI expanded its network of coordinating centers from twelve in 1970 to seventy by 1976. Efforts were made to provide Indians with legal titles to their communal lands: over 600,000 hectares of Chiapas jungle were recognized as belonging to the Lacandón tribe, while the Seri recovered traditional rights over Tiburón Island in the Gulf of California. In October 1975 the government organized the first National Congress of Indian Peoples in Pátzcuaro, which in turn created the National Council of Indian Peoples. Inevitably, the Congress was called on to hail Echeverría's Indian policies, while the new council was immediately coopted by the National Peasant Confederation, which forms part of the ruling party. But it was a daring experiment in that Indians who were separated by language, geography, traditions and levels of development were able to communicate—albeit in Spanish—and identify their common problems.

In the hope of changing traditional *mestizo* disdain for Indian culture, Echeverría also created a new department to promote Indian handicrafts and ordered that the presidential residence of Los Pinos be redecorated in "typical" Mexican style, with Chinese vases and Persian carpets replaced by Indian weavings, paintings and pottery. To the distress of Mexico's European-oriented elite, women attending state dinners for such visitors as Britain's Queen Elizabeth and the Shah of Iran were urged to wear regional Indian costumes instead of the latest Dior creation. Echeverría had a broader nationalist purpose in promoting respect for Indians, even seeing the campaign as a symbol of the government's new identification with the Third World. Indian culture and folklore nevertheless became more visible and accepted among the urban middle classes.

In the academic and bureaucratic worlds involved with Indians, new ideas were aired. Traditional anthropologists who saw the Indian question in strictly cultural terms tended to favor the isolation of the Indians, with the government—and specifically the INI—acting as their protector and principal interlocutor. Marxist sociologists, denouncing this as a "zoological" approach aimed at preserving Indians as objects of research, argued that a separate culture blocked the "proletarization" of the Indians. The only viable policy, the Marxists believed, involved bringing the Indians into the money economy by providing them with health, education, modern farming techniques and jobs. A third line of thinking also emerged: Some liberal anthropologists insisted that the survival of Indian groups enriched Mexico as a whole and that the integrationist approach of the past was wrong. The government should provide essential assistance, but without paternalism and manipulation. It should recognize Mexico as a multi-ethnic society and grant the Indians greater autonomy to run their own affairs. In other words, social development need not imply cultural integration.

Some of these ideas were tested under López Portillo. Programs were initiated to bring drinking water, health clinics and subsidized grain to the most marginalized regions, which included most Indian communities. At the same time, while another twenty-one INI coordinating centers were opened, greater emphasis was given to bilingual education with the idea of preserving autochthonous languages and local culture at the same time as providing a working knowledge of Spanish. As part of this bicultural drive, Indian-language radio stations were opened in areas already within reach of Spanish-language broadcasts, and school books were published in forty languages and eighty dialects. In addition, with some 25,000 bilingual teachers working in remote villages by 1982, a new generation of community leaders was born: some exploited their influence to become *caciques,* but others were able to deal more confidently with nearby *mestizo* power centers.

Although himself a *criollo,* López Portillo seemed to have a paternalistic fascination with Mexico's Indian roots. "Mexico is distinguished from the rest of the world by our ethnic groups," he once told a visiting group of Indians. "What would Mexico be were it not for what you signify and represent? Almost nothing!" On another occasion, he noted: "It is painful to see how, as one climbs higher into the sierra, our Indian groups are to be found, where they have fled injustice and slavery." And he added: "Brother Indians, if any cause is evident in the country, it is the Indian cause. And if to anyone we owe justice—justice as great as your neglect, justice as great as your pain—it is precisely to you." López Portillo's idea of integrating the Indians was that they should contribute to—rather than surrender before—the national culture and thereby help in the fight for "both national identity and national independence."

But this more sensitive language could not transform the condition of the Indians. At one meeting, Espiridión López, a leader of the Mayo Indians of Sonora, asked the President in frustration: "What is the point of having a President dedicated to solving our problems and integrating us with the rest of the population if those officials charged with carrying out the solutions are the very same people who are exploiting us?" When Miguel de la Madrid was campaigning for the presidency in 1982, he once again heard a litany of complaints, not only about the loss of communal lands, the discriminatory system of justice, the shortage of water and the oppressive weight of *cacique* bosses in Indian areas, but also about government policy. "The paternalism of the government, of anthropologists, of political parties and of the churches has taken the initiative away from us," Apolinar de la Cruz, spokesman for the National Council of Indian Peoples, told De la Madrid. "It has corrupted generations, it has blunted our ethnic and class consciousness. Because of paternalism, even public works and services impoverish and indebt us more than they benefit us. And as if that were not enough, paternalism becomes a vicious circle: it aims to protect us until we are ready to act on our own, but it prevents us from developing a capacity to look after ourselves."

De la Madrid pledged to break this tradition by adopting "an Indian policy with the Indians rather than for the Indians," and he too spoke of the importance of preserving Indian culture. "We must respect your culture and your way of life," he told a group of Huichol Indians. "To create a national culture does not mean imposing uniformity. Rather, it means recognizing the diversity and wealth of expressions that comprise Mexican culture. You are part of Mexican culture. If we lose something of Huichol culture, not only the Huicholes but all of us will lose." Still further from the traditional objective of assimilation, De la Madrid noted: "We must recognize a veritable federation of nationalities within the Mexican nationality."

Consolidation of this preservationist thesis revived a simmering controversy over the role of foreign anthropologists and missionaries working in Indian communities. Mexico had long been embarrassed by the fact that most original academic work on the country's Indian culture had been carried out by foreign scientists and, almost as a defense mechanism, leftist academics in Mexico often charged them with being CIA agents or looters of the country's pre-Hispanic ruins. With cultural nationalism on the rise in the 1970s, it became increasingly difficult for foreign—and particularly American—universities and archaeologists to obtain permission to excavate in Mexico. Moreover, concern began to grow about the activities of American Protestant evangelists among Indian communities.

The principal target of criticism was the Summer Institute of Linguistics, a branch of the Wycliffe Bible Translators which was dedicated to translating the Bible into Indian languages and converting Indians to

Protestantism. Paradoxically, the Institute was invited to Mexico in 1936 by Cárdenas, who felt Protestantism might break through the Catholic barriers to modernizing the Indians. Its missionaries, in fact, were the first to write down many of the Indian languages and in this way made an important linguistic contribution. But in tiny Indian communities where Catholic and semi-pagan religious beliefs form an essential part of an entire vision of life, conversions divided villages and eroded their cultural stability. In San Juan Chamula in Chiapas, hundreds of new converts and several missionaries were chased from the community and fled to nearby San Cristóbal after they turned against its traditional deities and rituals.

When the government abandoned its objective of integrating the Indians, the Institute was suddenly seen to be carrying out, in the words of one INI document in 1981, "ethnocide and cultural expropriation." Under pressure from anthropologists as well as the Council of Indian Peoples, a forty-year-old agreement with the Institute was revoked in 1979. Early in 1983, the De la Madrid government announced the Institute's eviction from Mexico. But actually nothing happened. Some of the older missionaries had married Mexicans and had Mexican children and, as individuals, could not be expelled. The U.S. Embassy intervened to counsel against any precipitous action that could be interpreted as religious persecution. Finally, some conservative officials in the Interior Ministry felt the Institute did a useful job in neutralizing the activities of left-leaning Catholic priests. As a result, the Institute continues its work as demands for its expulsion grow.

Still greater disarray was caused in late 1983 when the new director general of the INI, Salomón Nahmad Sitton, was jailed for allegedly taking the equivalent of a $30,000 kickback on the purchase of cloth to be donated by Cárdenas' widow to Indian communities of Oaxaca. Not only was Nahmad highly respected by fellow anthropologists for his honesty and dedication, but he had also won the affection of many Indian groups. There were increasing signs that he was the victim of political infighting within the government. Nahmad belonged to the new school of anthropologists who opposed, in his words, "paternalistic, incorporativist and integrationist policies" that treat Indians "like children." But his efforts to implement a new policy—he had already transferred control of the INI centers among the Yaqui and Chontal Indians to the local communities—were viewed as a threat by entrenched bureaucratic interests. Many leading intellectuals therefore protested Nahmad's arrest, while Indian community leaders began a sit-in at the INI headquarters demanding his release as well as the appointment of an Indian as his successor.

Instead, Miguel Limón Rojas, a political bureaucrat with no previous experience in Indian affairs, was named to the post, inheriting an organization that had lost the support of the most progressive anthropological lobby as well as the most active Indian groups. De la Madrid insisted that Indian policy would continue to seek "a balance between integration of the Indian into development and respect for his cultural identity, a balance which avoids degrading paternalism and promotes his dignified participation in society." But skepticism ran deep. Nahmad himself was released after six months in jail. "There is the fear that Indians and peasants might achieve just living conditions, but the greatest fear is of their rebellion," he said. "It's not that I'm in favor of violence, but the Indians have no alternative when blocked by lack of understanding and bureaucratic obstacles." After his arrest, the INI moved to recover direct control over Maya, Tarahumara, Mixtec and Nahuatl radio stations thought to be too independent. And, not for the first time, many Indian leaders concluded that the politics of "Indianism" was more important to officials than were the Indians themselves.

II

"The Indians are the peasants who live off the worst land in a country of poor land," Fernando Benítez, a writer who has dedicated much energy to recording Mexico's Indian heritage, once noted. "But the real problem is not the Indian himself. Rather it is his relationship with the system: the Indian and something else—the Indian and the land, the Indian and the forests, the Indian and coffee, the Indian and corn and so on. Everything that he owns or produces is the subject of theft or fraud."

In reality, there is no consensus on the correct definition of an Indian in Mexico, with blood, language, costume, territory and economic status used variously as gauges. Strangely perhaps, blood is the least reliable test since most Mexicans have some Indian blood and many "full-blooded" Indians now form part of *mestizo* society. Language and traditional costume, on the other hand, will clearly identify an Indian, although there are Indians who speak Spanish and wear Western clothes who retain the traditions and beliefs of their ancestors. "An Indian is any individual who feels he belongs to an Indian community, who conceives of himself as an Indian," Alfonso Caso, the founder of the INI, once explained. "This group consciousness can only exist when its culture is totally accepted, when the same ethical, aesthetic, social and political ideals are shared, when the individual participates in the collective sympathies and antipathies and collaborates in its actions and reactions."

But the most important factor appears to be whether society treats him —and exploits him—as an Indian: he may be rejected by his community, but not accepted by the outside world; and he may suffer racism even in a country where no color line exists. As Carmen Borja, an articulate young Indian woman, told De la Madrid during his election campaign: "The eyes of the *mestizos* and of the ordinary people of the city are filled with contempt or curiosity or pity when they see us." Not surprisingly, the Indian has defined the *mestizo* as his greatest enemy. "The worst plague that affects us is the *mestizos,*" one Tarahumara leader once said. "No one can do anything against them because they are strong. They rob, they kill our people, they enslave and rape our daughters, they use our land to grow marijuana, they make us drunk." The *mestizo* merely personifies the entire outside world, contact with which the Indian fears but frequently cannot avoid.

The Nahuas, Otomís and Mazahuas of the central highlands, the Zapotecs and Mixtecs of Oaxaca and the Mayas of the Yucatán and Chiapas are all too numerous and dispersed to remain isolated. From the time of the Colony, their worlds were forced to relate to the power centers of new colonial cities. They preserve their languages and cultural identity, but they also travel on buses, work on private farms, depend on markets in nearby towns and trade with *mestizos.* Even though the Indians in these semi-arid regions no longer control resources worth taking from them, like many other peasants they remain permanent targets of exploitation. If the Indian community produces surplus corn, beans or vegetables, almost automatically it falls victim to an intermediary who may buy the crop on credit even before it is planted or may charge an exorbitant rate for transporting the goods to market. Indian women who carry their own weavings to the nearest town find they must pay bribes to local police to "rent" a street corner.

Similarly, their cultures are besieged by new influences. Many Indian villages are reachable only by rough track, yet trucks somehow get through to supply their little stores with Coca-Cola, canned food, beer, cheap firewater and other products of civilization, all of which are sold at prices higher than in urban areas. Radio and in some cases television advertising serves to reinforce this new consumption, showing a world that is also coming within reach. Unavoidably, the Nahuas, Otomís and Mazahuas who live closest to Mexico City are being absorbed by the *mestizo* way of life faster than most Indian groups. There are said to be 1.5 million Indians living in urban areas, half in Mexico City itself. In some cases, Nahua villages on the outskirts of the capital have been virtually overrun by the expanding metropolis. In other cases, Indians come to Mexico City in search of work, and although they return regularly to their villages, they pick up Spanish and adopt different habits. Since many Indian men no longer wear their traditional costumes, they are barely distinguishable from other peasant migrants working on building sites or sweeping streets. Indian women—mainly Mazahua and Otomí—wrapped in shawls and carrying tiny babies can be seen selling fruit or chewing gum on crowded sidewalks or simply begging from passersby. Their need to survive physically inevitably threatens the survival of their culture.

For the Mayas, the growth of tourism on the Yucatán Peninsula has brought a different form of relief from their enslavement by henequen. The crop was introduced after the War of the Castes of the mid-nineteenth century as the agricultural solution to the region's thin topsoil, and after the large henequen haciendas were broken up in the 1930s, the Indians continued to grow it on small plots. But since World War II, synthetic fibers have shattered the world demand for henequen. Because no other suitable crop has been found to grow in the area, the government continues to subsidize its production, processing and marketing as well as the survival of some 57,000 Maya *ejidatarios* and their families. This subsidy—$30 million in 1983—has been the price of social peace in the region, but it has not alleviated severe poverty and chronic malnutrition. When construction of Cancún on the Caribbean coast began in the 1970s, thousands of Maya men soon found new jobs, first on building sites and later in hotels. They left behind wives and children to look after their plots and moved abruptly into a strange new world where even the language and habits of the *mestizos* were dominated by those of the "gringo" tourists.

On the Pacific coast, a similar phenomenon has occurred with Acapulco, which since the 1950s has drawn tens of thousands of Nahuatl-speaking Indians from the nearby poverty of Guerrero state. Some simply bring their fruit to the local market or hawk their handicrafts along the beaches and then, after a few days, return to their communities. But others have settled in hillside slums and, exposed to television and other cultural pressures, have gradually turned their backs on their past. Once their children attend an urban school, they refuse to speak the language of their parents and grow up as *mestizos*.

Indians nevertheless only leave their ancestral homes, temporarily or permanently, when local conditions effectively expel them. The 20,000 Mazatecos of Oaxaca were physically dislodged by development when their communal lands were flooded by the Alemán Dam in the 1960s. A new dam on the Balsas River threatens to flood the Guerrero villages that produce most of the *amate,* or bark paintings, sold elsewhere in Mexico. In 1981, after the Chichonal volcano erupted and covered the region in lava and ash, the Zoques of western Chiapas were dispersed over a large area and lost their territorial identity as a culture. Frequent droughts also decimate local corn production and force Indian men to migrate in search of the money needed to buy their families' corn. But there can be no greater disruption than the loss of communal lands: the larger ethnic groups that are most exposed to exploitation by the Western world are therefore also those most likely to migrate.

In many regions, however, Indian communities remain trapped in a colonial system that finds its expression in the figure of the *cacique,* the local boss who controls their economic and political relationship with the rest of Mexico. The *cacique* may be the principal local landowner, he may own all commerce in the town that dominates an Indian region or he may purchase all the crops produced by the Indians. (One *cacique* of the Chamula region of Chiapas was once described as "the owner of the candles, the incense, the liquor, the Coca-Cola and the lives of the Indians.") In some places, the *cacique* is himself an Indian. Whatever the case, the essence of the matter is the Indians' chronic indebtedness to the *cacique,* the fact that they are continually working to pay off their debts to him. To forestall any challenges to his power, the *cacique* will maintain his own corps of *pistoleros* and strong political links with the state government. He is the person who at election time can deliver overwhelming Indian support for the ruling party and can make sure that "agitators" from opposition parties are run out of the region.

In the case of the Triqui Indians of western Oaxaca, local *caciques* intent on exploiting timber reserves on communal lands have stimulated decades of intratribal violence by providing different communities with guns. As the Triquis fight out their internal differences, the *caciques* not only enrich themselves but also maintain effective political control. In the early 1980s, supported by leftist and civil rights groups elsewhere in Mexico, a Triqui Combat and Unification Movement was formed, but several Triqui leaders were murdered when the movement tried to run candidates in municipal elections. "With political power," the Indian leader Apolinar de la Cruz explained, speaking of the phenomenon nationwide, "the *caciques* prevent our remote villages from being provided with adequate food, health, education and communications because it is evidently easier to control a hungry, sick and ignorant people."

Like much of Mexico's rural population, the Indians suffer from parasites, respiratory ailments and such tropical diseases as malaria, all aggravated by chronic malnutrition. Alcoholism, however, is perhaps their most serious affliction. In some areas of Guerrero, intoxication is an essential part of many traditional ceremonies. In the arid regions of Hidalgo state, for example, Otomí children are given *pulque*—the fermented, nutritious juice of the maguey cactus—from an early age. In Oaxaca and other regions, Indian men spend their minimal savings on *mezcal,* frequently becoming indebted to the local *cacique* in the process. Elsewhere, numerous versions of rough *aguardiente* or firewater are readily available. The sight of drunk or even unconscious Indians in the *mestizo* towns closest to their homes is therefore tragically familiar. And when they sober up, they are vulnerable to extortion, accused of running up bills or buying animals or even committing crimes during their stupor.

Outside their communities, Indians have few places to turn for assistance. Some Catholic bishops, among them Samuel Ruiz of San Cristóbal, Arturo Lona of Tehuantepec and José Llaguno of the Tarahumara region, have long been identified with Indian interests, channeling outside assistance to them and denouncing to the rest of the country the repression and exploitation they suffer. Some local INI representatives also win the trust of Indian groups by showing willingness to confront the rest of the official bureaucracy on their behalf. Those who help the Indians, however, are generally suspected of radicalism: after taking office as governor of Chiapas in December 1982, for example, General Absalón Castellanos identified his three greatest problems as "the INI, the doctors of Comitán and the diocese of San Cristóbal." (The doctors were involved in helping Guatemalan refugees who had crossed into Chiapas to flee army repression in the Guatemalan highlands.) Similarly, because he spoke out against repression by government-backed *caciques* in his Oaxaca diocese, Bishop Lona was accused of supporting a leftist coalition that won the municipal elections in the Zapotec region of Juchitán in 1980.

Not infrequently, however, an Indian leader's feelings of resentment toward the *mestizo* world are awakened by his first contact with the INI itself, when he discovers that decisions affecting his community have already been taken by local bureaucrats. Compared to other centers of power, the INI is too weak to protect Indians against state or municipal police or to help defend them in the courts before judges vulnerable to corruption and political pressure. At times, INI officials have even tried to integrate Indian villages into the national judicial system, which only further undermines their autonomy. Indian leaders frequently complain that monolingual Indians are tried in Spanish without interpreters, routinely convicted and then left to linger for months or years in jail without recourse to appeal.

In few areas has this internal colonialism survived more cruelly than in Chiapas, which borders on a similar social structure in Guatemala. Many of the "colonialists" are descendants of German migrants, but the Luttmann, Gissemann, Bernsroff and Pohlenz families of the Soconusco Valley long ago allied themselves to the wealthy *mestizo* politicians whose haciendas dominate the more mountainous regions of the state. Today, about 35 percent of the state's farmers own only 1 percent of the land, while 1 percent of the landowners control 45 percent of the territory. But growing population pressure among the fourteen Indian groups in Chiapas has created new tensions. In some cases, communal lands have been stolen by *caciques*. In other cases, Indians have been able to rent scrub, but once it has been cleared for planting, the land has been recovered by its owner and used for cattle grazing, provoking angry clashes. No longer able to maintain themselves on their remaining plots, the Tzeltales, Tzotziles, Tojolabales, Chamulas and other Indians are forced to provide the cheap labor needed by privately owned cotton and coffee plantations, transported in crowded trucks, earning the equivalent of one dollar per day and sleeping in unhygienic wooden shacks known as *galerones*.

There is a tradition of Indian insurrection in Chiapas, and while the Tzotzil and Tzeltal uprising of 1712 and the Chamula siege of San Cristóbal in 1869 could not occur today, land and political problems frequently lead to violence, with mostly Indians the victims. Because the Army, state police and *caciques* have maintained tight control over the state to prevent emergence of an organized Indian movement, a highly publicized march by some five hundred Indians from various Chiapas villages to Mexico City in October 1983 came as a surprise. Their demands—for the arrest of assassins of Indians, for the release of jailed Indians, for higher wages—were familiar, but in political terms it seemed unthinkable that the state governor had "allowed" the Indians to carry their petitions as far as the National Palace. Federal authorities stepped in with new promises and persuaded the Indians to return home peacefully. Yet the very presence of proud but impoverished Indians in the capital city struck the rest of society like a momentary pang of conscience.

The Indians who fled to the jungle, mountain and desert "zones of refuge" following the Conquest did so in order to retain the independence of owning and working their land. The land—the concept of a territorial base—is an essential part of any Indian group. But eventually even these safe havens were penetrated by civilization. In the jungles of the Sierra Madre west of Chihuahua, the long-isolated world of some 70,000 Tarahumara Indians is being disturbed by timber companies that have no interest in the welfare of the native population. In Nayarit and Jalisco, new roads are suddenly making the remote mountain farming and cattle lands owned by the Huichol Indians accessible to—and therefore coveted by—*mestizos*. Even the Chiapas forests ceded to the Lacandones by Echeverría in the 1970s are being exploited by outsiders. As the land is lost, the cultural identity is unavoidably eroded.

In the deserts of Sonora, the resource that gave value to the land of the Yaquis was water. From the time of the Conquest, the warrior Yaquis had stubbornly refused to accept defeat and through much of the nineteenth century fought off white settlers encroaching on their land beside the Yaqui River. At one point, half the tribe fled to Arizona and many others were deported to the Yucatán, but the remaining Yaquis organized frequent and often bloody uprisings against the *yoris,* or whites. Finally, in 1936, just a decade after the last revolt, President Cárdenas gave them title to 750 hectares of land—a tiny part of what they had once owned—and recognized their right to self-government. But after the Alemán administration built dams on the Yaqui River and channeled its water into irrigation canals, the Indians lost access to the most vital element of their survival. Today, surrounded by the most productive land in Mexico, the Yaquis live in pitiful poverty. "Is this the Revolution?" a Yaqui elder asked General Cárdenas thirty years after he had recognized the tribe's communal lands. The story goes that Cárdenas could not hold back his tears.

From the Cucapas close to the United States border to the Mames on the border with Guatemala, the stories about the welfare of the Indians have an almost monotonous ring: the Indian tribes speak different languages, follow different traditions, worship different gods and wear different clothes, yet they share a common economic and social fate. De la Madrid once referred to "their intolerable and shameful condition," but his good intentions could do little to alter it. The Indians remain imprisoned not only by poverty but also by an entire system of exploitation from which the only apparent escape is surrender to the *mestizo* way of life.

III

Perhaps the only thing not stolen from the Indians has been their soul, their inaccessible world of strange languages and dialects, of hidden pride and strong hierarchy, of deep religious sensitivity and powerful ritual, of mystery and magic. It is the continuity of communion with this past—not the past of museums and statues but the past of spirits and beliefs—that has protected Indian culture from destruction. Destiny is predetermined by the gods, customs are established by ancestors and monitored by their spirits, problems are answered by shamans or traditional priests and discipline is maintained by elders. Dominated by fatalism, life involves following the footprints of the past. "Innovators are unknown in this world which copies itself indefinitely and almost automatically," wrote Fernando Benítez. And it is a world in which material suffering is more than compensated for by spiritual reward.

The strength of this culture is evident in its influence over the rest of *mestizo* society, visible not only in food, colors and language but also in traditions, beliefs and behavior. Even among the Indian groups scattered across the nation there are powerful themes and attitudes that unite them. Religion and nature are always interwoven, artistic expression is essential to their identity, loyalty to the community is unquestioned and wealth is shared. Their legends, passed on by word of mouth, tell of the origins of the earth, sun and moon and the birth and death of ancient gods. Their ethnocentricity is complete; their religious beliefs and myths assure them that they are at the center of the world.

Conversely, the dispersal of Indian communities ensures a great variety of cultural and religious expressions. Many groups numbering just a few thousand members preserve their language and costumes accompanied by their array of gods, while even the larger tribes are broken up into village-states with their own distinct visions of life. Among the Zapotecs of Oaxaca, for example, forty-two different dialects are spoken and communities just a mountain apart can barely understand each other. The 800,000 or so Nahuas, on the other hand, are spread over sixteen different states, from Guerrero, Puebla and Veracruz to as far north as Jalisco and San Luis Potosí, sharing a common language but few customs and beliefs.

This variety is also expressed in the hand-woven costumes and artisan work of the Indians across the country. In many areas today, Indian men wear traditional clothes only for religious festivals, but their wives and daughters do so proudly on a daily basis, seeing their clothes as extensions of their identity. Their weavings not only will distinguish a particular community in any ethnic group but will also be imbued with religious significance. Similarly, the paintings, carvings, and, above all, masks made by many Indian groups will be linked to similar cycles of nature or religious occasions, yet will vary sharply in style from one region to another.

Indian communities have survived, however, because of their internal religious and political cohesion. Functioning almost like theocratic societies, they subject their members to the strict rules and beliefs dictated or interpreted by elders and shamans. Most Indian groups were converted to Christianity by Dominican, Jesuit or Franciscan missionaries during the sixteenth and seventeenth centuries, but abandoned stone chapels in remote parts of the country bear witness to the neglect that followed. Eventually, even the Church accepted the Indian syncretism of Christianity and paganism, with ancient deities often assuming the formal identity of Roman Catholic saints but preserving their traditional powers, invariably linked to the weather, the harvest, physical health, defense against outside enemies and devotion to the dead. The variety of gods is enormous, although worship of the "Indian" Virgin of Guadalupe provides a powerful unifying thread among most Indian groups. The seemingly drab world of mud roads and mud huts, then, comes alive through magical legends that reinforce the philosophy, religion and social mores of the people.

Typically, in the case of the Yaquis, not only religious authority but also internal government and external contacts are in the hands of the elders. Although numbering only 22,000, the Yaquis are divided into eight communities, each run by a governor who is chosen for one year and by four elders who are named for life. The governor need not be an elder, but he must be renowned for his honesty and morality because he controls the community's water and land and serves as a judge. Further, all dealings with the *yoris* must be approved by the assembly of the eight governors and thirty-two elders which meets every Saturday under a tree at Pueblo Vicam, the traditional capital of the tribe. On one occasion, in 1983, the personal envoy of the governor of Sonora was refused permission to address the Yaqui leaders because the governor had not come in person. In this group there is an accumulation of native wisdom and lore that holds the society together.

The Indian community is in turn a projection of the family structure. Women rarely have a religious role and therefore, with the exception of the matriarchal society of the Juchitán area, are considered social inferiors. Their lot is to work, cook, have children and to suffer beatings in silence when their husbands are drunk, while their daughters are rarely allowed to attend school even when one exists in the community. Women also play a key role in the family economy, visiting nearby markets while their men are in the fields and being responsible for the sale of weavings or vegetables. Still more important, many beliefs and traditions are kept alive by women, not least those relating to their own purity and humility. A 1981 INI study recorded the advice that a Nahua mother from the Sierra de Puebla gave to her daughter: "When you look at the world, think that everything is looking at you. The trees are looking at you and so are the stones on the road. The eyes of the sun are fixed on you. That's why you should be clean. You should walk with elegance, your step should be soft so as not to hurt the earth. Hold your head up high and your hair in place. If men look at you, lower your eyes, but never stoop, not even when you're old. If you stoop, you'll shrink and become ugly. Everything is looking at you. That's why your image must be good."

The family is dominated by the eldest male, usually the grandfather or great-grandfather, who owns all the wealth and exercises all authority. Marriages between teenagers are still often arranged by the fathers of the future spouses—marriages outside the community take place, but are rarely approved—and confirmed through the exchange of gifts. In some cases, a wife must literally be stolen by a young suitor, with intense negotiations between the two families then preceding the formal wedding. Among the Seri, the father of the bride traditionally receives a bow and arrows, skins and meat as well as a promise to be looked after in old age by his future son-in-law. Young boys are naturally expected to emulate their fathers as hunters, fishermen or farmers and, not infrequently, they are discouraged from attending school, since "unnecessary" knowledge will eventually tempt them to migrate from the area. But attitudes vary depending on experience: a bilingual teacher who has remained loyal to his community will often succeed in filling his classroom.

No world is more full of magic than that of the Huicholes, who inhabit remote mountain villages in Jalisco and Nayarit and whose religious beliefs form a cosmic vision of life in which all of nature plays a part. They farm corn and own cattle, but an extraordinary amount of their time is devoted to the ritualistic preservation of their faith, which, since they chased out the Franciscan missions in the seventeenth century, includes only such odd remnants of Christianity as two Christs. In the panoply of deities, Nacawe, goddess of fertility, is the most important. To fit Christ into their culture, they gave him the role of a surveyor who came to measure the land and count the mountains and rivers. Every detail of their costumes, including the feathers in their broad-brimmed hats, has special meaning. Everything about their five religious centers, which to outsiders look like a sad collection of mud-floored shacks, has great significance. For them, even animals, plants, rocks and rivers are sacred.

Each spring, Huichol men go on a pilgrimage of over a hundred miles to the desert hills of San Luis Potosí which they consider to be their holy land. There they collect the hallucinogenic peyote plant which is essential to the religious fiestas that follow upon their return home. Their artwork—brightly colored "paintings" made of wool—reflect the three symbols of life: the peyote, the god of food-gathering peoples; the deer, the god of hunting peoples; and corn, the god of farming peoples. Comprehension of the origin and meaning of life itself is passed on from father to son through the poetry of legends. The Huicholes are gentle and humorous people, but naturally suspicious of all outsiders, who, if they come uninvited, are automatically ostracized.

Living in poverty, every Indian group has invented and preserved its own paradise which is lit up by the colors, candles and fireworks that seem inseparable from religious fiestas. The widespread use of masks, which may represent animals, spirits or historical, religious or mythical figures, underlines the importance of symbols that either threaten or protect. Similarly, dances ostensibly centered on the image of a Catholic saint have additional meanings indecipherable to outsiders. Alcohol is frequently an essential vehicle for communion with the spirits, although hallucinogenic plants, such as the peyote and the "magic" mushrooms of Oaxaca that became fashionable among U.S. hippies in the late 1960s, play the same role.

Because good health is a gift of the gods, medicine, magic and religion are inseparable, and understandable only to the *curandero,* or medicine man, who often doubles as the shaman. The inherited knowledge of herbal medicine that *curanderos* possess enables them to cure many ills, but they often do so in the context of magical beliefs and rituals. Such widespread ailments as the *espanto,* or shock, and the *mal de ojo,* or evil eye, can only be cured through ceremonial cleansing, the technique for which varies with each Indian group. Some *curanderos* will use a fresh egg to draw out the evil spirit, while others will appear to remove animals from patients' stomachs. Magic, both black and white, contributes significantly to sustaining an entire way of life. In this introspective world that they alone can understand, the Indians find the freedom and rewards denied them in the outside world.

The Indians' identity, then, will survive as long as their culture can resist the onslaught of individualism, materialism and consumerism inherent in modern development. Under siege, it is slowly giving way. Each new generation includes more Indian children who will eventually pass over to the *mestizo* side. Religious festivals are celebrated with less dedication than twenty or thirty years ago. "They prefer to watch television," complained Jacinto Gasparillo Anica, president of the Nahua Supreme Council, referring to the Indians of Guerrero, "rather than participate in the annual ceremony on May 2 asking for rain."

Yet, having withstood the military and religious conquests of the early sixteenth century, the disapproving protection of the Spanish Crown for three hundred more years, the loss of much of its territorial base in the nineteenth century, the integrationist efforts that followed the Revolution and the even more aggressive commercialism of the past four decades, Indian culture has proved its resilience. While lost traditions are mourned, many others survive. If the concept of a multi-ethnic nation is more widely accepted, Indians might be allowed a stronger political voice. But even if *mestizo* society fails to recognize the national patrimony represented by Indian culture, a distinct Indian identity will exist for many decades hence, keeping alive an essential part of Mexico that has been more readily recognized when dead.

11

The Social Crisis:
Catching Up with the Population

I

More than most Latin American countries, Mexico is formally committed to improving the lot of its population. The social ideals of the 1910
Revolution have been enshrined in the Constitution and in a thick body
of legislation, while the need to invest in political stability has spawned
a huge social welfare bureaucracy that spends billions of dollars annually. At this formal level, great progress has been made: the stated
objective is to end inequality and injustice, the people understand their
rights and the government has accepted its obligations.

But the reality is sadly different. More than seventy years after the
Revolution, Mexico's social profile is barely distinguishable from countries of the region that have had no revolution. The health of the rural
and urban poor is far below even the government's own minimum standards, with more than 30 percent of the population outside the reach of
state medical attention. Various degrees of undernourishment, including
acute malnutrition, affect 60 percent of Mexicans. Average schooling in
the country is around five years, with 15 percent of adults still illiterate,
while housing conditions for two-thirds of the population are blatantly
unsatisfactory.

The legacy of centuries of backwardness inherited by the Revolution
posed a challenge that no political system could quickly overcome. Even
the conservative attitudes of much of the peasant and Indian population
added obstacles to the process of social change. Yet it was better health
care, above all massive vaccination programs, introduced since the 1930s
that brought the greatest problem: infant mortality rates dropped suddenly, birth rates remained high and the country was swamped by a

surge in population. At the very time that Mexico initiated a period of rapid economic growth after World War II, its population began to rise rapidly—from 13 million in 1900 to only 20 million in 1940, but then to 51 million by 1970 and 77 million by 1984. Today, 56 percent of the population is under the age of 20. It became impossible for expenditures on health, education and other social services to keep up with demand.

More controllable variables also contributed. Successive governments were skillful in handling political pressures and preventing the demand for more radical social action from escalating into unrest. Their immediate priority was political stability rather than social justice, and though they built schools, hospitals and a large network of subsidies to appease the poor majority, those sectors with greater influence received more attention. If trade unions, peasant movements and urban squatter organizations had been stronger, the state would have felt obliged to do more. Even for those expenditures that have been made, the results have been tarnished by the chronic inefficiency, corruption and politicization of the social bureaucracy.

Yet no matter how large a regime's political commitment to combating entrenched poverty, social programs alone cannot alter a country's economic structure. In Mexico's case, the chosen economic strategy seems to work against social improvement. Not only has the economy been unable to create sufficient jobs—the most effective instrument for social amelioration—but it has also permitted and even promoted concentration of wealth. It can be no coincidence that Mexico and Brazil, the two Latin American countries that have enjoyed the fastest economic growth since the 1950s, display the most skewed distribution of income and wealth in the Americas.

During the steady growth of the 1960s, the purchasing power of Mexico's minimum wage increased 8 percent annually, but relatively few new jobs were created and therefore family income grew more slowly. During the more volatile growth of the López Portillo regime, an unprecedented 800,000 new jobs were created each year, but inflation eroded the real wages of those earning the legal minimum by 35 percent between 1976 and 1982. The fact that many of these new jobs survived the economic trauma of 1983 and 1984 contributed significantly to preserving political stability, yet the cost to the population at large was apparent in sharply reduced living standards. While open unemployment was held to around 12 percent in 1984, another 40 or so percent of the work force fell outside the formal economy into the vague category of "underemployed."

The assignment of resources within the industrializing economy also gave little priority to the creation of permanent jobs, with industrial and commercial assets concentrated in a small number of firms that employed relatively few workers. One study indicated that around 5 percent of commercial outlets controlled over 80 percent of sales, but employed only 40 percent of workers in this sector. Similarly, by definition, in capital-intensive industries, each new job cost between $250,000 and $500,000. The two booms and crises between 1970 and 1982 further strengthened large corporations to the detriment of small and medium-sized industry and commerce: both to grow and, subsequently, to avoid bankruptcy, they absorbed relatively more credit without creating or preserving a commensurate number of jobs. During the latest recession, it was the ability of small family businesses and the informal or parallel economy as a whole to absorb extra labor that provided a cushion of social security. Thus the rewards of expansion fell to the rich, while the burdens of recession rested on the poor.

In a country where the annual per capita income, some $2,000, is one-quarter that of the United States, the privileges enjoyed by the few must inevitably be financed by the many. According to government estimates in 1977, the wealthiest 20 percent of the population controlled 54.4 percent of all income. Some changes have taken place over the past thirty years, notably the expansion of the middle class, which has gained a greater share of income at the expense of both the top elite and the chronically poor: between 1968 and 1977, the income share of the top 5 percent fell from 27.7 to 23.9 percent, and that of the bottom 50 percent from 18.3 to 16.2 percent. But in practice even the middle classes—professionals, well-placed bureaucrats, middle-level company executives, owners of small businesses—still belong to the wealthiest 30 percent that earn 73 percent of the country's total income. Thus, while Mexico's very rich live in a style that would put all but a few American millionaires to shame and the middle classes enjoy the standards of suburban Americans, its majority lives in degrees of poverty ranging from mere survival to outright misery.

Mexicans working with the country's marginalized sectors soon conclude that their efforts are largely neutralized by the existing economic model. If people are unemployed, they receive no unemployment benefit from the state and must improvise a job or depend on relatives. If fortunate enough to earn the minimum wage, which most peasants and many workers do not, they are unable to feed or house their families decently. If they live in crowded shacks with open drains and contaminated drinking water, they are unavoidably condemned to poor health. Yet while the social crisis is a product of the economic model, no President since Cárdenas has sought to attack the problem at its roots, none has established redistribution of wealth as the centerpiece of his policies. Instead, social injustice has been accepted as the price of economic development: the pie must grow before it can be sliced differently.

To judge by rhetoric, the problem of chronic poverty has seemingly worried every administration. In his inaugural address in 1970, Echeverría noted: "There remain serious deficiencies and injustices that endanger our achievements. The excessive concentration of income and the marginalization of large human groups threaten the harmonious continuity of development." Six years later López Portillo said: "If I could make any appeal to the dispossessed and marginalized groups, it would be for forgiveness for not yet lifting them out of their misery. But I also say to these people that the entire country is aware and ashamed of our backwardness in this respect and for this very reason we will join together to achieve justice through law." In December 1982, it was De la Madrid's turn to concede: "Social inequality remains one of Mexico's most serious problems." In the midst of the worst economic crisis since the Revolution, he felt forced to add: "While the crisis continues, we cannot advance in the process of social justice. The immediate danger is a daily deterioration in the situation."

Even before these three Presidents, the state had responded institutionally to the social dimension of development. In the 1920s and 1930s, great emphasis was placed on building a national educational system. In 1943, a major step was taken to improve medical services for urban workers with the creation of the Mexican Social Security Institute (IMSS). In 1961, the Basic Foods Corporation, CONASUPO, was founded to ensure that the poor sectors were supplied with subsidized food and, later, with clothes and simple furniture. Since 1970, still more government instruments have appeared. Echeverría formed a Workers' Housing Institute, INFONAVIT, aimed principally at financing new housing construction for unionized workers. In the late 1970s, López Portillo channeled resources into a program for depressed zones and marginalized groups, COPLAMAR. Following political tradition, De la Madrid dismantled this monument to his predecessor, and COPLAMAR's functions were transferred to eight different ministries.

Beyond these key institutions, there are hundreds of smaller offices, funds and programs—including such oddities as the centuries-old national pawnshop known as the Monte de Piedad—which address specific social problems. Many deal with the depressed countryside, trying to promote production of assorted cacti, sisal and other native flora with commercial possibilities. More recently, a series of "integrated rural development" projects—known as PIDER programs—has been financed by the World Bank, with target communities assisted in cultivating new cash crops, raising productivity and improving the quality of life. Like his predecessors, De la Madrid also launched an Arid Zones Development Program, in this case using a $95 million loan from the World Bank to stop the spread of the desert and to improve economic opportunities and social conditions for 10 million people in these zones. Viewed in isolation at least, many of these programs are symbols of hope.

Still more important, subsidies have been used as an indirect form of income distribution. The price of corn tortillas, beans and cooking oil has long been held down by the government, helping those whose diets depend on these staples. Public transportation in Mexico City and most other urban areas is also subsidized, while free education and health care involve the transfer of resources from the government to the poor. With 25 percent of federal budgets devoted to "social development" and ten times more spent on education than on defense, the government's broad response seems impressive.

In practice, the social bureaucracy has displayed many of the ills that affect the rest of the government. Because resources are limited, they are invariably assigned where political pressures—rather than objective needs—are greatest. Although per capita income in Mexico City is five times higher than in Oaxaca, for instance, per capita social expenditure is nevertheless larger in the capital. Similarly, since organized labor is a key pillar of the ruling system, unionized workers are attended with greater care than the country's peasants. Federal and state government employees, now numbering some 3 million, are also successful at pressing for special health, shopping and other privileges. CONASUPO stores are even established in urban middle-class districts, providing subsidized goods to sectors that could afford to pay commercial prices.

Not infrequently, ambitious government programs are hampered by poor coordination between different offices. Apart from private medicine, health care is provided by three large organisms and dozens of semi-autonomous institutes. State governments have their own social welfare programs which at times duplicate the efforts of the federal bureaucracy. And when a President commits himself to a particular program, resources will often be reassigned arbitrarily from other programs to satisfy the immediate political requirement. Perhaps most depressing, the government's social welfare programs are riddled with corruption. Influence or bribes are required before workers can obtain housing credits from INFONAVIT. Basic grains assigned for distribution to the marginalized zones are frequently resold by officials before reaching their destination. The selection of medicines used by government hospitals may be influenced by kickbacks from pharmaceutical companies. And because of the risks of greater corruption, no system of food stamps has been developed to exclude the more affluent from the benefits of subsidies.

Despite the government's considerable effort in a period of rising birth rates, the final verdict on its social achievements must be provided by the existence—and, during the latest economic crisis, the growth—of unacceptable poverty. In 1970, 11.2 percent of the population was considered deeply impoverished, while 53.9 percent was living below the government's own minimum welfare standards. Sixty-four percent of the population received no medical attention, almost 50 percent did not consume meat or eggs regularly, 75 percent lived in homes without drainage and 70 percent of adults had not completed the six years of primary school education required by law. In reality, in health and education, these results showed slight improvement over the situation in 1960, and the results of the 1980 Census* were expected to suggest continuing progress. Yet gradual reduction in the percentage of Mexicans living below the poverty line could not disguise the fact that, in absolute terms, the number continued to grow.

The obstacles to resolving major social problems through the existing economic model are well illustrated by Mexico's chronic housing deficit. The right to a "dignified home" is now included in the Constitution, but the government looks principally to market forces to satisfy it. Unlike countries where housing construction is a key gauge of economic activity, Mexico has developed few mechanisms to encourage this sector. While the poorest peasants and slum dwellers must build their own adobe huts or wooden shacks, no CONASUPO-style program exists to advise them on basic design or to provide them with raw materials at cost. Similarly, young middle-class couples are unable to buy a house or apartment, not only because mortgages usually cover only 50 percent of the price, but also because interest payments, which can run up to 60 percent annually, are not tax-deductible. This in turn applies greater pressure on the price of rented property, and encourages speculation. Construction companies receive no fiscal incentive to build low-cost housing and therefore concentrate on either major government projects or homes for upper-income groups.

Different studies have provided wildly varying estimates of the dimensions of the problem. In the early 1980s, the housing deficit was put at

*Statistics in Mexico are unreliable, but the mishandling of the 1980 Census was unprecedented: beyond general population figures, no results had been published by 1984, forcing different departments to develop their own parallel social indicators.

4 million homes by the Budget and Planning Ministry, at 6 million by the National Consumer Institute and at 7.8 million by COPLAMAR. Further, in 1979, a now defunct National Housing Program estimated that some 10.9 million new homes would be needed between 1978 and 2000. Beyond dispute is the fact that new housing construction is lagging far behind demand and needs. INFONAVIT, the government's main housing program for workers, completed 316,000 low- and medium-cost homes between 1972 and 1982, and by the mid-1980s was still financing construction of only some 60,000 homes per year. Nationwide, another 100,000 or so new homes—excluding improvised rural and slum dwellings—were being built privately and by other government agencies each year. But the deficit—and therefore overcrowding among all classes—continued to grow. Neglected by social programs and seemingly resistant even to economic growth, this problem threatened to become a major cause of political irritation among the urban middle and lower classes.

A key factor in the housing crisis, as in other social problems, has been demographic pressure. With the population growth rate jumping from 1.1 percent in 1940 to 3.5 percent in 1970 and the total population rising by 150 percent over the same period, the government was simply unable to keep up: each year, more people received social services and more people also went without them. Successive governments refused to tackle the population issue. In 1970, with 2 million Mexicans being born every year, Echeverría campaigned for office with the motto that "to govern is to populate," and in his inaugural address he declared that "population growth is not a threat but a challenge." Yet, just three years later, he was persuaded to change his views by his administration's difficulties in alleviating social problems. Treading carefully to avoid political and religious mines, he finally launched a program euphemistically tagged "responsible parenthood."

By 1976, however, the idea of family planning had gained greater acceptability, enabling López Portillo to channel new resources into the campaign and to establish the goals of reducing the population growth rate to 2.5 percent by 1982 and 1 percent by the year 2000. The government saw the population problem in global terms, but it wisely avoided coercion or even indirect incentives, opting for a persuasive strategy built around the slogan "A small family lives better." Although the upper and middle classes had long practiced birth control, the government's program quickly satisfied a latent demand in poor urban sectors. Women in particular were sensitive to the problems of feeding, clothing and educating large families, and while older women found they could now avoid their sixth or seventh child, many younger women began planning their families from the moment they married. In the countryside, in contrast, not only was it physically more difficult to provide the service to tens of thousands of tiny communities, but the *machismo* of peasant men and the religious beliefs of women created additional obstacles.

Nevertheless, by 1984, the growth rate was down from its 1977 peak of almost 3.7 percent to 2.3 percent, and the program was proclaimed as one of the most successful so far in the Third World. The De la Madrid administration ratified the goal of 1 percent growth by the end of the century, noting that "population control is a key to our economic development." With television and radio soap operas, books, brochures and posters being used to disseminate information, priority was given to extending family planning to rural areas, where, as in most developing countries, the poorest couples still have the largest families.

Yet even the dramatic drop in birth rates brought little immediate relief to the government. With the country's population exceeding 77 million in 1984 and heading for 100 to 110 million by the year 2000, the number of new babies each year was virtually unchanged from 1970. Further, the government was still struggling to provide health care, education and housing for the 40 or so million Mexicans born over the previous two decades. Thus, while family planning should ease demand for social services by the end of the century, over the short to medium term the government still faces overwhelming obstacles in trying to improve the quality of life. The future performance and design of the economy will have a crucial impact on such variables as employment levels, food consumption and housing construction, all of which have so far failed to keep up with the population. But in the extraordinarily complex areas of health and education, the government will remain principally responsible for finding solutions.

II

The fact that the principal causes of death in Mexico—pneumonia and enteritis—fall into the category of avoidable diseases underlines the difficulty of separating health questions from broader socioeconomic problems. "Most health problems have their origin in the poverty, ignorance and insalubrity existing in the countryside and in urban slums," a COPLAMAR study noted in 1979. "A large part of the population lives in unhealthy conditions and in a state of undernourishment that make them particularly vulnerable to infectious and parasitical ailments." While vaccination programs have largely eliminated malaria, typhoid and measles as major causes of death, pneumonia and enteritis persist through poor hygiene and malnutrition. In the early 1970s, for example, the death rate from intestinal infections in Mexico was ten times higher than in Cuba and a hundred times higher than in the United States.

Not surprisingly, the highest death rates—dramatically higher in the case of children under the age of five, who still account for 29 percent of all deaths in Mexico—are to be found in the largely Indian and deeply impoverished states of Oaxaca, Chiapas, Guerrero and Puebla. Government officials concede that statistical data are poor, if only because many births and deaths in rural districts go unrecorded, but they estimate that infant mortality in these states runs at around 100 per 1,000, over twice the national average. Adding to the problems wrought by poor diets, contaminated drinking water and open drains, the number of hospital beds and doctors per capita is far lower than elsewhere in the country. In 1983, Chiapas' 2.5 million inhabitants had access to just 253 hospital beds and 521 doctors. The familiar circle is thus complete: these peasants are the unhealthiest because they are the poorest; and because they are the poorest, they cannot press for greater health care.

The socioeconomic indicators for Mexico as a whole hide sharp differences between regions and classes within the country. While current statistics show that over 20 percent of the total population eats no eggs or meat and 40 percent consumes no milk, in some states eggs, meat and milk are absent from the diets of 80 to 90 percent of the inhabitants. And while 40 percent of preschool children are considered healthy, only 10 percent fall into this category in the southeast. The impact of economic crises—either local droughts or nationwide inflation—will often be measurable in the food intake and even death rates of certain sectors of the population. In some remote districts, referred to technically as "supermarginalized," experts from the National Nutrition Institute have identified "generational holes": the age composition of a community will show gaps indicating crisis periods during which virtually all babies died.

Indirectly, by breaking down resistance to avoidable ailments, malnutrition is probably the principal cause of death and ill health. Once again, statistics vary: in 1983, the Nutrition Institute estimated that 66 percent of the population consumed less than the required minimum of 2,000 calories per day, while the Budget and Planning Ministry put this figure at around 40 percent; and the Institute estimated that 21 percent of Mexicans ate well, while the Ministry calculated only 18 percent. Still more alarming, the National Food Program (PRONAL) reported in 1983 that, after rising slowly between 1956 and 1966, nutritional standards in the country as a whole fell over the next decade, recovered during the late 1970s, but are again deteriorating, as evidenced dramatically in the falling demand for food among a growing population and the elimination of protein from the diets of many Mexicans. Even on the optimistic assumption that rapid economic growth will resume in 1985, the nutritional levels of 1982 will not be recovered until 1988, by which time the number of malnourished Mexicans will have risen from 30.5 to 33 million.

Once again, the nutritional crisis is inseparable from the broad economic policies that have been pursued since the 1940s. The perennial stagnation of agriculture has limited most peasant diets to corn tortillas and beans, and following the 1981 drought, consumption levels fell still lower. Yet two-thirds of the undernourished live in urban slums. Millions of peasant migrants have been persuaded by advertising to replace their traditional—and subsidized—diets with more expensive and still less nutritious "junk" food, such as sodas, cakes and potato chips. After the United States, Mexico is in fact the world's largest market for both Coca-Cola and Pepsi-Cola. According to the government, slum dwellers on the outskirts of Mexico City may suffer as much malnutrition as peasants in, say, Oaxaca. In contrast, in tropical coastal areas, where fruit grows wild, nutritional levels are higher.

The very process of industrialization has thus obliged the government to deal simultaneously with the symptoms of old poverty and new poverty, of rural backwardness and excessive urban growth. While the diseases most identified with underdevelopment could not yet be eradicated, the past forty years have also brought a sharp rise in ailments normally associated with developed societies. Heart disease, which ranked tenth as a cause of death in 1940, had risen to third by 1975, while cancer went from fifteenth to sixth place over the same period. Additional health problems have been caused by industrial and vehicular pollution of air, ground and water. Migration from the countryside has accelerated disintegration of the family nucleus, which in turn has stimulated alcoholism —said to affect 6.5 million Mexicans today—and the phenomenon of abandoned children, many of whom have become addicts of either narcotics or, more frequently, of paint thinner, glues and other substances that cause brain damage.

The sharp rise in life expectancy—from 37.5 years in 1930 to 64.4 years in 1980—and the accompanying drop in total death rates—from 230 per 10,000 in 1940 to 72 per 10,000 in 1975—nevertheless reflect the major effort made by the government to improve health standards since World War II. New health institutions had emerged from the Revolution and important campaigns against yellow fever, tuberculosis and malaria were launched in the 1920s and 1930s, but it was not until the 1940s that an entire welfare structure was founded. The key development was the creation of the Social Security Institute (IMSS) in 1943 as a gesture to organized labor, although coincidentally the government established the Ministry of Health and Assistance to attend those not covered by the IMSS. Subsequently, government workers were given their own social security institute (ISSSTE), and a child welfare system was formed, while Petróleos Mexicanos, the Federal Electricity Commission, the National Railroads, the Defense Ministry and the Navy all organized special health services for their employees.

The urban population was the principal beneficiary of these services. The IMSS, in particular, financed by contributions from workers, employers and the state, emerged as a powerful and wealthy organization, providing not only health services but also numerous other welfare benefits, such as recreational facilities, for around 32 percent of the country. The Health Ministry, in contrast, dependent entirely on the federal budget, had insufficient resources to tackle the endemic problems of a larger and poorer share of the population. In 1975, for example, while the IMSS had one doctor per 375 potential patients, each Health Ministry doctor was theoretically responsible for 4,087 people. Similarly, the IMSS had one bed per 776 members as against one bed per 2,695 people in the Health Ministry's hospitals. It was calculated that, in 1983, 58.5 percent of resident doctors were attached to the IMSS, 26.1 percent to the ISSSTE and only 25.4 percent to the Health Ministry.

The need to coordinate the often overlapping activities of these and other institutions led to the creation in 1983 of the so-called Health Cabinet, headed by the Health Minister, but the IMSS remained the dominating force. When the government sought to extend the family planning campaign to the countryside, the IMSS was the chosen instrument. And when, in the most important rural health program to date, COPLAMAR set up hundreds of small health clinics in marginalized regions in 1979, the program was financed and executed by the IMSS. By 1983, the IMSS was responsible for the health not only of its 5.8 million members and their families—totaling some 27 million people—but also of around 10 million impoverished nonmembers.

Poor planning has nevertheless plagued the health sector. In a country where almost half the population never sees a doctor, some 20,000 doctors cannot find jobs. During the 1960s and 1970s, many students were drawn to choose medical careers by the dream of a lucrative private practice. Subsequently unable to finance establishment of their own clinics, they were forced by the shortage of slots in government hospitals to work as laboratory assistants or as salesmen for pharmaceutical companies. But the government shared responsibility, since it subsidized state universities to produce doctors who could not be absorbed. Finally, in the late 1970s, measures were taken to restrict the intake of medical undergraduates. In 1983, fifty-seven medical schools, twelve of them private, graduated 14,000 young doctors, but only one-quarter of them found openings in government institutions. At the same time, there were three times as many student doctors as student nurses.

As in most developing countries, large multinational companies—American and Swiss in the main—dominate Mexico's pharmaceutical industry. In the past, they have been almost beyond government control. In theory, the Health Ministry tested all medicines before licensing for sale in Mexico; in practice, medicines were available which in the United States were either still at the experimental stage or had been withdrawn following identification of dangerous side effects. Similarly, the Commerce Ministry was charged with controlling the retail price of medicines, yet pharmaceutical companies developed ways of repackaging or renaming products to extend profit margins. In 1984, however, the government moved to reorganize the industry, to the vocal dismay of the foreign companies. New regulations required manufacturers of 400 "priority" medicines to display the generic name of a product as prominently as its trademark, with all similar medicines priced equally by the government. The health bureaucracy would also give preference to purchasing goods from Mexican companies, which currently control only 28 percent of the market. A total of some 24,200 medicines have nevertheless been approved for sale, and about 5,000 of these are readily available.

Compounding this problem, Mexicans frequently prescribe medicines for themselves without consulting a doctor. The tradition has its roots in rural sectors where, in the absence of both doctors and medicines, women inherit a knowledge of herbal cures which enables them to treat many ailments. But the medical bureaucracy has discouraged the use of medicinal herbs. In urban areas, where pharmacies are everywhere to be found, it is common practice for friends, relatives or simply the pharmacist himself to recommend medicines, including antibiotics, which can be bought over the counter without prescription. As a result, the urban poor consume too much medication for either their physical or their economic well-being.

The rapid growth of the health bureaucracy has combined with the increasing demand for medical attention to produce a service of patchy quality. The government's specialist hospitals maintain high standards and provide excellent attention for those with influential friends, yet ordinary Mexicans turn to the IMSS and the Health Ministry only when they cannot afford private treatment. The most frequent complaints are that outpatients must wait hours in crowded clinics before being received by overworked and "authoritarian" doctors, although stories of worse treatment abound. Exploiting this distaste for official services, many private clinics are to be found even in poor urban zones, where they claim to offer both faster and better attention. Most private medicine, however, is practiced by expensive foreign-trained doctors in more affluent residential districts, such as the Polanco neighborhood of the capital, where entire high-rise buildings are occupied by private clinics. The wealthy, on the other hand, fly to Houston for both regular checkups and emergency treatment. Nationwide, there are more private than government hospitals, although most are small and their coverage is limited to about 20 percent of the population.

In the marginalized zones where medical problems are most severe, the government must carry the load alone. Traditionally, health care has been provided by medical graduates who are obliged to serve one year in the field before receiving their formal certificate. The accompanying problems, however, are enormous. Rural clinics are often several hours' or days' walk from peasant villages, and not infrequently are poorly supplied with medicines. Many young doctors also face resistance from local peasants accustomed to being treated by herbal healers, or *curanderos,* who in turn warn patients against visiting the competing clinics.

When COPLAMAR launched its program to provide staple foods, improved housing, clean drinking water and basic health care to Mexico's 18 million poorest inhabitants in 1979, it faced many of these problems. But while food and housing standards remained virtually unchanged, construction by the IMSS of some 2,000 small health clinics in Mexico's most remote communities for the first time brought medical attention within reach of many poor peasants. Clearly, the socioeconomic environment—water pollution, ignorance and malnutrition—continued to condemn the population to ill health, yet where clinics were run by enthusiastic doctors or paramedics and were well supplied with medicines, death rates fell. It was through this new structure, maintained even after COPLAMAR was formally dismantled in 1983, that the government hoped to provide family planning to the rural poor.

The struggle to raise Mexico's health standards toward those of a developed country, however, will continue well into the twenty-first century. Rural poverty, undoubtedly the principal medical problem, is so much a part of more complex questions that it is likely to resist eradication for several decades. The government also has still to address the new health hazards posed by destruction of the urban environment and the lack of controls on industrial emissions: an environmental protection bureaucracy is in place, but it is politically weak and technically ineffective. And, despite the success of past vaccination campaigns, the government has yet to switch the focus of its health care from curative to preventive medicine.

III

Education also involves tackling the past and the future simultaneously, bearing the social obligation of eliminating illiteracy and ignorance as well as facing the challenge of preparing youths to develop the country's economy and safeguard its national identity. It is therefore of as much concern to economists and politicians worrying about the country's future as it is to parents anxious to see their children fare well in their careers. As in other social areas, while great progress has been achieved over the past forty years, evident in the 25 million students participating in different levels of the educational system in 1984, education in Mexico is still far from satisfactory.

At the heart of the problem are the seemingly conflicting pressures of quantity versus quality. Following the Conquest, education was placed entirely in the hands of the Roman Catholic Church, and though the clergy was unable to keep up with demand when the country's population began to grow, priests and nuns still provided the children of the country's elite with good schooling. Recognizing the Church's role in education to be a key instrument of its political influence, Benito Juárez established the principle of "compulsory, free and secular" education in the 1857 Constitution, although Church-run schools survived. As the nineteenth century drew to a close, growing awareness of the need for a national educational system resulted in a law declaring primary education to be obligatory in the capital. Yet, nationwide, probably fewer than 20 percent of the children were attending school at the time of the 1910 Revolution.

The 1917 Constitution once again asserted the monopoly of state-provided secular education, with priests and nuns specifically banned from operating their own schools. When the prominent intellectual José Vasconcelos served as Obregón's Education Minister between 1920 and 1924, a nationwide structure of state primary schools was founded. The question of quality, however, remained controversial, and efforts to suppress Christian education helped bring on the Cristero uprising in western Mexico in the late 1920s. But while in Mexico City and other large cities Church-run schools continued to exist, the government reaffirmed the principle of universal education. In 1934, the Constitution was even amended to define education as "socialist," aimed at giving students "a rational and exact concept of the universe and of social life." Angry protests finally brought its revocation in the 1940s, but in 1960 the government took the crucial step of introducing "free and compulsory" textbooks, which not only helped the poor but imposed a degree of uniformity on education.

Despite the unprecedented investment and the almost geometric increase in the number of schools, teachers and students, however, the architects of Mexico's new educational system could not have anticipated the population boom that began in the 1940s. As a result, Mexico has still to resolve the quantitative problem of basic education. In 1983 over 15 million children—87 percent of those eligible—were being attended by some 400,000 teachers in 76,200 primary schools. But 47 percent—75 percent in rural areas—would nevertheless drop out before completing the obligatory six years' schooling. Similarly, although school attendance has improved steadily, with average schooling said to have jumped from 3.3 to five years between 1970 and 1982, there is still 15 percent total illiteracy and 25 percent functional illiteracy.

Education has nevertheless served as a vehicle for social improvement and mobility. Many parents make great sacrifices to ensure that their children attend secondary school or even a university. But socioeconomic pressures also work against education. School attendance is lowest among Indians, peasants, migrants and slum dwellers. There are fewer schools per capita in poorer regions: some go years without teachers, while others have one barely educated youth teaching all six primary grades. Many uneducated parents also see little need for schooling, pressuring their children from an early age to earn their keep or to work in the fields. Primary school teachers, particularly in the countryside and in slum districts, note that pre-teenage children are frequently too undernourished to study, falling asleep in class because of hunger, and repeating grades until they drop out for reasons of boredom or frustration. With rare exceptions, the state neither seeks out and obliges children to attend school nor provides free milk and other staples to improve nutritional standards.

Successive governments have sustained—and financed at extraordinary cost—the principle that education is available to anyone who seeks it. In the 1970s, while population growth averaged 3.1 percent per year, enrollment in primary schools rose by 10 percent annually, with a special effort made to incorporate peasant children in small rural communities. Between 1970 and 1983, the number of students attending high school tripled to 3.3 million, while the number of university students quadrupled to almost 1 million during the same period. In 1960, of students entering primary school, one out of forty-three graduated from a university, but twenty years later the ratio had improved to one out of nineteen. The Autonomous National University in Mexico City (UNAM), accommodating some 320,000 undergraduates and pre-university students during the 1983–84 school year, is a monument to this egalitarian ideal. While many youths consider that they have a right to a university education, the government prefers to see ambitious—albeit academically unqualified—youths struggling for space on the campus than joining the restive army of the unemployed. In Greater Mexico City, though, the dropout rate from the UNAM and other state universities is 69 percent.

Administrative, economic and political problems have accompanied this dramatic expansion of education. The Education Ministry's 950,000 employees—mainly teachers at all levels—account for almost three-quarters of all central government employees and everything from training them and monitoring their performance to assigning them and paying them is a bureaucratic nightmare. The 600,000 or so primary and secondary school teachers also belong to a powerful and conservative union (SNTE) which has been run since the early 1970s by an old-style political boss, Carlos Jonguitud Barrios. The SNTE forms part of the pro-government labor movement—Jonguitud himself served as governor of San Luis Potosí state between 1979 and 1985—but it strongly defends its own interests and has resisted efforts to improve teaching standards. In contrast, some university teachers and administrative workers belong to the SUNTU coalition of leftist unions which have paralyzed institutions on numerous occasions in order to press wage demands.

While the state has achieved many of its quantitative targets, academic standards at all levels have suffered, and from a political point of view, even primary school education is no longer an effective instrument for inculcating basic national and moral values in children. Among the stated purposes of government education are promotion of honesty, hard work, a spirit of service, nonviolence and nationalism as well as respect for the family, the authorities and the law. But because these ideals often clash with those propagated at home or on television, schools are seen to be failing in their responsibility. Whenever the government goes beyond teaching the "three R's," it faces angry protests from parents' associations. In 1974, the Echeverría administration provoked an outcry when it modernized primary school textbooks to include some analysis of "capitalism" and "imperialism" and warm references to the Cuban Revolution. A decade later, there were still demands for revision of the most controversial social science textbook and for restoration of religious education in public schools.

The problem of quality has become still more urgent in higher education. Research is poorly financed and generally not oriented toward designing "alternative technologies" suitable for Mexico's level of development. Little effort is made to guide undergraduates toward the courses most needed by the economy, with the resulting surplus of doctors, lawyers, economists and architects and a chronic shortage of chemists, physicists, mathematicians and other scientists. The relatively easy entrance to universities and the overcrowding of classrooms have in turn eroded teaching standards. Many companies complain that they must retrain economists, engineers and agronomists who have graduated from a university. The government itself is a huge employer of graduates, and while inefficiency can be disguised, senior officials are also sensitive to the poor quality of their staffs.

But qualified teachers are difficult to find. Of the UNAM's 26,000 lecturers and professors, one-third have less than two years' experience. Absenteeism, a chronic problem, was aggravated by the latest economic crisis, since many professors—a Ph.D. was earning between $400 and $600 per month in 1984—were forced to moonlight in either the public or the private sector in order to sustain their families. As potential centers of dissent, most universities are also permanently exposed to political manipulation by both government and leftist parties. Since the brutal crushing of the 1968 student movement, the government has gradually brought the UNAM under tighter control. Leftist groups have come to dominate the university workers' union and classes are frequently disrupted by "solidarity" meetings on behalf of every imaginable cause, but student activism has posed no challenge to the government. When provincial universities—such as those of Sinaloa, Puebla and Guerrero—have come under the influence of the Unified Socialist Party of Mexico (PSUM), "punitive" cuts in subsidies provided by both federal and state authorities have soon been reflected in poorer education.

One result of this phenomenon has been a parallel expansion of private education. The country's elite continued to send their children to private —often Church-run—schools without interruption throughout this century, but over the past thirty years the urban middle classes have followed suit. Today, few medium-level bureaucrats would think of placing their children in a government school. Private schools have therefore multiplied in residential neighborhoods, while private universities— among them, the Autonomous Technological Institute of Mexico (ITAM) and the Ibero-American, Anahuac and La Salle universities in

Mexico City, as well as the Guadalajara Autonomous University and the Monterrey Institute of Technology—have expanded, particularly since the 1970s. Although they still account for only 14 percent of university students, 120 of Mexico's 260 institutes of higher education are now in private hands. Further, the state has recognized the need to provide scholarships for top students at U.S. and European universities and, when they return with doctorates and master's degrees, to attract them to government work.

This educational focus, in turn, has had a "denationalizing" effect on an influential sector of urban youth. For example, middle-class children attending schools where fluency in English is greatly emphasized do not receive the kind of nationalistic education still encouraged in state-run schools. In some institutions operated by Americans and other foreign nationals, the history of the United States or the British Empire may be stressed more than that of Mexico. Increasingly, senior officials in government are persons who have been educated first privately and later abroad, and who therefore have minimal direct experience of the country's more acute social problems. Thus, while the quantitative approach had the worthy objective of "democratizing" education, the need to find quality education in private schools has had the effect of widening the cultural gap between the elite and the majority.

The post-1982 economic crisis complicated the situation. Tuition fees in private schools jumped beyond the means of many middle-class parents with two or three school-age children, while the cost to the government of sending scholars abroad for postgraduate studies became exorbitant. The government therefore felt great pressure to improve the standard of state education to levels acceptable to the middle classes and to find ways of enabling state universities to produce the elite students that previously graduated abroad. For the first time, the search for excellence became the regime's principal educational priority.

In response, the De la Madrid government grandiosely proclaimed a "Revolution in Education," even though economic and political limitations permitted little more than a gradual reform. The first step was to decentralize education by transferring resources and responsibility for education to state governments, initially at the primary and teacher-training levels. By reducing bureaucratic obstacles, education could be designed to fit the varying needs of different regions. Since this would also weaken the centralized power of the teachers' union, the plan was strongly resisted by the SNTE leadership. If implemented, it could convert education into a key political issue in provincial elections, above all in more developed northern states where the PRI was already facing mounting opposition. Decentralization could widen the educational differences between different regions, with the poorest states assigned the role of dealing with the most backward sectors of the population.

In higher education, the problems were more severe. In 1984, the central government provided 91 percent of the resources of federal universities and 61 percent of the funds of provincial state-run universities, but this was insufficient to satisfy demand. The UNAM alone received $360 million, but turned away 60,000 prospective entrants. Limited by its own budget restrictions, the government urged universities to generate more income of their own, either through higher tuition fees or research contracts. But while the influx to primary school should peak by the late 1980s, the number of students receiving higher education will double to almost 2 million by 1990 and continue to grow after that. Currently spending five times more on primary than on higher education, the government may by then be able to reallocate some resources. But the political pressure to meet quantitative targets will remain strong. The UNAM's rector, Octavio Rivero Serrano, warned late in 1983: "We cannot renounce university education for the masses because this is one of the country's social conquests."

Yet the quality issue cannot be postponed. To date, the government has barely explored the educational possibilities of television and it has paid insufficient attention to vocational training, which can better prepare youths to enter the job market. At present, Mexico produces five professionals for every technician, when, ideally, the ratio should be reversed. In trying to improve the standards of higher education, its options are also limited: it can continue to send graduates abroad for master's degrees and doctorates, though risking an increased "brain drain" because of Mexico's devalued salary scales; or it can stimulate and expand smaller elitist universities and existing research institutions, such as El Colegio de México and the Center for Economic Studies (CIDE). But if it does neither, the vacuum will be filled by private universities that will propagate political values which the state does not share.

The educational policies adopted in the coming years will have a fundamental impact on the future shape of Mexico. The government cannot forget that half the country's children still fail to complete the legal minimum of six years' schooling, but it must also prepare the designers, engineers, computer technicians, economists and even politicians of the next generation. While emphasis on quantity worked in the past to the detriment of quality, the government cannot allow a new focus on quality to neglect still-unsatisfied quantitative requirements.

I 2

The Family Safety Net

I

The family's survival as a powerful and deeply conservative institution has been crucial to maintaining Mexico's political stability. Today it is the single most powerful reason why economic crisis has not translated into social unrest. It is through the family that traditions, values and religious beliefs are passed on. Much of the informal economy that sustains millions of Mexicans revolves around family farms, stores, mechanics' shops, restaurants and other small businesses. The extended family offers a structure of support to the young, the aged, orphans and visiting relatives, as well as greater security—a meal, a roof, even a job—than that provided by the state. In reality, society reflects the family. But the paternalistic and authoritarian structure of the family also seems to prepare Mexicans to accept the hierarchical social arrangements that prevail in the country at large.

The continuing strength of the family is all the more remarkable in a country that has been convulsed by social change over the past forty years. The population boom and accompanying migratory wave disrupted many rural families as sons and daughters went looking for work, leaving older parents and grandparents behind in the *campo*. The children of middle-class and affluent families began traveling and studying abroad, learning foreign languages and adopting American fashions. Industrialization and urbanization also shattered a once dominant provincial way of life, spawning new attitudes and behavior. The role of the Church and religion diminished among the new middle classes. Sexual freedom grew and easy access to birth control methods freed many poorer women from "permanent" pregnancy, gradually altering the man-woman relationship. Every day, there are more professional women, divorces, unmarried mothers, abortions and abandoned children.

Yet the family has changed less than the country. For most Mexicans the family remains the pivot of their lives. It is not a matter of choice: it is simply the way society is organized. Over 90 percent of Mexicans still live in a nuclear family, and while traditions and social pressures vary between regions and classes, they are united by their adherence to the tribal rules of each extended family. Closed to outsiders, the family is enormously self-sufficient. Interwoven attitudes toward sex, social rituals and religion are shaped at home. The full range of passions—of love, hate, jealousy, devotion and violence—can be lived out in the family. Social life involves being with relatives, children have no reason to play with anyone but siblings and cousins, and new spouses are viewed as intruders. Mexicans need few friends because they have many relatives.

On birthdays and saints' days, on weekends and during vacations, family groups gather almost instinctively. They wander through city parks with their platoons of children, they drive in caravans of dangerously overcrowded cars for picnics in the countryside or they congregate at the home of a grandfather; there is never a reason—or even an excuse —to be alone. Among the poor, an entire family, including cousins and nephews who have arrived from the countryside, will live under a single roof. More affluent families often build homes for their married children in the gardens of their estates or buy up adjacent houses on the same block. The only substitute for a relative is a *compadre*—the godfather of a man's child—but even he is accepted because spiritually he has joined the family.

Those with jobs look to place unemployed relatives: in homes with extensive domestic service, the maid, chauffeur and gardener may belong to the same family; on the floor of a small factory, most of the staff will often be related; in an office, cousins or sisters-in-law of secretaries have the best chance of filling an opening. Within the government, nepotism at the highest levels may be frowned upon, yet entire families will be brought into the bureaucracy by some relative with influence. Many of the largest economic groups in the country are still family businesses, bequeathed like a hacienda from father to son, with numerous relatives assured places in top management. But more is involved than a simple duty to look after a relative: the very insularity of the family teaches Mexicans to distrust society as a whole and they feel safer—less vulnerable to betrayal—if surrounded by relatives.

At the heart of the powerful emotions and simmering neuroses that maintain the family's cohesion is the relationship between men and women. And in many ways this has not changed since pre-Hispanic times. Under the Aztecs, women had numerous obligations, but few rights: they prepared food, went to the market, collected water and firewood and wove clothing; they looked after children, taught them a sexual identity, social and moral values and how to worship the gods. They could not choose their husbands—this was usually done by their fathers—but they were expected to have many children and, if proven barren, could be returned to their families. The religious importance of procreation was evident in the Aztec perception of childbirth as a battle, with women who died during labor themselves becoming warrior deities called Cihuateteo. Whereas female infidelity was considered an aberration worthy of public execution, men were permitted several wives and mistresses. There even existed prostitutes, known as Ahuianime, or "happiness givers," who were protected by the goddess of pleasure, Tlazolteotl.

At the time of the Conquest the Spanish, unlike the Pilgrim Fathers, landed in the New World without their wives, prompting them to take —often to kidnap—Indian women as mistresses, thus perpetuating into the Colony the submissive role of women under the Aztecs. But the Spaniards also brought their own religious prejudices and sexual ambivalences: women were required to make a home and procreate as well as to provide pleasure to men, but the same woman was not expected to do both. Once women arrived from Spain to marry the more prominent colonizers, mistresses remained essential and infidelity became institutionalized. The deeply rooted concept that women are inferior, that their purpose is to serve men, was thus reinforced throughout the Colonial era.

During the Revolution, women loyally accompanied their men as they wandered from battle to battle, cooking for them, caring for their wounds and not infrequently burying them. But even this social disruption did not release women from their assignment as abnegated wives and mothers. To men, the very idea that women might play some other, more public role was viewed as a threat. In 1938 Colonel Crescencio Trevino Adame, a veteran of the Revolution, warned President Cárdenas against giving women the vote. "Women are in this world to care for the home and not to get involved in politics, neither to meddle in the affairs of men nor to work in offices, above all government offices," he wrote in a letter. "This thing that they are talking about, this women's vote, would be madness." Women were finally given the vote in 1953 but, with rare exceptions, they voted as instructed by their husbands, and the reform had no impact on the family structure.

Today, during civil marriage ceremonies, the judge still frequently reads from a letter by a nineteenth-century politician, Melchor Ocampo, in which he defined the respective roles of husband and wife: "The man, whose sexual attributes are principally courage and strength, should and will give protection, food and guidance to the woman. The woman, whose principal attributes are abnegation, beauty, compassion, perspicacity and tenderness, should and will give her husband obedience, pleasure, assistance, consolation and counsel, always treating him with the veneration due to the person that supports and defends her." This text is no longer an obligatory part of the ceremony, but it is generally omitted only upon special request, which, if coming unilaterally from the bride, is itself cause for suspicion.

The inspiration for these precepts, however, was religious, echoing an Epistle of St. Paul read at church weddings, which urges the groom to love his wife as "saintly and immaculate" and the bride to respect and obey her husband. Even though Melchor Ocampo was an anticlerical liberal, he recognized that many of the attitudes of the Mexican family are founded in religion. As a political force, the Church has lost much of its influence, yet the Bishops' Conference claims that 92 percent of Mexicans have been baptized into the Catholic Church. Because of separation of Church and State, only civil weddings are legally valid, but over 70 percent of couples also marry in church—"under the two laws," as it is phrased—and 9 percent marry only in church. Many poor couples in fact make common-law marriages, but among the middle classes it is considered improper to cohabit until after the religious ceremony. Priests are also invariably on hand for funerals, even those of senior government officials who belonged to the anticlerical political system. Several Presidents—Avila Camacho, Alemán and Díaz Ordaz among them—are buried in consecrated ground.

Mexicans in general are not devout. Church attendance, particularly in urban areas, is falling, as is the ratio of priests to population. Attitudes toward divorce are changing: thirty years ago, a middle-class woman who left her husband for another man would find herself ostracized by her own family, but today divorce is rarely viewed as a sin. The growing use of birth control devices also suggests indifference to specific Church strictures. Even abortion is common among poor women who consider themselves good Catholics, although resistance from the Church has blocked efforts to legalize the practice.

Yet religious beliefs, customs and superstitions—more than the institution of the Church itself—form an intrinsic part of family culture. In the countryside, the local priest—known affectionately as *el padrecito,* or "little father"—is a powerful community leader, influencing women who turn to him for advice and support and assigning men the responsibility of buying the fireworks, flowers and food for popular religious festivals. Still more important, both the Bible and the Church foster the traditional man-woman relationship, endorsing the domination of men, while expecting women to emulate the abnegation, modesty and gentleness of the Virgin Mary, represented powerfully in Mexico as the Virgin of Guadalupe. The lines of authority thus take on a moral quality: an obedient woman is a good woman, while an independent woman must somehow be motivated by some sinful intention.

At risk of caricature, a typical Mexican family can still be stereotyped. The father is the undisputed figure of authority who has little respect for —or communication with—his wife. He expects to be served royally at home, but he spends much of his time and money drinking with friends or visiting his mistress. He pays minimal attention to his children, although he attaches great importance to having a male firstborn who carries his name. The mother, rejected as a wife and a lover by her husband, tries to alleviate all her frustrations through her children, above all pampering her sons in search of allies against the father and of substitutes for his affection. When her children marry and leave home, she struggles to maintain her authority, since her only possible role is as a mother.

Male offspring in turn soon learn that both mother and sisters attend to their wishes, but they resent their father's repression and neglect of the family and come to worship their mother as a long-suffering saintly figure. As they grow up, these attitudes are reflected in their sex life. Their first sexual experience is invariably with a prostitute or a maid, but they seek a maternal figure for a wife. Yet she not only falls short of the "perfection" of their own mother but, cast in the role of "pure" procreator, she is also rejected as a satisfactory sex partner. The young husband therefore seeks a "bad" woman—one unlike his mother—for his sexual distraction. And the cycle is repeated.

The idea of a strong family is inseparable from that of a family controlled by a paternalistic figure of authority. At its head is the figure of the grandfather or even great-grandfather, who serves as the defender of traditions and values as well as the arbiter of internal disputes and who, as the main property owner, can also use his relative economic power to preserve his authority. As they grow old, grandparents can expect to be cared for by their children and grandchildren and, in the case of surviving grandmothers, to be treated with special reverence. The chain of command, however, runs through the men of the family, with perhaps four generations carrying the same first name at any one time, each controlling his own family but accepting his place in the larger family structure. The young Mexican is thus born into a highly stratified institution dominated by power, hierarchy, loyalty and submission, and he knows that, with time, he will rise within it.

Yet, in many ways, this too is a mask. The real strength and stability of the family are provided by the women. Because of the large number of unmarried mothers and abandoned wives and children, about half the country's nuclear families are headed by women. Even in unbroken families, women resolve most of the problems: they are responsible and reliable, they provide continuity and they control the emotional environment. Above all, a mother determines the behavior and attitudes of her young son. "Be *macho* like your father," she urges him. While this *machismo* involves such concepts as defense of honor and physical courage designed to impress men, it is accompanied by a strong sense of sexual insecurity that is overcome only by treating women with a combination of distrust and repression. The Mexican man therefore remains emotionally undeveloped, unable to escape a dependent attachment to his mother, guilty about his sexual drives and obsessed by the fear of betrayal.

Women nevertheless waver between the conflicting roles—mother and lover—that they have been assigned. Daughters soon discover that they can almost seductively manipulate their fathers, while popular culture—women's magazines, television soap operas and Mexican movies—typecast women as submissive pleasure givers. They are also instructed by their unavoidably jealous mothers on the virtues of obedience, modesty, sexual repression and virginity. They see in their own family that they —rather than their brothers—are expected to be dutiful and responsible. They must therefore win their man with a suggestion of seduction visible through an image of respectability: through flirtation, they can control the relationship until the moment of conquest. After marriage they are taught to tolerate the shortcomings of their once-idealized husbands. As one popular saying puts it: "That man isn't perfect, but he's yours." It is upon these imperfections that they can eventually build their own power base inside the new family.

II

Among the Indians and peasants of Mexico, family customs have barely changed in centuries, with the cycle of life almost reduced to a ritual in which roles are predetermined. Families are large, not only because birth control is nonexistent and offspring amount to "as many as God decides," but also because more children mean more farm hands and greater security when parents grow old. Life is tough, and from an early age everyone is assigned a job in the home, the sons helping their father in the fields and the daughters sharing the duties in the home. Young girls care for their siblings: as early as the age of seven or eight, they will carry their baby brothers strapped to their backs. Discipline is strict, misbehavior is punished physically and communication within the family is minimal: discussion would suggest options, and options would imply a questioning of the father's authority.

The woman's role is nevertheless crucial, not only because she works incessantly but also because she transmits to her children the religious beliefs, legends and customs that help preserve family and community life. In a few regions of Mexico, notably around Juchitán, women dominate commerce and even exercise political influence, but in general the peasant woman learns the virtues of silence and modesty. She shies from talking to strangers, and she would not join her husband at the table with a visitor. Among some Indian groups, marriages are still arranged, with the bride's family expected to provide a dowry of sorts. In the rural southeast, because male members of a family must object to a daughter's leaving home, she may even be taken by force by her boyfriend, with peace restored between the families only after their first child is born. If an unmarried daughter becomes pregnant, it is usually possible to oblige the boy to marry her. Boys usually marry in their late teens; girls marry between the ages of fourteen and sixteen and are still having babies by the time they become grandparents.

The poverty of the rural sector has led many parents to accept the migration of their teenage sons as a way of supplementing the family income. Some young men leave home to pick crops in the United States or in more prosperous agricultural regions of Mexico, at first following some relative who has settled in the United States or has experience in following the harvests. Many then return in the fall to pick the family's own corn. Others head for urban areas, again usually inspired by the "success" of some relative who will accommodate them, initially seeking temporary jobs on construction sites and eventually looking for more stable employment.

Parents are more reluctant to allow a daughter to leave the *campo,* not only because she may be needed at home but also because cities are viewed as centers of sin. Economic pressures are nevertheless strong. If an aunt or cousin is already well established in the city and promises to watch over her and if the daughter pledges to return home regularly with a share of her earnings, permission is often forthcoming. The jobs open to a barely literate teenage girl, though, are limited: she may find a job in a textile sweatshop or on a factory assembly line, but almost certainly she will end up working as a maid.

The impact of city life on young migrants is striking. Many experience a sense of liberation when they escape the authoritarian dictates of their fathers, but they confront a new feeling of insecurity in the noise, size and anonymity of the larger cities. On any day, groups of men in straw hats and *huarache* sandals can be seen walking in single file along the streets as they might along a narrow mountain path or standing in horror as they ponder how to cross a busy downtown avenue. On weekends, maids on their days off are immediately distinguishable as they wander nervously arm in arm through Chapultepec Park in Mexico City, their eyes lowered shyly to avoid any suggestion of encouragement to passing boys.

The change is difficult. Many employers pay less than the legal mini-mum wage and dismiss those workers who complain. Maids find them-selves working as hard as they did at home and, on occasion, even become the targets of sexual molestation by the adolescent sons of their employers. Yet, with time, they learn to function in the city, becoming more fluent in the slang of the urban poor, trying different foods and eventually buying cheap city shoes and clothes. Television serves as a bridge between old and new cultures, introducing the world of consum-erism and exposing them, through the endless passions of soap operas, to different standards of morality. (In the 1960s, a weekly romantic comic book, *Lágrimas y Risas,* serialized the story of an Indian girl, María Isabel, whose simple virtues were rewarded when she married the rich husband in the house where she worked as a maid. The story, later made into a *telenovela* and a movie, was said to have convinced many peasant girls to migrate.) With girls, a key stage is passed when they cut their long hair and begin to wear makeup. They remain distrustful of men, yet dream romantically of marriage. When they visit home, their changed lifestyle is immediately noticed and criticized: their fathers question their morality, while their mothers insist they are needed around the house. Soon they begin to find excuses not to visit their parents.

The principal hazard they face is pregnancy. Caught between the competing female models of temptress and mother, many eventually have sexual relations with a boyfriend who holds out the promise of marriage. Few use birth control devices, viewing such a premeditated approach to sex as sinful while justifying the spontaneous passion of premarital sex. But when they become pregnant, they are invariably abandoned, left alone to choose between some back-street abortionist or, more likely, having the child. Once pregnancy becomes apparent, they often lose their jobs and must then make a new choice: they can return to their home villages, face the wrath of their fathers and leave their baby to be brought up by its grandparents; or they can move in with relatives in the city until after the birth and then look for a home that will employ a maid with a baby. The number of single-parent families runs into the hundreds of thousands.

The problem of male irresponsibility is particularly acute in urban slums. Minimal wages are often drunk away, while alcoholism leads to wife-beating and reduces sexual relations to an act of near-violence, both used as expressions of male authority. Pregnancy is an additional instrument of control: a pregnant wife is proof of virility and a protection against infidelity. Many men therefore strongly oppose the use of birth control methods, and wives are often forced to attend family planning clinics in secret. "Men only think of themselves," Guadalupe, a forty-two-year-old mother of nine, recounted. "If you get pregnant, that's your problem. But it's too much to be pregnant, to care for the kids, to look after your husband, to manage the money, to work and then as soon as you've had one child, here comes another. That was my life: one after another. My God, I would cry, why do you send me another when you know I can't look after it?" The language popularly used by poor women well illustrates their point of view: making love is when they are "used" by their men, they are "sick" when they are pregnant and "cured" when they give birth.

The incidence of men abandoning wives and families and moving in with another woman is considerable, with the result that both men and women frequently have several children by different spouses. No less often, many men continue to rule their own household but also somehow maintain a mistress and a separate bevy of children. Adultery is so widespread that sociologists consider it the norm among men. It is rare for a poor woman either to risk infidelity or to abandon her husband, even when she is neglected or mistreated. Some women in fact prefer to be pregnant, in the belief that they can hold their man in this way. Girls have also been known to use pregnancy to force boyfriends to marry them. But these are exceptions. The example of men abusing women with impunity soon teaches boys to regard women as chattels.

The proliferation of family planning clinics in urban areas has brought some relief to women, yet the continuing high rate of illegal abortions illustrates the educational gap still to be bridged. Statistics are unreliable, but population experts estimate that between 1 and 2 million abortions take place every year. Since only around 15 percent of women can afford the $100 to $150 cost of a medically supervised abortion, most are carried out in unhygienic surroundings or are self-induced; as many as 140,000 women are thought to die annually from resulting complications. One medical study presented to the Mexican Congress in 1983 noted that 60 percent of the beds in gynecology and obstetrics units of government hospitals were occupied by victims of improvised abortions, while abortions were the fourth-highest cause of maternal death. The study also pointed out that, of women who have aborted, 86 percent were practicing Catholics, 65 percent were married to or living with the man who helped to conceive the child and 70 percent had other children. In contrast to more developed countries, most women seeking abortions were not single girls trying to "correct" a mistake, but rather mature women motivated by the despair of their existing family environment.

The problem of abandoned children is more severe in large cities. In theory, laws protect the children of both common-law marriages and of husbands who leave their wives, but it is rarely possible to oblige men to contribute toward the upkeep of a former household. In the *campo*, the problem is less serious because some family member will always take in an orphan or unwanted child and bring him up as his own. In slum neighborhoods, a child abandoned, neglected or mistreated by his parents may prefer the freedom of street life, learning the tricks needed to beg, steal or earn enough pesos to stay alive. Once left to his own devices, he will often join one of the gangs of similar children—mainly boys, many of them pre-teens—who live in the ghettos of downtown Mexico City. Addicted from an early age to glues, paint thinner and other toxic inhalants as well as alcohol, these *olvidados*— "forgotten ones," as the late Spanish movie director Luis Buñuel once named a film about them —are condemned to a life of poverty and crime. Government rehabilitation programs do exist, but they involve only a tiny proportion of affected children, who, unless successfully reintegrated into a stable family environment, have no choice but to return to their street communities following treatment.

Even in the cities, however, the tribal instinct remains strong. Migrants from the same state or even the same town group together in the refuge of the same *barrio,* while every overcrowded slum shack houses several members of the same extended family. The shortage of alternative housing and the high cost of rents contributes to perpetuating this, yet it provides the structure of security and authority to which many migrants are accustomed. The precarious economy of the poor also revolves around family ventures, from children somehow contributing to the household budget to cousins helping each other run a stand in a market.

The hardship of urban life and the economic crises of recent years have even strengthened the importance of the family. Hundreds of thousands of tiny family businesses—from cobblers to fruit-juice vendors, from mechanics to flower-growers—have been formed or expanded to absorb the newly unemployed. In times of trouble, the family closes ranks to ensure its survival. When a breadwinner loses his job or a couple can no longer pay the rent, some member of the family can be expected to provide an interest-free loan or to make room for more in an over-crowded bedroom. "Where one eats, two can fit," the saying goes. Trying to minimize the impact of an economic crisis in 1977, President López Portillo noted that Mexican families could be relied on "to add more water to the pot of beans" to feed a needy relative. Thus even the government looks to the family as the principal social welfare system.

III

Greater affluence transforms social behavior. The dramatic expansion of the middle classes, above all since 1970, has led a growing number of urban Mexicans to adopt a more liberal lifestyle. Economic difficulties and material expectations have prompted more middle-class women to work, which in turn has given them the freedom to seek divorces from unhappy marriages that might previously have continued. Coincidentally, there has been a steady rise in the educational level of urban women, with more women not only attending universities but also eventually finding jobs of responsibility in public and private sectors. "I was brought up in the nineteenth century and my daughter has been raised in the twenty-first century," explained one wealthy woman who two decades ago "discovered" women's liberation. Even among men of this class, there has been a gradual, often reluctant, acceptance of the greater independence of women.

In politics, women are also more visible. Although only one woman was in De la Madrid's Cabinet—Victoria Adato de Ibarra as Attorney General for Mexico City—and only one of thirty-one governors was a woman—Griselda Alvarez in Colima—the government feels pressured to pay at least lip service to the idea of sexual equality. In 1975, an equal rights amendment was attached to the Mexican Constitution. Women are beginning to vote differently from their husbands, and frequently against the government because they are more aware of the impact of inflation of family budgets. In 1982 Rosario Ibarra de Piedra became the first woman to run for the presidency, winning almost half a million votes

on behalf of a small leftist party. In 1984, the PRI chose Irma Cué de
Duarte to be its secretary-general, the party's second-highest post.

In middle-class circles, the easy availability of family planning methods since the mid-1970s has also broken the traditional link between sex
and procreation and, in the process, has reduced women's dependence
on men. Middle-class couples now have an average of two children,
compared to five among poorer families, while unmarried women no
longer feel prisoners of either the fear of pregnancy or the institution of
virginity. Two decades ago, some doctors would lecture women on morality if they sought family planning advice. A decade ago, a few doctors
still made a lucrative business out of repairing the hymens of wealthy
girls who were expected to be "pure" on their wedding night. Today,
girls from the same class often initiate sexual relations while in their late
teens.

The social revolution that has taken place in the United States has had
enormous impact on the middle classes bent on copying the American
way of life. Children of Mexico's wealthier families routinely attend
summer camp, high school or university in the United States, while most
middle-class families have vacationed at least once north of the border.
No less important, Mexico's tourist resorts have adjusted to the tastes
of American visitors, which Mexican youths happily adopt, while
American television programs and movies have helped make divorce,
sexual freedom, youthful rebellion and the use of drugs seem more
acceptable. Equally, such Mexican family traditions as making an altar
on the Day of the Dead, delivering gifts from the Baby Jesus on Christmas Eve and exchanging presents on Epiphany are being replaced by
Halloween and Santa Claus.

Militant women's movements in the United States and Europe have
also spawned similar, though smaller, groups in Mexico. Since the
early 1970s, numerous feminist currents have emerged, and while still
scoffed at as *locas*—"crazies"—by many men, feminists have become a
permanent, vocal and highly political lobby. More recently, a less repressive attitude toward sex in general has led to greater tolerance of
male and female homosexuality, which in the past was regarded as a direct threat to *machismo* and therefore derided. In practice, police still
carry out frequent *razzias* of male prostitutes, but growing tolerance
in affluent and intellectual circles of larger cities has enabled many men
and women to admit their homosexuality publicly for the first time, on
occasion even on television, a degree of openness unthinkable some years
ago.

While attitudes have changed, the inner workings of most middle-class families have not. Almost by definition, a middle-class home will have a maid and a wealthier residence may have as many as four maids as well as a gardener, one or two chauffeurs and perhaps a night watchman. As a result, the role of the wife is often to manage the staff rather than personally carry out the domestic chores of cleaning, washing and ironing. For working women, maids serve as in-house baby-sitters, often more involved in the upbringing of children than the mothers. Even feminist activists can concentrate on broader ideological questions since maids deal with the domestic duties that often cause male-female frictions in the United States. Women who do not work, on the other hand, have time on their hands which can be devoted to socializing or caring for their children. And for many women, their lives still revolve around their mothers, who visit frequently, proffer advice and provide a refuge in times of marital crisis.

The availability of domestic service also determines the behavior of middle-class children. Social and economic pressures require the majority of young men and women to live at home—and, indeed, to sleep at home every night—until they are married. (Neither studio apartments nor singles bars exist in Mexico: the first are unnecessary and the second are considered improper.) Long before then, both boys and girls become accustomed to being attended hand and foot; as a result, they learn none of the skills—shopping, cooking, cleaning, gardening, even bed making —that would enable them to live alone. This in turn brings unexpected tensions to new marriages: the bride has little idea how to run the new home, while the groom expects his wife to care for him as dutifully as his mother did a few days earlier. Thus, even if the newlywed is an attractive professional woman, she is soon under pressure to become a hausfrau, and she in turn pressures her husband to provide her with the necessary support system of maids and chauffeur.

Many daughters of wealthy families still see their lives as following traditional patterns. Unlike their mothers' generation, they may live and study abroad for a time, forced to look after themselves and free to engage in more liberated sexual behavior than at home. Yet upon their return to Mexico, they invariably move in again with their parents, accepting tighter discipline and dating only boys from other wealthy families. Many of those who attend private universities study, as they put it, "M.M.C."—*mientras me caso,* or "until I get married"—and indeed express sentiments of despair if still unmarried at the age of twenty-five. A generation ago, wealthy girls were warned that "overeducation" would be a stigma when searching for a husband. Even today girls from this class rarely venture beyond courses in communications, archaeology and anthropology. Once married, most seek to "fulfill themselves as women" by having children almost immediately.

As with the urban poor, domination by the father remains the norm in both middle- and upper-class families. Although wife-beating is less frequent, the institution of the mistress—variously known as *la casa chica,* "the little home," *el segundo frente,* "the second front," or *La querida,* "the loved one"—is more formalized. Not infrequently, the relationship with a mistress may last years or a lifetime, becoming as institutionalized as a marriage and known not only to the man's friends but also to his wife and children. But sometimes a man's secret life may be exposed only upon his death, when the mistress or mistresses and accompanying children show up at the funeral or are named in a will. It is rare, however, for a Mexican marriage to break up as a result of male infidelity, certainly not before the couple's children are grown. Following a divorce, in a faithful reflection of prevailing attitudes, the children are more willing to accept their father's new partner than any suggestion of a blemish on their mother's "purity" through her remarriage. Similarly, widows are expected to remain faithful to their late husband, whereas widowers are not so constrained.

The Mexican man's propensity for adultery is exceeded only by his fear of being cuckolded. Brought up to believe he has almost pro-prietorial rights over his wife, he is fiercely jealous: among the rich, arguing threats to her security, a man may forbid his wife from driving alone and insist that she always be accompanied by a chauffeur. Few economically secure men find it in themselves to encourage a wife who wants to work. In the past, a working wife implied humiliatingly that her husband could not afford to keep her. Today resistance stems from concern not only that wives might be attracted to other men, but also that, economically and intellectually, they will become less dependent on their spouses and eventually owe loyalty to an organization other than the home. Among the more affluent classes, probably more marital problems stem from the professional interests of wives than from the philandering of husbands.

It is unusual for even upper-class Mexican women to have institution-alized extramarital relationships comparable to those of married men, for fear not only of violent reprisals but also of the impact of the breakup of their marriage on their children and parents. But it is less rare for these women to break the loneliness, boredom and frustration of their lives through casual affairs, often with young men or gigolos. These take place with the utmost discretion, with perhaps only an intimate girlfriend acting as accomplice in maintaining the secret. In any event, the traditional double standards apply: society views male infidelity as "normal" and female unfaithfulness as a moral aberration. When a draft reform of the Penal Code proposed depenalization of adultery in late 1983, the principal protests were heard from men who argued that it constituted an assault on the sacred institution of matrimony. Even though the existing penalties—up to two years' imprisonment and up to six years' suspension of civil rights—are never applied, the proposed reform was dropped by the government.

The conservative traditions of the Mexican middle classes are strongest in small provincial cities, where the weight of public opinion is still felt and appearances still count. There, education of girls is particularly neglected: girls are brought up to be wives and mothers. Courting involves a lengthy romantic ritual in which neatly dressed suitors with presents in hand must gradually win over their future in-laws and chaperones are assigned to accompany young couples on dates. If several sons move to Mexico City to study, their mother may follow to preserve their home environment. Marriages generally take place between the sons and daughters of "decent" or "known" families—"people like us," mothers will remark—with an unspoken racism apparent in the concern that offspring should not be too *mestizo*-looking. After marriage, the new brides happily abandon their maiden names, adopt the possessive *Señora de* So-and-So and re-enact the lives of their mothers. Among this provincial bourgeoisie, neither premarital sex nor divorce is common: the extended family remains a powerfully authoritarian institution, tied to the land and traditions, its internal strength perpetuating its external influence over local society.

It is only among some middle-class women coming of age in the late 1970s and early 1980s in large cities, notably the capital, that major changes of lifestyle have occurred. Educated and professional women still comprise a small minority, but they represent a generation that is being forced by economic necessity and intellectual restlessness to work, no longer just as secretaries, but often as journalists, academics, economists and even politicians. They therefore study for lifetime careers. Their attitudes toward marriage are also different. Having traveled or studied abroad and achieved economic independence at home, many are determined to find a husband willing to share domestic responsibilities and accept a working wife. If no such modern spouse is forthcoming, they are willing to resist social and family pressure to marry "anyone" before the age of twenty-five. And if they marry the wrong man, they are likely to seek an early divorce. Some leave home and share lodgings with other working girlfriends, even at the risk of upsetting fathers. But because young men distrust liberal women, the number of couples living together before marriage remains low.

The noisy activism of the small groups of organized feminists—probably fewer than 1,000 women, most of them left-leaning intellectuals—has helped society accept the changing role of middle-class women. Most of these women do not in fact identify with feminist militants, yet the fact that they prefer to work rather than stay at home categorizes them as feminists in the eyes of many men. The feminists themselves, while invariably belonging to the educated middle classes, pay less attention to such questions as "equal pay for equal work" and adequate representation in the government than to the socioeconomic exploitation suffered by the great majority of poor women. They have established a Rape Advisory Center, they have led the campaign for legalization of abortion and, almost alone, they have carried out studies on the fate of women factory workers, maids and Indian women. Yet in practice, through their quarterly magazine, *fem,* television appearances and occasional demonstrations, their proselytizing has been directed mainly at the government and the ruling elite.

The government itself is sensitive to the stabilizing function of the family in society and has sought to preserve key symbols of family integration. In 1983, the De la Madrid administration proposed depenalizing abortion as a logical first step toward dealing with the problem. The wave of criticism that followed prompted the administration to withdraw its plan. It was reluctant to confront the Roman Catholic Church, which, through assorted militant pro-life groups, was obliged to campaign against the reform. But it also responded to complaints that legalization of abortion constituted another dangerous step in the destruction of traditional values. As with the proposed depenalization of adultery, the loudest opposition came from men who clearly recognized that they had most to lose from changes in family mores.

The question whether the family would disintegrate if male authoritarianism were to ease remains largely academic. While some men now accept the principle of formal equality of the sexes, symbolized by more women in "nonthreatening" public positions, they continue to object strongly to changes in women's role in the family. And though some women are determined to assert their personal and professional identities, the majority still unconsciously accept the dictates of their fathers, brothers, husbands and even sons. Male domination is perceived as the price of maintaining traditions, morality and security. Through the conservative family structure, therefore, much of the good and the bad of old Mexico is reappearing in the new, more modern Mexico.

13

Mexico City:
Magnet and Monster

I

For the world's largest urban center, Mexico City is in the most impractical of settings. Situated 7,400 feet above sea level, it is ringed by mountains and volcanoes, set in an earthquake zone, gradually sinking into its soft subsoil, far from water, food and energy supplies and, literally, short of oxygen. Yet so strong has been the traditional domination of the country by its central highlands—from Teotihuacan through Tenochtitlan to Mexico City itself—that the capital has continued to grow beyond its ability to function. Today, it is not only the country's political capital but also its industrial, financial, commercial, entertainment, cultural and even religious capital. With a population of 17 million in 1984, it has become a case study in the chaos that awaits other developing nations where the rush to industrialize has stimulated a mass exodus from depressed rural to fast-growing urban areas, where the worst of underdevelopment has combined with the worst of overdevelopment.

People flocked to Mexico City because the country's economic strategy since the 1940s obliged them to do so. Resources were poured into industry, commerce and urban construction, while agriculture was neglected. Problems were then compounded by poor planning in every area —from industrial location to water supplies—as well as by the prohibitive cost of keeping up with the population. Yet people kept coming— even after industrial jobs were no longer automatically available—because the city still resolved many of their problems. Jobs could be found, schools were nearby and health services were accessible. Migration to the capital created an option of social mobility that could never exist in the countryside.

But chaotic growth has not obliterated Mexico City's character and charm. Its very growth reflects its hospitality, always allowing one more person through the door to find a niche and make a living. Its energy and spirit somehow isolate the pleasure of living there from the pain of its noise, traffic and pollution. The humanity of the city constantly protrudes through the façade of seemingly insoluble problems: architectural jewels from both the pre-Hispanic and Colonial past have survived, museums, theaters and concert halls are always crowded, social and intellectual elites flourish, shocking contrasts and delightful discoveries feed conflicting feelings of despair and hope. And everywhere the sheer power of El Gran Tenochtitlan, as it was once called, can be felt, not only controlling its own huge population but also holding together the rest of the country.

But this more poetic dimension does not explain two puzzling phenomena—that successive governments should have done so little to slow the city's growth; and that the population could accept the steady deterioration of the quality of urban life without major outcry. A form of collective hypnosis seems to have embraced both government and inhabitants as the city's population has multiplied, its environment has been destroyed, its services have been swamped, its finances decimated and its natural resources exhausted. In 1960, all the necessary socioeconomic ingredients for rapid urban growth were in place; by 1970, officials and citizens alike could already recognize the signs of urban macrocephalus; and by 1980, the city was overwhelmed by people and problems. But at no stage were new industries, construction programs or squatter settlements banned to forestall this disaster. Nor did discontent express itself in riots or protests. Short of a total breakdown of public services, above all of water supplies, no strategy can now prevent the capital's population from doubling to 30 million during the final two decades of the century.

What distinguishes Mexico City from other Third World urban disasters is neither the immediate cause nor the nature of its problems: industrialization has stimulated migration in many countries, while numerous cities are scarred by pollution, traffic jams and slums. Mexico City stands out because a centuries-old tradition of centralized power was followed by an unprecedented burst of growth since 1940. It is different because no other city in the world is larger today.

Nomadic tribes wandered through the region at least 20,000 years ago, but it was not until around 200 B.C. that Teotihuacan converted the central highlands into the focal point of Mexican political culture. Over the next thousand years, migration to the area increased, and by the time the Aztecs founded Tenochtitlan on an island in Lake Texcoco in 1325, the Valley of Mexico was well settled with towns and villages. The Aztecs went further, forcing a vast area of Meso-America to recognize Tenochtitlan as its military, political, religious and commercial capital, and after the Conquest in 1521 this fact alone convinced the Spanish to build Mexico City on the same site. With all business operations conducted in Tenochtitlan and all pilgrimages and, literally, all roads passing through, the conquistadors thus inherited an entire system of control. This political decision was reinforced by the area's natural resources. At the time of the Conquest, some 60,000 people were crowded onto the islands of Tenochtitlan and Tlatelolco, but the Valley of Mexico already sustained a population estimated at some 1.5 million.

Within a century of the Conquest, the dispersal of the Indians and, even more, their decimation through disease reduced the valley's population to just 70,000. But Mexico City remained home to viceroys, archbishops and the entire Spanish aristocracy, and the vast colony of New Spain was administered efficiently from there. Enough of Mexico's gold and silver stayed behind to convert the capital into an elegant colonial city. "Without doubt, Mexico must be one of the most beautiful of the cities founded by Europeans in either hemisphere," the traveler Alexander von Humboldt wrote in 1803, marveling at its stone edifices, wide avenues and "grandiose plazas," and adding that Lake Texcoco and its surrounding villages reminded him of "the most beautiful lakes in the Swiss mountains."

Following Independence in the early nineteenth century, when the valley had only about 350,000 inhabitants, roughly one-tenth of the country's population, the concept of centralized power was endorsed when Mexico City was declared a Federal District. In the decades that followed, Mexico City was twice occupied by foreign powers—by the United States and by France—and it was not until the second half of the nineteenth century that it resumed its growth, first when the magnificent Paseo de la Reforma was built from the downtown area to Chapultepec Castle and later when chronic drainage problems were resolved. Coincidentally, the dictatorship of General Porfirio Díaz reasserted Mexico City's political influence, ensuring for the first time since the Colony that all key decisions affecting any part of the country were once again taken in the National Palace.

Urban change first came with the Revolution. Until 1910, with fewer than 500,000 inhabitants, Mexico City remained a quiet neocolonial capital dominated by churches and palaces and surrounded by picturesque Indian villages where the wealthy had weekend homes. But during the conflict, both peasant migrants and wealthy landowners began moving to the capital to escape violence elsewhere in the country. The poor crowded into downtown tenement buildings, while elegant new neighborhoods appeared to house the more affluent. In 1930, the population reached 1 million, and although revival of the land reform program slowed urban migration during the decade, Mexico City grew to 1.5 million by 1940. Already it exuded the bustle and excitement of a large metropolis, but traffic moved smoothly along its broad tree-lined avenues and even social problems seemed less visible than today. Many elderly *chilangos,* as the inhabitants of the capital are known, can still remember waking up daily to crisp clean air and blue skies, with the snow-capped volcanoes, Popocatepetl and Iztaccihuatl, visible over the pine forests surrounding the city. Then, over the next four decades, the city was transformed.

In reality, the simultaneous growth and destruction of the Mexican capital were merely consequences of a more significant economic change wrought by World War II. The shortage of manufactured goods previously imported from the United States and Europe stimulated local business, creating new jobs that "pulled" peasants toward the capital. At the same time, worsening rural conditions "pushed" peasants out of the countryside. After the war, industrialization for "import substitution" became official policy and encouraged continuing peasant migration to the cities. As Mexico City expanded, its magnetic force grew: both foreign and domestic investment were drawn to the largest market and migrants went where jobs were to be found. Between 1940 and 1970, when the city's population jumped to 8.3 million, half its growth came from migration, while half the migrants in the entire country were heading for Mexico City.

Compared to the push for development, urban planning and ecological concerns seemed irrelevant: middle-class housing projects and migrants' slums sprawled chaotically in all directions, while factories poured industrial wastes into the rivers and the atmosphere with impunity. The emerging debate in developed countries about the need for birth control and environmental protection in the Third World was viewed suspiciously as an effort to slow Mexico's economic expansion. Thus, as the capital grew, its natural support system was destroyed: between 1950 and 1970, the city's wooded areas were reduced by 20 percent and its agricultural zones by 50 percent.

By the 1960s, because the city was growing horizontally rather than vertically, the population could no longer be contained within the limits of the Federal District and spilled over into the contiguous state of México. Soon the urban population inside the state of México was growing faster than that of the Federal District. This brought additional management problems. While the metropolis continued to function as a single urban unit, it was now governed—without coordination—by two administrations and two budgets. The Federal District was divided into sixteen "delegations," but Greater Mexico City also included fifty-three semi-autonomous municipalities in the state of México. Because the governor of the state of México is elected, he was under more pressure to balance his budget and impose higher taxes than was the mayor of Mexico City, who, as a presidential appointee, could subsidize public services with federal funds.

In the 1970s, the metropolis continued growing by 7 percent annually, its population exceeding 14 million by 1980. The concentration of all expressions of power also became acute. Not only was 21 percent of the population occupying just 0.1 percent of the national territory, but Greater Mexico City also accounted for 38 percent of the Gross Domestic Product (GDP), 48 percent of manufacturing industry, 45 percent of commercial activity, 52 percent of services, 60 percent of transportation and 69 percent of bank assets. Half the country's university students were in the capital, most television programs came from Mexico City and all successful political careers passed through the federal bureaucracy.

Although the Echeverría and López Portillo administrations preached the virtues of decentralization, in practice neither reduced the capital's magnetic pull or halted the deterioration of its environment. In the late 1970s, the principal concern of Mayor Carlos Hank González was to appease middle-class complaints about traffic problems, and he embarked on a massive spending program that included construction of new highways and expansion of the subway system. But the resulting jobs merely attracted hundreds of thousands more peasants to the city. Rather than raising land taxes and water rates, the city's traditional sources of revenue, Hank González paid for the program by borrowing. Thus, while in 1970 the city's own revenues covered 61 percent of its budget, by 1982 all but 21 percent of its budget was provided by the federal government and the city owed $2.3 billion abroad. When De la Madrid's new mayor, Ramón Aguirre, took office in December 1982, the capital was effectively bankrupt and dreams of addressing the urban crisis with expensive new programs were indefinitely postponed.

II

A brownish smog covers the Valley of Mexico most days of the year. Because the city is surrounded by mountains, thermal inversion frequently traps the pollution within the urban bowl, while the region's sunshine and thin air generate a particularly pungent photochemical smog. Daily, some 11,000 tons of metals, chemicals, bacteria and dust are poured into the atmosphere, darkening the air before returning to earth, sometimes as "acid rain." Visitors complain of burning eyes and sore throats or muse nervously about the innumerable toxic substances being breathed in. Yet locals have come to accept air pollution as an inescapable feature of life in the city. By now, the measures necessary to combat it seem beyond the political and economic resources of the government. To deal with each major cause of air pollution would involve resolving even more complex related problems.

During the early months of each year, the city is regularly assailed by dust storms coming from the east and northeast. In part, they are the result of deforestation of over 70 percent of the valley but, more seriously, they also blow in from the dried-up bed of Lake Texcoco. The drainage of the lake decades earlier had seemed necessary to prevent flooding and permit expansion of the city, but this disturbed the valley's entire ecological balance. Because some city sewage systems flow into the area and improvised open-air toilets are common, the dust often contains dried excrement and bacteria. Yet little can be done to prevent the *tolvaneras,* as the storms are known. Dry during the winter and muddy during the summer rainy season, the "lake" is unsuitable for urbanization (although many slums now stretch into it), while its highly saline soil prevents its surface from being farmed or reforested.

Inadequate garbage collection and disposal facilities for the 8,000 tons of refuse produced daily by the city add to air pollution. In poor districts of the capital, where garbage trucks pass only occasionally, locals are forced to burn refuse in the hope of combating rats and flies. On the seven large open-air city dumps, biochemical fumes occasionally spark smoldering fires that may last for several weeks, at times forcing evacuation of nearby neighborhoods. More than the enormous cost of buying additional trucks and building new disposal plants, which in the long run could finance themselves, the greatest obstacle to resolving the garbage problem is the amount of money being made out of existing arrangements.

The city's garbage collectors belong to a powerful organization that controls the resale of anything of value that is thrown away—principally metals, timber, plastics and bottles. With more trucks, they would still concentrate on affluent residential areas that have more "valuable" waste and provide hefty tips for the removal of garbage. Once all "valuables" have been removed, truck crews transport their loads to city dumps, where another organization takes over. (Private garbage trucks do not have access to these dumps and frequently scatter their loads in the Ajusco and other wooded areas near the capital.) Under the control of a tough and wealthy boss and his "corporals," an army of *pepenadores,* as the professional scavengers are known, again sifts through the garbage, separating out everything of minimal worth. Thousands of people earn their living from—and build their shacks inside—the dumps, while some of the bosses become powerful enough to be chosen as federal deputies by the ruling PRI. Resistance from these entrenched interests to a more industrial solution to garbage is therefore considerable and, in the name of political appeasement, the environment is allowed to suffer.

More serious than dust and burning garbage are the emissions from the 60,000 or so factories of all sizes installed in the valley. In the northern suburb of Azcapotzalco, for example, a refinery owned by the state oil monopoly, Petróleos Mexicanos, spews out sulphurous fumes. Beside the ring road known as the Periférico, cement factories operate without interruption. In the northern Vallejo and Naucalpán districts, where most of the city's factories are concentrated, visibility is frequently down to one mile. In the southern exit to the city, a paper factory produces a powerful smell that often reaches a nearby zone of government hospitals. Anti-pollution laws exist obliging factory owners to install filters, but immediately new problems arise: industrialists either pass on the costs of such controls to consumers or pay off government health inspectors to ignore violations of environmental standards.

The pre-eminent culprit, however, is the internal-combustion engine. In 1984, the government calculated that the 2.5 million vehicles circulating in the Valley of Mexico accounted for 75 percent of air pollution. The local auto industry has resisted pressure to install anti-pollution devices in new models, while the government has been reluctant to invest in "cleaner" high-octane gasoline. Sulphur, carbon monoxide and lead pour into the atmosphere from vehicles that are themselves often old and poorly serviced. United Nations studies point to pollution between three and six times above recommended safety levels. Once again, though, the real cause of the problem is to be found elsewhere, specifically in the public transportation system and the distribution of the urban population.

The majority of industrial workers live in the east of the city, in Netzahualcóyotl and other sprawling slums close to Lake Texcoco, while most industrial jobs are to be found in the northern suburbs of Vallejo, Naucalpán and Azcapotzalco. The middle and upper classes tend to live in the northwest, west and south, but work in government buildings or private offices in and around the center. Most people therefore cross a large part of the 500-square-mile urban area each day going to and from their jobs. In 1983, a total of some 22 million journeys were recorded in the capital each day.

Inexplicably, the problems of public transport have never been properly addressed. A subway system was initiated in the mid-1960s by President Díaz Ordaz, construction was halted under the Echeverría administration, resumed halfway through López Portillo's government and continued by De la Madrid. But its sixty-five miles of lines are designed in such a way that, even if going from east to north, commuters must often pass through the city center. The subway still accounts for only about 20 percent of daily trips and most travelers depend on buses, yet there are only some 6,000 units on the roads—half as many as estimated to be necessary, and less than one-third of those needed by 1988. Many are in poor condition, spewing out thick columns of black diesel smoke. In September 1981, with controlled fares discouraging bus owners from investing in new units and complaints about the service growing, the city government took over the buses, but it too was soon overwhelmed by the cost of running them.

For those who rely on public transport, each day is an odyssey, involving four or five hours of standing in line or hanging perilously to the sides of buses or being crushed in the subway. During his election campaign in 1982, De la Madrid heard testimony from workers who left home at 4:30 A.M. in order to be at the factory gate by 7 A.M. At one point he conceded: "The inhabitant of Mexico City is increasingly irritated, frustrated and desperate over transport conditions." The only compensation is that both subway and buses remain extraordinarily cheap: in 1984, 180 people could travel by subway or 60 people by bus for the equivalent of one dollar and in both cases the authorities spent more collecting the money than they received.

Such is the discomfort of public transport that, at the first opportunity, Mexicans buy an old car to drive to work or on weekend outings. The middle and upper classes, who would not contemplate using public transport, frequently possess two cars or more to satisfy family needs. The number of vehicles has therefore grown out of all proportion to available space on the city's roads. Aggravated by the fact that cars often carry only one person, traffic moves at an average of ten miles per hour during much of the day. Even the chauffeur-driven wealthy may take ninety minutes or more to reach their place of work. During the rainy season, flooded underpasses, blackouts of traffic lights and poorly trained policemen produce traffic jams that take hours to disperse. Political demonstrations—such as a sit-down protest by student teachers at the critical intersection of the Paseo de la Reforma and Insurgentes Avenue one day in 1983—can paralyze huge areas of the city. Finding a parking place is an additional nightmare. With parking lots both expensive and in short supply, drivers search for their own spots. In exchange for a tip, many policemen "look after" and accommodate cars often parked two or three deep from the sidewalk, further snarling the flow of traffic.

Air pollution is principally a function of the high number and low speed of cars in the city, with 90-decibel noise pollution added by buses, trucks and not a few old cars. The entire traffic problem must therefore be tackled first. Even without pollution, it has become a factor of contention between government and population: on average, transportation consumes 15 percent of income and 30 percent of hours awake. Should present trends continue, the number of vehicles in the city will exceed 5 million by 1990. At that point, air pollution will be intolerable and the hours wasted daily by commuters even more costly.

But by building highways and parking lots and by long subsidizing the cost of gasoline, the government tried to resolve the problem through cars when the answer lay elsewhere: in 1984, 5 percent of vehicles—buses, trolley-buses, taxis and *pesero* collective taxis—carried 84 percent of all passengers, while 95 percent of vehicles—private cars—accounted for only 16 percent of daily trips. The irony is that successive governments have accepted the principle of subsidizing transportation, but seemed reluctant to confront private car owners. Now officials believe the answer must lie first in doubling the number of buses in service and extending the subway to eighty miles by 1988 and then "punishing" the use of cars in the city during the week, either through exorbitant parking fees or special taxes. In the short term, such a policy would involve the political cost of angering the middle classes. Yet the long-term consequence of inaction will be a city unable to communicate with itself.

III

An official report in 1982 estimated that 10.3 percent of the metropolitan population lived in extreme poverty and a further 22.6 percent were unable to satisfy their basic needs. Other studies indicated that 40 percent received no health care, 51 percent were without running water in their homes and 49 percent of workers earned less than the legal minimum wage. These statistics in turn translate into an almost stereotypical description of urban poverty in any developing country.

In most cases, the affected are migrants with minimal education who live on the fringes of the money economy, working occasionally on construction sites or improvising a living by shining shoes, selling news-papers, cleaning cars, breathing fire on street corners or inventing new ways of garnering a few pesos. They and their large families subsist on beans and corn tortillas and live in one-room wooden or cardboard shacks without running water or drainage. Their immediate surround-ings are either dusty or muddy and permanently strewn with garbage, with open drains and stagnant pools aggravating chronic respiratory and gastrointestinal problems. Schools are usually within reach, but many children are sent out to beg or work at an early age. Crime is rampant, but police rarely bother to combat it.

Yet even in the absence of almost all public services, the principal demand of some 5 million urban poor in Mexico City is to own a piece of land, as if carrying with them their frustrated dream of a tiny plot in the *campo*. As in the countryside, land tenure problems in the city are severe. In a nation where the government intervenes in most areas of public life, market forces have defined land policy. Deforestation has taken place with impunity, rural areas of the city have been occupied by private developers and everywhere land speculation has pushed up real estate prices. The shortage of low-cost housing—city authorities estimate a deficit of some 800,000 units—has inflated rents beyond the budgets of the poor, while high interest rates and fear of a rent freeze have dis-couraged construction of private housing projects for low-income groups.

Migrants to the city have no choice but to squat on government or private land and build their own dwellings. Netzahualcóyotl, located inside the state of México but very much part of Greater Mexico City, was first "invaded" in the 1960s and now has a population exceeding 2 million. Other improvised settlements cover much of the northeast and east of the capital as well as pockets in more affluent neighborhoods. More recently, with available land in traditional migrant zones already occupied, squatters have begun spreading up the western hills of the cap-ital where private construction firms had planned more expensive homes.

The very act of squatting is conflictive. In some cases, squatters are forcibly evicted from private land by heavily armed police soon after they arrive. More often, invasions are carried out before dawn by groups organized and led by an experienced activist with enough influence or money to hold police at bay. The long struggle to persuade the authori-ties to "regularize" the land and provide services then begins, although years of petitioning may lie ahead. Often, installation of services is delayed until legal titles are distributed; in the meantime, the squatters steal light by tapping the nearest electricity line, carry water in buckets from a public tap and dig holes for their personal needs. The drive for self-improvement, though, is strong. After initial savings are spent on a television, wooden shacks are gradually replaced by stone or brick walls as the campaign to secure ownership of the plot continues.

Since expropriation of private land by the government may be necessary, the key variable is the pressure that each community can apply. In doing so, it must walk a narrow line between being ignored and repressed: poorly organized squatter colonies need not be attended to, but those that become too militant are considered a threat. The experience of the 2nd of October Camp illustrated the dilemma. In 1975, some 500 families seized empty land in the Ixcacalco sector of the city under the leadership of Francisco de la Cruz, an Indian from Oaxaca who had migrated to the capital twenty years earlier and had eventually graduated from the UNAM as a lawyer. He was a good organizer and soon the squatters had built their own cement-block factory, a health clinic and a three-floor community hall where their weekly bulletin was printed. De la Cruz had political ambitions of his own, and after trying to unite several squatter communities around the demand for land titles, police moved in to grab him. He managed to flee, but several shacks were burned as a warning.

After the change of government in 1976, De la Cruz returned to find his leadership challenged and the authorities exploiting the division. De la Cruz then took a gamble. Sensing political differences between Mayor Hank González and the then president of the PRI, Gustavo Carvajal, he invited Carvajal to visit the community and he even considered running as a PRI candidate in the 1979 congressional elections. But the alliance soon broke down and De la Cruz lost his protection. The following year, he ran unsuccessfully for governor of Oaxaca on behalf of the Socialist Workers' Party (PST), and when he began to use the squatter organization to protect a fleet of "pirate" taxis in exchange for regular fees, he overstepped the tolerated limits of independent power. In April 1981, De la Cruz was arrested, 3,000 police, including 500 on horseback, entered the camp and bulldozers followed. Within one week, the 2nd of October Camp had disappeared and De la Cruz was beginning a long prison term.

Despite the government's determination to prevent squatters from becoming a political problem, a National Urban Popular Movement, known by its acronym, CONAMUP, has been formed by numerous militant slum organizations. By campaigning for specific demands and avoiding close identification with leftist parties eager to coopt them, they have often been successful. Their demands are mirrors of their needs: drinking water, drainage, electricity, paved streets, garbage collection, better security and, most consistently, distribution of land titles. Many squatter leaders are themselves members of the PRI and, fully aware of the repressive potential of the regime, pointedly seek sponsors and protectors among congressmen and politicians of the ruling party.

Yet, with the exception of some disturbances linked to increased bus fares in Netzahualcóyotl in 1981, Mexico City's slum belt has witnessed no riots or looting sprees. The question inevitably arises whether the government will address the needs of the urban poor without the threat of a political explosion. The Federal District's resources are more limited than ever, but in the more affluent past its priorities were also not properly focused. At a time, for example, when the city's water shortage was impeding rapid expansion of supplies to slum areas, Mayor Hank González ordered elegant new fountains built near his home in a residential neighborhood. While postponing programs to pave the streets of new migrant settlements, he spent exorbitantly on new highways elsewhere in the capital. Even the argument that slum-improvement programs merely encourage squatters looked weak against the reality of continuing migration to the city. So long as Mexico City offers more hope than the *campo*—or, indeed, than other urban areas—migrants will keep coming.

IV

Mexico City has lost much of its staid turn-of-the-century elegance, but its soul has survived the metamorphosis. It is not immediately visible because it has fled the cacophonous traffic, crowded streets and advancing neighborhoods of middle-class consumers. Yet it can still be found in a handful of old communities and, more important, in the lives of ordinary—usually poor—Mexicans. The traditions that distinguish Mexico City from other large cities—the Colonial architecture, the markets, the food, the music, the dedication to family and leisure, the almost stylized formality, even the preference for a slow pace of life—keep its body and soul alive.

In the middle of the world's largest city, many communities display the characteristics—and isolation—of small towns. In part, this is a function of the difficulty of traveling within the capital: a lucky minority of Mexicans live, work and socialize in their own neighborhoods and thereby give stability and identity to their *colonia*. But the phenomenon also reflects the city's pattern of development. For centuries, the area surrounding the seat of government in the Zócalo exuded a strong personality of its own, while a rural way of life went on unchanged ten to fifteen miles away in such Colonial villages as Coyoacán, San Angel, San

Jerónimo and Xochimilco. As the metropolis expanded and besieged these communities with modern suburbs and broad highways, these *pueblos* retained their individuality.

Coyoacán and San Angel both existed before the Conquest and until the 1930s were still separated from downtown Mexico City by fields: a trip to the capital, elderly Mexicans recall, was a major outing. Today the villages survive as jewels of Spanish Colonial architecture, with shaded plazas, sixteenth-century churches, cobbled streets and huge mansions hidden behind adobe walls five feet thick. San Angel has been more invaded by the modern world, if only because real estate speculation has forced many poorer Mexicans to leave the district. But Coyoacán retains an almost provincial atmosphere, with its twin plazas, market, church, bandstand, iron benches and ramblas all offering a mood of quiet self-sufficiency. Here rich and poor live side by side, a millionaire's home next door to a store selling tacos and tortillas. Many artists and writers are also drawn to Coyoacán, able to stay in touch with the old Mexico of strong tastes, smells and colors without abandoning the capital.

Other pre-Hispanic villages, such as Tacuba, Ixtapalapa, Azcapotzalco, Tlanepantla and Tlalpán, have fared less well against the onslaught of highways, factories and squatters, although Texcoco, separated from the city by the expanse of dried-up lake bed, still retains some Colonial traits. To the south, the large plazas and sixteenth-century churches of Xochimilco recall its independent past, and to this day thousands of visitors hire boats every weekend to travel the canals separating "floating" gardens that were built long before the Aztecs arrived. Entire families take food and drink along with them as musicians, photographers, florists, cooks and vendors of everything from balloons to shawls float alongside in search of business. But even here, the polluted water of the canals is yet another reminder of the disregard of many Mexicans for the environment.

A tougher ghetto spirit survives in the inner-city communities of Guerrero and Tepito. Living conditions are poor, with most people crowded into *vecindades,* single rooms off a galleried inner courtyard. (These were the setting for Oscar Lewis' classic sociological study *The Children of Sánchez.*) But chronic poverty has also taught the locals to live off their wits, with the *colonias* producing many of the country's best boxers and entertainers. Tepito is also the traditional home of Mexico's smugglers, and every imaginable item of *fayuca,* or contraband, from Japanese watches to Yorkshire cloth, can be bought there. But it is the strong sense of local pride that makes the two *colonias* so different from other poor neighborhoods. Like clans everywhere, they speak their own slang, while family influence and community loyalty run deep, obliging the authorities to treat them with rare respect. Any local boy being chased by police, for example, can be assured a hiding place in the Casbah-like maze of *vecindades*. Outsiders are allowed in to spend their money, but are automatically viewed with distrust.

A few blocks away is the Plaza de Garibaldi, which is taken over each night by hundreds of mariachi musicians, street vendors, foreign tourists, police, pickpockets and Mexicans young and old intent on indulging in sentimentality. The setting itself is not special, with crumbling nineteenth-century buildings held together by newly painted façades, yet the mood is intense, as if constantly hovering between laughter and tears, embraces and violence. Mexicans are drawn by the plaza, not only on birthdays and paydays and other special occasions, but also when the need for release arises, when music and alcohol must be mobilized to deal with a personal problem or an existential dilemma. Men come to serenade a girlfriend or to get drunk with a group of buddies, they wander around the square or they sit at tables in bars; but for all, the cathartic purpose is the same. Outsiders may view the plaza as a tourist attraction, but it serves a more important function for those seeking spiritual—if not physical—escape from the travails of the city.

The area around the Zócalo is a world unto itself. Mexico has been ruled from the huge square ever since the Aztecs founded Tenochtitlan, and today, even amidst noise and traffic, it retains much of its grandeur as a symbol of power. Beside the sixteenth-century Metropolitan Cathedral and the seventeenth-century National Palace are the excavated ruins of the pre-Hispanic Templo Mayor as a constant reminder of the past. In the center of the Zócalo flies a huge Mexican flag, while on numerous political or patriotic occasions each year the President presides from the Palace balcony over marches or gatherings of 1 million people or more. During September—coinciding with Independence Day celebrations—and over Christmas, the Colonial buildings around the plaza are transformed by portraits and designs in colored lights. The narrow streets leading off the plaza are reminiscent of a Mexico fifty years ago, with tailors, jewelers, bookshops and Spanish restaurants wrestling for space. Everywhere there are churches built with the stone of razed Aztec temples, as well as stunning Spanish palaces that have been converted into banks or government offices without sacrifice of their ornate exteriors.

More modern Mexico City is lacking in character. The capital's most elegant avenue, the Paseo de la Reforma, is being transformed as old stone mansions make way for high-rise buildings with reflecting windows. The Zona Rosa, or "Pink Zone," with its restaurants, discotheques and nightclubs, is the favorite gathering point for affluent young Mexicans looking for echoes of Chelsea or Greenwich Village, and only Indian beggars remind one that its setting is Mexico. The district of Polanco, crowded with expensive stores and modern apartment blocks, could be in any Western city. When the capital expanded in the 1940s, the wealthy moved to the nearby foothills known as the Lomas de Chapultepec, constructing rambling arabesque homes set in quiet shaded streets. As the economy prospered and the city spread, the entire western slopes, including many of its ravines, were covered with new homes. In the late 1970s, one symbol of the economic boom was the construction fever in the Bosque de las Lomas district, where each extravagant new house cost at least $500,000.

Probably no section of the capital seems less identifiably Mexican than the endless sprawling neighborhoods of characterless middle-class homes in Satellite City to the north. The zone is a monument both to the middle-class Mexican's desire to own his home and to his fascination with the American way of life. Beside the multi-lane highways are huge shopping malls that are reachable only by car. The architecture of most houses could be described as modern utilitarian, although wealthier families have followed the American example of building homes around the golf courses of private clubs. Even the concentration of bilingual schools—teaching as much English as Spanish—emphasizes the mood of a rising middle class bent on self-improvement.

In contrast, the real soul of Mexico City is on display every Sunday in Chapultepec Park. In a city with little greenery, the park is the playground of 1.5 million people each weekend, many of them seeking respite from their slum homes. Enough come by car to clog the entire area's parking space, but most arrive by subway, carrying bags of food in one hand and trailing children with the other. Frequently, family groups stake out a corner by hanging brightly colored balloons between trees, and while lunch is warmed on an improvised campfire, a game of soccer or baseball ensues. But the park is for everyone. Young couples go there to flee the prying eyes of relatives, teenage maids on their days off look hopefully for a prospective husband and children in their thousands run freely. They visit the zoo, go rowing on one of three boating lakes, attend a concert or play in an open-air theater, spend money in an amusement park, sleep in the shade or sign up for open-air classes in everything from carpentry to hairdressing, from painting to doll-making. At every step, there are merchants, Indian women selling fruit or tacos, ancient photographers with box cameras, youths waving plastic helicopters or straw hats. Despite the crowds and bustle, the mood is relaxed, as if the entire occasion were a ritual.

Concentrated in the same area are the principal museums of the capital. The most important is the National Museum of Anthropology, because it contains the official past that Mexicans struggle to assimilate. Within walking distance are also the Museum of Modern Art, the Rufino Tamayo Museum, the Museum of Colonial Art in Chapultepec Castle and the Museum of Natural History, all of them cheaper to visit than the price of an ice cream. The proliferation of museums recording everything from popular art to foreign interventions also seems to symbolize the grandeur with which Mexico City still views itself: it has been savaged by chaotic growth, overrun by people and intoxicated by pollution, but it insists on preserving the cultural dignity of a great city.

V

Monopolizing political power, the government is primarily responsible for what happens next to Mexico City, but its options are limited. It cannot turn back the clock and rectify a development strategy that stimulated urban migration by concentrating on industry and neglecting agriculture. It cannot even stop the clock and win time to confront the phalanx of accumulated problems. It now recognizes the mistakes committed by previous governments, yet it faces such acute short-term problems that neither the ideas nor the resources for a long-term approach are available. At most, the De la Madrid administration can hope to bequeath a capital in 1988 that has deteriorated no more than the one it inherited six years earlier. But the most optimistic of planners have shied from forecasting solutions to any of the city's fundamental problems by the year 2000.

The most serious of Greater Mexico City's myriad deficits is water. Almost everything the city needs—food, energy and raw materials for industry and construction—is already carried at great expense to the mountain plateau where the capital is located, but the shortage of water is fast reaching crisis point. In reality, the problem is national: not only does Mexico have few large rivers, but 80 percent of its population live more than 4,000 feet above sea level, where only 20 percent of total water supplies are to be found; and of this population, 28 percent live in Mexico City.

Traditionally, the city obtained its water from its own subsoil, but this resulted in entire neighborhoods sinking by as much as nine inches a year. Expensive new techniques were developed to deal with the problem: many old churches began leaning precariously and were straightened; new high-rise buildings were constructed on special foundations that would permit them to sink with the city; and subway lines were placed inside metal tubes that "float" in the soft subsoil. When underground supplies became seriously depleted, water was pumped hundreds of miles from the Lerma and Cutzamala rivers. To keep up with the rising population and replenish the subsoil deposits, the government is required to increase outside water supply by 40 percent between 1984 and 1988. And to satisfy an estimated 60 percent rise in water demand by the end of the century, multibillion-dollar plans to tap the Tecalutla and Amacuzac rivers were drawn up.

Forced to fill buckets at communal faucets and carry them to their shacks, perhaps a mile away, the 2 million or so people without running water in their homes have long recognized the precariousness of this lifeline. In contrast, in wealthier neighborhoods, cars and sidewalks are still washed and gardens watered daily, with consumption per capita estimated at forty times higher than in poorer parts of town. But while government publicity campaigns urging conservation of water and even a sharp hike in water tariffs in 1983 failed to reduce wastage, the repeated suspension of water supplies to affluent districts during the months preceding the 1984 summer rainy season provoked alarm. Families began buying additional tanks, private water-supply trucks that normally worked only poor neighborhoods made their appearance outside mansions and couples interested in purchasing a house inquired first about the availability of water. The government rushed to repair leaking mains, but the water deficit could not be covered. In private, city officials warned that the lack of water would be more effective in stopping the capital's growth than any government strategy.

The problem of draining the metropolis is posing new health hazards. In poor neighborhoods with open sewers, high rates of infant mortality are attributed mainly to water pollution. In some cases, chemicals have been seeping through the soil and poisoning once pure subsoil deposits. A huge drainage system built in the late 1970s carries much of the city's waste to the Salado River some eighty miles away, but this flows into the Tula River and its waters are used to irrigate farms supplying the capital with vegetables. Since this waste is untreated, it too includes chemicals that are now being found in market food. With the entire ecological balance of the Valley of Mexico being disturbed, drastic measures are called for. One United Nations expert estimated that a massive reforestation program in the area would make the capital self-sufficient in water within twenty years. But most plans contemplate huge sewage treatment plants and recycling of water for industrial and agricultural purposes, although in the short term they are beyond the city's budget.

Before the De la Madrid administration could dream of new investments, it sought to strengthen the city's threadbare finances by absorbing its $2.3-billion debt and ordering sharp hikes in real estate and other taxes. Yet in 1983 the city could still finance only 18 percent of its expenditure with its own revenue, while its $3-billion budget for 1984 concentrated most resources on public transportation and offered no hope of tackling such endemic problems as air and water pollution, floods, blackouts, garbage disposal and slum housing.

The sharp rise in urban crime that followed the 1982 economic crisis, however, stirred middle-class protests and prompted the government to spend heavily on the city police. In the past, despite its poverty and overpopulation, Mexico City was considered a safe metropolis for all except slum dwellers: street assaults were rare, while homes were burglarized only if empty. But incidents of crime grew by 37 percent in 1983 and, with conversation over dinner increasingly monopolized by the subject, it became a positive obsession of the middle and upper classes. Having little faith in the city's 27,000-strong police force, they began to adopt their own security measures, hiring private armed guards to hover at front entrances or blocking off streets and placing checkpoints at each end. (The ordinary policeman earns less than $200 per month and is therefore more interested in supplementing his income than in risking his life by fighting armed criminals.)

In the absence of an electoral escape valve, the fear, anger and frustration of many *chilangos* over life in Mexico City are growing. Most of the country's educated, wealthy and politically literate are concentrated in the city, yet they have no voice in the management of urban affairs and no influence over the choice or policies of the mayor and his sixteen "delegates." Opposition parties have long demanded direct elections for the city government but, unwilling to permit the Federal District to fall into opposition hands, the government has looked for less risky forms of representation. Under López Portillo, Mayor Hank González organized a network of block committees that elected delegates to a city council. But in practice neither the committees nor the council had any power. When De la Madrid perpetuated the system in 1983, manipulation of the committees by the PRI was so blatant that the "elections" were ignored by most people.

Over the long term, the destiny of Mexico City may depend more on the policies adopted outside the capital than on those of the city government. By the year 2000, 75 to 80 percent of Mexicans will be living in towns and cities. With a successful family planning program, the country's total population may stand at around 110 million; and with the rural population expected to remain fairly static, 40 million people will be born in—or migrate to—urban areas during the final two decades of the century. The pressing questions are where they will live and how their basic needs can be satisfied. In 1977, a National Urban Development Plan projected optimistically that by the end of the century Mexico City would have 20 million inhabitants, Guadalajara and Monterrey would have 5 million each, eleven cities would have populations of around 1 million, while there would be seventy-four smaller cities with between 100,000 and 500,000 inhabitants each. By 1984, with the capital's population already 17 million, these projections seemed unrealistic.

The idea of deconcentrating and dispersing the population remained valid, but new urban settlements would have to follow government and industry, which, in the past, have resisted decentralization. No one has suggested challenging tradition by moving the capital, and even efforts to dispatch some government offices to the provinces have failed. When the National Coffee Institute was sent to Jalapa in 1977 as an experiment, its top executives kept their homes and offices in the capital: most ambitious politicians are also rising bureaucrats who feel lost if far from the center of power. In 1980, the state oil monopoly, Petróleos Mexicanos, saw no contradiction in building a new 52-floor headquarters in downtown Mexico City, hundreds of miles from its nearest oil well. Similarly, despite fiscal incentives to invest in "new" regions, many large companies have until recently continued to expand their operations in Mexico City, attracted by subsidized water, energy, transportation and proximity to their main market.

One of De la Madrid's first measures was to announce that no new industry would be authorized in the capital. The government later warned that factories poisoning the environment would be moved out of the city, although it failed to disclose which industries would be affected, when this would take place and what incentives would be provided. A broad development plan was also designed for the so-called Central Region, covering the states—México, Hidalgo, Morelos, Querétaro, Puebla and Tlaxcala—that traditionally send most migrants to the capital. In theory, by establishing new industry in these states, Mexico City's environment would be protected from further damage, while new jobs would keep migrants in their home states. But in practice, most migrants are now drawn by the labor-intensive services sector, which accounts for 50 percent of economic activity in Mexico City.

Perhaps the only way to temper the capital's growth is to make the city less attractive to migrants and more uncomfortable for its residents. The limited government resources that will be available in coming years could be channeled overwhelmingly into investments in agriculture, industry and urbanization in distant regions. But this would involve considerable political risk. The entire system of alliances and interest groups revolves around the concept of centralized power. The largest concentrations of rich, middle class and poor are to be found in Mexico City, each with a potential to destabilize society if their expectations were permanently disappointed. Yet, if in the past the capital was the natural product of a specific development strategy, its continued and chaotic growth in the future will be attributed to a political decision not to stop it.

I4

The Other Mexicos

I

Without strong central governments, a stable nation would not have been forged from the Indian tribes, regional warlords, rebellious generals and self-made entrepreneurs scattered over the mountains, deserts and distant cities of this large territory. But from the Aztec Empire to this day, the provinces have resisted and resented this alien domination. While politics, business and culture are concentrated in the capital and even the image of the "typical" Mexican reflects the idiosyncrasies of the *chilango,* different regions have stubbornly maintained strong independent personalities. True federalism may exist only in the country's official name —the United Mexican States—and in the letter of the Constitution, but history, religion, culture and economics have made it possible for a multitude of different identities to be embraced by a single nation. The mere mention of a provincial city or region, in fact, conveys a distinct image that somehow must fit into the larger mosaic.

The struggle between centralism and regionalism has been and will remain a constant of Mexican history: centralism has dominated because it is politically more efficient, but regionalism has survived because it is culturally more natural. Thus, while the Aztec Empire and the Spanish Colony demanded submission to Tenochtitlan and Mexico City, neither was fully successful in subjugating the provinces. Conversely, the extreme weakness of the governments following Independence facilitated the loss of half of Mexico's territory to the United States, the near-secession of the Yucatán and Baja California and the occupation of the country by French troops. This in turn led even *provincianos* to recognize that Mexico's "territorial integrity" could only be preserved by strong government.

In the late nineteenth century, two men from Oaxaca, Benito Juárez and Porfirio Díaz, began the process of nation-building, with the concepts of President, government, state and nation gradually blending into a single central pillar of stability. While regional unrest subsequently contributed to the revolution against General Díaz, the victorious northerners—Carranza, Obregón and Calles—who controlled Mexico from 1915 to 1935 were equally intolerant of any challenges to their authority. A convenient justification was formulated: since regionalism could be construed as a threat to national unity, provincial opposition to the ruling group in Mexico City should be suffocated.

Since then, central control has been perpetuated through an array of instruments. Since the late 1930s, the government's purpose in weakening the Army was to forestall regional military rebellions, and to this day zone commanders are regularly rotated to prevent them from establishing local power bases. Similarly, state governors are chosen by the President and they remain highly dependent on instructions from the Interior Minister, who, when necessary, can orchestrate their impeachment and ouster. The federal security apparatus, also run by the Interior Ministry, ignores state lines and frequently acts without informing the local authorities. Even the PRI, theoretically a national party, is run largely from the capital, with the result that all successful political careers must pass through Mexico City.

The federal bureaucracy also retains vast and arbitrary administrative powers. Businessmen in the provinces complain that it favors entrepreneurs in the capital, while states protest that the federal budget has traditionally taken more than it returns. Most state and municipal governments have insufficient resources to deal with the problems—roads, public transportation, housing, water supply and drainage systems—of most immediate concern to local populations. Unlike the federal government, which has strengthened its role in the economy through deficit spending financed from abroad, state governments cannot raise foreign credits without the Finance Ministry's permission. For a long time, most highways and airline routes began and ended in Mexico City, as if intended to avoid direct communication between regions.

Culturally, the provinces have done better in resisting the homogenizing force from the center. In the long run, this too may be a losing battle: increasingly, television projects Mexico City's vision and tastes across the country, while most artists and intellectuals are sooner or later coopted by the capital. But, owing largely to the strong cultural heritages bequeathed and preserved by various Indian groups, states and regions can still be identified through their traditional costumes, dances, music, poetry and food. Only an expert could recognize the geographic origin of each costume, mask and dance, but every *chilango* can distinguish the varying accents or argots of Spanish spoken in, say, Mérida, Veracruz or Chihuahua. In fact, not only personalities, but also physical characteristics—physiognomy, height and racial mixture—vary from region to region.

In sentimental terms, regionalism has been kept alive by the emotional power of smells, tastes, sights and sounds. Even in Mexico City, despite widespread ignorance of and indifference to political developments in the provinces, millions of *capitalinos* maintain nostalgic ties to some distant home: migrants of all classes will boast unabashedly of the virtues of their *tierra*, returning whenever feasible; some choose their friends from among other migrants from the same state; a few import regional traditions through special associations, gathering on weekends to eat, dance, gossip and even wear costumes as they might have done years earlier back home. There are restaurants with regional food, shops with regional handicrafts and nightclubs with regional music. Some states also organize annual festivals in Mexico City, as much to draw tourists to the provinces as to maintain a symbolic presence in the capital.

Political loyalties are often channeled along regional lines. The first move of an aspiring provincial politician is to find someone from his home state who is higher up the federal ladder and is willing to act as a sponsor. Often unrecognized by outsiders, groups of officials from the same state may quietly monopolize different corners of the bureaucracy. The regional links of the President are also important. After the "northern" Presidents, for instance, Portes Gil was identified with Tamaulipas, Cárdenas with Michoacán, Alemán and Ruiz Cortines with Veracruz and Díaz Ordaz with Puebla, and in each case they surrounded themselves with fellow *provincianos*. The last three Presidents have been *chilango* bureaucrats, but Echeverría's perspective was changed by marrying into the powerful Zuno family from Jalisco, while López Portillo was proud that his grandfather once served as governor of Jalisco. Even De la Madrid, who moved to Mexico City at the age of three, stressed his links with his native state of Colima, which has been favored during his administration.

The perspective from the provinces, however, remains one of suffocating control and indiscriminate imposition by Mexico City. While justified in the years following the Revolution, overcentralization of politics has now become a source of instability at election time. The President often picks PRI candidates for state gubernatorial elections from among old friends or politicians who have made their careers inside the federal government and have little local prestige or following. Some governors further bruise local sensibilities by surrounding themselves with officials who, although born locally, are better known in Mexico City, where they plan to resume their political ascent when the provincial sojourn is over. Opposition parties, in contrast, invariably choose a well-known local figure as their candidate and can exploit regional pride in their campaign against the PRI. To date, no gubernatorial election defeat has yet been recognized by the PRI, but violent protests have frequently followed suspected frauds. In mayoral elections in several large provincial cities where candidates have been picked in a similar fashion, opposition victories have been recognized.

Despite the growing political cost of this practice, however, no President has been willing to surrender the power to name his proconsuls. Instead, recent governments have sought less political ways of appeasing the provinces. Road and telephone communications between different states have vastly improved, and airline passengers are now able to fly between, say, Monterrey and Guadalajara without passing through the capital. Key ministries have opened regional offices authorized to handle fiscal and other problems that previously demanded trips to Mexico City. Control of some federally funded rural development programs has passed to state governments, while some states have attracted industrial investment without mediation by Mexico City. Arguing that efficient management required greater decentralization, De la Madrid proposed that states administer the federal education budget, which in several cases implied a doubling or tripling of resources handled by a governor. Decentralization of administration, however, is not synonymous with decentralization of power.

The problems and perils involved in transferring authority away from both Mexico City and state capitals were well illustrated by a municipal reform initiated by the De la Madrid administration in 1983. Since democracy exists only if it functions at a grass-roots level, the idea was to strengthen both the political and the economic autonomy of municipalities by guaranteeing opposition parties a voice in municipal councils and, more important, authorizing municipalities to collect and keep local land taxes. The enormous contrasts among the country's 2,377 municipalities made a single uniform policy impractical: they range from impoverished villages of 500 inhabitants to prosperous cities like Guadalajara and Monterrey with populations of around 3 million each; and while some large northern states have a half-dozen municipalities, Oaxaca alone has 570.

From an administrative point of view, some small municipalities are so poor that they must continue to depend on state governments and federal programs for basic services. But from a political point of view, both state governments and Mexico City have an interest in holding on to the purse-strings of larger municipalities in case they fall into opposition hands. Coinciding with the municipal reform, in fact, were victories in several northern state capitals by the conservative PAN party, while the government was forced to resort to fraud to block other opposition triumphs in cities bordering on the United States and nearer the capital.

Every federal government must therefore strike a balance between surrendering political control and stirring provincial resentment, between defending the national interest and accommodating the dramatically different characteristics and personalities of each region. The task is far from simple. Some social anthropologists have recognized around two hundred regions within Mexico's thirty-one states. Others, arguing that regionalism transcends local folklore to reflect the broad cultural, economic, political and religious features of larger areas, have identified eight different regions: those states immediately surrounding Mexico City; those in western Mexico within Guadalajara's sphere of influence; the Gulf coast states, notably Veracruz; the agricultural states of northwestern Mexico; the industrial centers of northeastern Mexico; the cities bordering on the United States; the Yucatán Peninsula; and the southern states of Chiapas and Oaxaca. But even the most cursory look reveals at least three distinct Mexicos: the *mestizo* and Colonial center, the modern Americanized north and the old Indian south.

II

Controlled by the Aztecs and then conquered and converted by the Spanish, Mexico's central highlands have long been dominated by the capital. They supply Mexico City with its food, its cheap labor and, increasingly, its industrial products, they accept the cultural and political leadership of the capital and they benefit from their proximity to the nation's largest market. It is not a homogeneous area. Several mutually unintelligible languages—Nahuatl, Otomí and Mazahua among them—are still spoken, while the huge mansions of Mexico City and the impoverished communities of rural Guerrero mirror the economic contrasts it embraces. Different cities retain their own personalities: Cuernavaca as a relaxed spa, Puebla as an ultra-Catholic stronghold, Pachuca as a dour mining town, Toluca as a new industrial center. But, spread over a wide area, these semi-arid mountainous states—Hidalgo, Tlaxcala, Puebla, Morelos, Guerrero, México and Querétaro—comprise a distinct *mestizo* region.

Industrial development and improved communications have accelerated the absorption of these states by Mexico City. The capital's congestion has spawned a generation of new factories in the industrial zones of Toluca, Querétaro, Puebla and Cuernavaca, although their corporate headquarters invariably remain in Mexico City. Highway construction has further integrated nearby rural areas, facilitating the temporary or permanent migration of peasants to urban slums. Some local business groups exist, particularly in the state of México, but they exercise their influence directly in Mexico City rather than independently. Similarly, with the exception of the Zapatistas of Morelos during the 1910s, these states have shown no instinct for rebelling against the capital. But the federal government maintains a tight hold: just as the mayor of Mexico City is appointed by the President, no opposition party has been allowed to win political control over a major city in the region.

The imprint of history is no less visible in the two other central regions of Mexico. In a sense, Guadalajara and Veracruz have little in common with each other or, indeed, with Mexico City. But these were Mexico's most important cities during the eighteenth and nineteenth centuries, and as such their economic and political destinies were interwoven with those of the capital. In their different ways, Guadalajara and Veracruz are therefore very "Mexican" cities, proudly regionalist but rarely questioning their identification with the central government. Neither city possesses industrial groups of national importance that might challenge Mexico City's business giants. (Even Veracruz's most important industry, the TAMSA steel complex, has its headquarters in the capital.) While both cities have a tradition of producing skilled politicians, they have preferred to infiltrate the central government and exercise their influence from within.

Guadalajara has long been the country's second-largest city, and its sphere of influence includes its own state of Jalisco as well as nearby Colima, Nayarit and Michoacán, although these rural areas have in turn helped feed the provincial mood and attitudes of Guadalajara itself. Certainly, other Mexicans have an almost cliché image of the *tapatío,* the native of Guadalajara. He has been brought up in a strongly Catholic family, dominated by conservative traditions and *criollo* pride in its Spanish ancestry. He is a strong believer in private enterprise and is quick to defend his honor or *machismo* with a gun. He considers it socially essential to marry into a "known" family, to live on the west side of town and to be well versed in the works of such *tapatío* native sons as the painter José Clemente Orozco and the writers Juan Rulfo and Agustín Yáñez. Outsiders—*mestizos,* Jews and Arabs—are generally unwelcome in aristocratic circles, but French and Spanish migrants are accepted as contributing to the "whiteness" of the city. Politically intolerant of socialist thought and culturally scornful of the moral laxity of American liberalism, Guadalajara society has tried to resist modernizing influences.

Even in business, the city has proved conservative, maintaining a structure of family firms and rarely entering into partnerships with transnational corporations, diversifying into huge conglomerates or assuming the risks of borrowing abroad. As a result, during the boom of the late 1970s, none of the new industrial groups that changed Mexico's economic profile came from this region. But, during the economic crisis that followed, the region's prior caution helped cushion the impact of the slump. For the old families, in fact, wealth is like breeding: it should be neither brazenly exhibited nor politically exploited. Even newer entrepreneurs have tended to be unadventurous, preferring the safety of real estate development to investment in industry. One exception is the Canadá Shoe firm, which was built up by a family of poor cobblers into the city's largest group.

Guadalajara does not try to compete with the capital, its regional pride quietly satisfied by seeing such distinctly *tapatío* products as tequila and mariachi music adopted as popular symbols of Mexican nationalism and its painters and writers improving the culture of the nation as a whole. Politically, the region has reacted against the center only when it has perceived threats to its Catholic and conservative way of life. It played a marginal role in the War of Independence and the Revolution, but the government's efforts to restrict religious freedom and impose secular education in the 1920s provoked the bloody Cristero uprising throughout the region. Guadalajara itself was not the scene of open conflict, but it provided weapons, money and refuge to the rebels and its bishop took to the hills rather than obey a government order to leave the country, while the city's Catholic aristocrats were forced to celebrate mass in hiding. In the late 1930s, distrustful of the radicalism of the Cárdenas administration, local conservatives founded the ultra-Catholic Autonomous University of Guadalajara (UAG) and played a key role in forming the opposition National Action Party (PAN), a movement that still retains strong, if informal, links with the Catholic Church. The PAN, however, has never won the mayoralty of Guadalajara or the governorship of Jalisco.

In the early 1970s, Guadalajara again felt besieged by the Left, and although the threat came from disenchanted radicals inside its own universities, the local elite immediately blamed Mexico City. In the past, leaders of the Guadalajara Student Federation (FEG) had collaborated with local politicians in controlling student activism, but after the unrest of 1968 a new Revolutionary Student Front (FER) appeared which soon formed urban guerrilla units. Not only did this movement coincide with Echeverría's new leftist rhetoric, but there were also signs that the President's local in-laws, the powerful Zuno family, were somehow involved in the agitation. The result was a serious crisis in relations between Guadalajara and the central government, with local business leaders even calling on the Army to restore order in the city. While the guerrillas were subsequently wiped out by federal security police, the entire episode greatly strengthened extreme rightist and neo-fascist forces within Guadalajara, many of them closely linked to the UAG and its movement of students and alumni known as *los tecos*.

Physical change, however, has come to Guadalajara. A permanent pall of smog and large new slums bear witness to the industrialization and accompanying migration that have doubled the city's population to around 3 million since 1970. To visitors from the capital, Guadalajara still seems slow-moving, but its elegant downtown area is now crowded with cars, while broad new avenues have extended the suburbs and gradually absorbed such nearby towns as Tlaquepaque, Zapopán and Tonalá. *Tapatíos* warn themselves against following Mexico City's example, and many signs of urban blight have already appeared. But the city still retains much of its provincial formality, closing down for long lunches much as Mexico City did forty years ago. It is this rhythm as well as the region's temperate climate that over the years has attracted thousands of American retirees to settle in Guadalajara and nearby communities beside Lake Chapala. They live in virtual isolation from the *tapatíos*, but are tolerated because they are quiet and respectable and, in the end, want to share rather than change Guadalajara's traditional way of being.

In contrast, in a country almost obsessed with introspection, Veracruz and the Gulf coast are Mexico's windows to the world through which a great variety of influences have passed. Cortés himself founded Veracruz when he arrived there from Cuba in 1519, and subsequently gold and silver left for Spain and colonizers arrived from Europe through the port. Later, migrants—Caribbean blacks, Arabs, Spaniards and other Europeans—settled in the area, giving the city a cosmopolitan and multiracial air that it retains to this day. The influence of Cuba, where ships would call en route from Spain to Mexico, is particularly felt. The vegetation, climate and even geographical shape of Cuba as well as the island's Afro-Iberian racial mixture are all repeated in Veracruz state. Cuba is also present in the way locals speak Spanish, in the dark coffee and strong cigars, in the music and food and in the tradition of holding a noisy pre-Lenten carnival.

Veracruz is not, however, a bustling port. Floating in the muggy heat of sea level, it has seemed happy to leave hard work to the more competitive environment of the central highlands. The *jarochos*—as Veracruz locals are known—like to boast of the "good life" they enjoy, rarely shedding their white *guayabera* sport shirts for suits and lingering over long seafood lunches under the whitewashed arches of the main square or in the former slave town of Mandinga to the accompaniment of the harps and guitars of troubadours. When *chilangos* arrive from the capital, they feel out of place: their accents sound strange, their pace is too fast and they cannot dance like the *jarochos*.

A succession of less welcome visitors to Veracruz have turned the port into a symbol of nationalism and strengthened its links to the central government. After Cortés came Sir Francis Drake and other buccaneers intent on grabbing gold and silver destined for the Spanish court, but still more invaders followed Independence: the French took the port during the so-called Pastry War of 1837; U.S. troops landed there in 1847 en route to Mexico City; the French, British and Spanish occupied Veracruz in 1861, the French then staying on to install the Emperor Maximilian; and in 1914, at the height of the Revolution, U.S. Marines again seized the city. Thus, in Mexico's struggle to defend its very existence as a nation, "Four Times Heroic Veracruz," as it is known, has always been present as both the farthest outpost and the first line of battle.

While the city of Veracruz has changed little, the Gulf coast region has been transformed over the past decade by the oil industry. This area that for centuries had Veracruz as its capital now has other centers of economic power spread around a 1,000-mile crescent. Tampico and Poza Rica have been important oil towns for several decades, but the new oil finds of the mid-1970s moved the focus of development south toward Coatzacoalcos, Villahermosa and Ciudad del Carmen and drew migrants —peasants seeking jobs and businessmen seeking fortunes—from all over. Yet the Gulf region is politically important only because the Oil Workers' Union is still run from Ciudad Madero, near Tampico. Most other decisions affecting the oil region are taken in Petróleos Mexicanos' headquarters in Mexico City, while any residue of local tradition and cultural pride outside the city of Veracruz has been poisoned by the chaotic and greedy rush of the oil boom.

The federal government views the Gulf coast region with a certain proprietorial interest, not only benefiting directly from its oil wealth but also seeing its energy, water, territory and agricultural resources as offering a long-term answer to the problem of the overcrowded highlands. Though decentralization of the population has not taken place, all studies of the ideal location for the "new cities" of the twenty-first century point to Veracruz and other Gulf coast states. In the late 1970s, a special effort was made to attract new industries to the region by building a natural gas pipeline up the Gulf coast from Villahermosa and by designing new industrial ports for Tampico and Coatzacoalcos. While resistance to leaving Mexico City remained strong, Veracruz and the Gulf began to symbolize an important development option for Mexico: to tackle the new "frontier" of the coastal lowlands.

III

At the time of the Conquest, there were no major pre-Hispanic civilizations in the inhospitable mountains and deserts of northern Mexico. The area was therefore colonized—first by missionaries and miners, later by farmers and industrialists—rather than conquered. As a result, it is the one region of Mexico that is not overshadowed by its past. Some Indian tribes survive—among them, Yaquis in the Pacific lowlands and Tarahumaras in the Sierra Madre—but most of the vast empty north has been populated and developed over the past hundred years.

Since then a different country has appeared where people are more daring and efficient, more outspoken and informal, even taller and whiter than most Mexicans. Their struggle to survive is reflected in their tough character. They are hard-driving self-made men who have tamed nature by turning rocks into cities and desert into fertile land, no less proud of their achievements than they are jealous of their independence. While most Mexicans remain hypnotized by the old, norteños reach out for the new, borrowing techniques and attitudes from the United States without crises of identity. They feel that they represent the new Mexico, and even more than resenting the meddling by Mexico City, they despise the political and bureaucratic ways of the chilangos.

Old mission posts testify to the efforts of the Spanish Crown to colonize a region which at the time included the Texas, Arizona, New Mexico and California of today. But it was only after the loss of these territories in the mid-nineteenth century that the north began to develop, first around such old mining towns as Durango and later through cattle ranching. By the turn of the century, Porfirio Díaz already viewed the relative autonomy of the north as a threat, and set out to destroy the fiefdoms of the Pesqueira family in Sonora and the Terrazas family in

Chihuahua. The large northern landowners were soon ready to turn their economic and political power against the Díaz dictatorship, and in the Revolution that followed, change came for the first time from the north. Madero's family owned land in Coahuila, Durango's most infamous son was Francisco "Pancho" Villa, Carranza had served as governor of Chihuahua and, finally, the Sonora "dynasty" of Obregón, Calles and De la Huerta took over. Yet even these *norteños* never truly integrated the north politically. To this day, few northerners are attracted by careers in the PRI or the federal bureaucracy, while the center retains a special respect for the stubborn independence of the northern states.

The north's principal power is economic, and its most recent clashes with Mexico City have taken place in this arena. In the northwest, the irrigated coastal plains of Sonora and Sinaloa account for much of the country's winter fruit and vegetable, rice, wheat and sorghum production. Such cities as Culiacán, Los Mochis, Ciudad Obregón and Hermosillo are strongholds of wealthy conservative farmers who believe fervently in the work ethic and the profit motive and have no time for the agrarian populism emanating cyclically from the capital. In the early 1970s, their resistance to Echeverría's stepped-up land reform program provoked a wave of agitation by semi-official peasant organizations that climaxed in the expropriation of some 90,000 acres of irrigated private land outside Ciudad Obregón. Echeverría was clearly anxious to demonstrate his loyalty to the peasant cause, but he seemed no less determined to punish the "insubordination" of the wealthy northerners. They absorbed the blow and, while still deeply distrustful of Mexico City, the farmers of the Yaqui Valley personify the one dynamic sector of Mexican agriculture.

The rebellious frontier spirit brought another problem to the federal government in the 1970s, when Culiacán became the center of a multibillion-dollar narcotics trade. Peasants in the inaccessible mountains of Sinaloa happily multiplied their incomes by growing marijuana and opium poppies, while powerful drug rings in Culiacán packed the marijuana and processed the heroin that was smuggled by land, sea and air into the United States. The resulting gang warfare and massive corruption convulsed the once quiet provincial city and prompted the direct intervention of the Army, which finally brought the problem under some control. Even now, the *federales* still maintain a permanent presence in Culiacán and other narcotics cultivation areas of the north, in the belief that local police cannot be trusted to attack the problem.

In practice, the personalities of different cities mirror the interests of their own business groups. Yet from their Stetson hats and cowboy boots to their defense of private enterprise and opposition to state intervention, wealthy northerners have much in common. During the agitated period under Echeverría, strong political links between the farmers of the north-west and the industrialists of the northeast were forged. Both felt threat-ened by the President's verbal radicalism and they joined forces to com-bat the perceived threat of Communism. Both also had strong economic ties to the United States and, out of fear, initiated the flight of capital that subsequently brought on the 1976 currency devaluation. Political leadership was provided by the millionaires of Monterrey.

Monterrey traces its foundation to 1596, but it was not until three hundred years later that it began its transformation into Mexico's se-cond-largest industrial center and third-largest city. Since then, the story of Monterrey has been inseparable from that of the Garza and Sada families, which, through intermarriage, eventually formed a powerful tightly knit clan. Starting with a brewery, the two families built up a huge business empire that not only included steel, glass, chemicals and finance but also served as a motor for the city's general economic growth. Further, the Monterrey Group, as it was known, came to symbolize the industrious no-nonsense approach of the *regiomontano* inhabitants of the city. They emphasized education, ambition, initiative and profit, and paid scant attention to such "socialist" concepts as trade unions, urban planning and environmental protection. Such was the city's commitment to money that the *regiomontanos* earned a reputation elsewhere in Mex-ico for penny-pinching meanness. But the results of their labors gave them a strong sense of regional pride that translated into distrust and disregard for all outsiders, above all politicians and bureaucrats sent by Mexico City to meddle with their "freedom."

As early as 1934, their opposition to "socialist education" earned them the fierce rebuke of General Calles, who referred to them on one occasion as "capitalist Jews . . . allied to the clergy" and denounced their "voracity and egoism." (Although by then strong Catholics, the Garza and Sada families were of Sephardic Jewish origin.) Between 1940 and 1970, the pro-business policies of successive governments assured good relations between Monterrey and Mexico City, but these soured again when Echeverría began attacking the Group as a prime example of conserva-tive capitalism. As in Guadalajara, the appearance of urban guerrillas in Monterrey in 1971 was blamed by the local elite on Echeverría. After the head of the Monterrey Group, Eugenio Garza Sada, was murdered by leftist guerrillas in 1973, the city's business community became convinced that Communism was about to engulf Mexico. Garza Sada's heirs felt so vulnerable that they broke up the Monterrey Group into the Alfa

Group, chaired by his nephew, Bernardo Garza Sada, and the VISA Group, run by his son, Eugenio Garza Lagüera. Echeverría in turn held the "fascists" of Monterrey responsible for the wild rumors that accompanied his final days in office.

Duly convinced of Monterrey's determination to defend itself against the central government and anxious for a symbol of his desired rapprochement with the private sector as a whole, López Portillo therefore began wooing the *regiomontano* industrialists as soon as he took office. They responded with enthusiasm and relief, investing, expanding and diversifying in such a way that the Alfa Group in particular soon carried the flag of business confidence throughout the country. Eventually, when Alfa overborrowed and overspent itself into bankruptcy, López Portillo responded loyally by approving government loans to bail out the conglomerate. But it was too late. With Mexico's own financial collapse completing the demise of Alfa in 1982, Monterrey could once again blame the central government for its problems.

Monterrey had long disguised its ugliness with bustle and dynamism, but now many of its chronic social and urban ills were suddenly exposed by the slump. Unable to keep up payments on its $5-billion foreign debt when domestic demand evaporated, the city's major corporations were forced to close factories and lay off thousands of employees, from U.S.-educated MBAs to construction workers. Sorely short of resources, the city government fell further behind in providing water, electricity and paved streets to local slums, while air pollution seemed to hang more pungently in the arid valley. The innate self-confidence of the *regiomontanos* somehow survived intact: they set about rebuilding local industry, convinced that through hard work they would once again become the envy of Mexico City.

By 1983, a new political mood appeared to be spreading across northern Mexico. Middle-class disenchantment with the federal government had been visible in growing anti-PRI votes throughout the country in the 1970s. In the early 1980s, anger at the economic crisis was compounded in the north by regional factors. Better educated, fed and housed than the rest of the population and influenced by the sight of U.S. democracy at work nearby, northerners began demanding a more open political debate and a freer electoral process. When the PRI campaigned with old-fashioned revolutionary rhetoric and the PAN addressed the immediate concerns of the middle classes, the ruling party suddenly began to lose. Because anti-government sentiments seemed indistinguishable from regional pride, Mexico City was uncertain how to respond.

It was nevertheless the PAN's victory in Ciudad Juárez on the border with the United States that most alarmed the government. The prospect of a string of border cities falling into the hands of the conservative pro-American PAN seemed like a threat to the country's sovereignty. It reawakened both fears about the political vulnerability of the northern border and latent doubts about the patriotism of the *fronterizo* population. But successive governments had in fact contributed to this "denationalizing" process: while the border cities have always existed as a function of their proximity to the United States, Mexico City has done little to incorporate them into the rest of the country.

Long after the border was fixed in 1848, such towns as Tijuana, Nogales, Ciudad Juárez and Matamoros were still little more than border crossings. As the American side of the border developed, the Mexican side became important as a safe haven from American law and morality, protecting fugitives and providing prostitution and gambling. During Prohibition, Ciudad Juárez not only exploded with bars but also served as the bootlegging center for much of the American Southwest. By the 1920s, the reputation of the Mexican border towns was already established: American authorities complained that they were centers of crime and sin, while Mexico City despised them as "de-Mexicanized" beachheads of the country's peaceful conquest by the United States.

The fortunes of the border cities nevertheless remained tied to the United States. Just as Prohibition brought a boom and the Depression a severe slump, World War II helped them enormously, with hundreds of thousands of Mexicans crossing north to work and as many Americans—above all, servicemen—crossing south for diversion. In the 1950s and 1960s, while a continuing American demand for stoop labor pulled Mexican peasants north, tighter border controls swelled the Mexican border population. The cities remained service economies, always looking for new ways of drawing tourists. To the traditional fare of prostitution, gambling and risqué nightclub shows were added bullfights, horse racing, narcotics, contraband and even quickie divorces. To the distress of officials in the capital, this was the only Mexico that millions of Americans saw.

Between 1940 and 1980, excluding those hundreds of thousands seeking illegal entry into the United States each year, the permanent population of the eight main border cities—Tijuana, Mexicali, Nogales, Piedras Negras, Ciudad Juárez, Nuevo Laredo, Reynosa and Matamoros—expanded more than twentyfold to 3.4 million. This growth in turn prompted federal authorities to recognize that an entirely new border phenomenon now existed. From the late 1960s, federal aid was therefore channeled toward addressing such chronic problems as housing, water supplies, roads, schools and hospitals. To appease local shopkeepers who saw most *fronterizos* spending their money across the border, they were given permission to import foreign goods duty-free for resale in the Mexican border cities. Finally, taking advantage of U.S. trade legislation, the government began encouraging the establishment of "in-bond" border factories—known as *maquiladoras*—which imported raw material duty-free and exported finished products, with U.S. tariffs paid only on the value added.

These programs had the effect of improving life at the border, but, paradoxically, they did little to reduce the region's dependence on the United States. The *maquiladora* program expanded rapidly as the promise of cheap nonunionized labor attracted hundreds of electrical assembly plants, textile factories and myriad other labor-intensive operations. In the process, tens of thousands of new jobs were created in a zone that previously had no industry. The boom also brought problems: it stimulated migration to the border cities, but because young women comprised over 90 percent of *maquiladora* employees, male unemployment actually increased. (In the mid-1980s, this phenomenon prompted the *maquiladoras* to seek more male workers, even though they are more likely to form unions.) Further, the number and employment levels of in-bond plants proved highly elastic, reflecting economic developments in Mexico: when rising inflation and wage levels were accompanied by a fixed exchange rate in both 1975 and 1981, many plants closed; after the devaluations of 1976 and 1982, many more opened up. By 1984, they provided some 150,000 jobs but surprisingly little long-term security.

Accepting their vulnerability, the border cities have learned to live off their wits, adjusting to ever-changing tastes and economic climates. Since more liberal laws and attitudes north of the border put quickie divorces out of business and closed down many Mexican red-light districts, they have tried to attract ordinary tourists in search of a Mexican meal, a bargain handicraft item or simply a day-trip to another country. But the loosely patrolled border also permits a spectrum of illicit activities. The economies of Tijuana and Ciudad Juárez are buoyed by the dollar incomes of maids and laborers who cross daily or weekly to work in San Diego or El Paso. All border cities harbor *coyotes* who guide undocumented migrants into the United States. Tighter controls over illegal migration by U.S. authorities may eventually reduce the flow of poor Mexicans to the border cities. But at any one time, drugs, oil and cattle are also being smuggled north, while consumer goods and firearms—some destined for Central American revolutionary movements—are being shipped south. Like border cities worldwide, these have a special appeal for those seeking lax laws and quick profits.

The problem of the region's cultural absorption by the United States, however, remains acute. Its population lacks a distinct personality, since migrants have come from all over the country. A new generation born at the border is now growing up without even sentimental attachment to some *tierra* deeper inside Mexico. While almost everyone has been to the United States, few have visited Mexico City. English is widely spoken, with English signs to be seen everywhere and Anglicisms creeping into local Spanish. A majority of adult *fronterizos* work for American companies or families, consume American products and watch American television programs. In fact, popular Mexican culture—food, music and handicrafts—is kept alive more by the demand of American tourists and itinerant migrants than by the tastes of locals.

Community leaders in the border cities resent the perception that the region is somehow less Mexican than the rest of the country. They see themselves acting as a dike against the onslaught of American culture and boast proudly that they are in fact "Mexicanizing" the American border states. If the idea of providing cheap entertainment to American tourists is bruising to national dignity, they blame the fact that, despite promises and programs, the federal government has failed to integrate the region—economically, culturally or, indeed, politically—with the rest of Mexico. The links to the United States are the result of need rather than choice: American products are purchased because Mexican products are unavailable.

Once again, the government has launched a border development program, but both resources and options are limited: its most important measure in 1983 was to renew Baja California's status as a duty-free zone for a further six years, thus recognizing its economic ties to the United States. More worrisome to the regime is the loosening of the border's ties with Mexico as a whole. Aware that this leads to rejection of the ruling PRI, the government began giving priority to "Mexicanizing" education and culture at the border, subsidizing celebrations of traditional festivals and emphasizing such key dates in the nation's calendar as Independence Day and Revolution Day. Such is the competing appeal from the north that the "reconquest" will be difficult: at the border, while Mexico seems more a concept, the United States is very much a reality.

IV

If the north is viewed by Mexico City as a disturbing force for unpredictable change, the regionalism of the south is deeply rooted in the past and, as such, strongly resistant to modernization. If the north is dynamic and developing, the south is static and impoverished. And if the north turns outward for influences, the south looks inward to preserve the status quo. The area's basic profile was shaped during pre-Hispanic times and its attitudes and behavior today can be explained in no other context: attached to the land of their forefathers, caught up in ancient traditions and squabbles, the *sureños* resented the impositions of the Aztecs six hundred years ago just as they regard *chilangos* as interfering foreigners today.

The Maya Empire had disintegrated long before the rise of the Aztecs, but the Mayas were never fully subjugated by the armies of Tenochtitlan, and in the sixteenth century they valiantly—and vainly—fought to hold off the extending fist of the Spanish conquistadors. During the Colony, the isolation of the Yucatán—it was closer and more accessible to Cuba than to Mexico City—reinforced the tradition of independence among the new *criollo* families of Mérida. But the rebellious spirit of the Mayas did not die, and in the mid-nineteenth century they rose up again in the War of the Castes, prompting the besieged elite of Mérida to offer to become a colony of the United States or Britain in exchange for protection. The Mayas were eventually put down with great loss of life, and the Yucatán was converted by the Díaz dictatorship into a virtual slave state. Today, its social plight is dismal. The region has no industry and most Maya peasants are reduced to bare subsistence farming on their *milpas* or the cultivation of henequen, which the government must buy at subsidized prices.

Despite deep poverty, the language, culture, religion and pride of the Mayas survives. The *mestizo* population of Mérida—to the mixture of Maya and Spanish is added an important dose of Arab migrant blood —also has a strong sense of regionalism. The *yucatecos* even distinguish themselves from the "Mexicans" and refer to their state, with only a touch of irony, as the Republic of Yucatán. Physically, they are much as their forefathers were portrayed in paintings and carvings: stocky, with large heads, receding foreheads and distinctly Maya aquiline noses. In character, they are dignified, stubborn and deeply distrustful of outsiders. Instinctively, they resist the dictates of Mexico City: the PRI lost the municipal elections in Mérida to the PAN in 1964, and five years later it preferred to face riots and resort to fraud rather than accept its defeat in gubernatorial elections. More recently, the PRI's selection of a general from Mexico City rather than a popular native son as the candidate for the 1982 gubernatorial elections again offended local sensibilities: two years later, the government felt pressured to dump the general and appoint the local favorite as governor.

The central government and the *chilangos* in general, however, have also distrusted the *yucatecos*. Theirs is a strategically located state and their record of rebellion and opposition makes their nationalism suspect. When some years ago Mexico's representative at a Miss World competition jokingly remarked that she came from the Republic of Yucatán, newspapers in the capital reacted with indignation, as if happy to see their prejudices toward the peninsula's inhabitants confirmed. Mexico City at times has even seemed anxious to maintain the Yucatán's isolation: Mérida was not connected to the national railroad system until 1950.

To the west, Oaxaca has proved no less difficult to govern, not least because of the state's large, highly fragmented Indian population. Through Benito Juárez and Porfirio Díaz, its influence over the rest of Mexico was felt strongly during the late nineteenth century, but today it is an introspective state, still dominated by its Mixtec and Zapotec past. Each of Oaxaca's 570 municipalities represents a village or community that existed at the time of the Conquest and subsequently refused to merge with its neighbor. In some rural areas, each extended family group has its own tradition of self-rule. Much of the violence that plagues the state stems from disputes between adjacent Indian villages over communal land rights. The resistance of rural Oaxaca is therefore less to interference from distant Mexico City than to acceptance of the "colonial" state government in the city of Oaxaca. But such is its poverty, with its eroded hills barely able to sustain an annual corn crop, that many peasants are forced to head for the more buoyant economies of Puebla or Mexico City.

In the fertile Isthmus of Tehuantepec, more serious problems appeared in the 1970s when the Student-Worker-Peasant Coalition of the Isthmus (COCEI) took up the cause of peasants whose communal lands had been occupied by large landowners. Riots in the city of Oaxaca in 1976 prompted the federal government to send in the Army and replace the local governor with a general, but rural tensions persisted. In 1980, Leopoldo de Gyves, a COCEI candidate supported by the Communist Party, won the mayoralty of Juchitán, the dominant town of the isthmus, and was allowed to take office as a symbol of López Portillo's new political reform. But his relations with the state government soon deteriorated: De Gyves complained that Juchitán was being denied its rightful share of the state budget, while PRI officials claimed it had become a center of subversion and even arms-smuggling to Central America.

Finally, on the eve of elections for the Oaxaca state Congress in August 1983, a violent clash between the respective supporters of PRI and COCEI candidates gave the federal government the opportunity to act: the Oaxaca Congress removed De Gyves and replaced him with a temporary municipal council. But the ousted mayor and his followers refused to leave the town hall and, perhaps fearing that armed resistance would lead to a bloodbath and a serious blemish on its image, the government decided not to evict them before the end of De Gyves' three-year term. Instead, when municipal elections were held in Oaxaca in November 1983, the PRI simply made sure that its candidates won in every village, town and city in the state, including the thirteen municipalities in which strong COCEI candidates were nominated. A few days before the PRI's new mayor in Juchitán was to take office, the Army ousted the COCEI from the town hall.

Despite the central government's intervention, the roots of the problem are regional. The fact that the people of Juchitán are of mainly Zapotec descent—a warrior tribe that was never conquered by the Aztecs—was essential to understanding their militancy. The local land disputes involved squabbles between *caciques* as well as broader ideological issues. After the violent ouster of the COCEI, even the Unified Socialist Party (PSUM) concluded that the affair could be explained only in a local context and it opted not to mount a major protest against the government in Mexico City. The ingredients for continuing grass-roots instability in Oaxaca remained in place, but it seemed unlikely to spread beyond traditional zones of friction, posing a constant headache to the state government and no challenge at all to federal authorities.

In Chiapas, a centuries-old tradition of regionalism has suddenly acquired greater strategic significance because the state borders on Guatemala and serves as Mexico's buffer with Central America. For the first time in decades, Mexico City is now looking to its deep south with concern. Until 1830, Chiapas was part of Guatemala and to this day, with its stunningly beautiful mountains and lakes, its large coffee and cotton plantations and its communities of impoverished Indian peons, it has more in common with Guatemala than with neighboring Oaxaca. In the eighteenth and nineteenth centuries, there were Indian uprisings, but in recent decades the state has been characterized by acute economic exploitation, social neglect and tight political control. The Indian peasants are merely required to vote for PRI candidates at election time but are otherwise without political voice. So long as political trouble was limited to occasional massacres of Indians trying to recover stolen communal land, the federal government paid minimal attention to Chiapas.

In mid-1981, however, the problems of Central America spilled into Chiapas when some 2,000 Guatemalan Indian refugees crossed into Mexico while fleeing a Guatemalan Army offensive. These first refugees were forced to return home, but as political violence escalated in Guatemala, more and more entered Mexico and were allowed to build improvised settlements in fields and woods close to the border. By late 1982, some 40,000 Guatemalans had arrived in Chiapas. Coincidentally, thousands of Salvadorans were also entering Mexico illegally through Chiapas, but they came across in small groups and pressed on to Mexico City or the United States. The Guatemalans, in contrast, arrived in communities, some of which had been "organized" by leftist guerrillas. With weapons being smuggled into Guatemala from Mexico, with "radical" priests involved in aiding the refugees and with Guatemalan military patrols occasionally entering Mexico in hot pursuit of guerrillas, the government feared contagion of Chiapas by Central America's political unrest.

The De la Madrid administration therefore designed a two-pronged strategy for the state: tighter security and improved welfare. Its objective was the repatriation of the Guatemalan refugees, and while it could not deport them without provoking a major international outcry, it moved quickly to isolate the border refugee camps and discourage new refugees from entering the country. But on April 30, 1984, Guatemalan soldiers entered Mexican territory and killed six refugees. Mexico therefore decided to relocate the refugees, officially numbering 46,000, to Campeche state. In the process, three more refugees were killed, this time by Mexican troops who were in charge of the forced eviction. At the same time, to improve its own ability to react to a border security problem, the government found the funds necessary to complete a 278-mile strategic highway running through the Lacandon jungle along Mexico's border with Guatemala. The road will eventually open up the area for oil exploration and the construction of hydroelectric dams, but its principal purpose was political. Increasingly, Chiapas has been viewed through the prism of Central America.

In public, greater emphasis was given to the socioeconomic aspects of the Chiapas Plan, although this too was motivated by the political need to defuse potential sources of unrest. In 1983, an unprecedented $900 million was spent on new schools, health clinics, nutrition and road construction programs. Subsequently, an integrated development plan for the entire southeast—comprising not only Chiapas and Oaxaca but also Veracruz, Tabasco, Campeche, Yucatán and Quintana Roo—was announced by the administration amid promises to improve the living standards of the country's poorest region.

But Mexico City's overriding concern remained Chiapas and its border to the south. As with the country's northern border, the government once again found itself caught between the seemingly conflicting needs to strengthen the region's autonomy and to secure its political loyalty to the center. The two borders had little else in common: in the north, relative prosperity tempered by an economic crisis, an outflow of migrants, a stable border and the political pressure of living beside a powerful democracy; in the south, chronic poverty aggravated by political uncertainty, an influx of refugees, a worrisome border and the "demonstration effect" offered by nearby revolutions. But even in a country built around centralism, a vital part of government remained that sought to manage the problems, accommodate the idiosyncrasies and pacify the mood of the provinces in order to maintain the national consensus. With the regions literally divided among themselves, however, the central government retained the final word.

15

Culture for Some and for Many

I

Intellectuals are perhaps the most privileged elite in Mexico. Academics, writers, painters and musicians of minimal renown inherit the right— even the duty—to participate in politics, to give opinions on subjects far removed from their areas of talent, to sit in judgment on the regime, even to denounce the system. The government in turn promotes their reputations, finances their cultural activities and tolerates their political dissidence, preferring the price of appeasing or coopting intellectuals to the perils of ignoring or alienating them. It is a strangely incestuous relationship, rich in posturing and ritual, obscured by radical language, frequently denied by both sides and long ago demonstrated to be mutually convenient.

Society as a whole has not benefited from this arrangement. While bureaucrats and intellectuals play the politics of culture in a small corner of the national stage, they have surrendered the cultural development of the broad mass of the population to the commercial interests that control radio, television, movies and comic books. In the case of the television network Televisa, it may involve the greatest cession of power by the state since the Revolution. But the trance has not been broken: the government seeks to influence writers and artists because it looks to the quality of the players rather than the size of their audience; and intellectuals, recognizing the centralized nature of power in Mexico, consider it more useful to influence the government than public opinion.

The role of the intellectual is highly institutionalized. To achieve this status, he must express interest in the problems of contemporary society, he must believe that he has a duty to pontificate on a variety of political subjects and he must harbor ambitions of exercising power directly one day. A less elegant definition might be someone who signs anti-American protests, writes a weekly column in a newspaper and dreams of becoming an ambassador. Recognition comes more easily to those on the left of the national conscience: simply by contributing toward the cost of publishing the declarations of an obscure Mexican Committee of Intellectuals and Artists for the Defense of the Sovereignty of Our Peoples, a writer can appear as a signatory and graduate as an intellectual. A politician with strong academic credentials will be respected as an intellectual if he has a liberal record, but he may be denigrated as a technocrat if conservative. Right-wing intellectuals do exist, but they must become famous as artists and writers before their political views are heeded. Nonetheless, the most important definition of an intellectual is that he should be recognized as such by the government. By deciding he is important enough to be wooed as a friend or persecuted as a foe, the ruling class perpetuates his role in society.

In Mexico, that role has traditionally been played close to power. Artists, sculptors and musicians provided the Aztecs with a cultural framework that gave cohesion to their militaristic and theocratic state. After the Conquest of Mexico, the Spanish Crown passed responsibility for the promotion and censorship of literature, painting, music and architecture to the Roman Catholic Church and the Inquisition. As in Spain, most cultural expression was religious and most Colonial writers and artists were priests. The concept of intellectual freedom was nonexistent: thought and creativity were expected to be supporting pillars of religion.

Mexico's intellectual tradition was therefore rooted in three centuries of Catholic dogmatism. Early in this century, when the Revolution finally broke the spell of the Church, the switch of loyalties to Marxism took place easily. "We are the sons of rigid ecclesiastic societies," the novelist Carlos Fuentes once lamented. "This is the burden of Latin America—to go from one Church to another, from Catholicism to Marxism, with all its dogma and ritual." Thus Marxism became the new creed, intellectuals its new priests and dissidents its heretics.

After the Revolution, the state began using culture to promote a sense of national identity, and it assigned the new generation of intellectuals an important responsibility. José Vasconcelos, a prominent philosopher, founded the country's modern educational system while serving as Obregón's Education Minister. The writers Martín Luis Guzmán and Mariano Azuela, the composers Silvestre Revueltas and Carlos Chávez and the muralists Diego Rivera, José Clemente Orozco and David Alfaro Siqueiros began producing works inspired directly by the Revolution. Even the fact that Rivera, Siqueiros and dozens of other artists were members of the Mexican Communist Party was no impediment to their painting radical murals in government buildings. The emerging political system saw the need to incorporate the artistic Left, while intellectuals felt no conflict of principles in working for the government.

In practice, both benefited. In an essentially authoritarian political system, approval or at least acceptance of the regime by the intellectual elite served to endorse the power of the ruling group, while the strongly nationalist content of much of the art of the period was an effective substitute for revolutionary measures. The government learned that leftist and anti-American rhetoric appeased the intellectual Left and became a useful weapon against domestic conservatives. Although intellectuals had little interest in direct association with the official party, they considered the Revolution's original promise of social justice to be a worthy objective and preferred employment or sponsorship by the state—by universities, the National Institute of Fine Arts or perhaps the diplomatic service—to dependence on the private sector. Those who sniped at the regime acted as harmless escape valves for discontent, but many accepted the principle of working for change from within the system.

The intellectual appeal of Marxism remained powerful throughout the 1920s and 1930s, with the romantic heroism of the Spanish Civil War catching the imaginations of writers and artists in Mexico no less than in Europe. Many young Mexican intellectuals, among them the poet Octavio Paz, traveled to Paris at the time, while Cárdenas won over the Mexican Left by openly supporting the Spanish Republican cause. At home, it was a period of intense search for the country's historical, philosophical and ethnic roots and it produced several cultural *caudillos* who, while not famous abroad, exercised crucial influence over later generations: Manuel Gamio and Alfonso Caso, both archaeologists and writers, helped rescue Mexico's pre-Hispanic past and Indian present; Alfonso Reyes, Daniel Cosío Villegas and Jesús Silva Herzog, Sr., philosopher, historian and economist, respectively, kept alive liberal thought against mounting Marxist pressure.

In the early 1940s, the intellectual world was convulsed by disputes inside the international Communist movement. Trotsky's expulsion from Moscow, the Moscow Trials and Trotsky's murder in Mexico City provoked violent purges among Mexico's Communists, while the Soviet Non-Aggression Pact with Hitler accelerated intellectual disillusionment. In the 1940s and 1950s, most Mexican writers and artists maintained a vaguely socialist discourse, but they no longer identified with Moscow. Many were also too young to remember the Revolution, and favoring a less dogmatically nationalist view of art, they opened themselves to new foreign influences. Many Spanish Republican intellectuals came to Mexico as exiles and their presence was soon felt in education and publishing. The cultural supplement of the daily *Novedades* served as an important display window for new writers. Mexico was governed by conservative pro-business administrations, but cultural figures were still heard on the problems of the country and they enjoyed the intellectual freedom of having shaken off Stalinism and adopted no new dogma.

A critical turning point came in 1959 with the Cuban Revolution, which revived faith in a radical political option for Latin America. When the United States tried to topple the new regime in 1961, Mexican academics, writers and artists immediately closed ranks behind Cuba, establishing support for the Castro regime and *La Revolución* and criticism of the United States as permanent precepts of most Mexican—and Latin American—intellectuals. In Mexico, however, they did not equate their defense of Cuba with advocacy of an "armed struggle" at home. Nor were they interested in changing their relationship with the Mexican state. Nonetheless, largely as a result of the government's fear of the Cuban example, the traditional modus vivendi broke down in the 1960s.

As early as 1960, President López Mateos had differentiated between thought and action—between intellectual and political freedom—by jailing the Communist muralist Siqueiros, purportedly for organizing anti-government protests. But López Mateos' refusal to break ties with Cuba won him intellectual support and he freed Siqueiros before leaving office. His successor, Díaz Ordaz, distrusted the very idea of intellectuals, presuming all to be enamored of the Cuban Revolution and enemies of the Mexican state. Long before the anti-government student movement and subsequent massacre of Tlatelolco on October 2, 1968, confirmed their low opinions of each other, communications between government and intellectuals had broken down. Díaz Ordaz silenced the intellectuals at home but paid a high price abroad: when Octavio Paz, pursuing a career as a diplomat while writing poetry and essays, resigned in protest as Mexico's ambassador to India, intellectuals around the world joined him in blackening Díaz Ordaz's name. To Díaz Ordaz's subsequent chagrin, the intellectuals—political scientists and historians—eventually had the last word on his administration at home.

In 1970, President Echeverría, a consummate politician, immediately tried to woo them back with his promise of reform. In the process, he also demonstrated that, while dangerous foes, intellectuals were easy to befriend. He first disarmed the Left by adopting its rhetoric and then installed several well-known leftists or nationalists within or close to his administration. The impression was created that an entire national renaissance was about to take place. The works of writers, painters and movie directors considered enemies by Díaz Ordaz were suddenly brought before the public. Siqueiros was rehabilitated and given the status of a national institution before his death in 1974: Echeverría personally inaugurated the artist's Polyforum, a huge building covered inside and out with murals. He also persuaded Carlos Fuentes to become Mexico's ambassador to France in 1975, pointedly drawing a contrast with Octavio Paz's resignation under Díaz Ordaz.

Many prominent political scientists, sociologists and writers were in turn flattered by invitations to "advise" the President on domestic and foreign policy, and while their counsel was usually ignored, their sudden proximity to power was a dizzying experience. (Cosío Villegas once remarked that Mexican Presidents needed intellectuals "not to advise them but to furnish them with articulate reasons for decisions they have already taken.") They naturally denied that they had been tamed or bought. Instead, they justified their support for the regime by arguing, in the words of one leading writer, that the country faced a choice between "Echeverría or fascism." But they were well rewarded for their new responsibilities and they enthusiastically accepted invitations to accompany the President on his frequent world travels. During a visit to Cuba, Echeverría pointed to his traveling court of intellectuals and noted: "As for our political opponents, we put them on a plane and take them with us so they can see what we're doing." On another occasion, on just twenty-four hours' notice, he demanded that a plane be filled with leading academics, writers and artists, who then joined him in Buenos Aires at an official dinner.

Echeverría was happy to be praised by intellectuals, but proved less tolerant of their criticism. In the early 1970s, the editorial pages of the newspaper *Excelsior* had become a leading forum for political thought and analysis, much of it supportive of the government's reformist posture. But when, in 1976, its columnists began turning against the mounting inconsistencies and demagoguery of his administration, Echeverría promptly orchestrated an internal mutiny against the daily's editor, Julio Scherer García. Among many intellectuals who lost a forum was Octavio Paz, who had edited *Excelsior*'s literary monthly, *Plural.* The irony was that Echeverría had overestimated the importance of both the praise and the criticism of intellectuals and, like Díaz Ordaz, had underestimated their power of revenge. Before he left office, *Excelsior*'s toppled elite had regrouped in a new political weekly, *Proceso,* which appeared in time to publish a ferocious epitaph on his six years in office.

López Portillo, himself a former university professor and occasional novelist and painter, felt greater identity with the worlds of philosophy and the fine arts, and before his inauguration he reassured offended intellectuals of his sympathy. Soon afterward, he followed Echeverría's example by filling the intellectual quota in his administration, naming Víctor Flores Olea, a former dean at the UNAM, as Under Secretary of Education and later ambassador to UNESCO and Gastón García Cantú, an obsessively nationalist historian, to the National Institute of Anthropology and History. (A minor setback came when Carlos Fuentes resigned his post in Paris to protest the appointment of former President Díaz Ordaz as ambassador to Spain.) The choice of the historian and "intellectual" politician Jesús Reyes Heroles as Interior Minister was particularly applauded, and he recognized the need to create a new intellectual mouthpiece to replace *Excelsior*. He therefore approved funding for a new left-leaning daily, *Uno más Uno,* and official advertising helped support several smaller publications, among them *Nexos,* a cultural monthly, as well as *Proceso* and *Vuelta,* Octavio Paz's new literary magazine. Intellectuals were once again able to express their own —and read each other's—views in the confident belief they were being influential.

Money was a key factor in sealing the relationship between intellectuals and the state. Already under Echeverría, university salaries were sharply increased and an entire generation of young academics received scholarships to study abroad. Publishing expanded dramatically, with many leftist authors finding themselves in print for the first time. The oil boom of the late 1970s released still more funds for culture. The price of this was that the President's sister, Margarita, and his wife, Carmen Romano de López Portillo, were allowed to run the arts much as they pleased and, at times, with disastrous results. But the intellectual world prospered as never before. Painters were exhibited, writers published and academics given research grants: as a class, intellectuals lived better in Mexico than in the United States or Western Europe, moving in circles of influence at home and frequently traveling abroad.

With little interest in confronting the government, they channeled their political energy into fighting among themselves over abstract foreign policy issues. López Portillo's support for Nicaragua's Sandinista regime and El Salvador's leftist revolutionaries and his warm ties with Cuba were warmly applauded by the bulk of Mexico's intelligentsia. For most, loyalty to Cuba, Nicaragua and *La Revolución* remained articles of faith that resisted arguments about political freedom: in revolutionary terms, Fidel Castro enjoyed infallibility and intellectuals flocked to Havana with all the reverence of a pilgrimage to the Holy See. Cuba in turn learned to exploit this loyalty, flattering Mexican—and other Latin American—poets, novelists and painters with attention, inviting them to the island for conferences and recognizing their works with prizes.

In the early 1970s, some Mexican writers, including Carlos Fuentes, became disenchanted with the lack of cultural freedom in Cuba. But they withheld public criticism of the Castro regime, accepting the view that Washington's hostility had blocked adoption of more liberal policies. By the late 1970s, however, a small, vocal group of intellectuals began challenging Cuba and the revolutionary "myth." Led by Octavio Paz, whose socialist idealism had been eroded first by Moscow and then by Havana, they argued that nothing justified suppression of freedom in Cuba. They chose to ignore the impact of U.S. foreign policy and insisted that Cuba had merely replaced the political dictatorship of Batista with that of Castro and economic dependence on the United States with "enslavement" to Moscow. They dismissed as sophistry the familiar reasoning that bourgeois democracy was an obstacle to social and economic "liberation" by a revolutionary state. In the early 1980s, after radicalization of the Nicaraguan Revolution, they applied the same criteria to the Sandinistas and warned unpopularly of the Stalinist instincts of El Salvador's Marxist guerrillas.

Such was the polarization between these points of view that no serious debate ensued. The majority and the minority took to exchanging epithets, pointedly excluding each other from appearing in their respective publications or attending their conferences and seminars. They also mobilized Latin American, European and American intellectuals as weapons in their dispute. Many exiled Latin American intellectuals as well as the Colombian Nobel laureate, Gabriel García Márquez, who kept a home in Mexico City, were openly sympathetic to Cuba and lent their names to statements criticizing U.S. policy. On occasion, Cuba's hand was also visible. In 1982, a so-called Dialogue of the Americas in Mexico City purported to bring together Latin American and U.S. intellectuals for a free exchange of views, but it became bogged down in anti-American clichés, prompting García Márquez to disassociate himself from the gathering. When the same group of pro-Cuban intellectuals organized a poetry festival in Michoacán in 1983, Octavio Paz and his friends successfully organized an international boycott of the event, publishing a list of prominent names—including Günter Grass, Czeslaw Milosz, Allen Ginsberg, Ted Hughes and Jorge Luis Borges—who would not be attending.

The principal obstacle to Miguel de la Madrid's good relations with the intellectual Left was the economic crisis that he inherited. The problem was less that a stiff austerity program brought increased hardship to the country's peasants and workers than that funds were not available to cushion the impact on the living standards of intellectuals. He recognized the need to give the government a voice among intellectuals, and intellectuals some identification with the administration: Reyes Heroles was named Education Minister, the writer Enrique Florescano took over the Anthropology Institute and Flores Olea became Under Secretary in the Foreign Ministry. But the slump brought a sharp drop in new book titles, sales of paintings and university budgets: in dollar terms, the salaries of top professors fell from $2,000 to $600 per month in less than two years. Suddenly short of personal and institutional resources, intellectuals were losing a crucial symbol of their importance.

De la Madrid was helped by the perennial disagreements within the intellectual Left. In December 1983, a dispute among staff members of the daily *Uno más Uno* led to the walkout of a group of prominent journalists and intellectuals amid fresh recriminations about sectarianism and dogmatism. The dissidents established a new daily, *La Jornada*, as a forum for "the most diverse sectors of society," excluding those dominated by "ideological conservatism, narrow commercialism or extra-national alliances"—as well as those appearing in *Uno más Uno*. Confident that recovery of the economy would permit a rapprochement with his intellectual jury, De la Madrid continued financing not only *Uno más Uno* but *La Jornada* and other intellectual outlets. Recent history suggested that governments which respect intellectual freedom to dissent can count on support for the system as a whole. One minister once complained to a group of leftist economists: "You can't agitate with your left hand and earn with your right." But in fact, until intellectuals themselves begin to question the propriety of their privileged position within society, no government has reason to fear them.

II

With the arts so tied to politics, three key periods in Mexico's post-Columbian history have left distinct cultural imprints. For four centuries, European influence was crucial. Indian culture survived among the population at large, but the elite world of writing, painting, music and architecture was dominated first by Catholic Spain and later, in the nineteenth century, by France and England. Then, after the 1910 Revolution, art became powerfully nationalist and stubbornly introverted, rescuing the country's pre-Hispanic roots and using social realism to mirror contemporary political conflicts. Finally, since the 1950s, Mexico's economic development has opened the arts to greater outside—often American—influence. Artistic expression remains peculiarly Mexican, but it is freer than in the past, able to develop new techniques and address universal themes without renouncing Mexico as a font of inspiration.

It is in classical music that the least syncretism has taken place. And it is in this area of the fine arts that Mexico has contributed least to the world. The pre-Hispanic tradition of popular religious music survived the Conquest and gradually absorbed the melodies and rhythms imposed by Catholic missionaries. It remained simple, repetitive and at times hypnotic music, dominated by percussion and flutes and aimed at accompanying worship or religious dances. Only among the Colonial aristocracy did the European idea take root that music could also be listened to for its own sake. Few compositions from the period survived the closure of monasteries during the liberal reforms of the mid-nineteenth century. After the Revolution, a new generation of "nationalist" composers, notably Silvestre Revueltas, Carlos Chávez and later Manuel Ponce and José Pablo Moncayo, sought to incorporate a "native force" and create classical music that seemed distinctly Mexican. By the 1950s, a strong reaction against the folkloric content of their works led classical music, dance and opera in Mexico once again to follow Europe and the United States.

Perhaps because classical music is considered a poor instrument of political propaganda or perhaps because musicians are rarely activist intellectuals, no recent government has shown interest in promoting musical education and creativity. Instead, governments have preferred to sponsor autochthonous and regional music and to project Mexico's image abroad through Amalia Hernández's Folkloric Ballet Company. During the late 1970s, substantial sums were spent on bringing leading world orchestras to Mexico and Señora López Portillo formed a new Mexico City Orchestra, but the capital's Conservatory of Music had to struggle to stay open. The country's top conductor, Eduardo Mata, gained experience and recognition by leaving Mexico, eventually becoming permanent director of the Dallas Symphony Orchestra. Today, no new classical music is distinctly Mexican and no Mexican composer of universal music has won recognition.

In contrast, Mexicans have always expressed themselves comfortably, enthusiastically and imaginatively in painting, and their talent has long been acclaimed abroad. During the Colonial period, Mexican painters were constrained by the European tradition of portraits and religious themes, but they bequeathed a great body of work that once covered the walls of palaces and churches and today fills scores of museums. In the nineteenth century, the new European vogue of painting landscapes and battle scenes also reached Mexico, prompting José María Velasco and his followers to look to their own country's valleys and volcanoes and recent battle for Independence for inspiration. But their style remained entirely European.

After the Revolution, a truly Mexican school of painting finally emerged, not only adopting the powerful colors of popular culture and the muralist tradition of the pre-Hispanic civilizations, but also looking at both Mexican history and day-to-day life through nationalist, revolutionary and often Communist eyes. Using their oils and murals to scourge the brutality of the Spanish conquistadors and their Catholic allies and to romanticize the country's Indians and peasants, the leaders of this school—Rivera, Siqueiros and Orozco—transformed the Mexican art world. They inspired other painters—Juan O'Gorman, Frida Kahlo, Pablo O'Higgins and Gerardo Murillo, known as "Dr. Atl," among them—who became figures of importance in their own right. In the 1930s, the art world also recognized the extraordinary talent of José Guadalupe Posada, a prolific and satirical engraver who had died penniless in 1913. For the first time, Mexican art was influential beyond the country's border: Rivera, Siqueiros and Orozco had disciples in the United States and all three were invited to paint murals in American cities.

Such was the political and artistic dogmatism of this movement that painters who felt drawn by abstract or purely aesthetic styles were ostracized. Rufino Tamayo, at the time a young painter from Oaxaca, felt obliged to go to New York in 1936 and did not return to live in Mexico until thirty years later, long after his work had won recognition in the United States and Europe. Carlos Mérida, a Guatemalan who came to Mexico during the Revolution, also spurned social realism and was consequently ignored by the militant art establishment. At the time, it seemed, the only valid themes were evil priests and heroic Indians, revolutionary hats and rifles, cacti and volcanoes. But both Tamayo and Mérida would outlive the three great muralists and witness the dismantling of the "cactus curtain" that isolated Mexican art from outside influence.

From the 1950s, young painters began to shake off the restrictions inherited from the Revolution. Unlike their musical colleagues, they did not turn violently against Mexican themes; rather, they began to approach the shapes and colors of Mexico with a new freedom. Since then, Mexican painting has flourished. Tamayo and the young Francisco Toledo, both from Oaxaca, gave flight to a magical and sensual surrealism inspired by the fruits and animals of their native state. Mérida, finally winning renown as an old man, produced abstract canvases that recalled pre-Columbian art. Gunther Gerzso, another abstract painter of great talent, also claimed to be influenced by pre-Columbian art and the dramatic spaces of the Mexican landscape. Mexican colors—bright yellows, pinks, blues and greens—were no less evident in the works of Pedro Coronel, Ricardo Martínez and Luis López Loza. In contrast, José Luis Cuevas, the self-proclaimed *enfant terrible* of Mexican art, made his name in Paris and addressed the universal theme of "the anxiety and loneliness of man today" through drawings and engravings of deformed Goya-like figures.

Behind these names, there are several thousand—some estimate around 15,000—painters, engravers and sculptors living off the arts in Mexico. There are also dozens of museums and hundreds of commercial galleries being sustained by the government and, indirectly, by the artists themselves. Special auctions of Latin American art at New York's Sotheby Parke Bernet helped to stir interest in contemporary Mexican painting abroad and, particularly, to inflate the price of works by the country's best-known painters. Tamayo's *Boy with Watermelons* sold for $200,000 in 1981, many of his other canvases routinely fetch around $100,000 and there are collectors and investors ready to pay five-figure sums for the works of Cuevas, Toledo, Mérida and Gerzso.

The cycle of architecture in Mexico in many ways paralleled that of painting. A tradition of grandiosity stretched back to pre-Hispanic times when pyramids and temples were shrines and even symbolic stepping-stones to the gods. When these were razed by the Conquest, Indian stonemasons were immediately mobilized to build the magnificent churches and palaces of the Colony. The essence of this style—churrigueresque façades, thick adobe walls, fine archways and staircases, elegant balconies looking onto inner patios and hidden gardens—was preserved until, in the late nineteenth century, the dictator Porfirio Díaz sought to enhance his prestige with such neo-baroque creations as the Palace of Fine Arts and a new Congress building, which, unfinished in 1910, eventually became the Monument to the Revolution. From the 1920s, architecture then adjusted to the political mood of the epoch, with the state constructing large utilitarian buildings decorated with populist murals and sculptures. As with painting, architecture then entered an innovative period in the 1950s, achieving dramatic and exciting results by blending many of the colors and shapes of traditional Mexico with modern styles and techniques imported from abroad.

Pedro Ramírez Vázquez first broke through the mold with his daring use of reinforced concrete in the design of the new campus of the National University, the National Museum of Anthropology and the Aztec Stadium. Coincidentally, Luis Barragán was developing a new style for private residences, using reflecting pools, hidden gardens, freestanding walls and unexpected colors to create a fresh concept of space. His best-known works are the huge three-faced multicolored towers at the entrance to Satellite City north of Mexico City. These two men created schools of followers, but other young architects continued studying and traveling abroad in search of ideas and techniques. The results can be seen in the wild, often clashing styles evident in such new residential districts of the capital as El Pedregal and Bosque de las Lomas, where everything but temerity is on display. A new approach to public buildings, using cement with white marble chips and counterposing heavy walls with angles and spaces, was developed by Abrahán Zabludovsky and Teodoro González de León, who designed the INFONAVIT Housing Fund Building, El Colegio de México and the Tamayo Museum. The modern style carries echoes of old Mexico, taking from the past to assimilate the future.

Mexican literature, unlike painting and architecture, found more difficulty in breaking free of the intellectual restraints imposed first by religion and then by the Revolution. From the Colonial period, only the plays of the Mexican-born Spaniard Juan Ruiz de Alarcón and the love poetry of the seventeenth-century nun Sor Juana Inés de la Cruz are still widely read today, while the post-modernist poets Ramón López Velarde and José Juan Tablada were among the few nonpolitical writers to emerge from the nineteenth century. Novels of importance appeared only after 1910, with Mariano Azuela's *The Underdogs* and Martín Luis Guzmán's *The Eagle and the Serpent,* but they and their emulators remained hypnotized by the Revolution. A small group of poets known as the Contemporaries, which included Xavier Villaurrutia, José Gorostiza and Salvador Novo, reacted against this political fervor in the 1930s, although not until after World War II did the epic surrender to a more sociological, psychological and occasionally surrealist treatment of contemporary themes.

The theme of Mexico was not abandoned. In the 1950s, Juan Rulfo produced the novel *Pedro Páramo* and a collection of short stories, *The Burning Plain,* both books of magic surrealism set in the Mexican provinces. Carlos Fuentes, who has lived most of his life outside Mexico and of the country's authors is perhaps the best known abroad, also writes mainly about Mexico. He first won acclaim with his novel *Where the Air Is Clear,* and he followed with *The Death of Artemio Cruz,* an allegory of the corruption and abandonment of the ideals of the 1910 Revolution and, more recently, with *Terra Nostra* and *The Hydra Head*. Other writers, among them the poets Carlos Pellicer and Jaime Sabines and the novelists José Revueltas, Vicente Leñero, Jorge Ibargüengoitia, Gustavo Sáinz and Carlos Monsiváis, also rarely ventured far from strongly Mexican subjects. Perhaps only the works of Octavio Paz, Ali Chumacero, José Emilio Pacheco, Homero Aridjis and other poets could be considered universal, but even Paz's principal impact has come through collections of political and philosophical essays, such as *The Labyrinth of Solitude, Another Mexico* and *The Philanthropic Ogre,* rather than his erudite poetry.

Mexico's most widely read author, Luis Spota, deals so exclusively with Mexican topics that he is virtually unknown abroad. His novels routinely sell 50,000 or more copies, and in the mid-1970s he found a formula for fictionalizing the inner workings of Mexico's political system. Since he timed his books to coincide with key moments of the country's six-year political cycle, even foreign diplomats used them as primers to understand the system at work. Spota's peers did not consider him of literary importance, but none could dispute the political influence of his novels. His success—and that of other leading novelists—underlined the fundamental importance of fiction in a society dominated by secrecy, discretion and loyalty. With most academics, political analysts and journalists unwilling or unable to write with unrestrained frankness about the government or the system, the Mexican public turns to fiction to understand reality. As one writer put it, "journalists use the truth to tell lies and novelists use lies to tell the truth."

III

The high standard of art and literature contrasts dramatically with the mediocrity of mass entertainment in Mexico today. In a country where the average adult receives only five years' schooling, the political implications of this situation are ominous. Recognizing the links between culture and nationalism, successive governments have poured resources into the fine arts. Yet they have neglected mass entertainment, leaving the hearts and minds of most of the population to commercial exploitation. Thus, while Mexican culture is well preserved in museums, galleries and bookstores, traditional values are being decimated in the country's homes by the revolution in mass communications. Rather than serving as an arena for Mexican creativity, popular entertainment has become a broad avenue for cultural penetration by the United States.

Such is the legacy of Mexico's several pasts—pre-Hispanic, Colonial and revolutionary—that a distinct folk culture still survives, above all in the food, clothes, music and handicrafts of the countryside. It is this old *típico* Mexico that the new middle classes and urban poor are increasingly replacing with more aggressive, consumerist and imported entertainment. The problem stems less from the disappearance of folklore than from the failure of a new, authentically Mexican popular culture to emerge. Both government and the cultural elite share responsibility. Leftist intellectuals who are quick to denounce commercial television are disdainful of using the medium to reach a wider audience. And when Octavio Paz marked his 70th birthday in 1984 with a series of wide-ranging television interviews, he was accused of selling out to Televisa. Similarly, the government sees no contradiction in financing newspapers and magazines read by an elite minority and allowing commercial interests to provide the "gutter press," illustrated stories and *fotonovelas* that are read by millions.

What the ordinary Mexican reads appeals either to his morbidity or to his sentimentality, rarely to his intelligence. Two weekly newspapers, *Alarma* and *Alerta,* which between them sell almost a million copies, concentrate on covering violent crimes. At one point in the 1970s, *Alarma* published a separate *fotonovela* in which the most depraved crimes were re-enacted; this *Casos de Alarma* was selling 1.2 million copies weekly before it was finally closed by the government. Numerous other widely circulated booklets tell their stories of violence, drugs, prostitution and corruption through drawings or photographs, appealing mainly to the semi-literate male of the urban slums. The same format is used by "heartbreak" comic books that are bought by maids and other poor urban women. Long the most successful was *Lágrimas y Risas—Tears and Laughter*—but many others, using a vocabulary of only some 300 words, focus on the familiar themes of sex, romance, betrayal and tragedy.

The argument has been made that the 70 million comic books and *fotonovelas* sold each month represent an important stage in the population's passage from illiteracy to literacy. The government has adopted the format to promote family planning and nutrition programs, and the talented political cartoonist Eduardo del Río, known by the pen name of Rius, has also used the comic-strip technique to explain Marx and Lenin "for beginners." But the vast majority of these booklets have the opposite effect. Rather than consciousness-raising, they work within the confines of their readers' existing culture, reinforcing such "ideals" as male domination, female obedience, admiration for money and respect for the authorities and, no less strictly, avoiding any suggestion of political or social comment or dissent.

The government is more directly responsible for the dismal state of Mexico's movie industry. It not only owns the country's principal studios and most movie theaters, but also controls the Cinematographic Bank, which provides financing for most productions. The degeneration of the industry is perhaps all the more notorious since, during the late 1930s and the 1940s, Mexican movies enjoyed a golden era. Some movies were broadly didactic, recounting the appearance of the Virgin of Guadalupe and the exploits of Emiliano Zapata, Pancho Villa and other revolutionary heroes. Many were exciting musical melodramas about the Mexican *charro,* or cowboy. During this period, the industry also produced numerous figures of importance beyond Mexico: the renowned cameraman Gabriel Figueroa, who later shot several films for Luis Buñuel, himself then a resident of Mexico; directors Emilio Fernández, Julio Bracho and Fernando de Fuente; actresses Dolores del Río and María Félix; actors Pedro Armendariz and Mario Moreno, known as Cantinflas; and the singing stars Jorge Negrete and Pedro Infante.

The industry benefited from the shortage of entertaining—rather than propaganda—movies from the United States and Europe during World War II, and Mexican movies also became popular elsewhere in Latin America. But by the 1950s, with Hollywood once again shaping cinema tastes worldwide, the old Mexican *charro* movies lost their appeal. Private production companies faced new financial and labor problems, and by the late 1950s the government stepped in to buy the huge Churubusco Studios from the Azcárraga family. No renaissance followed, and in the 1960s Mexican film crews were kept busy mainly by foreign movies being shot in Mexico, among them a whole genre of cowboy films made in the desert of Durango. The low quality of the movies exhibited in Mexico also reflected the government's fear of political and moral subversion. Censorship remained tight, with only cheap and banal entertainment considered appropriate for the masses.

A brief spring took place under Echeverría between 1970 and 1976. He named his brother Rodolfo, a professional actor, to run the Cinematographic Bank and gave him ample resources. Long-censored movies like *Rosa Blanca* (recounting the 1938 expropriation of foreign oil companies in a strongly nationalistic and anti-American tone) were released to the public and a new generation of directors—among them, Felipe Cazals, Gustavo Alatriste, Paul Leduc, Alberto Isaac, Arturo Ripstein and Alfonso Arau—were permitted to tackle previously sensitive political and social issues. Echeverría himself called on them "to produce great human themes, to engage in social criticism," and he promised "to say thanks and goodbye" to the commercial producers who had dominated the past.

The industry responded with enthusiasm. New movies mocked the hypocrisy of family mores and ridiculed the corrupt paternalism of the ruling party. Others dealt with the misery of slum life and a few even included unusually frank sex scenes. Leduc's film version of John Reed's book *Insurgent Mexico* offered a new interpretation of the Mexican Revolution, portraying it as an often chaotic conflict between bands rather than an epic struggle between good and evil. Cazals was even more daring: in *Canoa,* he re-created an incident in 1968 when a conservative Catholic priest incited fanaticized peasants to lynch a group of leftist students; in *El Apando,* he exposed the violence of life inside the capital's infamous—and now closed—Lecumberri jail. The *nouvelle vague* demonstrated, to the surprise of many critics, that the state could make serious and critical movies that avoided intellectual esotericism and in many cases became box-office hits.

This burst of creativity was short-lived. It ended with the installation of the López Portillo administration. In 1976, the President's sister, Margarita López Portillo, the Director General of Radio, Television and Cinema, withdrew official support for movies which she considered morally or politically dissolute. She offered no alternative policy and decimated the industry by hiring and firing six different heads of the Cinematographic Bank in as many years. The result was that old-time private producers filled the vacuum left by the government and once again began producing movies of great banality. A large number—35 percent, according to one estimate—dealt with the problem of illegal migration to the United States and were targeted at Mexican and Chicano audiences in the American Southwest. Others were simply vehicles for sexual titillation. With talented "new" directors unable to find work at home, not one noteworthy domestic movie was made during the entire López Portillo administration.

After the change of government in 1982, De la Madrid appointed the director Alberto Isaac to head a new Cinematographic Institute, which was charged with rescuing the industry. It faced problems of both quantity and quality. By law, at least 50 percent of films shown must be Mexican-made; in practice, the average was closer to 10 percent, most of them in the low-level category and having no appeal for middle- and upper-class audiences. Moreover, because of the economic crisis only minimal resources were available for the improvement of films. The institute began by encouraging small independent producers and giving them access to larger theaters. To demonstrate its new concern for quality, it provided half the $3 million financing for John Huston's film version of Malcolm Lowry's classic novel *Under the Volcano*. But the industry's principal activity remained that of providing technicians and studios for American and European producers, who in 1983 alone made some twenty movies on Mexican locations. For the foreseeable future, the country's moviegoing public would have little choice but to see foreign—mainly American—films.

The success of the *charro* movies of the 1930s and 1940s was due to the extraordinary popularity of Mexican music at the time: many of the movies were simply vehicles for the singers Jorge Negrete, Pedro Infante and Javier Solís. This too was a new phenomenon. Until the turn of the century, Mexican popular music was still largely a function of Indian and religious festivals and was unknown abroad. During the Revolution, *corridos* and *música ranchera*—Mexico's country-and-western music— were used to sing the tales of life at the war front. Only when radio arrived in the late 1920s could music from one region be heard all over the country. The invasion of Mexico City by Guadalajara's mariachi music began soon afterward. The most important composer of the period, Agustín Lara, brought gentler, more poetic and melodic songs from his home state of Veracruz. In the Yucatán, another singer-composer, Guty Cárdenas, added sentimental boleros to the musical fare. Never before had Mexico's popular culture been so influential. While the country showed no political interest in the rest of the continent, Latin Americans sang Mexican songs and watched Mexican movies.

Since the 1950s, Mexican popular music has stagnated: the same styles and even the same songs have been repeated for four decades, and most "new" music imitates Caribbean salsa, American rock or the protest music of Argentina and Chile. For this, musicians blame commercial radio stations and record companies. From the very beginning in Mexico, radio was viewed principally as an advertising medium, and once a successful formula was found, there seemed to be no need to encourage musical innovation. Today, closely tied to record companies, radio stations play American-style music for middle-class audiences and mariachi and salsa songs for poorer audiences. The government, interested only in maintaining a firm control over news broadcasts, has not recognized popular music as an important expression of national identity among the population at large.

Nowhere is the government's failure to understand the dynamics of mass entertainment more blatant than in its handling of television. Television—and particularly the near-monopoly, Televisa—has become the country's Ministry of Culture, its Ministry of Education and its Ministry of Information. It is changing consumption patterns, social models, daily language and political opinions. With the average child spending more time in front of the television than he does in the classroom, the tastes and values of the coming generations are being shaped more by advertisers than by government, teachers or family. Among 30 to 40 million regular viewers, materialistic expectations are being raised that have no hope of being satisfied. Yet the state has failed to recognize the socio-cultural revolution that is underway.

Television began as a business when the Alemán administration handed out the first concessions to established monied families and retained no role for the government: in 1950, Channel 4 was opened by the O'Farrill family, which owned the Novedades newspaper group; in 1952, Channel 2 was founded by the Azcárraga family, already leaders in radio and cinema; and the same year, Alemán gave the concession for Channel 5 to his own family. In 1955, the three companies formed Telesistema Mexicana, with each channel aiming at a different economic and cultural group. The government saw no political threat in this monopoly. Telesistema's wealthy shareholders had no interest in criticizing the regime, and Emilio Azcárraga, who came to dominate the company, initially avoided the political risks of news broadcasts by contracting *Excelsior* to read its own stories on the air. In 1958, the government authorized the semi-autonomous National Polytechnic Institute to open Channel 11 as a cultural station, but in practice it lacked the resources to develop good programs or even to beam its signal beyond a tiny radius around the capital.

In the early 1970s, the government became more directly involved in television. Telesistema remained politically loyal to the government, but its values seemed to clash with the cultural nationalism being promoted by the Echeverría administration. In 1972, the government bought Channel 13, a station founded just four years earlier by a cabaret owner, Francisco Aguirre, who had gone bankrupt trying to compete with Telesistema. Channel 13 immediately built expensive new studios on the outskirts of the city and recruited left-leaning intellectuals to provide quality programming. But few had previous experience in the medium and many were disturbed by the tight censorship exercised by the Interior Ministry. Their dull programs received dismal ratings and soon intellectuals gave up the experiment.

Commercial television, meanwhile, was flourishing. In 1973, Telesistema changed its name to Televisa after absorbing Channel 8, founded by the Monterrey Group in the late 1960s. Control of the market was

assured through its fare of music, sports, soap operas—or *telenovelas*—
and a great variety of cowboy, comedy and crime series bought from the
United States. Looking to the middle classes, Televisa founded Cablevi-
sión S.A. to bring American network programs into Mexican homes. A
strong demand for Mexican programs continued abroad, with Televisa
exporting its *telenovelas* throughout Latin America and creating the
Spanish International Network (SIN) to carry its programs to Hispanic
audiences in the United States. As the owner of the Aztec Stadium and
the principal stockholder in Televisa, Emilio Azcárraga, Jr., who succeeded his father in the early 1970s, was also a certain beneficiary from
Mexico's decision to host the 1986 World Soccer Cup. Televisa's balance
sheets remained tightly held secrets, but the key to its success was
evident: to provide viewers with what they wanted—and to have frequent
advertising breaks.

Azcárraga has no compunction about declaring himself a member of
the ruling PRI and noting that his "only boss is the President of the
Republic." Programs that are politically or sexually too explicit are
automatically kept off the air, news programs are subject to tight self-
censorship and discussions of social issues are broadcast around midnight. But the disaster that struck Channel 13 when it fell within Margarita López Portillo's empire between 1976 and 1982 indirectly
threatened Televisa. The President's sister hired and fired a series of
corrupt friends and obsequious acolytes as directors general of the station—seven in just six years—and the resulting chaos merely underlined
Televisa's domination of the market: its channels were receiving 96
percent of the ratings.

Criticism of Televisa began to grow among intellectuals and in some
government circles. The principal complaint was that Televisa was
"denationalizing" the country by presenting the American way of life as
a new ideal reachable through obsessive consumption. Most *telenovelas*
deal with unreal wealthy families; cartoons, crime series and movies
shown on Mexican television are made in—and portray life in—the
United States; and studies show that the favorite television personalities
of young boys are Superman, Spiderman and Batman and of young girls,
Wonder Woman. American football and baseball enjoy more airtime in
Mexico than soccer. In the hands of American advertising companies,
about half the models used on television are European or American in
appearance, including many seductive blue-eyed blondes. In a country
where less than 5 percent of the population is of pure Caucasian blood,
the message is that things go better for white fair-haired "foreigners"

than for the short dark Mexicans. Advertising also concentrates on such nonessentials as liquor, beer and cosmetics and, for children, candies, cakes, chewing gums and sodas of minimal nutritional value.

In June 1981, the government's National Consumer Institute tested 1,800 primary school children in Mexico City on their comparative knowledge of "television reality" and "national reality" and came up with dramatic results. The children, who were found to spend an average of 1,460 hours in front of the television as against 920 hours in school each year, provided correct answers for 73 percent of questions about television and only 38 percent of questions about the country. For example, 92 percent knew that a duckling used to advertise chocolate cakes said "Remember me" and only 64 percent identified Father Miguel Hidalgo as author of the phrase "Viva la Independencia!"; 96 percent recognized television cartoon characters, but only 19 percent the last Aztec emperors; 98 percent identified Superman, while only 33 percent knew who Emiliano Zapata was; 96 percent recognized a local television character and only 74 percent could name the then President, López Portillo; and 77 percent identified the trademark of Adams Chiclets and only 17 percent spotted the Monument to the Revolution. More children also knew the times of television programs than the dates of religious festivals, including Christmas.

At the height of Mexico's financial crisis in August 1982, Azcárraga learned that López Portillo was under pressure to nationalize television —by canceling Televisa's concessions—during his final State of the Union address on September 1. Azcárraga, a flamboyant and outspoken man, is said to have confronted López Portillo, who, having lost the element of surprise, denied any such intention. But after the President used the occasion to announce nationalization of private banks, leftist intellectuals and politicians campaigned anew for expropriation of Televisa, arguing that it was the principal cultural and political foe of the state. Azcárraga in turn broke up many of Televisa's production, recording and publishing functions into independent companies to protect them in case of takeover.

Azcárraga himself believes that culture and education are the responsibility of the government, but he has responded to threats to his empire by sponsoring more educational programs. In the late 1970s, the telenovela format was used with great success to promote government family planning programs. Televisa and the Children's Theater Workshop have converted "Sesame Street" into "Plaza Sésamo" to spread traditional family values among Latin American children. Under an arrangement with the Finance Ministry, Channel 2 broadcast a late-night series of concerts, operas and plays. After the 1982 financial crisis affected revenues for Channel 8, Televisa created a new cultural channel that carried no advertising and worked closely with the National University, the haven of Azcárraga's leftist critics. Finally, when the faltering Alfa Group was no longer able to sustain the Rufino Tamayo Museum, Televisa took over its management and, through intensive advertising on television, drew unprecedented crowds to exhibitions of Picasso, Matisse, Diego Rivera and David Hockney. Even in the venture of taking the fine arts to the masses, Televisa proved more effective than the government.

The state's inability to compete with Televisa reflects its own antiquated view of the country. Mexico has become a nation of television watchers, with even the poorest semi-literate viewers receptive to the sophisticated stimuli of programs and advertising. Television is now the principal influence on the cultural, political and economic attitudes of the population at large. The government's traditional responsibility for transforming society is being challenged by Televisa, which, in many cases, preaches values that conflict with those proclaimed by the regime. Even in the narrow area of party and electoral politics, the ruling PRI has still to use television effectively as a way of reaching the disenchanted urban middle classes.

How should it respond? The state has demonstrated with Channel 13 that it cannot compete with Televisa and is ill prepared to run a nationalized television system. It already has free access to 12.5 percent of Televisa's airtime for cultural, educational and other public interest programs, but has rarely filled its quota. Some politicians argue privately that banal *telenovelas* and the like contribute to stability by diverting attention away from social problems. "It's better to use tearjerkers than tear gas," one politician said, adding: "If the nanny keeps the children quiet, why change her?" But other officials feel impotent in face of Televisa, as if the entire country were running ahead of the system. In the past, the political and intellectual elite was able to define culture's role in society because it faced little competition. Today, the contradiction is growing between the government's commitment to cultural nationalism in the fine arts and its resignation to a popular culture increasingly alienated from Mexico. But it has discovered no way to deal with the dilemma.

16

"...And So Close
to the United States"

I

The asymmetry of power determines how Mexico and the United States view each other. Differences of history, religion, race and language serve to complicate their relationship, to contrast their ways of doing things, to widen the gulf of understanding that separates them. But all these variables are overshadowed by the inescapable and unique fact that a vulnerable developing country shares a 2,000-mile border with the world's richest and strongest power. When confronting its northern neighbor, history has taught Mexico that it has few defenses.

Contiguity with the United States has proved a permanent psychological trauma. Mexico cannot come to terms with having lost half of its territory to the United States, with Washington's frequent meddling in its political affairs, with the U.S. hold on its economy and with growing cultural penetration by the American way of life. It is also powerless to prevent these interventions from taking place, and is even occasionally hurt by measures adopted in Washington that did not have Mexico in mind. And it has failed to persuade Washington to give it special attention. Intentionally or not, Mexico has been the target of American disdain and neglect and, above all, a victim of the pervasive inequality of the relationship.

The emotional prism of defeat and resentment through which Mexico views every bilateral problem is not simply the legacy of unpardoned injustices from the past. Contemporary problems—migration, trade, energy and credits—also involve the clash of conflicting national interests, with Mexico approaching the bargaining table deeply sensitive to its enormous dependence on American credit, American investment,

American tourists and even American food. Good faith alone could not eliminate these contradictions, but underlying tensions are kept alive by Mexico's expectation that it will be treated unfairly. Its worst fears are confirmed with sufficient regularity for relations to remain clouded by suspicion and distrust. As the local saying goes: "What would we do without the gringos? But we must never give them thanks." Mexico must depend—but cannot rely—on its neighbor.

In a sense, this posture is one more Mexican mask kept in place by politicians and intellectuals. Living next to the United States has brought Mexico economic opportunities and has enabled the country to save on defense expenditure. (Mexico's inability to defend itself militarily against the United States is also useful politically: it has reduced the country's need for a large army and has thus contributed to domestic political stability.) Few Mexicans express hostility toward Americans as individuals and many openly admire those American qualities—above all, honesty, efficiency and democracy—that seem lacking in Mexico. Mexico's growing middle classes enthusiastically adopt American consumer patterns, make sure their children learn English and vacation when possible in the United States. Poorer Mexicans stream across the northern border into a strange land that offers them the hope of finding jobs that are not available at home. There is no consensus: no single image captures how Mexicans see the United States.

Ambivalence runs still deeper. Nationalism and even anti-Americanism are also natural by-products of the relationship, serving Mexico both as an aggressive response to the past and as a defensive shield against the present. It is not an ideological reaction. Successive governments, whether left-leaning or conservative, have felt duty-bound to articulate a nationalist posture, not only to camouflage deeply felt frustration and impotence at Mexico's dependence, but also as a way of strengthening a sense of national identity. Nationalism is an inward-looking phenomenon that cannot prevent unneighborly acts by the United States but enables the country to survive the blows. It perpetuates the belief that Mexico is owed a historical debt by the United States which allows it to ignore American "favors" and to rage against American offenses without costly reprisals.

Yet Mexico's emotional nationalism is also tempered by realism. It recognizes that it needs good relations with the United States and that it cannot risk the economic and political repercussions likely to flow from alienating Washington. It knows that a stable and prosperous Mexico serves the United States' best interests, but it also understands that its autonomy is limited: economically, it would be thrown into chaos if, even indirectly and unofficially, the United States encouraged a credit, trade or investment boycott; and politically, it could be destabilized if Washington defined any Mexican regime as a threat to U.S. national security. In practice, its nationalism must be a controlled ritual, reduced largely to rhetoric and occasional displays of independence in foreign policy.

Aware of the basic rules of their relationship, of their need to deal with each other daily on a multitude of different subjects at various levels, of their common interest in maintaining a stable relationship, the two governments—even the two countries—still fail to communicate effectively. Mexico might come to accept its dependence on the United States if it felt that it received respect. Because the United States is powerful, it cannot comprehend Mexico's obsession with respect. All too often the two governments talk past each other. When Mexican Presidents or politicians address American audiences, they invariably speak in conceptual and philosophical terms, almost begging for respect and understanding rather than demanding concessions on specific topics. American officials, in contrast, rarely grasp the psychological dimension of the relationship and ignore Mexico's nationalist cries for attention, preferring instead to focus on the concrete issues which they believe define the state of relations. The feeling that they are condemned to live beside each other is shared by both countries.

II

The relationship has always been one-sided. The United States achieved its independence almost fifty years before Mexico and, in the process, helped make Mexicans aware of themselves as a nation in the late eighteenth century. In the political confusion that followed Mexico's own independence in 1821, the new republic was too weak to prevent the United States from seizing Texas, New Mexico, Arizona and California in 1848. Yet, less than two decades after the United States had thus defined the shape of its neighbor, Mexico looked to Washington for the military and political support needed to topple the Emperor Maximilian and oust the French occupation force. The sense that Mexico's destiny was in the hands of the United States fed deep insecurities. Even the conservative dictator General Porfirio Díaz, historically viewed as pro-American because he opened the doors to Yankee entrepreneurs, later encouraged investment by France and Britain to counterbalance growing U.S. control of the economy. (It is Díaz whom many credit with authorship of the lapidary remark "Poor Mexico! So far from God and so close to the United States.") A century ago the government learned to juggle the advantages and perils of living next to the United States. Since then, Mexico's relations with the world—and quite often its internal relations —have been a function of its relations with the United States.

The Revolution did not resolve these self-doubts, but the concept that the United States posed a permanent threat to Mexico's political, economic and cultural independence became an important ingredient in a new and stronger national identity. Little recognition of this was apparent to the north. The role played by the U.S. ambassador Henry Lane Wilson in the overthrow of the first revolutionary government of Francisco I. Madero in 1912 left a deep bruise of resentment. When in 1914 President Wilson sent troops to occupy Veracruz in the belief that he was aiding opponents of the Huerta dictatorship, rebels under Carranza demanded their withdrawal, seeing the American "assistance" as simply one more intervention. Just two years later, American troops indeed returned in pursuit of Pancho Villa. The dispute with foreign oil companies was a running sore in relations over the next two decades, yet the principal motivation for their expropriation in 1938 was not a conflict over wages but the insulting and arrogant way in which they negotiated with President Cárdenas. The presumption that Mexico could not expect respect from the United States came to provide a permanent—if implicit —justification for nationalism.

For a quarter-century after World War II, Mexico suppressed its sentiments toward the United States in the name of promoting domestic economic development and avoiding any appearance of involvement in the Cold War. But it kept alive a sense of pride by pursuing a symbolically independent foreign policy in Latin America. At a time of growing economic dependence on the United States through investment, trade and tourism, Mexico was the only Latin American country to refuse to sign a military assistance agreement with the United States. Mexico also turned down direct economic aid because of the political conditions usually attached to such assistance, and never accepted Peace Corps volunteers offered under the Alliance for Progress. Even Díaz Ordaz, perhaps the most anti-Communist Mexican President since the Revolution, was forced to temper his instinctive pro-Americanism.

When in 1970 President Echeverría mobilized nationalism in response to domestic economic and political problems, Mexico's latent feelings toward Washington again resurfaced. There were specific motives—the 10 percent import surcharge imposed by the Nixon administration in August 1971 came as a severe blow to Mexico's exports—but Echeverría, like many incoming Mexican Presidents, was also seeking a different relationship. "It seems inexplicable that the daring and imagination used by the United States to resolve complex problems with its enemies cannot be employed to resolve simple problems with its friends," he told the U.S. Congress in 1972. In private, he tried to convince Washington that his reformist rhetoric was aimed at neutralizing domestic leftists and therefore served American interests. Even his efforts to reduce Mexico's dependence on the United States through closer association with the Third World and other power blocs seemed largely aimed at nudging Washington to pay more attention to Mexico. But no psychological breakthrough was achieved, Echeverría's frustration and Washington's impatience grew steadily and mutual suspicion remained intact.

After Mexico discovered massive oil wealth in the mid-1970s, the government seemed certain that the United States would change its attitudes. When this did not occur, the new President, José López Portillo, made no secret of his feelings. On one occasion in October 1978, he was kept waiting for an hour to meet a group of U.S. newspaper editors in Tijuana. "I represent 63 million human beings," López Portillo told them, visibly irritated. "We have three thousand kilometers of common frontier and many problems. Maybe one of the problems is that we are not given priority or respect. I had hoped that this meeting would take place under the auspices of friendship, respect and consideration. Possibly we just don't know each other well enough."

This historical lack of understanding was well symbolized by López Portillo's difficult personal relationship with President Carter. When Carter the engineer vetoed the purchase of Mexican natural gas in 1977 for the mundane reason of overpricing, López Portillo the intellectual considered he had been humiliated—in his words, "left hanging by the paintbrush." The offense was not the decision itself but rather the seemingly offensive way in which the disagreement had been handled by Washington, above all by the then Secretary of Energy, James Schlesinger, who had publicly predicted that Mexico would be forced to lower its price. Instead, Mexico used some of its surplus gas in its own industry and stubbornly burned the rest. Two years later, it felt vindicated when a new gas export agreement, albeit for a smaller amount, was signed at double the original price rejected by Washington.

Receiving Carter in Mexico City in February 1979 with the still unresolved gas dispute clearly in mind, López Portillo tried to explain Mexico's sensibilities: "Among permanent, not casual, neighbors, surprise moves and sudden deceit or abuse are poisonous fruits that sooner or later have a reverse effect. Consequently, we must take a long-range view of ourselves. No injustice can prevail without affronting decency and dignity. It is difficult, particularly among neighbors, to maintain cordial and mutually advantageous relations in an atmosphere of mistrust or open hostility. . . . A good neighbor policy presupposes a general climate of opinion in which respect prevails over prejudice and intelligence over sectarianism." Referring to Mexico's new oil finds, he added: "Mexico has suddenly found itself the center of American attention—attention that is a surprising mixture of interest, disdain and fear, much like the recurring vague fears that you yourselves inspire in certain areas of our national subconscious. Let us seek only lasting solutions—good faith and fair play—nothing that would make us lose the respect of our children."

The visiting contingent from Washington failed to recognize the deep anxiety that motivated the speech. Instead, the White House press corps focused on Carter's own undiplomatic remark that he had suffered "Montezuma's revenge"—diarrhea—during an earlier visit to Mexico City, while Carter aides complained that López Portillo had used the occasion to lecture his guest. The Mexican President was dismayed that the underlying purpose of his speech had been misunderstood, and after Carter's departure for Washington, he called a press conference to elaborate. "Because we are friends, we can be frank," he explained. "Because we are ready to hear the truth, we have a right to speak the truth, our truth." But the psychological gulf between the two men continued to widen and, more than any of the numerous bilateral problems that they discussed, it defined the mood of relations during the four years they coincided in office.

By then, little remained of the special relationship that both governments had sought to project in the 1950s and 1960s. "Our relationship is special because we are neighbors," Mexico's Foreign Minister, Jorge Castañeda, said before López Portillo's visit to Washington in September 1979. "But this does not mean there is a closer relationship or that the moral ingredient or sympathy may be more powerful." On another occasion, Castañeda was still franker: "I discount the possibility of any sudden, newly discovered or rediscovered good will, sympathy or moral consideration on the part of the United States that could change its basic attitude toward Mexico. The past history of U.S. policy, its present-day prepotency, its selfishness and conservative mood will not allow for such a change." Not surprisingly, Washington viewed Castañeda as an anti-American leftist, but the real issue lay elsewhere: nationalism had been fanned by Washington's refusal to join a host of other industrialized nations in acknowledging Mexico's new importance.

Mexico's obsession with symbols was quickly understood by Ronald Reagan. (Mexicans still recall that President Truman laid a wreath at the

Monument to the Child Heroes in 1948 on the centenary of their death resisting the American occupation of Mexico City, while President Kennedy was no less effective in winning over Mexicans by kneeling before the image of the Virgin of Guadalupe during his visit in 1962.) It was to be expected that accession to the White House of a conservative augured clashes with a nationalist Mexico openly sympathizing with left-wing revolutionary movements in Central America. Yet when López Portillo met Reagan in Ciudad Juárez, just three weeks before the latter's inauguration, the two men immediately got on well. Perhaps Reagan's California years had made him more sensitive to Mexico, perhaps Reagan understood that Carter's mistakes were more of style than substance or perhaps Reagan simply felt at home with a fellow *macho simpático* —López Portillo gave his guest an Arab stallion and Reagan gave his host a hunting rifle—but somehow the chemistry between the two men was right. From the moment he took office, Reagan instructed his cabinet members to treat Mexico with special deference. As a result, despite sharp disagreements over Central America and a host of unresolved bilateral problems, U.S.-Mexican relations were perceived to have improved.

After visiting Camp David in June 1981, one of four occasions that they met in just one year, López Portillo paid tribute to Reagan's understanding: "What is really important about these meetings is less the restatement of problems than the will to resolve them. And the attitude we found now was highly positive, friendly, respectful, considerate, interested." He elaborated in a tone rarely heard from a Mexican President: "What really counted in this interview was the climate and the attitude. An absurd tension, derived from incomprehension, has been broken. There is comprehension and there is respect. And when we are treated with respect, we know how to respond with respect. And, gentlemen, we were treated with respect and, even more, with friendship and affection. And that is highly satisfactory."

But the surprising honeymoon between the Presidents could eliminate neither the tradition of distrust between the two governments nor the inherent differences in their policy perspectives and objectives. Among State Department veterans who represented the institutional memory, there remained a deep residue of irritation toward Mexico, formed over the years by the belief that Mexico will almost dogmatically resist cooperating with Washington on foreign policy issues. Many conservative ideologues in the Reagan administration were angered by Mexico's Central American policy and, frustrated by Reagan's refusal to pressure López Portillo more directly, hoped Mexico's economic crisis in 1982 might soften its rhetoric. "With the wind out of its sails, Mexico is likely to be less adventuresome in its foreign policy and less critical of ours," a confidential memorandum prepared by the State Department's Office of Inter-American Affairs noted. "It would be unrealistic to expect, however, that even an economically chastened Mexico will compromise its prickly independence in any fundamental way."

Within Mexico, attitudes were no less entrenched, not only within the Foreign Ministry but also in the press and, predictably, among leftist intellectuals. Many officials viewed Reagan's personal charm as a poor disguise for Washington's innate ill will toward Mexico. After the first of several devaluations of the Mexican peso in 1982, the officials became convinced that the State Department was responsible for a series of television reports and newspaper articles questioning Mexico's political stability. It was not the first time that U.S. media had been viewed as instruments of an anti-Mexican campaign and, at a time of economic chaos, the United States was more than ever a convenient and familiar scapegoat. Taken together, the media coverage, the attitude of Mexican business circles with close ties to the United States and indiscreet remarks by some American officials all led López Portillo to believe that his government was being destabilized.

Much of the complexity of U.S.-Mexican relations stems from the fact that governments handle only a small part of the country-to-country relations. Because these broader relations are also more dynamic, governments often find themselves reacting to—rather than anticipating—problems. On the border, Mexicans and Americans have learned to live side by side, perceiving their local interests as in many ways compatible and openly resenting interference by Mexico City or Washington in their natural interdependence. Similarly, businessmen, bankers, farmers, oil drillers, tourist operators, contrabandists, drug traffickers, artists and intellectuals from both countries deal with each other routinely. The relationship between U.S. transnational corporations and their Mexican subsidiaries, defining policies that affect both countries, takes place unmonitored by either government.

Within each bureaucracy, different aspects of bilateral ties are handled by literally hundreds of departments and agencies. Formal ties are managed by the Foreign Ministry and the State Department, but governors of states on both sides of the border regularly discuss the practical problems of neighborhood. (Even here, the differences between the two countries are apparent: while the U.S. governors belong to different parties and often disagree among themselves, the Mexicans display extraordinary unanimity, carefully briefed by the federal government on what they can or should say.) Direct and frequent contacts are maintained between Mexican and American trade, financial, environmental and justice officials. Mexico's Interior Ministry, which is in charge of all security matters, works closely with the Federal Bureau of Investigation and the Central Intelligence Agency, exchanging information on the activities of the Soviet, Cuban and other socialist bloc embassies in Mexico City.

The highly centralized nature of power and the overwhelming importance of its relations with the United States enable Mexico to interrelate and coordinate these myriad contacts. The relative autonomy of different corners of the U.S. bureaucracy and a lesser sensitivity to Mexico often result in mixed signals emanating from Washington. On the day that Carter arrived in Mexico City in February 1979 for the purpose of stressing Mexico's importance to the United States, the local U.S. Trade Office closed its doors, complying with a decision taken by the Department of Commerce two years earlier. Viewing the world through the prism of its own system, Mexicans found it inconceivable that the two events were not related.

Few issues of substance are handled directly by the Mexican and American ambassadors in their respective capitals, but the asymmetry of power is once again evident: the Mexican ambassador in Washington is an unimportant diplomatic figure, with rare access to the White House; the U.S. envoy to Mexico City dominates the local diplomatic scene and meets frequently with the President. (The practice of Mexican Presidents meeting privately with U.S. ambassadors sometimes complicates relations: the ambassador reports on his conversation to Washington, but the President may overlook informing his Foreign Minister. Washington may then presume agreement on issues which the Mexican Foreign Ministry still considers subject to negotiation.) And while Washington has generally been indifferent to the choice of the Mexican ambassador, Mexico has always carefully scrutinized the U.S. representative for political significance.

From Mexico's point of view, the ideal ambassador is a political appointee of sufficient renown to give Mexico status and with the necessary clout to get through to the White House during moments of crisis. The appointment of experienced career diplomats—Robert H. McBride and Joseph J. Jova—by the Nixon and Ford administrations meant that relations with Mexico were handled through diplomatic rather than political channels. In contrast, since 1977, the ambassadors have been political appointees, although none of sufficient stature for Mexico to feel flattered.

Carter's first ambassador to Mexico, former Wisconsin governor Patrick J. Lucey, claimed that his inability to speak Spanish was more than compensated for by his close ties with the President. But he alienated the powerful American business community in Mexico by failing to lobby on its behalf and his political standing in Washington was eroded when a former congressman from Texas with no regional experience, Robert Krueger, was appointed Coordinator of Mexican Affairs. Lucey's successor, Julian Nava, a little-known academic from California, fared even worse. He was fluent in Spanish and was appointed during the 1980 election campaign for the sole reason that he was a Mexican-American, but he had no influence in Washington and was considered ineffective by Mexico. When Reagan appointed as his ambassador John Gavin—the former actor who was best known in Mexico for his television spots advertising Bacardi rum—Mexicans felt no less slighted, with some officials suggesting that Cantinflas, the Mexican comic star, should be sent to Washington in reprisal.

As the personification of American power and the heir to a tradition of diplomatic meddling in Mexico, the U.S. ambassador is, ex officio, the preferred and predictable target of anti-American sentiments. He will be routinely baited by leftist commentators, and should he publicly criticize Mexican affairs, he is certain to be lambasted. In 1972, Ambassador McBride made the seemingly harmless suggestion that Mexico's new Foreign Investment Law could discourage a capital inflow, but he was berated by the press for "threatening" Mexico with an investment boycott. In March 1976, during a Washington symposium, Ambassador Jova quoted a Mexican author's remark that Mexico's political system is "one of monarchical succession, no matter how democratic, it is monarchical." Once his words were reported in Mexico, they provoked collective indignation, including a reference by then presidential candidate López Portillo to "apparent efforts to destabilize Mexico through mocking criticism." Ambassador Lucey, perhaps because he spoke no Spanish, recognized the virtues of being "seen but not heard." But Ambassador Nava's belief that his Mexican extraction gave him special insight into Mexico—"Some Mexicans don't know what to do about an [American] ambassador who understands them," he once remarked—earned him the reputation of being both American proconsul and Mexican traitor.

Every U.S. ambassador is at one time or other tempted by the illusion that he can change Mexico's attitudes toward the United States, but none in recent memory took up the challenge in a manner more designed to upset Mexico than John Gavin. During his first year at his post, he expressed his disapproval of Mexican policies only in private. After

Mexico's economy went into crisis early in 1982, he became less cautious. Appearing on an ABC television report, "Mexico: Times of Crisis," Gavin noted that many Mexicans wondered whether the country's institutions were strong enough to withstand the economic collapse. Feeling besieged by economic problems, López Portillo was infuriated by the remark and even threatened to declare Gavin persona non grata. Ironically, Foreign Minister Castañeda, whom Gavin considered his principal foe within the Mexican government, dissuaded the President from the action, warning of its serious implications for U.S.-Mexican relations.

After the change of Mexican administrations, Gavin resumed his public interventions, adopting a paternalistic tone in scolding Mexico for its nationalist responses to the United States. "Those elements within Mexican society which cannot find any excuse for drawbacks or failings other than to blame the United States only denigrate and demean their own splendid country and their own noble people by this craven process," he told the American Chamber of Commerce in Mexico City in July 1983. "In times past, the routine seemed to be that attacks on the United States were perfectly all right because they were, after all, 'for internal consumption.' In other words, the slanders, the libels, the scurrilous nonsense were only to be heard in Mexico and so, of course, were acceptable. Well, I would like to invite the people who still think that way into the twentieth century." In effect, he was saying: "Why don't you Mexicans grow up and become more like us?" His patronizing style only served to perpetuate the cliché image held by many Mexicans of the "ugly American."

Successive Mexican governments have come to expect diplomatic, economic or political pressure as a natural function of the bilateral relationship, but arm-twisting must be carried out quietly and discreetly if it is to be effective. The mere suggestion of public pressure releases all the country's nationalist suspicions. When seventy-six U.S. congressmen denounced Echeverría as a "Communist" in a letter to President Ford in 1976, Mexico saw this as punishment for its new links to the Third World and unleashed a wave of radical rhetoric. After Mexico's oil finds of the mid-1970s, every American move was read as an attempt to control the country's new energy resources, with the government eventually limiting oil shipments to the United States to 50 percent of total exports as an act of self-protection.

Years later, differences over policy towards Central America were accepted so long as Mexico was treated as an equal partner. When, in 1983, Washington's UN ambassador, Jeane J. Kirkpatrick, warned that Mexico's economic crisis made it vulnerable to a Central American "domino effect," De la Madrid's new Foreign Minister, Bernardo Sepúl-veda, sniped back: "Mrs. Kirkpatrick seems to think that she is still teaching kindergarten." The following year, General Paul F. Gorman, chief of the U.S. Southern Command in Panama, told a Senate Commit-tee that within ten years Mexico would be the United States' "No. 1 security problem," adding that it had "the most corrupt government and society in Central America" and was already "a center for subversion." Mexican officials publicly mocked his ignorance about the country. Still more dramatically, when Jack Anderson published a column "exposing" alleged corruption by De la Madrid on the day the President was to meet Reagan in May 1984, Mexican officials saw it as a barely disguised official reprisal for the country's independent policy towards Central America. The column provoked an outpouring of nationalistic resentment towards Washington.

While Mexico has vainly demanded to be understood by the United States, however, it has made little attempt of its own to understand its neighbor. "If a country exists which has had, has and will have a need to study the United States, that country is Mexico," the Mexican histo-rian Daniel Cosío Villegas once wrote. "Nevertheless, one of the Mexi-can's most disconcerting traits is his Olympian intellectual disdain for the United States, which he secretly envies, while blaming it for all his ills and which he has never tried to understand." Specifically, most Mexicans assume that not only the executive branch but Congress, the judiciary, the state governments and even municipal authorities in the United States are all subservient to the President. Every "anti-Mexican" incident—from a protectionist trade measure in Congress to the beating of an undocumented Mexican by a Houston policeman—therefore seems politically motivated and serves to reinforce a conspiratorial view of the United States.

This vision helps feed Mexican nationalism, but it serves the country poorly when dealing at a more practical level with its northern neighbor. Many top Mexican officials—including those educated in U.S. schools—have a more sophisticated knowledge of the United States, but the Mexi-can bureaucracy as a whole has not learned to distinguish between the different lobbies and interest groups that are frequently behind policies objectionable to Mexico. Unlike other Latin American countries, Mexico has rarely hired an experienced U.S. lobbyist, on the grounds that this would be undignified. The Mexican Embassy in Washington has also been reluctant to make its voice heard on Capitol Hill. On a few occa-sions, Mexican business groups affected by U.S. trade legislation have felt obliged to launch publicity campaigns of their own in Washington.

Some officials simply hope that a pro-Mexico Hispanic lobby—analogous to the Israeli and Irish lobbies—might one day appear in Congress, although Mexican efforts to develop strong political links with the Mexican-American community have been fraught with problems. The Echeverría administration encouraged Chicano leaders to visit Mexico and strengthen ties with their "homeland," but differences among the myriad Mexican-American organizations prevented any institutional relationship from developing. Mexico was also made aware that its "interference" in American political affairs could serve to justify Washington's meddling in Mexico. During a visit to Washington in September 1979, López Portillo arrived at the White House from a meeting with Chicano leaders who asked him to convey a message to President Carter. Before he could do so, a visibly annoyed Carter interrupted with the remark: "Next time, tell them to get in touch with me directly."

Presidents, foreign secretaries and ambassadors may momentarily affect the atmospherics of bilateral relations, but they can neither rewrite history nor transform suspicion into trust. In 1983 and 1984, De la Madrid was anxious to avoid public disputes with Washington that could disturb his efforts to attract foreign bankers and investors back to Mexico. Yet, the more blatant Mexico's economic dependence on the United States, the more the country needed to deny it. Even praise of De la Madrid's economic policies from American officials was therefore counterproductive at home. Further, like so many of his predecessors who had also begun by trying to court the United States, De la Madrid became more outspoken with frustration—specifically over U.S. policies toward Central America and Latin American debt problems—as his administration proceeded.

Yet, with the asymmetry of power an accepted reality, the tone of relations is established by the past more than the present and by attitudes more than issues. "To attain the level of mutual respect and maturity that marks our present relationship," De la Madrid could not resist reminding Reagan when they met in August 1983, "we had to pass through bitter experiences and suffer hostility and misunderstanding." Still more philosophically, López Portillo told Carter in 1979: "We do not view our history as one that uselessly anchors us, like so many pillars of salt, to a burden of resentment." Yet Mexico's "burden of resentment" has grown in recent years and seems unlikely to be lifted until Mexico perceives a change in U.S. attitudes. Washington, while willing to help in times of crisis, has assigned little priority to assuaging Mexico's feelings. Perhaps only by recognizing and respecting their deep cultural, religious and philosophical differences could the neighbors become friends. But their very differences in strength prevent even this from occurring.

III

When United States and Mexican Presidents meet, as they do most years notwithstanding the state of relations, a series of concrete bilateral issues are always discussed. Some, such as migration and trade, are permanent items, too complex and dynamic to be resolved and too important to be ignored. Others, such as debt crises, energy exchanges, fishing rights and the narcotics traffic, are more immediate problems and more susceptible to answers. Since the mid-1970s, regional questions—particularly the violent instability of Central America and Mexico's criticism of Washington's response to the crisis—have featured prominently as Mexico has adopted a more activist foreign policy. Yet all topics are somehow interwoven by the thread of neighborhood. At times, officials in both countries have even debated translating this very real interdependence into linked solutions to various problems. While this has not proved possible, seemingly unrelated problems unavoidably influence each other by contributing to the mood of relations.

The oldest problem—the century-old question of illegal migration—is the most insoluble, not only because opinions are deeply divided on both sides of the border, but also because "solutions" would require the assumption, by one or both countries, of high political risks. From the Mexican point of view, there is embarrassment that, more than seven decades after the Revolution, hundreds of thousands of people must leave the country each year to work in the United States, but Mexicans quietly celebrate the informal "reconquest" of territories lost in the nineteenth century. Mexico insists that the silent invasion is smaller than claimed in the United States, but it fears the social and political consequences of mass deportations or a sealing of the border, although neither is probable. While some officials favor working out a guest-worker program with the United States, recent governments have preferred the less perilous path of protesting the mistreatment of Mexican laborers in the United States without accepting responsibility for controlling the exodus of undocumented migrants.

In the United States, there is still greater ambivalence. A perception exists that the United States is being overrun by illegal migrants and that any measure, however costly, is warranted. During periods of recession, the labor movement automatically blames migrants for high unemployment. The Anglo population also fears that the United States' traditional values, culture and even language are being subverted by new waves of migrants, around half of whom are Mexicans. But the farms of the Southwest and the "sweatshops," restaurants and construction sites of all major cities west of Chicago depend on cheap Mexican labor to remain profitable, with the farmers comprising a powerful Washington lobby. Americans of Mexican descent also argue that, in the absence of a national identity card, the idea of which is strongly opposed by Congress, new legislation placing sanctions on the employers of illegals will inevitably result in job discrimination against them.

Involving so many "push" and "pull" factors in both countries, the migration issue has long resisted solution. A small Mexican population remained in the territories seized by the United States in 1848, and after 1880 the expansion of agriculture in the West stimulated the first major influx from the south. The "pull" of agricultural and railroad maintenance jobs during World War I then coincided with the "push" of economic hardship and political chaos during the Mexican Revolution. Although the U.S. Border Patrol was formed in 1924, this migration continued steadily until the "pull" of jobs evaporated with the Depression. Some 500,000 to 800,000 Mexicans moved to the United States between 1910 and 1930, and about 400,000 returned home between 1930 and 1933. By 1940, the United States' war economy once again needed Mexicans, and from 1942 an official Bracero Program permitted them to work north of the border for specific periods. Many Mexicans nevertheless traveled without permits, and after the war the first mass deportations began, climaxing with Operation Wetback of 1954, during which over 1 million Mexicans were rounded up and forced home. By the time the Bracero Program ended in 1964, not only had 4.6 million temporary permits been issued, but a strong tradition of working north of the border had been reinforced in much of rural Mexico.

Since then, the number of Mexicans crossing into the United States has grown steadily, though at a pace responsive to economic conditions in the United States and Mexico. The statistics on the subject have varied widely and have proved vulnerable to political manipulation. Americans alarmed by the phenomenon have pointed to the dramatic rise in the number of undocumented aliens returned by the Border Patrol to Mexico—55,000 in fiscal 1965, 277,000 in 1970, 680,000 in 1975, 950,000 in 1980 and 1.05 million in 1983—but these figures do not record how many Mexicans were detained on more than one occasion. While 90 percent of undocumented aliens apprehended by the U.S. Immigration and

Naturalization Service are Mexican nationals, this statistic reflects how enforcement activities are concentrated along the Mexican border. In the early 1970s, the then head of the INS, General Leonard Chapman, stirred fears by claiming that 4 to 12 million illegals were living in the United States, but he had no statistical basis for his estimate.

Under pressure from organized labor, and without consulting Mexico, the Carter administration sent a new Immigration Bill to Congress in August 1977 and soon discovered the complexity of the issue. With no consensus in either Congress or the country at large, Carter opted in 1978 to appoint a Select Commission on Immigration, which, required to report in March 1981, conveniently kept the problem out of the 1980 election campaign. Mexico, confident that internal differences would continue to block passage of new legislation, felt free to acknowledge the United States' legal right to control immigration, but pointed to its own constitutional prohibition on stopping Mexicans from leaving the country and refused to cooperate with border enforcement. "It is our job to take decisions in our territory," López Portillo once noted, "and our decisions can in no way limit the freedom of movement or settlement of the Mexicans." More practically, no President could be expected voluntarily to close what is widely viewed as an escape valve or to renounce the estimated $1 billion or so in annual remittances from undocumented Mexicans.

While the Select Commission on Immigration was at work, Mexico embarked on its own study of the phenomenon, aimed essentially at separating facts from myths. Until then, most related studies had been carried out by American academics in the United States. Mexico's Labor Ministry polled 62,500 homes in 115 communities and for the first time obtained its own data on migrants with residence in Mexico. Many of the results were not surprising: 84 percent of migrants were men, 77 percent were between the ages of fifteen and forty, their 4.9 years of schooling was significantly above the national average, 90 percent came from the mainly arid states north of Mexico City and 75 percent traveled to either California or Texas.

Other results had greater political implications. Of almost 1 million migrants identified in December 1978, 48 percent were in Mexico, either on vacation or between crops, thus underlining the temporary quality of much of the migration. Figures indicating that only 3.2 percent of migrants were unemployed before traveling north and that 77 percent found a job within two weeks of reaching the United States enabled Mexico to argue that it was neither exporting unemployment nor taking jobs from Americans. Government consultants inferred that not more than 900,000 undocumented workers whose usual place of abode was in Mexico were present in the United States at any one time in 1978, far below previous estimates.

Perhaps for fear of becoming involved in the search for a solution, Mexico made surprisingly little use of these studies. When the U.S. Select Commission issued its report in 1981, it offered its own guess—without any reference to the Mexican poll—of between 3 and 6 million illegal migrants, an estimate that included persons from countries other than Mexico. The political issue was then reopened by the U.S. economic recession, and after the Reagan administration dropped its own immigration proposals, it endorsed a bill presented by Senator Alan Simpson and Representative Romano Mazzoli in March 1982.

The bill aimed to control illegal migration by strengthening the Border Patrol and placing sanctions on employers of undocumented aliens, but it also recognized the humanitarian and legal obstacles to mass deportations by designing a program to grant amnesty to all illegals who could prove permanent residence in the United States. Mexico was never consulted about the planned legislation, but bipartisan support for the measure seemed strong, and when it failed to win approval in 1982, an amended version was resubmitted in 1983 and was again passed by the Senate. In October 1983, fearing that the Democrats might lose Hispanic votes in 1984, the Speaker of the House, Thomas P. O'Neill, Jr., abruptly withdrew it from consideration, but under pressure he allowed it to be taken up again the following summer. On June 20, 1984, the House finally adopted its version of the immigration bill by 216 votes to 211, a minimal margin that reflected the emotions stirred up by the issue.

But before the bill could be sent to the White House, a compromise version reconciling the House and Senate bills required negotiating, raising hopes in Mexico that U.S. electoral passions would block a final agreement. The Senate contemplated granting permanent residence status to illegal aliens who entered the United States before January 1, 1977, and temporary status to those arriving before January 1, 1979; the House offered temporary permits, which could become permanent after two years, to those living continuously in the United States since January 1, 1982. Still more important, to appease the American farming lobby, the House offered a guest worker program under which temporary migrants could stay in the United States for up to 11 months at a time, as well as a transition period allowing farmers three years to comply with the new law. After that, employers of undocumented aliens would be subject to fines and, in the Senate bill, possible imprisonment. Further, while the House leadership said it would not accept the Senate version, President

Reagan declared he would not sign the House version. And supporters of *any* version feared that the tiny majority of June 1984 had already disappeared.

Nonetheless, the approaching specter of a migration clampdown came as a shock to Mexico. Migration experts had frequently reminded the government that some new legislation was unavoidable, but officials had gambled that it would be perennially blocked by internal differences within the U.S. Congress. Further, having long refused to discuss the migration issue with Washington, Mexico had no grounds for complaint. In fact, during the lengthy debate on Capitol Hill, the likely impact of the bill on Mexico was not even raised. Under media pressure to protest, Mexican officials merely reiterated that they would defend the "rights" of Mexicans in the United States, but in private they expressed the hope that a guest worker program and a transition period included in any new law would forestall the need to absorb those accustomed to traveling north each year. They also argued that the legislation would be impossible to implement, and sought solace in projections of the United States' long-term needs for cheap labor which could be supplied by Mexico. But, impotent to affect the outcome, the government understood that successful application of a new law could have serious political and economic repercussions for Mexico.

In the past, Mexico had tried to link the migration and trade issues by arguing that less protectionism by the United States would mean fewer illegal migrants from Mexico. "We prefer to export products rather than people," López Portillo once noted. But this was no more than a useful political posture. Not only did Mexico's export industries lack the capacity to absorb the underemployed hundreds of thousands that worked north of the border, but neither organized labor nor protected industries in the United States had any interest in transferring jobs or market opportunities to Mexico. Any special trade deal for Mexico was blocked by U.S. legislation and by the General Agreement on Tariffs and Trade (GATT), which Mexico had refused to sign for fear of exposing its own protected industries to outside competition. Mexico's demand for greater access to the U.S. market became a perennial feature of presidential meetings, but little progress was recorded.

The irony is that bilateral trade has expanded dramatically in recent years. Two-thirds of Mexico's total trade has traditionally been with the United States, and in 1981, when two-way trade exceeded $26 billion, Mexico became the United States' third-largest trading partner, the result of both rising oil exports and massive imports of capital goods from the United States. Between 1982 and 1984, because of import controls forced on Mexico by its financial crisis, the country actually recorded large surpluses in its trade with the United States. From Mexico's point of view, the unbalanced nature of the commercial relationship had been disguised by oil. In 1982, Mexico became the United States' single largest foreign supplier of crude, but its non-oil exports had stagnated. This was blamed on the "new protectionism"—such nontariff barriers as voluntary quotas, arbitrary quality controls and punitive anti-dumping measures—being exercised by the United States against leather, textiles, cement, steel and other products that developing countries were able to export.

The longest-running battle has involved exports of winter vegetables and fruits which compete directly with Florida farmers. In 1978, Florida producers formally charged that Mexican tomatoes, eggplants, cucumbers, peppers and squash were being dumped on the U.S. market, and after the suit was rejected eighteen months later by a Carter administration clearly anxious to appease Mexico, Mexican farmers continued to claim that health, quality and packaging controls were still used to limit exports. Mexico also routinely protests when the United States eliminates any of its products from the Generalized System of Preferences (GSP), although this is done only when they are earning $53 million annually in sales and are considered "fully competitive." Further, Mexico still exports about half of the 3,000 products on the GSP list, while only fifty-five of these are subject to import duties.

The greatest complication has stemmed from Mexican export subsidies that expose products to countervailing duties in the United States. Protection against "unfair competition" is permitted by GATT, with duty applied once the American plaintiff proves injury. But for non-GATT members like Mexico, a provisional duty is imposed as soon as the complaint is filed, and though removed if damage is not proven, it disrupts production and marketing programs. Because duties are levied on Mexican exports of leather wearing apparel, ceramic tiles, balloons, iron castings and specialized steel, some exporters have forgone the subsidy to avoid the duties. In 1984, with Mexico arguing that it needed to export in order to maintain interest payments on its foreign debt, Washington agreed to apply the GATT "injury test" to Mexican products affected by dumping charges. But efforts to draw up a broad bilateral trade agreement remained blocked by differences over "permissible" levels of Mexican protectionism and constraints imposed by U.S. trade legislation.

Running through Mexico's relationship with its neighbor is ambivalence about a special relationship. On trade, Mexico would welcome a one-way arrangement. But when mention was made in the late 1970s of a North American Common Market, tying together the economies of the United States, Canada and Mexico, Mexico immediately balked, fearing that it would lose control of its economy and energy resources. In practice, ambivalence is still apparent: Mexico was anxious to prevent the United States from relying excessively on Mexican energy, but since world oil prices began to fall in June 1981, it has looked to the United States to take more of its crude. In August 1981, Petróleos Mexicanos signed a five-year contract with the Department of Energy to supply 50,000 barrels a day to the U.S. Strategic Reserve, and a year later in the midst of the country's financial crisis, it signed another twelve-month contract to provide 110,000 barrels a day to the Strategic Reserve. Including commercial sales, by 1983 half of Mexico's exported oil—750,000 barrels a day—was flowing to the United States.

Mexico's economic dependence on the United States has continued to grow in recent years, but its oil boom and subsequent financial bust revealed a new U.S. vulnerability to economic development in Mexico. The United States had come to count on the security of Mexican oil, but many American companies also enriched themselves by exporting to Mexico, real estate companies profited from the exodus of Mexican capital and commerce in the American Southwest counted Mexicans among their best clients. When the Mexican peso collapsed and the country's foreign exchange reserves evaporated in August 1982, economic activity in the border states immediately sagged, exporters of everything from oil rigs to private jets lost their markets, even Americans —many of them tax evaders—who had invested in fixed-interest dollar accounts in Mexico learned they would be repaid in devalued pesos. Only the oil relationship was unaffected.

At the time, the United States' weakest flank was in fact Mexico's $80-billion foreign debt, but the Reagan administration was slow to recognize this situation. When Mexico's Finance Minister, Jesús Silva Herzog, flew to Washington on August 13, 1982, and confronted Treasury Secretary Donald Regan with Mexico's imminent bankruptcy, he was told: "Well, that's your problem." But Silva Herzog pointed out the massive exposure of American banks in Mexico. In the frantic weekend of negotiations that followed, prompted largely by the threat to the American banking system and the international monetary structure, the Reagan administration pledged $1 billion in advance payment for oil, $1 billion in Commodity Credit Corporation guarantees and $985 million toward a $1.8 billion loan from the Bank of International Settlements. Subsequently, Washington pressured commercial banks and the International Monetary Fund to provide new long-term credits at a time when Mexico was unable to keep up payments on its existing debt.

The way Washington handled the negotiations, however, forestalled any expressions of appreciation by Mexico. Mexico resented the fact that its proximity to the United States had facilitated the flight of capital which brought on the financial crisis. It felt humiliated that its dream of increased economic independence from the United States had once again been shattered. Most of all, the López Portillo administration believed that the United States had taken advantage of Mexico's prostration by negotiating an unjustly tough deal. On at least one occasion during the talks, Silva Herzog announced plans to return to Mexico rather than accept the American terms. Eventually Reagan himself intervened to improve Washington's offer and Mexico reluctantly agreed to sell its $1 billion worth of oil at just $25 per barrel, below the going rate, and at 20 percent interest, above the market price. "We flew home relieved but strangely ungrateful," one Mexican official recalled later. "Washington had saved us from chaos, yet it did so in an uncharitable manner." Even at such a critical moment, the substance and style of the relationship seemed inseparable.

IV

Feeling imprisoned historically and economically by the United States, Mexico has used a series of lesser political issues as loudspeakers for its nationalism. Its strong influence over local media and the discipline of its political apparatus enable the government to switch on nationalist "shows" at its convenience: issues that in one year become tests of national honor may be ignored the next year. Major "victories" have therefore been recorded on problems of little consequence to the United States and of great symbolic weight to Mexico. Even when disputes disappear as quickly as they appear, leaving no permanent mark on bilateral relations, the high-pitched media coverage that invariably accompanies these instant crises provides a useful catharsis for pent-up passions. It is as if Mexican politicians and journalists need some relatively simple issue on which to focus their infinitely more complex sentiments about the United States. When no such problem exists, it may be quite literally invented.

In the 1960s, this role was played by the Chamizal question. The problem had been created in 1864, when the Rio Grande, which marks the U.S.-Mexico border from the Gulf to El Paso, changed its course and passed 440 acres of Mexican territory to the U.S. side of the river. Mexico initiated efforts to recover the so-called Chamizal district outside El Paso, but despite favorable arbitration rulings, no progress was made. For a country that had lost half its entire territory a century earlier, recuperation of the Chamizal gradually became a point of principle and Presidents Kennedy and López Mateos finally settled the matter in June 1962. Two years later, amid great trumpeting in Mexico, the Chamizal was returned. In the late 1960s and early 1970s, another border issue— the high salinity of the Colorado River as it entered the farming valleys of northwestern Mexico—came to symbolize U.S. disregard and it too was partly resolved after simmering Mexican indignation prompted Washington to respond.

Narcotics became a sensitive political issue on both sides of the border. The problem began suddenly in 1969 when the Nixon administration carried out Operation Intercept, exhaustively checking all vehicles entering the United States from Mexico and paralyzing border traffic for days. While the Mexican government was angered at being given no prior warning, the implication being that it could not be trusted with the secret, Mexico soon became the scapegoat for its neighbor's entire drug problem. Mexican officials argued that the solution lay in attacking demand rather than supply, but under pressure from Washington, an anti-narcotics campaign launched in 1975 resulted in eradication of marijuana and opium poppy fields and the jailing of several hundred American traffickers. Instead of receiving thanks, Mexico found itself the target of a media campaign orchestrated by pro-marijuana groups that portrayed traffickers as innocent victims of Mexican torture and mistreatment. With the problem dominating bilateral relations and stirring passions in both countries, Washington finally proposed a prisoner exchange in 1976, which Mexico happily agreed to. But almost a decade later, the drug problem threatened to return as a bilateral issue, with the appearance of cocaine laboratories in Mexico for the first time.

In the late 1970s, with Mexico's self-confidence boosted by its new oil wealth, there were numerous occasions for flare-ups of Mexican nationalism, many of which went virtually unnoticed in Washington. A decision by the local office of the Immigration and Naturalization Service to build a spiked border fence at El Paso was presented by the Mexican press as a malicious plan to cause bodily harm to illegal migrants, although the "tortilla curtain," as it was tagged, was soon as full of holes as other border fences. A drought that severely damaged Mexican agriculture in 1980 was attributed by some officials to hurricane seeding by the U.S. National Ocean and Atmospheric Administration. On this occasion, embarrassed Mexican diplomats conceded privately that the nationalism was misplaced and the media "show" had taken off on its own. The following year, no credit was given to the United States for an excellent rainy season.

When an offshore Mexican oil well—Ixtoc I—blew in June 1980, Mexico used nationalism to hide its embarrassment. With 30,000 barrels a day spilling into the Gulf, Mexican press reports emphasized that Sedco, the drilling contractor responsible for the accident, was an American company—owned, conveniently, by the son of the then governor of Texas, William P. Clements. When floating oil finally reached Texas beaches, temporarily threatening tourism at South Padre Island, Mexico dismissed American efforts to obtain compensation, arguing that no international law covered the case and recalling that Mexico was the impotent victim of toxic air pollution from factories in American border towns. Good fortune rather than nationalism, however, saved Mexico from years of litigation in the United States: even though Ixtoc I was not capped until nine months later, the permanent damage that it caused was minimal.

After Mexico renounced all fishing agreements with the United States in December 1980 and began patrolling its 200-mile "exclusive economic zone," it was even able to savor some gunboat diplomacy against the United States. The problem arose from Washington's refusal to recognize that the 200-mile zone applied to tropical tuna, but it coincided with Mexico's new emphasis on developing its own neglected fishing industry. When the San Diego tuna fleet refused to buy licenses to operate in Mexican waters, the Mexican Navy responded by "arresting" a number of boats, seizing their nets and catch and levying stiff fines before releasing them. The United States then suspended all tuna imports from Mexico. But to some Mexicans the losses suffered by the fishing industry were more than compensated by the sheer delight at seeing American boats detained in Mexican ports, the closest that Mexico had ever come to recording a naval victory over its neighbor.

The one dispute that did provoke the wrath of the Carter administration was not strictly bilateral but rather Mexico's relatively minor role in the U.S.-Iranian drama. After his ouster in December 1978, the Shah of Iran began searching for a permanent home, and through the intercession of former Secretary of State Henry A. Kissinger and David Rockefeller, chairman of Chase Manhattan, López Portillo was persuaded to grant him a six-month tourist visa. The Shah arrived in June 1979 and rented a huge home in Cuernavaca, but four months later he flew to New York for medical treatment. Soon afterward, hostages were seized in the U.S. Embassy in Teheran, and when the Shah was ready to return to

Mexico, López Portillo refused him entry. The White House then persuaded Panama's ruler, Brigadier General Omar Torrijos Herrera, to receive him.

Carter, however, felt personally betrayed by López Portillo at a crucial moment in his struggle for political survival. Claiming that the Shah had been promised re-entry to Mexico, American officials "leaked" reports attributing López Portillo's volte-face to the Shah's refusal to invest in Mexico. In his only reference to Mexico in his memoirs, Carter recalled bitterly that López Portillo had demonstrated that he was not a man of his word. Feeling the heat of Washington's anger, Mexico explained that it had simply decided not to renew the Shah's six-month visa upon expiry December 9, one week after his planned return. The real reason was different. López Portillo had been ready to allow the Shah back, but was dissuaded by Foreign Minister Castañeda's argument that Mexican embassies around the world would become vulnerable to attack by radical Iranians, that Mexico had no reason to involve itself in Washington's foreign quarrels and associate itself with an unpopular exiled dictator who was totally identified with the United States.

The episode further poisoned personal relations between López Portillo and Carter, but left no permanent imprint on U.S.-Mexican ties. Symbolically, it marked an important turning point: through its greater involvement in Third World and Latin American affairs, Mexico now had its own interests to defend abroad. And its changing perception of its role in the world soon added complicated new dimensions to its relationship with Washington. By the early 1980s, while both Mexico and the United States sought to isolate bilateral trade and financial questions from broader political problems, their disagreement over Central America had become the most prominent feature of the relationship. It brought important adjustments on both sides: Mexico was no longer simply using a foreign policy issue to exhibit its independence from the United States; and Washington for the first time reluctantly came to accept Mexico as a valid interlocutor on a problem of strategic importance to the United States.

17

Foreign Policy:
Facing Central America

I

Mexico's foreign policy has traditionally been inward-looking, aimed at
shielding the country from outside pressures rather than expanding its
sphere of influence. Because these pressures have come only from the
United States, its policy toward the rest of the world has been shaped
by its relationship with Washington. For this reason, East-West issues
and even Third World problems long seemed irrelevant: Mexico looked
to the world as a defense against U.S. intervention and it ventured into
the world to display its independence from Washington. The resulting
policy of loud words and cautious action served Mexico well. It was
consistent with the country's history, it kept alive nationalism, it discouraged militarism, it appeased leftists both at home and abroad and
it allowed Mexico to challenge Washington in diplomatic forums without threatening fundamental U.S. interests in Mexico. Being a policy that
reflected the national interest rather than the whims of a single administration, it was also constant.

The fine-sounding principles that guide Mexico's foreign policy—
respect for national sovereignty, territorial integrity and self-determina-
tion, opposition to all forms of intervention and application of the international rule of law—are therefore more than juridical abstractions.
They comprise Mexico's principal guarantee against repetition of its
history, and when applied to other countries exposed to intervention,
they are seen to protect Mexico. But even these global principles are
applied selectively in the light of the country's own experience. Mexico
accepts its alignment with Washington in any confrontation with Moscow, but it refuses to view Latin America's problems in an East-West

context. From emotional as well as political points of view, it also has difficulty equating interventions by Washington and Moscow: American soldiers have entered Mexico on numerous occasions; Soviet troops have not.

Successive administrations in Washington have been both irritated and puzzled by Mexico's foreign policy. They have variously portrayed it as the product of unthinking anti-Americanism, immature *machismo* or naïve ignorance of the true danger posed by the Soviet Union and Cuba to Mexico's own stability. Occasionally, they have identified an expansionist and competitive motivation behind Mexico's foreign policy. More often, convinced that they have had only the best interests of the region at heart, they have failed to grasp that U.S. national interests do not necessarily coincide with those of Mexico.

With fresh memories of diverse American political and military interventions in Mexico during the Revolution, the Calles government in the 1920s sent weapons to aid rebels under General Augusto César Sandino who were fighting U.S. Marines in Nicaragua. According to official documents from the period, Washington wavered between blaming "Moscow's influence" and Mexico's ambition to install governments in Central America that were "not only friendly but subservient to Mexico and completely under Mexico's domination." But Calles' main objective was to discourage U.S. interventions by raising the cost of such adventures. Once the Marines were withdrawn by President Roosevelt, leaving a series of right-wing dictators to maintain order, Mexico lost interest in Central America.

Mexico's involvement in the Spanish Civil War, its first incursion into problems outside the region, was inspired by domestic concerns. It was opposed on principle to Nazi Germany's support for General Franco's fascist forces, but it also felt powerful emotional ties to a Republican Spain struggling to break free from an authoritarian tradition that Mexico identified with its own Colonial past. Taking the lead in denouncing the fascists, President Cárdenas secretly purchased weapons and ammunition for the Republicans and attempted unsuccessfully to supply some U.S.-made aircraft. After the defeat of the Republicans in 1940, Mexico accepted over 20,000 refugees, permitted a government-in-exile to be installed in Mexico City and refused to restore diplomatic relations with Spain until Franco's death in 1977.

In the 1930s, the government's priority was to consolidate its political and economic control of the country and its principal clashes with the United States and Britain stemmed from the expropriation of foreign railroad and oil companies. After joining the Allies in World War II,

Mexico began to recognize the opportunities as well as the threats posed by the outside world. In the late 1940s, its foreign policy was for the first time used to project an image of growth and stability that would attract foreign investment, credit and tourism. Since these were available largely north of the border, Mexico needed to maintain warm bilateral relations with Washington without abandoning any fundamental foreign policy principles.

As the economic partnership flourished, Mexico disapproved of much of U.S. foreign policy. It refused to accept the political and military role that Washington assigned Latin America in the Cold War and, along with only two other regional governments, maintained diplomatic ties with Moscow. Desirous of avoiding gratuitous involvement in East-West problems, Mexico turned down numerous opportunities to return to the UN Security Council after serving as a member for one year in 1946. It was particularly wary of Washington's hegemonic ambitions in Latin America. It signed the 1947 Inter-American Treaty of Mutual Assistance, known as the Rio Pact, creating a regional system of collective security, but has opposed all moves to apply the treaty. After the creation of the Organization of American States (OAS) in 1948, it embarked on a lonely crusade to prevent the United States from using it as an instrument of its own foreign policy. As a result, Mexico was often in a minority opposing Washington and, to this day, continues advocating fundamental reforms of the OAS Charter.

Even in its present form, the OAS has served Mexico, providing a public forum where it can defend its principles without assuming an obligation to confront the United States in any more perilous fashion. During the 1950s and 1960s, the independence of its foreign policy was built almost entirely around a series of votes. In 1954, only Mexico and Argentina opposed an OAS resolution which condemned Guatemala's left-leaning government and prepared the diplomatic way for the U.S.-backed invasion that ousted President Jacobo Arbenz. In 1965, Mexico was joined by just four other countries in opposing the OAS's creation of an Inter-American Peace Force to legitimize post facto the U.S. invasion of the Dominican Republic, with Mexico simultaneously sponsoring a resolution at the United Nations calling for withdrawal of the Marines. Washington in turn came to expect these stances and bilateral relations were not affected.

Over Cuba, Mexico eventually found itself completely alone in the regional body. To some extent, President López Mateos reacted to the sympathy stirred by the 1959 Cuban Revolution among Mexican leftists and nationalists. But he was also following tradition by challenging

Washington's application of the Monroe Doctrine to justify its new intervention in the region. In April 1961, the abortive Bay of Pigs invasion of Cuba provoked strong protests in Mexico (even the aging former President Cárdenas offered to help defend the island). In 1962, Mexico and five other countries opposed an OAS resolution suspending Cuba from the organization for "exporting" revolution to Venezuela. Two years later, Mexico was the only country to ignore a mandatory OAS resolution ordering all members to break relations with the Castro regime. Between 1964 and 1970, when Chile's new Allende government recognized the Castro regime, Mexico was Cuba's only formal link to Latin America.

Mexico was not motivated by ideological sympathy with Havana. When global issues were involved, as during the 1962 missile crisis, Mexico took Washington's side. The years of Mexico's greatest importance to Cuba coincided with the administration of Gustavo Díaz Ordaz, the country's most anti-Communist President in decades. When a 1967 conference of the Latin American Solidarity Organization in Cuba adopted resolutions calling for revolution throughout the continent, Mexico's Foreign Minister, Antonio Carrillo Flores, responded with a stern warning to the Castro regime. (Cuba has never sponsored guerrilla movements in Mexico, and to this day there is an explicit—though unwritten—understanding that neither government will meddle in the other's internal affairs.) But while relations were cool and trade minimal, preservation of formal ties with the Castro regime served as a vital symbol of Mexico's independence: it was a policy designed for Washington, not Havana.

Cuba was forced to suffer frequent humiliations at Mexico's hands in order to avoid total isolation. The most important feature of the relationship was Cubana de Aviación's twice-weekly flight to Mexico City, which permitted Cuban officials to travel to the United Nations without going through Europe and enabled thousands of American and Latin American leftists to visit the island. In practice, this Mexican gesture was less than generous. The Central Intelligence Agency was allowed to oversee the Mexican end of the air link, with all travelers to and from Cuba photographed at the Mexico City airport and their trips recorded with a huge stamp in their passports. Mexican authorities also cooperated with the CIA in tapping the telephones of the Cuban Embassy and the homes of Cuban diplomats and photographing everyone who entered or left the embassy. (Evidence was thus obtained of Lee Harvey Oswald's visit to the Cuban Embassy in Mexico City prior to his assassination of President Kennedy in 1963.) At one point, a member of the Mexican Embassy in

Havana was exposed as a CIA operator and expelled. Mexico made no effort to deny the charges.

Some of the symbols of Mexican foreign policy have verged on myths. In the early 1960s, because its foreign exchange coffers had been filled by American tourists and investors and remittances by braceros working in the United States, it could afford to ignore the Alliance for Progress and even mock the program as a new form of interventionism. Mexico refused to sign an agreement proposed under the Alliance for Progress guaranteeing American private investment in Mexico, and in 1966 the Agency for International Development closed its office in Mexico City. Between 1962 and 1971, Mexico received only $70 million in direct U.S. aid—much of it spent on bilateral border programs—compared to $1.4 billion channeled to Brazil and $744.7 million to Colombia. On a per capita basis, Mexico has received less aid than any other Latin American nation. It is also more economically dependent on the United States than any other.

At the time of the Alliance for Progress, President López Mateos tried to extend Mexico's vision beyond the region through a busy program of foreign travels that took him to Western Europe and Asia. This too was largely symbolic. He met Yugoslavia's Tito, India's Nehru and Indonesia's Sukarno, who at the time were building a neutral corner for newly independent former colonies, but Mexico neither joined the Non-Aligned Movement nor raised its voice in the Third World campaign for economic reform at the UN Conference on Trade and Development (UNCTAD). López Mateos' foreign policy served to promote his personal prestige at home and to demonstrate Mexico's independence to Washington, but it developed no new role for Mexico in the world.

Mexico's principal international initiative of the decade, the 1967 Treaty for the De-Nuclearization of Latin America, known as the Treaty of Tlatelolco, involved the much-publicized defense of a principle without assuming any political risk. The treaty, which included protocols to be signed by the nuclear powers and by countries with colonies in the region, aimed to keep nuclear weapons out of Latin America. It was never ratified by Argentina and Brazil, the only nations in the area suspected of having nuclear ambitions. But it permitted Mexico to embrace the cause of disarmament, and years later it earned the Mexican architect of the treaty, Alfonso García Robles, a share—with Sweden's disarmament advocate Alva Myrdal—of the 1982 Nobel Peace Prize, thus adding another symbolic rosette to Mexican foreign policy.

Mexico's strategy was to plant occasional banners on the international and regional diplomatic stage and then withdraw to the real world of its internal development and its relations with the United States. Succeeding the peripatetic López Mateos, Díaz Ordaz met several times with Presidents Johnson and Nixon, but traveled no further east than Washington. Elsewhere in Latin America, Mexico's economic and political profile was low, with South American governments feeling little identification with Mexico. To the extent that Mexico looked abroad at all, it looked north. Despite the importance of an independent foreign policy as a counterpoint to its economic dependency, Mexico—government, private sector and political groups—generally ignored the rest of the world just as the world ignored Mexico.

II

The more activist foreign policy adopted by President Echeverría between 1970 and 1976 was initially motivated by changing domestic circumstances. A recession exposed weaknesses in the postwar economic strategy and underlined the need to diversify export markets and support international economic reforms. Following the 1968 student movement, a more nationalist foreign policy also fitted into the strategy of winning over disenchanted leftists and intellectuals. Only later in his term did Echeverría's personal interest in projecting his image around the world add an ingredient of vanity that would eventually become indistinguishable from foreign policy itself.

Like many Presidents assuming office at a difficult domestic moment, Echeverría pledged not to travel outside the country "for two or three years." Just ten months later, he flew to New York to address the UN General Assembly. In the four years that followed, he visited thirty-six nations on thirteen different trips and a score of foreign heads of state also visited Mexico, including Queen Elizabeth II and the Shah of Iran. Echeverría recognized China in February 1972 and became the first Mexican President to visit either Moscow or Peking. Even though Mexico has no diplomatic relations with the Vatican, he sought an audience with Pope Paul VI during a trip to Rome. (The break with the Vatican came under Juárez in the mid-nineteenth century, and after anticlericalism was reinforced by the Revolution, no government has dared recognize the Holy See as a state.) Soon Echeverría began courting smaller Third World countries in an effort to provide leadership.

In his State of the Union address of September 1972, he explained his purpose: "For many years, we have acted with firmness but with caution. We are now contributing more direct actions in defense of our international principles. In the coming years, Mexico must assume a more important role in international affairs." As evidence of this, addressing the Third UNCTAD in Chile in April 1972, Echeverría proposed a Charter of the Economic Rights and Duties of States as a kind of economic corollary to the UN Charter itself. It added little to the ongoing debate between industrialized and developing nations, and when eventually approved by the UN General Assembly in 1974, the United States and other key industrialized nations cast negative votes. But the charter brought Mexico into the North-South debate and gave Echeverría a cause to promote during his travels.

As the obstacles to reducing Mexico's economic dependence on the United States became clearer, the political dimension to Echeverría's foreign policy grew more important and more controversial. His handling of relations with Chile in particular accelerated the polarization that marked the second half of his administration. Just as López Mateos felt overshadowed by Fidel Castro, Echeverría seemed compelled to compete with Salvador Allende, but he did so by embracing the Chilean experiment as if it were a natural successor to the Mexican Revolution. After his trip to Santiago, he received Allende in Mexico in December 1972, stirring the first conservative protests about his foreign policy. But this was compensated by the usefulness of the association with Chile among domestic leftists: Echeverría could sound radical and at the same time hold up Chile's democratic nonviolent example to Mexican youths more taken by the Cuban model.

After Allende's death in the September 1973 military coup, Echeverría responded almost emotionally, ordering the Mexican Embassy in Santiago to accept all political refugees who sought asylum and personally receiving Allende's widow, Hortensia Bussi, and several ousted ministers when they arrived in Mexico in exile. A few months later, he broke relations with the Pinochet regime and Mexico became the main center of propaganda activities against the dictatorship. Several thousand Chilean politicians, economists and academics were found jobs in Mexico's government and universities, and within two years the country's doors were again opened to thousands of Argentine and Uruguayan liberals and leftists in flight from military dictatorships at home. Echeverría clearly saw himself emulating General Cárdenas' treatment of Spanish Republican exiles, but the prominence given to many South American radicals stirred irritation among Mexico's business community and middle classes and eventually spawned a wave of anti-Communist xenophobia.

Following the Chilean coup, Echeverría became increasingly obsessed with foreign policy, viewing himself as a lonely voice in a continent increasingly dominated by pro-American military regimes. As evidence grew of the CIA's involvement in the ouster of Allende, Echeverría began openly criticizing the United States, referring routinely to "imperialism," language normally used only by leftists in the region. A special effort was also made to improve relations with Cuba. The CIA operation at the Mexico City airport was eliminated, and valuable real estate was donated for construction of a new Cuban Embassy building. In August 1975, at the end of a fourteen-country swing, Echeverría became the first Mexican President to visit Havana since the Revolution. He was given a rousing welcome by a government fully conscious of the impact this would have in Washington. Echeverría, still unable to shake off his innate anti-Communism, responded effusively: "I have seen socialism in some large socialist states. The leaders of those countries should come to Cuba to learn how to achieve socialism with sensibility, with humanity, with respect for human dignity."

By 1975, Echeverría considered himself a Third World leader worthy of greater recognition. He first promoted himself as a possible UN Secretary-General, traveling again to New York late in 1975 to address the UN General Assembly, and later appointed a loyal aide as ambassador to Norway with instructions to campaign on his behalf for a Nobel Peace Prize, supposedly for conceiving the Economic Charter. But Echeverría had failed to win a strong constituency in the Third World. Most Latin American governments shared Washington's disapproving view of his radical rhetoric, while political leaders in Africa and Asia noted that Mexico still refused to join either the Non-Aligned Movement or the Organization of Petroleum Exporting Countries. To them, it was blatantly apparent that Mexico remained economically dependent upon— and therefore politically vulnerable to—the United States.

Two incidents irreparably damaged Echeverría's international image. In 1975, following the execution of five Basque terrorists by the Franco regime, Mexico demanded the expulsion of Spain from the United Nations. The Security Council refused even to hear the case and, in the process, became convinced of Echeverría's unsuitability as Secretary-General. Soon afterward, in a misguided attempt to validate its Third World credentials, Mexico joined seventy-one other countries in supporting a UN resolution condemning Zionism as a form of racism. The resulting controversy underlined Mexico's vulnerability. Furious American Jewish organizations mounted a punitive tourist boycott of Mexico which cost the country heavily in foreign exchange and forced an embarrassed government to retreat from its position. When Foreign Minister Emilio O. Rabasa apologized to Israel during an improvised speech in Tel Aviv, however, he went too far and was fired.

From Mexico's point of view, the balance of Echeverría's adventuristic foreign policy was not entirely negative. It brought no significant change in the nation's trading patterns, it gave Echeverría a radical image that frightened away many potential foreign investors and it created unnecessary tensions with the United States. But it helped win domestic leftist support for the regime and thus contributed to political stability. It broke Mexico's political isolation in the world and accustomed Mexicans to thinking beyond the United States. Although Echeverría's successor, José López Portillo, gave immediate priority to patching up relations with Washington in early 1977, he too soon concluded that Mexico's national interest demanded an active and pluralistic foreign policy.

Paradoxically, it was through the accident of massive oil finds that López Portillo won the international recognition that Echeverría had so doggedly and vainly pursued. Within a year of taking office, the new administration was being courted by governments from across the globe. There was hardly a Western nation not eager to secure a special relationship with Mexico. It was enough for Mexico to be growing rapidly while most industrial economies were stagnating. But at a time of great uncertainty over the future of the world oil market, Mexico also possessed secure energy reserves far from the troubled Middle East. Before long, López Portillo began to savor the prominent role he had been assigned, traveling almost as extensively as his predecessor but being received with more attention. Overnight, Mexico had become important for what it was rather than for what it said.

The oil finds provided Mexico with a new opportunity to exhibit its independence from the United States. Determined that Washington should not regard it as its strategic energy reserve, López Portillo encouraged other industrialized nations, among them France, West Germany, Sweden, Canada and Japan, to step up investments in Mexico in exchange for long-term oil supply contracts. He also rediscovered many of the militant Third World positions advocated by Echeverría. In international debates on economic development, human rights, disarmament and the law of the sea, Mexico assumed a prominent role. In 1980, Mexico took a seat on the UN Security Council for the first time since 1946, as if suddenly ready to give opinions and cast votes on sensitive political issues as varied as the Middle East and southern Africa. For the first time, U.S.-Mexican relations began to include a multilateral as well as a regional dimension.

A psychological adjustment was also continuing. "The country must change its traditional purely defensive attitude toward the world," Foreign Minister Jorge Castañeda explained in March 1980. "The outside world is no longer, as we thought in the past, only a source of unmentionable ills which we cannot remedy. . . . Leaving home naturally involves risks. But to lock ourselves passively inside our house not only prevents us from defending it properly, but also will asphyxiate us. The modern world presents dangers but it also offers better instruments for defense . . . In this new historical-political context, Mexico can act with confidence. It must coldly evaluate its interests, acting with a sense of responsibility, soberly measuring its possibilities and strengths with neither false illusions nor unjustified and paralyzing fears."

At first, López Portillo traveled under the guise of finding new markets for Mexican products. After presenting a World Energy Plan to the United Nations in September 1979, he was able to promote this idea in various capitals. Finally, following the Brandt Commission's report on Third World poverty, López Portillo suggested hosting a high-level conference to revive the North-South dialogue initiated years earlier in Paris. Although President Reagan and leaders of other Western industrialized nations had little interest in the topic, they eventually participated in the twenty-two-nation North-South summit in the Mexican resort of Cancún in October 1981. (Reagan's only condition was the exclusion of Fidel Castro, who, as president of the Non-Aligned Movement, had a special claim to be invited. López Portillo reluctantly agreed to Reagan's terms and by so doing ran up a political debt to Castro. This was repaid two months later when Mexico secretly loaned $100 million to a financially squeezed Cuba.) The summit failed in its primary objective of initiating global negotiations on development issues at the United Nations, but it demonstrated Mexico's new power of convocation and provided López Portillo with his valedictory on the international stage. One year later, he made a final appearance before the UN General Assembly, but by then his own standing had collapsed along with the Mexican economy.

III

The most significant change in Mexican foreign policy in decades was brought not by oil but by political unrest beyond the country's borders in Central America. In its relations with the rest of the world, despite its higher profile, Mexico maintained its traditional caution, refusing to join the Non-Aligned Movement or OPEC and interested principally in impressing two familiar audiences: the United States and domestic public opinion. But in Central America, Mexico was forced to take risks as well as strike poses. Wary of violating its sacred principle of nonintervention, it moved slowly. As events to the south began to affect Mexico directly and the specter of an American military intervention in the isthmus reappeared, both López Portillo and his successor, Miguel de la Madrid, asserted Mexico's influence more confidently and even selfishly.

Throughout the century, Mexico's only interest in Central America has been political stability, because instability inevitably involved the United States in the area. Between the withdrawal of the Marines from Nicaragua in 1934 and the invasion of Guatemala by U.S.-backed forces twenty years later, Mexico barely looked south. With the exception of a brief rupture of diplomatic relations with Guatemala in 1959 after some Mexican fishing boats were attacked by Guatemalan aircraft, Mexico seemed content to see stability maintained by right-wing dictators. Several, including Nicaragua's General Anastasio Somoza Debayle, even paid official visits to Mexico during the Echeverría administration.

Economically, Mexico developed few interests in the area. During World War II, the absence of American products led to a brief flurry of trade, but the moment passed, and despite a much-publicized economic offensive in the region under Díaz Ordaz, by 1970 only 1.8 percent of Mexico's exports went to Central America. There was some Mexican investment in fertilizer and textile factories, but total Mexican capital in the region never exceeded $100 million.

In cultural terms, Mexico's presence was felt more strongly in the region. Many business, political, professional and even military leaders of the region had received training in Mexico. Still more crucially, Mexican popular music, movies, television soap operas and food frequently overwhelmed local traditions. In many ways, Mexico's relationship with the United States was mirrored in Central America's relationship with Mexico. As the closest neighbor, Guatemala particularly resented domination by its "Giant to the North," occasionally banning Mexican television programs as cultural imperialism and quick to identify malice in the course of routine Mexican neglect. Annoyed by Mexico's support for the independence of Belize, long claimed by Guatemala as part of its territory, successive Guatemalan governments learned to doubt Mexico's occasional expressions of good-neighborliness.

Mexico made little effort to provide political leadership to the countries to the south. In the early 1970s, both Venezuela and Brazil launched diplomatic offensives in the region, but even these were not considered challenges by Mexico. Central America was seen to "belong" to the United States, and neither the media nor official circles in Mexico were well informed about events to the south. Except for those living in Chiapas, few Mexicans had ever visited Central America. Until 1977, no Mexican airline flew into the region.

The López Portillo administration was slow to recognize the importance of the changes taking place in Nicaragua in the mid-1970s. Sandinista guerrillas had been active there intermittently since 1962 but, divided into three factions, they seemed to pose no threat to the Somoza dynasty. But in October 1977, after numerous setbacks and internal disputes, one rebel faction, known as the Terceristas—"those of the third way"—persuaded reform-minded clergy, liberal intellectuals and businessmen disenchanted with government corruption that only an armed insurrection could restore democracy. With respected Nicaraguans—the "Group of 12"—acting as its spokesmen, this faction obtained support from three key regional leaders: Venezuela's President Carlos Andrés Pérez gave money and weapons; Panama's strongman, Brigadier General Omar Torrijos Herrera, provided some weapons and training; and in Costa Rica, first President Daniel Oduber Quiróz and then his successor, Rodrigo Carazo Odio, permitted the country to be used as a springboard for attacks on Nicaragua.

After the murder of the opposition newspaper editor Pedro Joaquín Chamorro in January 1978, Mexico began to show interest in Nicaragua, though describing the war publicly as an internal question to be settled by Nicaraguans. Soon afterward, a Tercerista commander, Plutarco Hernández Sancho, established contact with Interior Minister Jesús Reyes Heroles, and a few months later another Sandinista faction, known as the "Prolonged Popular War" and headed by Tomás Borge Martínez, set up a parallel line of communications with the head of Mexico's ruling PRI, first Carlos Sansores Pérez and later Gustavo Carvajal.

The rebels were given some money—less than $1 million—for "travel expenses" and allowed to open propaganda offices in Mexico City, but Mexico preferred to stress its diplomatic profile. It refused to participate in a U.S.-led mediation team formed by the OAS after the first abortive Sandinista insurrection of September 1978, because it seemed aimed at perpetuating the Somoza regime. But it received hundreds of fugitive young street fighters in its embassy in Managua, and after the mediation effort broke down late in 1978, gave temporary asylum to seven members of the Group of 12, a move that was diplomatically acceptable and earned Mexico the gratitude of several men who later held key posts in the revolutionary government, among them junta member Sergio Ramírez Mercado and Foreign Minister Miguel d'Escoto.

By early 1979, with the Sandinista factions united and the Somoza regime looking increasingly vulnerable, Mexico cast around for some spectacular political gesture that would identify it with a victorious revolution and enable it to recover political ground lost to Venezuela, Panama and Costa Rica. By then, López Portillo's imagination had been fired by the Sandinista struggle,* and in secret negotiations with rebel commanders, he offered to break relations with Somoza at the moment most convenient to them. The rebels hoped the move could coincide with the launching of their final offensive, planned for late May. On May 18, López Portillo met in Cozumel with Fidel Castro—Castro's first visit to Mexico since the Cuban Revolution—and two days later he saw Costa Rica's President Carazo in nearby Cancún. Disturbed by Carazo's account of events inside Nicaragua, López Portillo decided to break immediately with Somoza. During his luncheon toast on May 20, without previously advising his new Foreign Minister, Jorge Castañeda, he made the announcement. One week later, the Sandinistas' final offensive began.

Having taken this gamble, Mexico was anxious for a successful dénouement. In contrast, the Carter administration suddenly developed fears of an outright Sandinista victory. When OAS Foreign Ministers met in Washington on June 17, Secretary of State Cyrus Vance proposed dispatching an Inter-American Peace Force to Nicaragua, with the formal brief of ending the fighting and the real purpose of excluding the Sandinistas from power. Castañeda, however, successfully blocked the interventionist initiative. With Mexico increasingly identified with the Sandinistas, López Portillo shipped some rifles and much ammunition to the rebels via Costa Rica and appointed an ambassador to the still-exiled new regime. Washington, meanwhile, tried to negotiate a peaceful transfer of power that would forestall collapse of the National Guard. This scenario also fell apart and on July 19, two days after Somoza fled to Miami, the Guard crumbled and the Sandinistas seized power. That evening, the new regime's cabinet flew to Managua from Costa Rica on board *Quetzalcóatl I,* López Portillo's presidential Boeing 727. Also on board was the U.S. diplomat William D. Bowdler, who had been charged with keeping the Sandinistas from taking over.

In the months that followed, having won a place among the godfathers of the Revolution, Mexico sent food, medicines, buses and other aid to Nicaragua. As Venezuela, Panama and Costa Rica grew worried over the radicalism of the Sandinistas, Mexico offered still stronger political

*Reflecting its narrow focus, Mexico saw no contradiction in inviting for a visit, in February 1979, El Salvador's President, General Carlos Humberto Romero, at a time of massive repression in that country.

support. During a visit to Managua in February 1980, López Portillo noted that the Mexican Revolution had brought freedom and the Cuban Revolution had brought justice, but Nicaragua offered the hope that "freedom, justice, equality and security can be combined to create a new option for the future." The Sandinistas were happy to exploit López Portillo's paternalistic enthusiasm, traveling frequently to Mexico City with long lists of requests. On occasion, the President would receive delegations of *comandantes* with the words: "Well, what do you need, *muchachos?*" Then he would order his ministers to help.

Though hypnotized by Nicaragua, Mexico was also gradually developing a broader Central American policy. In August 1980, it accepted a Venezuelan suggestion that the two nations jointly provide oil to Caribbean Basin countries with a 30 percent credit, a move that demonstrated their willingness to invest in stability. In the summer of 1980, top Mexican officials, including Castañeda and Carvajal, held their first secret meetings with Salvadoran opposition leaders, including several *comandantes* of the Farabundo Martí National Liberation Front (FMLN). Later, similar contacts were established with Guatemalan guerrilla leaders, not to provide them with support, but to establish lines of communications. Mexico also chose to ignore the polarizing impact of the Nicaraguan Revolution on the rest of Central America and placed a protective arm over Cuba. After receiving a hero's welcome during a visit to Havana in August 1980, a visibly moved López Portillo told Castro: "We won't allow anything to happen to Cuba."

When the Reagan administration took office on January 20, 1981, determined to draw the line on further leftist expansionism in the region, Mexico faced an entirely new challenge. A few days earlier, an unsuccessful final offensive by Salvadoran guerrillas had prompted the lame-duck Carter administration to resume military aid to the country's junta, but Reagan immediately went further by directly blaming the conflict in El Salvador on the Soviet bloc. Soon afterward, a White Paper purportedly proving Nicaraguan, Cuban and Vietnamese arms shipments to the Salvadoran rebels was circulated by the State Department among Washington's allies. In mid-February, the ambassador-at-large General Vernon Walters flew to Mexico City to show the evidence to López Portillo, who replied that social injustice and political repression—rather than imported subversion—were to blame for Central America's crisis. A few days later, to demonstrate that he was not intimidated by Washington's born-again anti-Communism, López Portillo told a visiting Cuban delegation: "Without doubt, the Latin American country most dear to us is our Cuba. Please send an embrace to the Comandante [Castro]."

From that moment, López Portillo's foreign policy was largely dedicated to opposing the United States in the region. Officials in Washington were irritated: they variously dismissed Mexico's position as appeasement of its domestic Left or romantic obsession with the idea of revolution, and they repeatedly warned that Mexico was not immune to infection by Marxist fever. But Mexico refused to view the crisis in East-West terms and explained the instability differently: the neo-feudal social systems of the past were disintegrating and could no longer guarantee political tranquillity; new structures would need to be forged, through either violence or negotiation, before stability could be restored. Mexico went still further: in the search for regional solutions to regional problems, the single greatest obstacle was direct or covert U.S. intervention and not Havana and Moscow.

Mexico had additional motives for its policy. López Portillo believed that Mexican influence over left-leaning nationalist sectors of the region gave it greater leverage with the United States. To gain that influence, it needed both to support the Sandinistas and the FMLN and to stand up to the United States. To win credibility for its "third option"—neither Washington nor Moscow—among the region's revolutionaries, Mexico also had to compete with Cuba. In the past, the region's leftists and even liberals turned to Havana because no other regime would heed them. But if they were pampered in Mexico City, they would be exposed to more moderate counsel. Specifically, Mexico felt that political pluralism and mixed economies were more likely to emerge if the Sandinistas and El Salvador's FMLN and its non-Marxist allies in the Democratic Revolutionary Front (FDR) were not abandoned to the Soviet bloc.

After the Reagan administration cut off economic aid to the Sandinistas in reprisal for their arms shipments to the FMLN, Mexico increased its support, including lines of credit, technical assistance, investments in joint ventures and donations of food and equipment worth $200 million in 1981 alone. When in 1982 Nicaragua could no longer keep up payments on oil imports from Venezuela, Mexico satisfied all its needs entirely on credit. In the case of El Salvador, Mexico opted not to break relations with the government, but made little effort to disguise its support for the FMLN and FDR. Opposition leaders used Mexico as their principal propaganda base and would meet frequently with Castañeda and other top officials to discuss their diplomatic strategy. Working in close coordination with the Salvadoran rebels, in August 1981 Mexico and France recognized the FMLN and the FDR as "representative political forces" that should participate in any negotiated settlement of the country's civil war.

One price of this policy was Mexico's increased isolation within Latin America. Prompted by Washington, ten regional governments denounced the Franco-Mexican declaration on El Salvador as "interventionism." Countries that originally supported the Nicaraguan Revolution—Venezuela, Panama and Costa Rica—were openly criticizing the Sandinistas for eroding democracy. Mexico was therefore forced to look elsewhere for allies. The ruling PRI is not a member of the Socialist International, but Mexico's call for negotiations in the region was endorsed by the worldwide social democrat movement. In 1979, the PRI had formed a Permanent Conference of Latin American Political Parties (COPPPAL) where leftist and liberal politicians—many of them exiled—could meet to denounce the continent's military dictatorships. This forum also helped to promote the idea of an alternative to United States policy in Central America. In Washington congressional Democrats began insisting that Mexico's voice be heard.

The Reagan administration decided that differences over Central America should not be allowed to poison bilateral relations with Mexico. It invited Mexico to participate in a Caribbean Basin Initiative along with Venezuela, Canada and, later, Colombia, although the cooperation bore no fruit. Secretary of State Alexander M. Haig, Jr., agreed to a Mexican request that he meet secretly in Mexico City in November 1981 with Cuba's Vice-President, Carlos Rafael Rodríguez. Administration officials also avoided public responses to López Portillo's frequent criticism of U.S. policy, aware that new rhetorical exchanges would follow.

But although willing to appease Mexico in symbolic ways of little importance, Washington was uninterested in a dialogue with leftists and began a three-pronged security offensive in the region: the Salvadoran junta was bolstered with massive military aid; Nicaraguan counterrevolutionaries were organized, financed and trained by the CIA for the purpose of toppling the Sandinistas; and military aid aimed to convert the Honduran Army into a buffer against leftists in both Nicaragua and El Salvador. The justification for this was provided by portraying Central America as the target of Soviet expansionism.

When López Portillo launched his most ambitious diplomatic initiative during a visit to Managua on February 21, 1982, he made a special effort to be even-handed, pointedly referring to his "friends" in Washington and his "friends" in Havana. He offered the services of Mexico as a "communicator" for a series of parallel negotiations—between Washington and both Cuba and Nicaragua and between El Salvador's warring parties—to bring détente to the region. He also took note of U.S. concerns, insisting that "the wind blowing through the zone does not represent an intolerable danger to the fundamental interests and national security of the United States" and criticizing his Sandinista hosts for spending "scarce resources" on an arms buildup that "worries neighboring and nearby countries." But he concluded: "The United States government should renounce the threat and use of force against Nicaragua. It is dangerous, undignified and unnecessary."

The Reagan administration listened politely to the Mexican proposal, but responded without enthusiasm: it had neither faith in López Portillo nor doubts about the policy it was pursuing. Haig sent General Walters to Havana for secret talks with Castro, but they amounted merely to a restatement of familiar positions. After two lengthy meetings with Castañeda, who also traveled to Havana and Managua, Haig presented a new negotiating position to the Sandinistas. But the fate of the initiative depended on the outcome of elections for a Constituent Assembly in El Salvador the following month. Had the elections been marked by massive abstentionism and disorder, Mexico's usefulness to Washington as an avenue to the FMLN might have grown. But when the large turnout at the polls enabled Reagan to proclaim a "victory for democracy," López Portillo's entire peace plan was forgotten and Washington's contacts with Havana and Managua were suspended.

By mid-1982, the United States felt that it had recovered the initiative in Central America. In El Salvador, an interim government was appointed by the Constituent Assembly; Costa Rica's incoming President, Luis Alberto Monge, was highly critical of the Sandinistas; Honduras' new civilian government was dominated by the pro-American army chief, General Gustavo Alvarez Martínez; and anti-Sandinista "contras" were making regular attacks on Nicaragua. The only setback was Venezuela's shift away from Washington's position, prompted by the exclusion of Christian Democrats from El Salvador's new government and by U.S. support for Britain in the Falklands war. This led López Portillo and Venezuela's President, Luis Herrera Campíns, to launch their first joint initiative in September 1982, calling on the United States, Honduras and Nicaragua to prevent open hostilities along the border between Honduras and Nicaragua. But the Reagan administration persuaded Costa Rica to host a meeting of regional governments—excluding Nicaragua—which presented its own peace plan and successfully torpedoed the Mexican-Venezuelan initiative.

By late 1982, López Portillo's ability to dictate Mexico's foreign policy had been seriously eroded, not only by his lame-duck status but also by the severe economic crisis that had undermined his domestic popularity. Several months earlier, Mexican business groups had complained to the

President about the arrest of three Nicaraguan business leaders, but some now even suggested that the country's economic crisis was Washington's reprisal for Mexico's foreign policy. Concern was voiced within the ruling PRI about the long-term impact of encouraging revolutionary forces in Central America and reports circulated that the incoming De la Madrid administration would not follow López Portillo's foreign policy.

The internal debate surfaced dramatically over the problem of Guatemala. Mexico had long applied a double standard when dealing with its immediate neighbor and, in contrast to its attitude toward El Salvador, had chosen to ignore both the massive repression and the growing guerrilla activity taking place next door. "Mexico will take no sides in the conflict," López Portillo once noted. "It is an internal problem and we view internal affairs in the context of nonintervention. We have no reason to take sides." Since the same argument could be applied to El Salvador, the key difference was Guatemala's location. Open support for Guatemalan rebels would create tensions that could force Mexico to militarize its southern border and risk destabilization of its frontier state of Chiapas. Further, a Marxist-Leninist regime in Guatemala would polarize political opinion in Mexico and invite a direct U.S. military intervention on Mexico's southern border. Thus, more than anywhere in Central America, stability—even under a right-wing military regime—remained Mexico's principal objective in Guatemala.

The test came when thousands of Indian refugees began fleeing to Chiapas in July 1981 to escape counterinsurgency sweeps by the Guatemalan Army. The first groups were deported at gunpoint by immigration agents acting on orders from the Interior Ministry. After protests by the United Nations High Commissioner for Refugees (UNHCR), the Foreign Ministry persuaded López Portillo to approve entry of Guatemalan refugees on the grounds that Mexico's tradition of asylum, its moral right to complain about mistreatment of undocumented Mexicans in the United States and the credibility of its entire Central American policy would otherwise be threatened.

The number of refugees rose rapidly to some 40,000 during 1982, but the Interior Ministry continued to view them with hostility, providing them with insufficient food and medical attention and frequently evicting them from improvised border camps. (Another 100,000 or so Salvadoran "illegals" were also in Mexico, but they were spread all over the country and thus posed less of a problem.) Senior Mexican Army officers met with their Guatemalan counterparts to assure them that Mexico was not harboring guerrillas. After several Guatemalan armed incursions into refugee camps brought a formal protest from Mexico's Foreign Ministry, Mexico's Defense Minister, General Félix Galván López, publicly denied that any such attacks had taken place. Since the Mexican government regarded the Guatemala problem as basically an internal affair of that country, the influence of the more liberal Foreign Ministry was minimal compared to that of the Interior and Defense ministries.

IV

Upon taking office, De la Madrid immediately reaffirmed the continuity of Mexican foreign policy. No less than his predecessor, he believed that the prospect of U.S. military intervention was the most serious threat to Central America. But the role of foreign policy in domestic affairs seemed to be changing. De la Madrid had sound economic reasons for not wanting to provoke Washington's ire and he inherited none of López Portillo's emotional ties to Nicaragua and the Salvadoran Left. More ominously, the domestic consensus that had long supported foreign policy was disintegrating. In the past, the traditional constituency for foreign policy was the Left, but now the business and political Right was also demanding to be heard, above all on the crucial questions of relations with both the United States and Central America. For the first time, a government had to conciliate strongly conflicting diplomatic, political and financial points of view at home before presenting itself to the world. The immediate result was a more middle-of-the-road foreign policy that, while consistent with Mexico's broader interests, pleased neither Left nor Right.

Like many incoming Presidents, De la Madrid moved first to correct some of his predecessor's mistakes. López Portillo's rhetorically confrontational approach had isolated Mexico within Latin America and had done nothing to temper the views or actions of the Reagan administration. To be effective, De la Madrid concluded, Mexico should speak in chorus with other Latin American countries and aim to persuade rather than provoke Washington. Further, Mexico could more easily pressure Cuba and Nicaragua to adopt more flexible postures if it did so in the company of other Latin American countries. The objective was to make Mexico more effective and less vulnerable in Central America.

At Mexico's initiative, the Foreign Ministers of Mexico, Venezuela, Colombia and Panama met on the Panamanian island of Contadora in January 1983 to look for solutions to the regional crisis. In subsequent meetings, the four conferred with the Foreign Ministers of the five Central American countries, and in July the Presidents of the so-called

Contadora Group countries met in the Mexican resort of Cancún. Soon "Contadora" became synonymous with the search for peace in Central America, duly endorsed by most Latin American countries, by the Socialist International and even, if only for the sake of appearances, by Cuba and the United States. In a matter of months, without seeming to change its policy, Mexico had ended its isolation on the Central America issue and had embarked on a less emotional dialogue with the Reagan administration.

Contadora was less effective in settling the region's problems. Because it was a forum of governments and the Salvadoran regime refused to discuss its internal affairs with others, one of the two main crises was largely ignored. The Contadora Four did take credit for averting a war between Honduras and Nicaragua, but they could neither persuade Honduras to admit that it was harboring anti-Sandinista rebels nor Nicaragua to accept that its radicalism had strengthened opposition to its policies: Honduras refused to negotiate with Nicaragua, and the Sandinistas scoffed at the idea of talking to the contras. The United States also continued to arm the Honduran Army and the rebel Nicaraguan Democratic Force, while the Soviet Union and Cuba poured weapons into Nicaragua. Soon, with fighting continuing unabated in El Salvador and inside Nicaragua's two borders, Contadora became bogged down in the exchanging of documents and discussion of peace plans. Lacking the political and military weight necessary to impose some solution, the four countries had little credibility as mediators.

In a narrow diplomatic sense, Mexico maintained familiar positions, though with softer language. To appease nationalist sentiment and avoid appearing subservient to Washington, it was still important for Mexico to criticize outside intervention in the region and to treat both Cuba and Nicaragua with special warmth. When in April 1983 an anti-Sandinista leader, Alfonso Robelo, tried to hold a press conference in Mexico City on the eve of a visit by Secretary of State George Shultz, he was promptly deported. When De la Madrid met Reagan in August 1983, he warned against "shows of force which threaten to touch off a conflagration." And when the United States invaded Grenada in October 1983, Mexico had no choice but to express its "profound concern" over—under López Portillo, it might have "condemned"—the intervention as a violation of the UN Charter and to demand the withdrawal of the Marines.

By 1984, however, De la Madrid was showing signs of frustration with Washington's militaristic approach to the region's problems and he too began adopting stronger language, language increasingly reminiscent of those of his predecessors. "Latin America needs a stable and pluralistic

Central America," he insisted. "The way to achieve this is clearly dialogue and negotiation and not confrontation and conflict, destabilizing
actions or the imposition of models from abroad by those who believe
they know best what the Central Americans want." Once again, the gulf
was widening. When President Reagan signed National Security Decision Directive 124 ordering the State Department to pressure Mexico to
cooperate with Washington in Central America, Foreign Minister Sepúlveda said it must have been prepared by a "minor official" who had "no
knowledge of the policy that the Mexican government has historically
had in internal and international affairs."

Sensing little comprehension in Washington, De la Madrid looked
south for new allies, not only on Central America but also on debt-
related problems, traveling to Colombia, Brazil, Argentina and
Venezuela early in 1984 in the hope of forming a lobby of Latin America's
principal governments. For the first time in twenty-five years, he felt,
these nations shared a common crisis and a common vision, and by
acting together they would bolster their negotiating position on political
and economic issues. Already assuming a leadership role in Latin America after only eighteen months in office, De la Madrid therefore spoke
for more than Mexico when he visited Reagan in Washington in May
1984. In speeches in the White House and on Capitol Hill, he not only
denounced "military solutions" in Central America but also warned of
the still more serious economic crises brewing elsewhere on the continent. A few days after this visit to Washington, Mexico joined Brazil,
Argentina and Colombia in jointly protesting a new rise in interest rates
on their huge foreign debt payments. After his talks with Reagan, De la
Madrid had remarked that they had learned "respect for one another's
truth," and he could even claim credit for promoting the first serious
talks between the United States and Nicaragua in two years, including
a brief visit by Secretary of State Shultz to Managua. Yet the perception
in Mexico was that the country was once again drifting into a period of
testy relations with the United States. What made this unusual was that
it was coming so early during De la Madrid's six-year administration.

While leftist and nationalist groups at home felt Mexico was displaying less firmness than in the past, conservative political and business
circles were already arguing that the government was going too far. They
accepted Washington's assertion that events in Cuba, Nicaragua, El
Salvador and Grenada formed part of a Soviet offensive in the region and
believed that, on such an East-West issue, Mexico was wrong to criticize
the United States. Inside the government, new conservative voices were
heard. Those in charge of the economy insisted that Mexico could no

longer afford a spendthrift foreign aid program, and they successfully pressed for a downward revision of terms on the Mexican-Venezuelan oil facility.

Since Nicaragua had been the principal beneficiary of Mexico's past generosity, it was the main target of the new austerity. De la Madrid told one worried *comandante* that Mexico would help "to the extent of its possibilities," but times had clearly changed. Several ongoing assistance programs were suspended, and at one point Mexico withheld oil shipments to pressure the Sandinistas to renegotiate their debt. In August 1983, it was calculated at $480 million, and agreement was reached that it would be repaid over eight years, with three years' grace on principal. A bankrupt Nicaragua was expected to pay around $50 million per year in interest and was obliged to start paying in cash or products for all but 20 percent of its oil imports from Mexico. A clause noted that breach of any part of the agreement would bring the suspension of all transactions until the problem was resolved, and on several occasions oil shipments were again delayed when Nicaragua's interest payments fell behind schedule.

Mexico never explicitly linked political and economic questions, but the Sandinistas soon concluded that oil was being used to pressure them to moderate their political positions. As they were unable to survive without Mexican oil, appeasement of Mexico became one reason for the Sandinistas' decision to slacken domestic political controls, call elections and request that dozens of Salvadoran rebel leaders and hundreds of Cuban teachers and technicians leave Nicaragua in late 1983. By using the oil weapon, however, Mexico risked losing its leverage with the Sandinistas: Nicaragua began looking for more secure sources of oil, notably the Soviet Union.

Mexico's traditionally conservative Interior Ministry also influenced areas of foreign policy. In order to restrict the inflow of Central Americans, the Ministry at first placed its Refugee Commission inside the Migration Department and began sealing off Guatemalan refugee camps in Chiapas, discouraging new migrants from entering Mexico and urging existing refugees to return home. (Thus, officials in charge of allowing in refugees were controlled by officials in charge of keeping out foreigners.) The ministry revoked the authority of airlines to give tourist cards to nationals of fourteen Latin American countries, most of them in the Caribbean Basin, and ordered Mexican consulates not to issue visas to travelers who "hope in this way to find a solution to social problems they suffer in their own countries, as has been the case with Guatemalans and Salvadorans." To justify these measures, Interior Minister Manuel Bartlett Díaz argued in a confidential memorandum that illegal migrants were taking jobs from Mexicans and creating "social pressures." Subsequently, the ministry ordered that foreigners should not hold posts in the public sector, and withdrew work permits for Argentine and Chilean exiles thought able to return home.

On matters of real rather than symbolic importance, the Foreign Ministry appeared to be losing influence. During a keynote speech early in 1983, Foreign Minister Sepúlveda sought to develop a broad concept of Mexico's "national security," but he was promptly reminded by the Interior and Defense ministries that this was their exclusive area of concern. Sepúlveda also disapproved of pressuring Nicaragua with oil, but at times found the Finance Ministry, Bank of Mexico and Petróleos Mexicanos acting independently. The Foreign Ministry particularly opposed the Interior Ministry's increasingly xenophobic approach to refugee and migration issues, noting that the reasons for keeping out Central Americans were identical to those given by the United States for keeping out Mexicans, and that squabbling between migration officials and the UNHCR threatened to escalate into an embarrassing international scandal. The Foreign Ministry was aware that Mexico's long tradition as a safe haven for political refugees had given the country a moral authority in international forums which the Interior Ministry was now gratuitously eroding. When, however, in April 1984, Guatemalan troops again entered Mexico and killed six refugees, even the Interior Ministry was obliged to react, ordering the withdrawal of some 46,000 refugees camping near the border to a valley in Campeche state.

One incident dramatized the ideological struggle beginning to affect foreign policy. By mid-1983, feeling the need to make a political gesture toward Cuba, Mexico planned to open a $50-million line of credit during a visit to Havana by Finance Minister Silva Herzog on September 5. But on September 1, during De la Madrid's first State of the Union address, Mexican security agents detained two Cuban diplomats for allegedly delivering a bomb to two Cuban exiles who had flown to Mexico City from Miami. Presented with the evidence by the Interior Ministry, De la Madrid felt under pressure to cancel Silva Herzog's trip. Cuba denied that a bomb was involved—it said one of the diplomats was carrying a self-destruct device in a briefcase—and considered itself the victim of a plot by either the CIA or rightist elements in the Interior Ministry. Cuba was given an additional reason to feel bitter toward Mexico: the two Cuban exiles were immediately deported, but the diplomats were held incommunicado for a week and tortured during interrogation by Mexican agents. Nonetheless, a crisis in relations served neither country's interest: De la Madrid ordered Silva Herzog to make his trip to Havana, Castro appeared at the signing ceremony for the line of credit and no public reference to the incident was ever made.

The unanswered question was whether the need to satisfy different domestic political currents would undermine the effectiveness of Mexico's foreign policy at home and abroad. A more conservative foreign policy alone would not appease domestic conservatives, but it would alienate liberals and leftists who give relatively more importance to foreign affairs. Similarly, simply by being, in De la Madrid's words, "objective and impartial," Mexico risked losing the trust of Cuba, Nicaragua, El Salvador's FMLN and other regional leftists without gaining credibility and influence in Washington. Mexico clearly cannot afford to withdraw from Central America, to allow the fate of a strategic region to be defined entirely by others. It also cannot endorse a U.S. strategy that appears to be feeding instability. Its only remaining option, therefore, was to remain politically aligned with revolutionary forces in the region. As in the past, the new government looked for alternatives, but found that Washington—and history—permitted none. In fact, only through continuity could Mexico's foreign policy remain a useful instrument of the political system and a faithful mirror of the country's national interest.

18

Shaping an Uncertain Future

I

Shocked by the extremes of wealth and poverty to be found in Mexico, many foreigners have long argued the inevitability of a new revolution. Many Mexicans, unversed in the mysterious ways of government, have also frequently doubted the resilience of their society. But nothing has proven more wrong than predicting the demise of Mexico's political system. Since its foundation in 1929, it has presided over the transformation of a rural society into a largely urban nation and it has adjusted to the quadrupling of the country's population. More recently, it withstood an intense anti-government movement in 1968, it survived a serious political crisis in 1976 and it defied expectations by maintaining stability during the post-1982 economic slump. Despite widespread disenchantment with the corruption, inequities and inefficiencies that characterize the system, no viable alternative has appeared.

Yet there is little room for complacency. Beneath the surface calm, the repercussions of change, growth and urbanization are subjecting society to unprecedented strain. As if all the moments of the country's history had been telescoped, Mexico is today preparing for the twenty-first century without having dealt with the legacy of the sixteenth century. The problems of underdevelopment are being compounded by overdevelopment, hopeless poverty is coinciding with excessive growth, the weight of the past is pulling against the magnet of the future. More complex than rich versus poor, urban versus rural or Right versus Left, the dilemma touches on the fundamental issue of Mexico's profile as a nation. A new head has been transplanted onto an old body—a Westernized, restless, individualistic and materialistic minority imposed on an Oriental, conformist, communitarian and traditional majority—and the relationship is uncomfortable.

Most people—the peasants, the urban poor, those living in smaller provincial cities—struggling to deal with their problems in Mexican terms, living the present in harmony with their own past, never question their identity as Mexicans. The middle and affluent classes, in contrast, are caught up in a rootless future, avidly adopting non-Mexican customs and values and in many cases even believing they have the option to become Americans. The immediate question is whether the system can design a single strategy that satisfies these two competing sectors. Still more fundamentally, can these contrasting Mexicos learn to coexist?

So far, the political system has merely mirrored the changes and contradictions evident in society as a whole. Control of the upper reaches of government has passed from experienced politicians who were in touch with the grass roots of society to technocrats more familiar with the workings of the world economy than with the political intricacies of Mexico. The new caste has introduced a more open—more "democratic" —political system, but it still depends on an antiquated and debilitated party to legitimize its power through the votes of peasants and workers whom it neither represents nor understands. The urban middle classes, whose very existence is the product of the growth and stability brought by the system, are able to vote increasingly against the ruling PRI thanks to the political reforms of recent years. Uncertain how to handle democracy, the new technocrats resort to the old technique of fixing election results: being inexperienced, they do so clumsily; being haughty, they refuse to turn to veteran *políticos* to do it for them.

The carefully nurtured consensus of interests that long held the system together has also been battered by change. The private sector's traditional faith in the government was seriously eroded by the Echeverría and López Portillo regimes, with the result that some provincial businessmen now openly back the conservative PAN in local elections. The labor movement, the most reliable pillar of the system, has been weakened not only by the latest economic crisis but also by the struggle to find a successor to the aging boss Fidel Velázquez. The Army has already seen old "revolutionary" generals replaced by younger, better-educated officers with a strong middle-class mentality who make little effort to disguise their disapproval of the way the country has been governed since 1970. The media are increasingly dominated by the television giant, Televisa, which constantly reinforces conservative, middle-class and even Americanized values. The Roman Catholic Church, which for decades supported the status quo by keeping out of politics, is raising its voice on public affairs in an effort to increase its share of power.

Spawned by growth, many of these problems were brought to the surface by economic contraction. With the exception of the Church, the components of the system had always enjoyed a privileged share of an expanding economic pie, but their allegiance began to waver when the rewards threatened to evaporate. During periods of expansion, above all in the 1970s, the middle classes were kept largely apolitical by a steady improvement of living standards, but they turned militant critics of the regime when their futures clouded over before them. For decades the tranquility of the nation as a whole was maintained by the creation of 500,000 or more new jobs each year, insufficient to eliminate chronic underemployment though enough to sustain the hope of economic mobility. Without growth, young Mexicans entered the work force with no stake to defend.

The economic crisis bequeathed to President de la Madrid in December 1982 was less dangerous than the stark future that he inherited. Many of the immediate symptoms of excessive and chaotic growth responded quickly to the traditional medicine of monetarist austerity, allowing the administration to claim proudly that the crisis had been controlled. But unlike previous incoming Presidents who were forced to cut spending for twelve to eighteen months before initiating their own periods of expansion, De la Madrid faced the prospect of prolonged stagnation, which in Mexico meant annual growth rates of less than 4 percent. No President since World War II has had to govern Mexico without steady, though cyclical, growth.

The problem was twofold. First, the resources necessary for a new burst of development were no longer available. Maximized oil exports and new foreign credits barely covered essential imports as well as interest payments on the country's $87 billion foreign debt. The vast capital that left the country between 1980 and 1982 seemed unwilling to return, while nontraditional exports, foreign investment and domestic savings provided too little for growth. Mexico covered interest due in 1983 and 1984 by holding down spending, imports and growth, but it was to pay out another $12 billion in interest in 1985, the year that the government hoped to reflate the economy. The debt itself will not be repaid—and the latest restructuring frees De la Madrid of this worry for the rest of his term. But new development funds will be scarce throughout the 1980s.

Secondly, the political implications of failing to recover traditional high growth rates place the country at a crossroads between assuming the risks of greater democracy, trying to perpetuate the existing system under more difficult circumstances or resorting to more open authoritarianism. All three options involve hidden perils. The key actors in the system prefer to see the status quo ante 1982 restored, but this would require a high level of government expenditure—to "service" its allies—which might be possible only if the United States, the International Monetary Fund and foreign banks felt a sudden need to subsidize Mexico's stability. Without such a subsidy, the supports of the system might be persuaded to remain in place with fewer benefits, but this would demand a degree of political leadership seemingly lacking in the new technocratic elite. In practice, the system held together in the early 1980s because no alternative existed, but its traditional beneficiaries were less inclined than before to invest in its survival. No one yet wanted the ship to sink, no one had tried to torpedo it, yet few were working to keep it afloat.

A more visible political challenge came from the resentful middle classes, without whose consent no regime has tried to govern since World War II. In theory, the government could permit greater democracy, allowing the middle classes to vote for the opposition PAN, recognizing its victories and auguring the emergence of a two-party system. But Mexico's entire stability has been built around the premise of a powerful, almost infallible central authority and, paradoxically, greater democracy could suggest disintegration of the country as well as the system. To compete for the electoral support of the middle classes, in contrast, would involve transferring resources from social welfare, rural development and even industrialization to the maintenance of currency stability, consumer spending and urban improvement, a policy that in 1984 seemed to be tempting the administration. But while bringing short-term political relief, this strategy would sow the seeds of a new financial crisis that could prove a still greater political disaster.

The cost of appeasing the middle classes would be the worsening of the living conditions of the great majority of Mexicans, who, although less able to articulate and organize their dissent, could not be expected to remain passive indefinitely. Inexplicably, as if denied access to the secret codes needed to operate the system, the new ruling technocrats surrendered many of the instruments that have proved effective in controlling the masses. The populism of the past was blamed for many economic ills, yet no substitute was found to sustain the political legitimacy of the "revolutionary" regime or to keep alive the hopes of the needy. Since political leadership was considered less important than good planning and administration, the lines of discipline and authority in the country began to blur. Even the perennial resource of nationalism was tapped in a timid way: fearful of alienating domestic conservatives and foreign businessmen through the use of standard anti-American rhetoric, the government discovered that emphasis on such patriotic symbols as the national anthem, flag and emblem failed to stir a sense of solidarity within the regime or the country.

When Mexico has run short of the political and economic resources necessary to maintain peace through manipulation, cooptation, populism and corruption, it has resorted to authoritarianism, and signs that frustration was leading to intolerance began to grow in 1984. Yet this option may be less readily available than in 1968, when it was last fully exercised. The middle classes have grown accustomed to a new degree of individual and political freedom and the system as a whole could even divide under the pressure of repression. The most persistent doubt is whether the Army would be willing to step in once again to "save" the civilian government. Politicians know surprisingly little about the thinking of the Army, but they contemplate the possibility that, in the face of political unrest, economic mismanagement and clear rejection of the government by the middle classes, the military might prefer to seize power rather than sustain an incompetent regime. It would not act unless a coup enjoyed broad support from key sectors of society, and as long as the government retained the political initiative, the Army posed no immediate threat. But it was no longer an assured servant of civilian authorities.

As Mexico moved irrevocably into a period of growing domestic uncertainty, Washington's understanding of the country became crucial. Historically, the United States' single overriding concern has been Mexico's stability, which, for decades, it could take for granted. But in recent years, the new fear has been that Central America's revolutionary fever could infect a Mexico weakened by economic troubles. Not for the first time, Washington is misreading its neighbor. The United States has frightened itself into imagining a Marxist Mexico on its southern border and has pressured the regime to move to the right to strengthen its defenses. Yet Mexico's immediate stability is endangered less by a rebellion of the masses led by the Left than by a mutiny of the middle classes inspired by the Right. By moving sharply to the right to defuse the latter threat and to please the United States, however, the government would disturb the political balance and risk stirring labor, peasant and student unrest. Political wisdom counseled against turning right and economic realities prevented the government from choosing left: if it did, the economy would be quickly destabilized by the flight of capital, hoarding and inflation, and the political mood of the country would be further polarized.

Recognizing the greater hazards of changing course, the new government tried to work the system along essentially traditional lines, hoping somehow to appease both key interest groups and the population at large without surrendering any of its power. Fear of political change has been a common feature of all administrations since Cárdenas, and even during the critical moments of the mid-1980s this instinct remained strong. Like so many of his predecessors, De la Madrid campaigned for office on a platform of change, promising new approaches to such perennial problems as land reform, corruption, electoral freedom and the state's role in the economy. But as he confronted the realities of power he gradually lowered his sights. It seemed cynical to hold out the hope of greater social justice at a time of tumbling real wages. The fight against corruption remained necessary, but elimination of the practice no longer appeared feasible. Greater democracy was a valid objective, but it suddenly involved unexpected risks. Reduction of the state's role in the economy was sabotaged by entrenched bureaucratic and political interests. In brief, De la Madrid discovered the limits of presidential power in Mexico. And, constrained by the cycle of his own six-year term, his main concern became the preservation of stability, his overriding ambition that of handing over power peacefully in December 1988.

With the system's political, economic and social perspectives blocked by short-term problems, little attention could be paid to long-term development questions. When the twenty-first century is contemplated, it is done so with fatalism. No former colony with a large indigenous population has ever climbed out of underdevelopment. No valid blueprint exists, no improvised plans seem to work. Even if Mexico's political system survives in its present form, its managers harbored few illusions that the country's deep social problems would be resolved before the year 2000: optimistically, it might resemble Greece; pessimistically, it will be more like India.

Economic growth will principally benefit the upper and middle classes, further skewing the distribution of wealth. Rural and urban poverty will remain endemic, with its accompanying problems of malnutrition, avoidable diseases, inadequate housing and functional illiteracy. Hundreds of thousands of Mexicans will still look for work in the United States each year. Governments will be obliged to address these problems through social welfare programs and assorted subsidies, but they will continue to regard industrial growth as the only way of lifting the majority of Mexicans out of poverty, even though this strategy has proved wanting in the past.

Fundamental issues of environment and resources are also being neglected. Although the country can feel confident that its long-term energy needs are satisfied, it faces a chronic shortage of water and agricultural land. Water supplies are suffering from overexploitation, pollution and wastage, while the quality of land is being deteriorated by deforestation, desertification and erosion. In large urban areas, air and water pollution is further evidence that Mexicans still regard the environment as a free and renewable resource rather than one that requires careful protection and preservation. The need to redesign Mexico's demographic profile to prepare for a still larger urban population is recognized, but this requires difficult decisions that may produce results only decades later and are easily postponed. Nowhere is this more apparent than in Mexico City, which, already difficult to manage and inhabit, is condemned to doubling its population by the early years of the next century. And the cost of feeding, housing, transporting and supplying the *capitalinos* will weigh more heavily on the country as a whole.

Struggling with so many problems of the past and the present, Mexicans face the future with ambivalence. The country's first century of independence suggests that long periods of stability are disrupted by mass bloodletting, while the record since the Revolution implies growing political maturity. But neither precedent is sufficient to illuminate the future. Uncertain whether to prepare for sudden violent change or for relatively uneventful continuity, Mexicans live from day to day. Ordinary Mexicans have always viewed the future with stoicism and seem less disturbed: they will deal with its challenges when they arrive. But the middle classes are gripped by doubts that undermine the very system that once brought them security. Even within the government, officials will temper their confidence in the survival of the system with quiet recognition of the unpredictability of the Mexican people.

The key variable is not how society will respond to the system but rather how the system will adjust to a both changing and unchanging country. In the past, the system gained its strength from a traditional society built around accepted cultural and political values. Then the middle and upper classes broke away from that society and demanded a system that would give their interests priority. Recent governments responded, rushing to modernize the country, economically through massive expenditure and indebtedness and politically by adopting more of the trappings of a Western democracy. But in the process Mexico became neither more just nor more stable. On the contrary, both economically and politically, it became more vulnerable to outside destabilization and thereby less independent.

The real strength and stability of Mexico remain in its people, in the ordinary Mexicans who preserve family and community traditions, whose material expectations remain secondary to their spiritual aspirations, whose nationalism is irrefutable because it is undeclared. Their future has little to do with governments and political systems. Their lives have a rhythm of their own. Even their expectations are limited. The recent boom was a "fiesta" and life returned to normal when it was over: they understood neither why it started nor why it ended but they adapted to both. A system that turns its back on this Mexico will balance precariously on the weak, unreliable pillar of an increasingly alienated sector of society. It will risk a backlash from the past.

The dangers of excessive economic growth became apparent in 1982, but the risks of too hasty political, social and cultural change are even greater. Few traditional societies have modernized themselves at high speed without instability or repression. In its soul, Mexico is not—and perhaps never will be—a Western nation. But by trying to make the country more superficially democratic, more Western, more "presentable" abroad, the system's roots in the population have weakened. It has become less truly democratic because it is less representative of real Mexicans. The more the system responds to the Americanized minority, the more blatant will be the contradictions within the country.

The issue is not whether Mexico should develop—it must develop— but rather whether it grows, changes and modernizes in harmony with the majority of its population. If the system turns inward, it can still tap the country's real strength. Mexico's history, religion and culture have made it a nation that since pre-Columbian times has existed on the scale of the gods. Mexico's greatness, at times hidden, lies waiting to be uncovered, but it can only prosper in its own context. Thus, Mexicans felt comfortable with the system when it was peculiarly Mexican, with its mixture of authoritarianism and paternalism, of cynicism and idealism, of conciliation and negotiation. But if it loses its originality, if it loses its national identity, it loses its way. Mexico produced the system and can therefore replace it. And a system that is not Mexican cannot survive. What will survive is Mexico.

Selected Bibliography

This bibliography represents, needless to say, only a small sampling of the vast literature on Mexico in both English and Spanish. Its aim is to present a range of books, mostly of general interest, that can provide more detailed or different insights into Mexico and the Mexicans than those offered by the present work. Mexican government documents have been omitted, although the Bank of Mexico's annual report and the President's State of the Union address delivered each September 1 are essential to those who follow Mexican developments closely.

English Language List

Alba, Francisco. *The Population of Mexico: Trends, Issues and Policies.* Transaction Press, 1982.

Azuela, Mariano. *The Underdogs.* New American Library, n.d.

Benítez, Fernando. *The Century After Cortés.* University of Chicago Press, 1965.

Brandenburg, Frank. *The Making of Modern Mexico.* Prentice-Hall, 1964.

Brenner, Anita. *The Wind That Swept Mexico.* University of Texas Press, 1971.

Cornelius, Wayne A. *Politics and the Migrant Poor in Mexico City.* Stanford University Press, 1975.

Díaz del Castillo, Bernal. *The History of the Conquest of New Spain.* Penguin Books, 1958.

Domínguez, Jorge, ed. *Mexico's Political Economy: Challenges at Home and Abroad.* Sage Publications, 1982.

Erb, Richard D., and Stanley R. Ross, eds. *United States Relations with Mexico: Concept and Content.* American Enterprise Institute, 1981.

Fagan, Richard R., and William S. Tuohy. *Politics and Privilege in a Mexican City.* Stanford University Press, 1972.

Fehrenbach, T. R. *Fire and Blood: A History of Mexico.* Macmillan, 1973.

Fuentes, Carlos. *The Death of Artemio Cruz.* Panther, 1974.

———. *Where the Air Is Clear.* Farrar, Straus & Giroux, 1971.

Gonzalez Casanova, Pablo. *Democracy in Mexico*. Oxford University Press, 1967.

Grayson, George W. *The Politics of Mexican Oil*. University of Pittsburgh Press, 1980.

Greene, Graham. *The Lawless Roads*. Penguin Books, 1947 and 1971.

Gruening, Ernest. *Mexico and Its Heritage*. Greenwood Press, 1928 and 1968.

Guzmán, Martín Luis. *The Eagle and the Serpent*. Peter Smith, n.d.

Hanson, Roger D. *The Politics of Mexican Development*. The Johns Hopkins University Press, 1971.

Johnson, Kenneth. *Mexican Democracy: A Critical View*. Allyn & Bacon, 1971.

Katz, Friederich. *The Secret War in Mexico*. University of Chicago Press, 1981.

Lawrence, D. H. *The Plumed Serpent*. Vintage, 1926/1951.

Levy, Daniel, and Gabriel Szekely. *Mexico: Paradoxes of Stability and Change*. Westview Press, 1983.

Lewis, Oscar. *The Children of Sanchez*. Vintage Books, 1961.

McBride, Robert H., comp. *Mexico and the United States*. Prentice-Hall, 1981.

Montgomery, Tommie Sue, ed. *Mexico Today*. Institute for the Study of Human Studies, Philadelphia, 1982.

Needler, Martin. *Politics and Society in Mexico*. University of New Mexico Press, 1971.

Padgett, L. Vincent. *The Mexican Political System*. Houghton Mifflin, 1976.

Paz, Octavio. *The Labyrinth of Solitude: Life and Thought in Mexico*. Grove Press, 1961.

———. *The Other Mexico: Critique of the Pyramid*. Grove Press, 1972.

Ramos, Samuel. *Profile of Man and Culture in Mexico*. University of Texas Press, 1962.

Ross, Stanley. *Is the Mexican Revolution Dead?* Knopf, 1966.

———, comp. *Views Across the Border*. University of New Mexico Press, 1978.

Rulfo, Juan. *Pedro Páramo*. Grove Press, 1959.

———. *The Burning Plain and Other Stories*. University of Texas Press, 1967.

Scott, Robert E. *Mexican Government in Transition*. University of Illinois Press, 1959.

Simpson, Lesley B. *Many Mexicos*. University of California Press, 1966.

Smith, Peter. *Labyrinths of Power: Political Recruitment in Twentieth Century Mexico*. Princeton University Press, 1979.

Tannenbaum, Frank. *The Struggle for Peace and Bread*. Columbia University Press, 1950.

Vásquez, Carlos, and Manuel García y Griego, eds. *Mexican-U.S. Relations: Conflict and Convergence?* UCLA Press, 1981.

Womack, John. *Zapata and the Mexican Revolution*. Knopf, 1969.

Spanish Language List

(All Refer to Mexican Publishing Houses)

Benítez, Fernando. *Los Indios de México* (5 vols.). Era, 1967–72.

———. *La Ciudad de México, 1325 a 1982* (3 vols.). Salvat, 1982.

————. *Lázaro Cárdenas y La Revolución Mexicana* (3 vols.). Fondo de Cultura Económica, 1977–79.

Cosío Villegas, Daniel, ed. *Historia Moderna de México*. El Colegio de México, 1977.

————. *El Sistema Político Mexicano*. Joaquín Mortíz, 1972.

————. *El Estilo Personal de Gobernar*. Joaquín Mortíz, 1974.

————. *La Sucesión Presidencial*. Joaquín Mortíz, 1975.

————. *Memorias*. Joaquín Mortíz, 1973.

El Colegio de México. *Historia General de México* (2 vols.). El Colegio de México, 1977–81.

Fuentes, Carlos. *Tiempo Mexicano*. Joaquín Mortíz, 1973.

Gamio, Manuel. *Forjando Patria*. Porrúa, 1916.

González González, José. *Lo Negro del Negro Durazo*. Posada, 1983.

Krauze, Enrique. *Caras de la Historia*. Joaquín Mortíz, 1983.

Meyer, Jean. *Los Cristeros*. El Colegio de México, 1977.

Meyer, Lorenzo. *Las Empresas Transnacionales en México*. El Colegio de México, 1974.

————. *México y los Estados Unidos en el Conflicto Petrolero, 1917–1942*. El Colegio de México, 1972.

————, ed. *México–Estados Unidos, 1982*. El Colegio de México, 1982.

Morales, Patricia. *Indocumentados Mexicanos*. Grijalbo, 1981.

Ojeda, Mario. *Alcances y Límites de la Política Exterior de México*. El Colegio de México, 1976.

————, ed. *Administración del Desarrollo de la Frontera Norte*. El Colegio de México, 1982.

Paz, Octavio. *Tiempo Nublado*. Seix-Barral, 1983.

————. *El Ogro Filantrópico*. Joaquín Mortíz, 1979.

Poniatowska, Elena. *La Noche de Tlatelolco*. Era, 1971.

Segovia, Rafael. *La Politización del Niño Mexicano*. El Colegio de México, 1975.

Solís, Leopoldo. *La Realidad Económica Mexicano*. Siglo XXI, 1970.

Suárez, Luis. *Echeverría en el Sexenio de López Portillo*. Grijalbo, 1983.

Tello, Carlos, and Rolando Cordera. *México: La Disputa por la Nación*. Siglo XXI, 1981.

————. *La Política Económica Mexicana, 1970–1976*. Siglo XXI, 1979.

Unikel, Luis. *La Dinámica del Crecimiento de la Ciudad de México*. Fundación para Estudios de la Población A.C., 1972.

————. *El Desarrollo Urbano en México*. El Colegio de México, 1976.

Villarreal, René. *La Contra-Revolución Monetarista*. Océano, 1982.

Index

abortion, 241, 246–7, 253
abrazo (embrace), 10
Acapulco, 209
adultery, 246, 251–2
agrarian policy, 180–9; of Alemán, 183, 184, 192–3; of Cárdenas, 182–3; of De la Madrid, 188, 189, 191; of Echeverría, 186–7; of López Portillo, 187–8; *see also* land reform
agrarian reform, *see* land reform
agricultural exports, 192, 193, 334
agriculture, 145; under De la Madrid, 197–8; López Portillo's policy, 195, 196; modernization of, 136; productivity in, 190–2; water and, 189–90; *see also* food production
Aguilar, Father Gerónimo de, 27
Aguirre, Ramon, 258
air pollution, 259, 260, 262, 370
Alamán, Lucas, 37
Alarma (newspaper), 308
alcoholism, 211, 246
Alegría, Rosa Luz, 128
Alemán Valdés, Miguel, 56–8, 87, 91, 312; agrarian policy of, 183, 184, 192–3; corruption and, 115, 136; the economy under, 135
Alfa Group, 146, 148, 285–6
Allende, Capt. Ignacio, 32, 33
Allende, Salvador, 346, 347
Alliance for Progress, 344
Almazán, Gen. Juan Andreu, 55, 108
Alpuche Pinzón, Gen. Graciliano, 82
Alvarez Martínez, Gen. Gustavo, 356
ambassadors, United States, 324–6
American Chamber of Commerce, 138
American Federation of Labor (AFL), 84
amparo agrario, 183, 184, 189, 192
Anderson, Jack, 132, 133
anticlerical campaigns (1920s), 50–1, 89

Anti-Reeleccionista Party, 41
Arbenz, Jacobo, 342
architecture, 305–6
Argentina, 360
armed forces, 91–3
Armed Revolutionary Movement (MAR), 102
Army, the, 91–3, 102, 186, 187, 275, 365, 368
arts, the, 302–7
Authentic Party of the Mexican Revolution (PARM), 96–100
automobiles, 260–2
Autonomous National University (UNAM), 59, 60, 234, 235
Avila Camacho, Manuel, 55, 89, 91, 115
Azcárraga, Emilio, Jr., 140, 313
Azcárraga, Emilio, Sr., 139–40, 155, 312–14
Aztecs, 16, 25–9, 240, 255–6

banks, 153; nationalization of, 68–9, 73, 88, 107; *see also* businessmen
Barragán, Luis, 306
Barragán Camacho, Salvador, 172, 174, 176, 177
Barra García, Félix, 127, 187
Bartlett Díaz, Manuel, 80, 361–2
Becerra Acosta, Manuel, 106
Benítez, Fernando, 207, 214
Bermúdez, Antonio, 162
Bernal, Ignacio, 25
Beteta, Mario Ramón, 175, 176
birth control, 225–6, 245, 246
Bonaparte, Joseph, 32
Bonillas, Ignacio, 48
border, U.S.-Mexico, 336–7
border cities, 287–9
Borge Martínez, Tomás, 351
Borja, Carmen, 208

Bowdler, William D., 352
Bracero Agreement, 56, 330
Brazil, 350, 360
bribes, *see* corruption
Bucareli Agreements (1923), 49, 159
Buendía, Manuel, 107, 125, 132 *n.*
bureaucracy, corruption and, 119–20
Business Coordinating Council (CCE), 87
businessmen, 87–8; corruption and, 115,
    122–4; *see also* private sector

Cabanas Barrientos, Lucio, 102
Cabrera, Luis, 52
caciques, 35; Indians and, 210–11, 212
Calles, Plutarco Elías, 15–16, 44, 48–55, 75,
    91, 115, 182, 285
Camarena, Lydia, 131
Campa Salazar, Valentín, 16, 57, 97, 101
Cancún, North-South summit in, 349
Cantú Peña, Fausto, 127
Carazo Odio, Rodrigo, 351, 352
Cárdenas del Río, Gen. Lázaro, 15, 18,
    53–6, 78, 91, 108, 142, 297, 341, 343;
    Indians and, 201–2, 213; land reform
    under, 182–3; oil industry and, 159–61
Cárdenas Lomeli, Rafael, 172
Carranza, Venustiano, 15, 44–8, 158, 182
Carrillo Flores, Antonio, 343
Carter, Jimmy (Carter administration),
    167, 195, 320–1, 324, 325, 328, 331, 334,
    338–9, 352
Carvajal, Gustavo, 264, 351
Caso, Alfonso, 207–8, 297
Castañeda, Jorge, 321, 326, 339, 349, 352,
    354
Castellanos, Gen. Absalón, 211
Castillo, Heberto, 98, 103–5
Castro, Fidel, 352, 353
Catholic Church, 29–30, 34, 35, 38, 50–1,
    89–91, 200, 253, 365; education and,
    232–3; the family and, 241–2; Indians
    and, 29–30, 211, 215; intellectuals and,
    296; the Right and, 108–10; *see also*
    churches
Cazals, Felipe, 309, 310
Cedillo, Gen. Saturnino, 55
Central America, 64, 292, 293; policy
    toward, 322–3, 329, 339, 349–63
Central Intelligence Agency (CIA), 343,
    344, 347, 355
centralism, 274–5
Chamber of Commerce, American, 138
Chamber of Deputies, 96–9
Chamizal district, 336–7
Chapman, Gen. Leonard, 331
Chapultepec Park, 268–9
Charter of the Economic Rights and
    Duties of States, 346
Chiapas, 292–4; Indians in, 212–13

Chicanos, 328
Chihuahua Group, 110
children, 247, 314; *see also* education;
    family
Chile, 346
Chinanteco Indians, 185
chingar, 13–14
Christianity, Indians and, 215–17; *see also*
    Catholic Church
Chumacero, Blas, 86
churches, 29–30, 50, 51, 89
Cinematographic Bank, 309, 310
Cinematographic Institute, 310–11
Ciudad Juárez, 287, 288
classical music, 303
Clements, William P., 338
Clouthier, Manuel, 111
COCEI (Student-Worker-Peasant Coalition
    of the Isthmus), 291–2
Coindreau, José Luis, 111
Colombia, 358, 360
Colonial period, 30–1, 114, 290, 296, 303;
    see also Conquest
Communist League 23rd of September,
    102
Communist Party (PCM), 16, 52, 53, 56,
    63, 98, 101, 102, 105, 297
Comonfort, Ignacio, 37–8
Conchello, José Angel, 109
Confederation of Industrial Chambers
    (CONCAMIN), 87
Confederation of Mexican Workers
    (CTM), 54–6, 84–6, 173
Congress, 68–9, 96–9
Conquest, the, 3, 4, 27–9
Conservatives, 37–9, 49
Constitution, 47, 50, 51, 68, 69, 158, 159,
    182
Contadora Group, 358–9
COPLAMAR, 222, 229, 231
corn, 22, 181, 190, 196
Corona del Rosal, Gen. Alfonso, 59, 70
Corral, Ramón, 40, 41
corruption, 113–33; under Alemán, 136; in
    armed forces, 91–3; De la Madrid and,
    115, 129–33; under Echeverría, 115, 126–7;
    influence and, 121–2; of the judiciary,
    119; López Portillo and, 115, 127–31; in
    the oil industry, 127, 128, 168; police,
    117–18, 130; private sector and, 115,
    122–4; social welfare programs and,
    223–4
Cortés, Hernán, 3, 4, 16–18, 26–9, 42
Cosío Villegas, Daniel, 299, 327
Costa Rica, 351, 352, 355, 356
Coyoacán, 266
creativity, 5–6
crime, 271
criollos, 31–3, 42

Cristeros, 50, 108, 109, 232
Cuauhtémoc, 3, 16–18, 28, 29
Cuba, 64, 281, 300–1, 342–4, 347, 353, 358, 362–3
Cuevas, José Luis, 305
Culiacán, 284
culture: Indian, 203, 214–18; popular, 307–15
curanderos (medicine men), 217
currency devaluations, 63, 64, 73, 136, 143, 144, 147–9

death, 6
decentralization, 277
de Gyves, Leopoldo, 291–2
de la Cruz, Apolinar, 205, 210–11
de la Cruz, Francisco, 264
de la Huerta, Adolfo, *see* Huerta, Adolfo de la
de la Madrid Hurtado, Miguel, 15, 16, 18, 19, 64–5, 68–76, 80–1, 83, 91, 110, 169, 253, 276, 310, 366, 369; agrarian policy of, 188, 189–90, 191; agricultural policy of, 197–8; bank nationalization and, 88; corruption and, 115, 129–33; the economy under, 73, 149–56; education policy of, 236–7, 277; election of, 69–72, 98, 99; foreign policy of, 357–63; Indians and, 205–7, 213; intellectuals and, 301–2; labor unions and, 85, 86, 176, 177; Mexico City problems and, 261, 271, 272; oil industry and, 175, 176, 179; social problems and, 222, 226; United States and, 327, 328
Democratic Revolutionary Front (FDR), 354
De-Nuclearization of Latin America, Treaty for the (Treaty of Tlatelolco), 344
D'Escoto, Miguel, 351
devaluations, *see* currency devaluations
Díaz, Félix, 43–4
Díaz, Porfirio, 39–41, 96, 157–8, 256, 283–4, 305, 318
Díaz del Castillo, Bernal, 27–9
Díaz Ordaz, Gustavo, 58–61, 73, 79, 84, 92, 184, 298, 300, 319, 343, 345
Díaz Serrano, Jorge, 65, 128, 131–2, 164–70, 174–7
distribution of income and wealth, 220–2
Doheny, Edward L., 158
Dominican Republic, 342
Dovalí Jaime, Antonio, 164
drug traffic, 337
Duarte, Irma Cué de, 249
Durazo Moreno, Arturo, 118–19, 132

Echeverría, Rodolfo, 309
Echeverría Alvarez, Luis, 15, 17, 61–3, 71, 74, 76, 78–80, 87, 90, 109, 258, 285, 286, 309–10, 326, 328; agrarian policy of, 186–7, 284; armed forces and, 92; background of, 61; corruption and, 115, 126–7; democratic opening of, 62, 101–2; the economy under, 62–3, 141–3; electoral reform under, 96–7; foreign policy of, 62, 319–20, 345–8; Indians and, 202–3; intellectuals and, 298–300; the Left and, 59, 62, 70, 73, 83, 84, 101–4; oil industry and, 163–4, 172; social problems and, 222, 225, 234
economic growth, 134–5, 147, 220, 366, 369, 371
economy, the, 20–1, 134–56; under Alemán, 57, 135; under Calles, 50; under Cárdenas, 54–5; under De la Madrid, 149–56; under Echeverría, 62–3, 141–3; under López Portillo, 63–4, 142–51; *see also* agriculture; banks; currency devaluations; labor unions; oil industry; private sector
education, 232–7; Catholic Church and, 232–3; higher, 234–7
ejidos, 180, 181, 183–4, 187–8, 190–2, 194
elections, 68–70; of 1982, 98–100, 110, 111
El Salvador, 64, 353–6, 359
embrace *(abrazo)*, 10
Encinas, Dionisio, 101
Espino, Everardo, 131
Espinosa Yglesias, Manuel, 139
Excelsior (newspaper), 104, 299, 300, 312
extramarital relationships, 246, 251–2

family, 7–9, 238–53; Indian, 215–16, 243–4; middle-class, 248–52; religion and, 241–2; stereotype of, 242–3
family planning, 249; *see also* birth control
Farabundo Martí National Liberation Front (FMLN), 353, 354
farmers, 120, 192–4; *see also* agriculture; land reform
fatalism (as national trait), 6, 7
father, role of, 242, 251
favors, exchange of, 122
Federal Electoral Commission, 95, 97, 100
Federal Security Directorate, 95, 102, 103
feminists, 249, 253
Ferdinand VII, king of Spain, 32, 33
fiesta, in national life, 9
fishing industry, 338
Flores Curiel, Col. Rogelio, 62, 78
Flores Olea, Víctor, 300
Flores Tapia, Oscar, 78
food industry, 194
food production, 194–8
Ford, Gerald R., 163–4

foreign debt, 64, 88, 134, 143–5, 148–55, 335, 360, 366
foreign exchange, 136, 148–50, 153
foreign investment, 40, 58, 135–8, 141, 142, 145–6, 153, 154, 348; in oil, 157–8
Foreign Ministry, 362
foreign policy, 58, 62, 64, 340–63; of Calles, 341; toward Central America, 322–3, 329, 339, 349–63; of De la Madrid, 357–63; of Echeverría, 345–8; of López Mateos, 342–4; of López Portillo, 348–9, 351–8; toward Nicaragua, 351–61; in the 1930s and 1940s, 341–2; principles of, 340–1; *see also individual countries*
foreign trade, 31–2, 40, 136, 147, 155; with United States, 333–6; *see also* agricultural exports; oil exports
fotonovelas, 308
France, 36, 38, 354–5
Franco, Gen. Francisco, 18
Fuentes, Carlos, 296, 299–301, 306–7

Galván López, Gen. Félix, 93, 358
Gamio, Manuel, 114, 201, 297
García Barragán, Gen. Marcelino, 59
García Cantú, Gastón, 17, 300
García Hernández, Hector, 176–7
García Márquez, Gabriel, 301
García Paniagua, Javier, 71–2, 82
García Robles, Alfonso, 344
Garrido Canabal, Tomás, 51
Garza Laguera, Eugenio, 286
Garza Sada, Bernardo, 146, 286
Garza Sada, Eugenio, 103, 139, 146, 285
Gascón Mercado, Alejandro, 104
Gasparillo Anica, Jacinto, 218
GATT, *see* General Agreement on Tariffs and Trade
Gavin, John, 325–6
General Agreement on Tariffs and Trade (GATT), 147, 333, 334
Generalized System of Preferences (GSP), 334
General Worker and Peasant Confederation of Mexico (CGOCM), 54
Gerzso, Gunther, 305
Gómez, Pablo, 105
Gómez Villanueva, Augusto, 187
González, Felipe, 18
González, José, 119
González, Manuel, 39
González, Gen. Pablo, 46
González de León, Teodoro, 306
Gorman, Gen. Paul F., 327
government expenditures, 140–2, 144
government officials, *see* bureaucracy, corruption and; politics
grandparents, 242

Great Britain, 37, 38
Group of 12, 351
Guadalajara, 279–81
Guadalupe-Hidalgo, Treaty of, 36
Guadalupe Zuño, José, 103
Guajardo, Col. Jesús, 46
Guatemala, 292, 342, 350, 357–8, 361–2
Guatemalan refugees, 211, 293, 357, 361–2
Guerrero, 102, 266–7
Guerrero, Vicente, 34
guerrilla groups, 95, 102–3, 281, 285
Gulf coast region, 281–3
Gutiérrez, Gen. Eulalio, 45
Guzmán, Martín Luis, 201

Haig, Alexander M., Jr., 355, 356
Hank González, Carlos, 127–8, 258, 264, 265, 271
Harding, Warren, 49
Health and Assistance, Ministry of, 229–31
health care, 219–20, 223–4, 226–32
Henestrosa, Andrés, 10
Hernández, Benito, 185
Hernández Galicia, Joaquín (La Quina), 86, 172–4, 176–8
Hernández Sancho, Plutarco, 351
Herrera Campíns, Luis, 356
Herrero, Gen. Rodolfo, 48
Hidalgo y Costilla, Miguel, 32–3
history, attitude toward, 14–18
homosexuality, 249
Honduras, 355, 356, 359
housing, 224–5, 247, 263–5
Houston, Sam, 35
Huerta, Adolfo de la, 44, 48, 50
Huerta, Gen. Victoriano, 43–5
Huicholes, 216–17
Humboldt, Alexander von, 32, 256

Ibarra, David, 148, 169
Ibarra de Piedra, Rosario, 99, 248–9
ICA Group, 139
illegal migrants (to U.S.), 329–33
Immigration and Naturalization Service, U.S., 330–1
IMSS (Social Security Institute), 222, 229–31
Indians, 3, 4, 22–33, 35, 39, 40, 42, 199–218, 275; alcoholism among, 211; *caciques* and, 210–11, 212; Cárdenas and, 201–2, 213; Catholic Church and, 29–30, 211, 215; in Chiapas, 212–13, 292–3; Christianity and, 215–17; during Colonial period, 30–1, 199–200; culture of, 203, 214–18; definition of, 207–8; De la Madrid and, 205–7; Echeverría and, 202–3; family, 243–4; López Portillo and, 204–5; *mestizos* and, 208–9, 213;

National Indian Institute (INI) and, 202, 203, 206–7, 211–12; religion of, 22, 29–30; Revolution and, 200–1; War of Independence and, 31–4; *see also individual peoples*

Industrial Development Plan, 146

industrialization, 56, 135, 137

inflation, 143, 147, 150, 152, 220

influence, political, 121–2

INFONAVIT (Workers' Housing Institute), 222, 223, 225

Institutional Revolutionary Party (PRI), 57, 75–82, 84, 271, 275, 277, 286, 290–1, 351, 355; bureaucracy and, 76–9; elections of 1982 and, 98, 99; opposition parties and, 95–100; peasants and, 185; political crisis in, 81–2; Presidents and, 68–73; the Right and, 108, 110–12; woman chosen secretary-general, 249

intellectuals, 295–302; Catholic Church and, 296; Cuban Revolution and, 298; De la Madrid and, 301–2; Echeverría and, 298–300; López Portillo and, 299–300; right-wing, 296

Inter-American Treaty of Mutual Assistance (Rio Pact), 342

interest groups, 67–8

Interior Ministry, 95–6, 362

International Monetary Fund (IMF), 63, 144–5, 149–53, 155, 335–6

investment, foreign, *see* foreign investment

Isaac, Alberto, 310

Israel, 347–8

Isthmus of Tehuantepec, 291

Iturbide, Col. Agustín de, 15–16, 34

Ixtoc I oil well, 338

Jackson, Andrew, 36

Jaramillo, Roberto, 104

Jaramillo, Rubén, 58, 186

jobs, 220–1

John Paul II, Pope, 89–90

Jonguitud Barrios, Carlos, 86, 234

Jova, Joseph J., 324, 325

Juárez, Benito, 37–9, 200

Juárez Blancas, Alberto, 86

judiciary, corruption of the, 119

Kehoe Vincent, Heriberto, 172

Kennedy, John F., 322, 337

Kirkpatrick, Jeane J., 326–7

Kissinger, Henry A., 338

Krueger, Robert, 325

Labor Congress, 86

Laborde, Hernán, 101

labor unions (labor movement), 48, 49, 54,

83–6, 105; corruption and, 124; *see also individual unions*

Lajous, Adrian, 150

land reform, 39, 42, 48, 49, 53–4, 180–9; Echeverría and, 284; *see also* agrarian policy

Land Reform Law (1983), 189

language(s), 11–14, 19–20; Indian, 214

La Quina (Joaquín Hernández Galicia), 86, 172–4, 176–8

Lara, Agustín, 311

Las Casas, Bartolomé de, 30

latifundios, 35

latifundistas, 180–2, 184, 187

Leduc, Paul, 309, 310

Leduc, Renato, 125

Left, the (leftist parties/movements), 97–107; Echeverría and, 59, 62, 70, 73, 83, 84, 101–4; guerrillas, 95, 102–3, 281, 285; internal divisions within, 104–5; *see also individual parties and movements*

Leñero, Vicente, 16

León Toral, José de, 51

Lerdo de Tejada, Sebastián, 39

Liberals, 37–9

Limantour, José, 40

Limón Rojas, Miguel, 207

literature, 306–7

Llaguno, Bishop José, 211

Lomas de Chapultepec, 268

Lombardo Toledano, Vicente, 54, 56, 84, 101

Lona, Bishop Arturo, 211

López, Espiridión, 204–5

López, Jacinto, 186

López, Maximiliano, 186

López Mateos, Adolfo, 58, 59, 61, 184, 298, 337; foreign policy of, 342–4

López Portillo, Carmen Romano de, 128, 300

López Portillo, José, 15, 17, 18, 20, 68, 70–4, 76, 79, 80, 90, 222, 225, 248, 258, 286, 310, 314; agrarian policy of, 187–8; agricultural policy of, 195, 196; armed forces and, 92–3; corruption and, 115, 127–31; the economy under, 63–4, 73, 142–51; foreign policy of, 348–9, 351–8; Indians and, 204–5; intellectuals and, 299–300; labor unions and, 84–5; oil industry and, 164–70, 174–6; opposition parties and, 97, 103, 107; United States and, 320–3, 325, 326, 328, 331, 336, 338–9

López Portillo, José Ramón, 128, 129

López Portillo, Margarita, 128, 300, 310, 313

Lucey, Patrick J., 325

Lugo Verduzco, Adolfo, 82

Luiselli Fernández, Cassio, 196

machismo, 8, 11
Madero, Francisco I., 15, 41, 43, 44, 319
Madero, Gustavo, 44
Madero, Pablo Emilio, 99, 109, 110
maids, 245, 250
male-female relationship, 8, 240–2; *see also*
    family; women
malnutrition, 227–8
Mancera, Miguel, 149, 150
maquiladoras, 288
Margain, Hugo B., 142
Martínez Domínguez, Alfonso, 62, 73, 78,
    79
Martínez Manatou, Emilio, 71, 78–9
Martínez Mendoza, Sergio, 172
Martínez Verdugo, Arnoldo, 99
Martínez Villicana, Luis, 189
Marxism, 106, 296, 297
mass entertainment, 307–15
mass media, *see* media, the
Mata, Eduardo, 303
Maximilian, Emperor of Mexico, 38–9
Mayapán, 24
Mayas, 23, 24, 36–7, 181, 209, 290
Mazzoli, Romano, 332
McBride, Robert H., 324, 325
media, the, 82–3, 365; corruption in,
    124–6; leftist, 106–7; *see also*
    newspapers; television
Medrano, Francisco, 186
Méndez Arceo, Sergio, 90
Méndez Docurro, Eugenio, 127
Menéndez, Mario, 104
Mérida, Carlos, 290, 291, 304, 305
Merino, Jaime J., 172
mestizaje (mixed-blood heritage), 3, 4, 8,
    14, 16–17, 20
mestizos, 3; Indians and, 208–9, 213
Mexican-Americans (Chicanos), 328
Mexican Bishops' Conference, 90
Mexican Businessmen's Council, 87–8
Mexican Communist Party, *see*
    Communist Party
Mexican Democratic Party (PDM), 89,
    98, 99, 109
Mexican Food System (SAM), 195–8
Mexican Managers' Confederation
    (COPARMEX), 88
Mexican People's Party (PPM), 104
Mexican War (1846–48), 36
Mexican Workers' Party (PMT), 98, 104,
    105, 107
Mexico City, 254–73, 278–9, 370; air
    pollution in, 259, 260, 262; communities
    of, 265–9; crime in, 271; dust storms in,
    259; garbage collection and disposal in,
    259–60; growth of, 255–8, 272; history
    of, 255–8; migration to, 254, 257;
    poverty and slums in, 262–5; public

transport in, 261–2; squatters in, 263–5;
    water supply of, 269–71
middle class, 221, 365, 367, 368; family,
    248–52
migration: to Mexico City, 254, 257; to
    the United States, 329–33; to urban
    areas, 244–7
missionaries, 29–30
mistresses, 246, 251
Mixtecs, 24
Moctezuma, 26–8, 113–14
Moctezuma Cid, Julio R., 170, 174
Mohammed Reza Pahlevi, Shah of Iran,
    338–9
Monge, Luis Alberto, 356
Monte Albán, 24
Monterrey, 285–6
Monterrey Group, 139, 285–6
Morelos, Jose María, 15, 16, 33
Morelos region, 42–3
Morones, Luis, 54
Mota Sánchez, Ramón, 130
mother, role of, 8, 13–14
Movement for Socialist Action and Unity
    (MAUS), 104
movie industry, 309–11
Moya Palencia, Mario, 71, 78, 95
multinational companies, 230
municipalities, 277–8
Muñoz Ledo, Porfirio, 78
MURO, 109
music, 303, 311

Nahmad Sitton, Salomón, 206–7
Napoleon Bonaparte, 32
Napoleon III (Louis Napoleon), 38
narcotics traffic, 337
National Action Party (PAN), 88, 89,
    96–100, 108–11, 280, 286–7, 365, 367
National Confederation of Popular
    Organizations (CNOP), 55
National Food Program (PRONAL), 197,
    198
National Indian Institute (INI), 202, 203,
    206–7, 211–12
nationalism, 18–20, 317–19, 327, 336, 337,
    367–8
Nationalist Revolutionary Civic
    Association, 102
nationalization: of banks, 68–9, 88, 107; of
    oil companies, 160–1
National Liberation Movement, 101
National Peasant Alliance, 186
National Peasant Confederation (CNC),
    54, 182, 185, 187, 189, 203
National Polytechnic Institute (IPN), 59,
    60
National Revolutionary Party (PNR), 52,
    75

National Sinarquista Union, 109
National University, see Autonomous
National University
Nava, Julián, 325
nepotism, 121, 129, 239
New Spain, 28, 29
newspapers, 308; corruption and, 124–6,
130; see also press, the
Nicaragua, 64, 300, 301, 341, 351–61
Nixon, Richard M. (Nixon
administration), 319, 337
northern Mexico, 283–9; border cities in,
287–9
North-South summit (1981), 349
nutrition, 227–8

Oaxaca, 291–2
Obregón, Alvaro, 44, 45, 49–51, 75, 115, 182
Ocampo, Melchor, 241
Ocampo Pact, 186
O'Donojú, Juan, 34
Oduber Quiroz, Daniel, 351
oil companies: foreign, 158–61;
nationalization of, 54–5, 160–1
oil exports to U.S., 326, 333–6
oil industry, 63–4, 145–7, 157–79, 348;
Cárdenas and, 159–61; corruption in,
127, 128, 168; De la Madrid and, 175,
176, 179; Echeverría and, 163–4; López
Portillo and, 164–70, 174; see also
Petróleos Mexicanos (Pemex)
oil prices, 143, 166, 169, 170
oil workers, 159
Oil Workers' Union (STPRM), 124, 159–60,
162, 163, 171–8; dissidents in, 172
Ojeda Paullada, Pedro, 71, 72, 78
Olid, Cristóbal de, 28
Olmecs, 23
Olympics (1968), 59
O'Neill, Thomas P., Jr., 332
opposition parties, 94–112; in Congress,
96–9; Interior Ministry and, 95–6;
leftist, 97–107; registration of, 97–8;
right-wing, 107–12; see also individual
parties
Opus Dei movement, 89, 109
Organization of American States (OAS),
342, 351
Organization of Petroleum Exporting
Countries (OPEC), 163, 166, 169
Orozco, Pascual, 41, 43
Ortiz de Domínguez, Josefa, 32
Ortiz Mena, Antonio, 74
Ortiz Rubio, Gen. Pascual, 52
Oteyza, José Andrés de, 78, 79, 148, 169,
170

Padilla, Ezequiel, 56
painting, 303–5

Palomino, Danzos, 186
Panama, 339, 351, 352, 355, 358
Party of the Mexican Revolution (PRM),
55
Party of the Poor, 102
Paz, Octavio, 7, 9, 298, 300, 301, 307
Pearson, Weetman D., 158
peasants, 180–2; family, 243–5; migration
to urban areas, 181, 184; organizations
of, 185–6; see also ejidos
peninsulares, 31–3
Pérez, Carlos Andrés, 351
Pérez Treviño, Manuel, 52
Pershing, Gen. John J., 45
Petróleos Mexicanos (Pemex), 121, 143, 145,
157, 161–79, 260, 272, 335; corruption in,
131–2; see also oil industry
pharmaceutical industry, 230
Pinochet, Gen. Augusto, 346
Pino Suárez, José María, 44
planning, attitude toward, 6
Plan of Ayala, 43, 45, 46, 47
Plan of Iguala (Plan of Three Guarantees),
34
Plan of San Luis Potosí, 41, 43
Plaza de Garibaldi, 267
PNR, see National Revolutionary Party
Polanco, 268
police corruption, 117–18, 130
Political Action Movement (MAP), 104
political parties, see Institutional
Revolutionary Party (PRI); opposition
parties
politics: the Church and, 89–90; historical
past in, 15–17; language in, 12–13;
technocrats and, 79–81; women in,
248–9; see also Institutional
Revolutionary Party; opposition parties;
Presidents
pollution, 369–70
popular culture, 307–15
Popular Party, 101
Popular Socialist Party (PPS), 96–9, 101
population growth, 136–7, 220, 225–6,
272
¿Por Qué? (weekly), 104
Portes Gil, Emilio, 52
poverty, 222, 224
Presidents, 12–13, 66–75, 276; as
all-powerful, 66; bureaucracy and, 76–7;
the Church and, 90; Congress and,
68–9; election campaigns of, 69–70;
interest groups and, 67–8; PRI and,
68–73; "spiritual mentors" of, 15;
succession of, 70–3
press, the, 82–3; corruption and, 124–6,
130; leftist, 104, 106–7
PRI, see Institutional Revolutionary Party
priests, 50, 51, 241–2

prisons, 119
private sector, 86–8, 135, 136; corruption and, 115, 122–4; dominating figures in, 138–40; the Right and, 108–11; *see also* banks; businessmen; foreign investment
Proceso (weekly), 106, 107
Protestant evangelists, 205–6
protest movement (1968), 59–61, 92, 101
public health, 226–32
public transport, 261–2

Quetzalcóatl, 15, 25, 26
Quintana, Bernardo, 139

Rabasa, Emilio O., 348
racism, 7
Ramírez Limón, Leopoldo, 131
Ramírez Mercado, Sergio, 351
Ramírez Vázquez, Pedro, 305–6
Ramos, Samuel, 7
Reagan, Ronald (Reagan administration), 148, 321–3, 332, 335, 336, 349, 353–6, 359, 360
Reform Laws, 38–9
refugees, Guatemalan, 211, 293, 357, 361–2
Regan, Donald, 335
regionalism, 274–8; *see also specific regions*
religion: family and, 241–2; of Indians, 22, 29–30, 214; *see also* Catholic Church
Revolutionary Party of National Unification, 55
Revolutionary Socialist Party (PSR), 104
Revolutionary Workers' Party (PRT), 98, 99
Revolution of 1910, 39, 43–9; Indians and, 200–1
Reyes, Gen. Bernardo, 43–4
Reyes Heroles, Jesús, 78, 95, 97, 172, 300, 351
Right, the, 107–12
Rio Pact, 342
Rivera, Diego, 16, 17
Rivero Serrano, Octavio, 237
Robelo, Alfonso, 359
Rockefeller, David, 338
Rodríguez, Gen. Abelardo, 52
Rodríguez, Carlos Rafael, 355
Rojas, Francisco, 80, 129
Roman Catholic Church, *see* Catholic Church
Roosevelt, Franklin D., 56, 161
Ruiz, Bishop Samuel, 211
Ruiz Cortines, Adolfo, 58, 115, 162
Rulfo, Juan, 306
Rural Credit Bank (BANRURAL), 190

Sáenz, Gen. Aaron, 52
Salinas de Gortari, Carlos, 79
SAM (Mexican Food System), 195–8

Sandino, Gen. Augusto César, 341
Sansores Pérez, Carlos, 351
Santa Anna, Gen. Antonio López de, 34–6
Satellite City, 268
Scherer García, Julio, 104, 299
Schlesinger, James, 320
schools: primary, 232–3; private, 235; *see also* education
Scott, Gen. Winfield, 36
Sedco, 338
Select Commission on Immigration, 331, 332
self-doubt, as national characteristic, 20–1
Sepúlveda, Bernardo, 80, 327, 362
sex, 242, 245–6
Shultz, George, 359, 360
Sicartsa steel complex, 142
Silva Herzog, Jesús, 79, 149–51, 335, 336, 362, 363
Simpson, Alan, 332
Sinaloa, 193
Sinarquistas, 51, 108, 109
Siqueiros, David Alfaro, 299
Social Democratic Party (PSD), 98
Socialist Workers' Party (PST), 98, 99, 104
Social Security Institute (IMSS), 222, 229–31
social welfare programs, 222–4
Somoza DeBayle, Gen. Anastasio, 350–2
Sonora, 193
southern Mexico, 290–4
Soviet Union, 297
Spain, 18, 38, 341, 347; *see also* Colonial period
Spanish Civil War, 18, 297, 341
Spanish Conquest, *see* Conquest, the
Spanish International Network (SIN), 313
Spota, Luis, 307
state governments, 275–8
status symbols, 10–11
STPRM, *see* Oil Workers' Union
student protests (1968), 59–61, 92, 101
Student-Worker-Peasant Coalition of the Isthmus (COCEI), 291–2
Summer Institute of Linguistics, 205–6

Tamayo, Ruffino, 304
Taylor, Gen. Zachary, 36
Teachers' Union (SNTE), 234, 236
technocrats, 79–81
Telesistema Mexicana, 140, 312
Televisa, 83, 124, 140, 311–15, 365
television, 83, 140, 245, 311–15
Tello Macías, Carlos, 79, 150–1, 155
Tenochtitlan, 26, 28, 255–6
Teotihuacan, 24–5
Tepito, 266–7
Terceristas, 351

Terrazas Zozaya, Samuel, 172
Texas, 35-6
Texcoco, 266
Tibón, Gutierre, 17-18
time, attitude toward, 6-7
titles, 11
Tlatelolco, 3
Tlatelolco, Treaty of, 344
Tlatelolco massacre (1968), 60-1
Tlaxcala, 27
Toltecs, 25
Torres Pancardo, Oscar, 172, 177
Torrijos Herrera, Brig. Gen. Omar, 339, 351
tourism, 136, 209
trade unions, see labor unions
transportation, 261-2
Trevino Adame, Col. Crescencio, 240
Triqui Indians, 210-11
Trotsky, Leon, 54, 101, 297
Truman, Harry S, 321-2
Tzotzils, 200

underemployment, 220
undocumented aliens, 329-33
unemployment, 220, 221
Unified Socialist Party of Mexico (PSUM), 98-100, 105-7, 110, 235, 292
unions, see labor unions
United Nations, 346-8
United Nations Conference on Trade and Development (UNCTAD), 344
United States, 56, 62, 92, 114, 193, 195, 316-39, 368; aid to Mexico, 344; ambassadors of, 324-6; attitude toward, 19, 327; border issues, 336-7; Central America and, 349-63; Chamizal question and, 336-7; drug traffic and, 337; fishing rights and, 338; illegal migration to, 329-33; Ixtoc I oil well spill and, 337-8; misunderstanding of, 327; Nicaragua and, 341, 351-61; oil exports to, 333-6; and revolution in Mexico, 43-5; and Shah of Iran, 338-9; trade with, 196, 333-6; see also individual U.S. presidents
universities, 234-7
Uno más Uno (weekly), 106, 107, 300, 302
urban areas, 244

Vallina, Eloy, 110, 139
Vance, Cyrus, 352
Vasconcelos, José, 52, 201, 232, 296
Vatican, the, 345
Vázquez Rojas, Genaro, 102
Velasco, Miguel Angel, 104
Velasco Agreement, 35, 36
Velasco Ibarra, Enrique, 82
Velázquez, Fidel, 71, 84-6, 365
Venezuela, 350, 351-3, 355, 358
Veracruz, 279, 281-2
Villa, Francisco "Pancho," 15, 41, 44-5
violence, 10
Virgin of Guadalupe, 90, 200, 215, 242
VISA Group, 286
Vivanco García, Pedro, 172

Walters, Gen. Vernon, 353, 356
War of Independence, 31-4
War of the Castes, 37, 181, 290
water supply, 369
White Brigade, 103
Wilson, Henry Lane, 44, 319
Wilson, Woodrow, 44, 45, 49, 319
women, 8-10, 238-53; Indian, 215-16, 240; middle-class, 248-53; in politics, 248-9; working, 251; see also family; maids; mistresses
Workers' Housing Institute (INFONAVIT), 222, 223, 225
World War II, 55, 56

Xochimilco, 266

Yaquis, 31, 213, 215
Yaqui Valley, 187, 190
Yucatán, 36-7, 290-1

Zabludovsky, Abrahán, 306
Zabludovsky, Jacobo, 83
Zapata, Emiliano, 15, 42, 43, 45-7, 180
Zapotecs, 24, 214
Zimmermann telegram, 47
Zócalo, 267
Zona Rosa, 268
Zuloaga, Gen. Félix, 37-8

About the Author

Alan Riding was born in Brazil and educated in England. In 1971 he began his career as a correspondent in Latin America—based chiefly in Mexico City—for publications including *The Financial Times* and *The Economist*. For six years he was Mexico bureau chief for *The New York Times* and from January 1984 to March 1989 Mr. Riding was the *Times* bureau chief in Brazil. He is currently based in Rome, where he lives with his wife and son and reports on the Mediterranean region for *The Times*.